D0871958

THE CIVILIZATION OF THE AMERICAN INDIAN SERIES
(List begins on page 341.)

THE CAYUSE INDIANS

The Authors

ROBERT H. RUBY is a practicing surgeon, who makes his home in Moses Lake, Washington. JOHN A. BROWN, a graduate of the University of Washington, is a member of the faculty of the Department of History in Wenatchee Valley College, Wenatchee, Washington. They also wrote *The Spokane Indians: Children of the Sun* and *Half-Sun on the Columbia: A Biography of Chief Moses*, both published by the University of Oklahoma Press. CLIFFORD M. DRURY, who makes his home in Pasadena, California, is a retired Presbyterian minister. He is the author and editor of many works on the early missionaries and settlers in Oregon.

The illustration on the front of the jacket is from a photograph of Cayuse Chief Fish Hawk, taken by Major Lee Moorhouse about 1900. It is reproduced through the courtesy of the Smithsonian Institution National Archives, Bureau of American Ethnology Collection.

UNIVERSITY OF OKLAHOMA PRESS

NORMAN

THE CAYUSE INDIANS
Imperial Tribesmen of Old Oregon

By Robert H. Ruby and John A. Brown

FOREWORD BY CLIFFORD M. DRURY

By Robert H. Ruby and John A. Brown

Half-Sun on the Columbia: A Biography of Chief Moses (Norman, 1965)
The Spokane Indians: Children of the Sun (Norman, 1970)
The Cayuse Indians: Imperial Tribesmen of Old Oregon (Norman, 1972)

International Standard Book Number: 0-8061-0995-5

Library of Congress Catalog Card Number: 74-177345

The Cayuse Indians: Imperial Tribesmen of Old Oregon is Volume 120 in The Civilization of the American Indian Series.

To
Robert Jr.
and
Bernice

Foreword
By Clifford M. Drury

Here is the fascinating account of a small Indian tribe, the Cayuses, whose lodges once were located at one of the busiest crossroads of the Old Oregon country. Proud and haughty by disposition, the Cayuses became involved in the turmoil of events that followed the coming of the white men—explorers, fur traders, missionaries, Indian agents, and settlers. The involvement of the Cayuses in such events as the Whitman massacre and the Indian wars that followed arose largely out of the accident of their geographical location. The Oregon Trail ran through their homeland. The mighty Columbia River, the great water highway of the Oregon country, bordered their domain. The clash between the culture of the red man and that of the white man was inevitable.

As the authors of this book clearly explain, never in the history of the United States has so small a tribe wielded so great an influence over so many years and at so great a cost to the white government as the Cayuse Nation. At the time of the Whitman massacre, in November, 1847, the tribe numbered fewer than four hundred individuals, including women and children.

The authors of this book are admirably qualified to write about the Cayuses. In recent years they have collaborated on a biography of Chief Moses and a history of the Spokane Indians. They have been indefatigable in their search for relevant facts bearing on the history of the Cayuses, dating from the aboriginal period and running through the nineteenth century to the time the remnant of the once-proud tribe was forced to move to a reservation. They have conducted interviews, consulted libraries and archives, and reviewed scores of books and journal articles. The extensive bibliography bears witness to the thoroughness of their research. The appendices, which form an important part of this book, contain five rare source documents.

In the Preface, after pointing out the deep involvement of the Cayuse tribe in "every important act in the drama of the Pacific Northwest," the authors state their theme: to do justice to the Cayuse Indians. As conscientious historians, the authors have produced an objective study of what happened. They have not drawn upon imagination to guess at what the Indians thought or did. They have told, in clear, documented accounts, what actually happened when the white men took by force what the Indians felt was rightfully theirs. This approach is one that can be accepted without hesitation. After reading this book, every honest inquirer should have strong feelings of sympathy for the Cayuses. The authors have not tried to gloss over the Indians' mistakes; but when the full story is revealed, we see that they were more sinned against than sinning.

This volume will be a valuable sourcebook for the history of the Northwest as long as libraries exist.

Pasadena, California
March 15, 1972

Preface

The Cayuse Indians are associated not only with the development of the range horse named for them but also with important events in history, among which the Whitman massacre is the most dramatic. The Cayuse Indians rode their horses to a position of power among tribes of the plateau lands in the Intermontane West and left in their sturdy mounts a legacy to the white frontiersmen who ultimately conquered the land. But the Indians also left a legacy of violence. The Whitman massacre was a cause of bitterness in both red and white communities for many, many years. Especially galling to the whites was the placing of responsibility for the event on members of their own race. We have written of the causes and effects of that oft-related tragedy, but with minimal detail. We mention little about white responsibility for the massacre because it concerns the Cayuse Indians only indirectly.

Seldom has a people as numerically small as the Cayuses played so important a role in the recorded history of a region. With their lodges pitched at a strategic time and place, sustained by a fierce pride and a drive for tribal perpetuation, they were involved in, if not epicentral to, every important act in the drama of the Pacific Northwest before they were forced behind the curtain of near oblivion on a reservation. We trust that we have done justice to the actors of this drama, which was set primarily within the nineteenth century, when their historic influence was greatest.

In preparing this volume, we have become indebted to many persons. We owe much to skilled and dedicated librarians: the staffs of the Huntington and Bancroft libraries; Hazel Mills, of the Washington State Library; Priscilla Knuth, of the Oregon Historical Society; Earle Connette, archivist of the Holland Library, Washington State University; Mildred Sherwood, archivist Richard Berner, documents librarian Miriam Allen, and microfilm librarian Mrs. Erven Kloostra, all of the Suzzallo Library of the University of Washington; the Reverend Wilfred Schoenberg, S.J., of the Crosby Library, Gonzaga University; Mrs. Bill Gullick, of the Penrose Library, Whitman College; Jane D. Hamm, librarian of the Umatilla County Library; and Hilda Schlicke, of the Eastern Washington Historical Society. We owe much to librarians Marie Kennedy, Pearl C. Munson, Mrs. Lawrence Bingham, and Irma McKenzie, all of the Moses Lake Library; Annie Koinzan, of the North Central Washington Regional Library; and Wenatchee Valley College librarians Audrey Kolb, Betty Jean Gibson, and Arvilla Scofield.

We especially thank the governor and committee of the Hudson's Bay Company for their permission to use the 1829 report of Samuel Black, chief trader at Fort Nez Percés. To Elmer Lindgard, archivist of the Federal Records Center in Seattle, we extend a special note of appreciation. For their assistance we also thank Harold Duck, acting superintendent of the Umatilla Indian Agency; David S. Hall, executive secretary of the Umatilla Confederated Tribes; Mary Half Moon and other residents of the Umatilla Indian Reservation who are cited in this work; and Cecil Pambrun. Thanks are also due Elizabeth Racy, who translated French documents for us, and Lavonne Carter, of the *Spokesman-Review*, who answered our many queries. Much assistance was given us by Mr. and Mrs. Purdy Cornelison, Bernice Perkins, Lila Lyons, George Smith, Elvin W. Barkhoff, Charles and Lea Hansen, Joe McAdams, Lois Ledeboer, Sally Probst, Frances Dussell, and the late Click Relander. Jack Cleaver, of the Oregon Historical Society, and Nancy Pryor, research consultant at the Washington State Library, rendered invaluable assistance. We thank Paul Stowell for his photographic work. We are also grateful to Angie Debo, who helped with this as well as with our earlier books. And we deeply thank Margaret Camp and Herbert Hyde for their patience and skill in helping shape our work into its present form.

Moses Lake, Washington   Robert H. Ruby

Wenatchee, Washington   John A. Brown

January 15, 1972

Contents

Illustrations

Maps

THE CAYUSE INDIANS

I
An Imperial Tribe

At the dawn of the nineteenth century in what is today eastern Oregon, large bands of horses, sometimes numbering four thousand head, grazed bunchgrass hills and valleys sloping down the majestic Blue Mountains. White men would one day call these animals cayuses, thereby paying the highest of compliments to their owners, the Cayuse Indians. These red men, whose wealth and pride lay in their horseflesh, received their name from French-Canadian employees of the fur companies who came to their country to trade. As did their prized possessions, the Cayuses freely roamed the hills and valleys buttressing the Blue Mountains, and because of the rocky nature of a portion of this land the traders called the Indians Cailloux, meaning "People of the Stones or Rocks," variously interpreted as "People of the Flint Rocks."[1]

In their native language the Cayuses' name for themselves meant "Superior People," and they wore it well. Many times both other Indians and whites described them as a proud and haughty people. But with all their pride they were never unmindful that in their mounts lay not only their nobility but also their mobility, making them monarchs of a vast Pacific Northwest region between the Cascade and Rocky mountains.

Before acquiring horses these people led a modest pedestrian life. Calling themselves Waiilatpus, they spoke the Waiilatpuan

---

1 Samuel Black, "Extracts from report by Chief Trader Samuel Black to the Governor and Committee of the Hudson's Bay Company, dated 'Willa Walla,' 25 March 1829" cited hereafter as "Report by Chief Trader Samuel Black"), Query 25.

tongue of the Penutin base of dialectic divisions formerly thought to have been distinct linguistic stocks including also the Northern Shahaptian, Lutuamian, and Nez Percé Shahaptian.[2] In an earlier day with their close Waiilatpuan neighbors the Mollalahs, the Waiilatpus, or Cayuses, dwelt in a small area in the shadow of Mount Hood, home of the legendary fire god and demons. The Mollalahs lived near the Deschutes River, a tributary of the Columbia, and the Warm Springs River, a Deschutes tributary (below present-day Kaskela, near South Junction, Oregon). The Cayuses were located along the headwaters of another Columbia tributary, the John Day River. Someday archaeologists may tell us where these people dwelt in the more distant past.

Much hardier than other Indians of the region, the Cayuses and Mollalahs lived in similar mat houses in summer[3] and mud-covered semisubterranean houses in winter, subsisting mostly by hunting, fishing, and gathering roots and berries. There were, however, differences between the two peoples. The more aggressive Cayuses were destined for expansion; the Mollalahs would be pushed out of their lands to find a new home in the Willamette Valley of western Oregon.

Early in the eighteenth century the Cayuses went to war. Like the Mollalahs, they fought raiders from the south. Yet their defensive posture was offset by one of offense, for in the ebb and flow of warfare they came to grips with the Snake peoples to the south and east.[4]

---

[2] Melville Jacobs, *Northern Sahaptin Grammar*, 93.

[3] Edward S. Curtis, *The North American Indian*, VIII, 80.

[4] The name Snake appears extensively in the popular designation of the Northern Paiute Indians. In "Linguistic Distribution and Political Groups of the Great Basin Shoshoneans," *American Anthropologist*, N.S., XXXIX, 4 (October–December, 1937), 625, Julian H. Steward says the Northern Paiutes are the same people A. L. Kroeber calls the Mono-Paviotso division of Shoshone Indians and that when Lewis and Clark reported Snakes on the Deschutes River and Peter Skene Ogden Snakes on the John Day River, the Indians were probably Paiutes.

Anthropologist Verne F. Ray states: "Sahaptin informants emphatically declare that they never used Snake as a tribal name, and that they are quite unaware of any such tribe. Instead, the term is used collectively for the Shoshone, Bannack, and Paiute. The name came into familiar usage among the whites because it is

There has been considerable controversy among anthropologists concerning the Snakes' role in the bifurcation of the Cayuses and Mollalahs sometime after 1780.[5] One anthropologist asserts that the Snakes, themselves under hammerings from the Blackfeet,[6] were forced northward, splitting the Cayuses and Mollalahs.[7] It was then, according to this anthropologist, that the Snakes drove the Mollalahs west, clearing the Columbia River's south bank of the Tenino Shahaptians, among whom were Tygh, Deschutes, and John Day bands occupying a stretch from The Dalles to the Umatilla River.[8] Salishan peoples living along and

the exclusive designation in sign language, the symbol being the same as that used for the reptile." Verne F. Ray *et al.*, "Tribal Distribution in Eastern Oregon and Adjacent Regions," *American Anthropologist*, N.S., XI, 2–4 (1938), 394.

The use of *Snake* for *Bannack* persists among chroniclers of the region, even though the two are separate entities. Although members of the Shoshonean family, the Bannacks are more closely related to the Utes. Frederick Webb Hodge (ed.), *Handbook of American Indians North of Mexico*, II, 606, defines *Snake* as follows: "A name applied to many different bodies of Shoshonean Indians, but most persistently to those of E. Oregon. . . . These Indians form one dialectic group with the Paviotso of W. Nevada and the Mono of S.E. California. The principal Snake tribes were the Walpapi and the Yahuskin." Descendants of the Snakes live in and around Klamath, Oregon. They are divided into the Walpapi, Paviotso, and Yahuskin bands. The Mono-Paviotsos live at Owens Valley, California. A handful of Snakes also reside among the Shoshones and Bannacks at Fort Hall, Idaho, as do a few Paiutes. An explanation of the origins of the confusion in names is contained in the opening chapter of Brigham D. Madsen's *The Bannock of Idaho*.

In a brief prepared for the U.S. Claims Commission, the Cayuses stated that their hereditary enemies were the Northern Paiutes, whom they identify as Snakes. *Before the Indian Claims Commission: Confederated Tribes of the Umatilla Indian Reservation, Petitioner, v. United States of America, Defendant. Petitioner's Proposed Findings of Fact and Brief (Claims One and Four). Claims Commission Brief*, Docket 264, 20, 23.

5 John R. Swanton says the Mollalahs and Cayuses were still together in 1780. *The Indian Tribes of North America*, 466.

6 James H. Teit, *The Middle Columbia Salish*, 101. See also Zenas Leonard, *Narrative of the Adventures of Zenas Leonard*, 25.

7 Lee Moorhouse, who served as agent on the Umatilla Indian Reservation, where the Cayuses lived in the nineteenth century, got from these people (before anthropologists began to explore the question) the story that it was the Snakes who separated the Cayuses and Mollalahs. Lucullus Virgil McWhorter, " 'Indian Henry' was of old Cayuse Tribe," clipping from *Portland* (Oregon) *Journal* in McWhorter Papers, 409. See also Joel V. Berreman, *Tribal Distribution in Oregon*, 58; and Teit, *The Middle Columbia Salish*, 100–110.

8 Indian tradition concerning the northern thrust of the Snakes has it that they inhabited the country adjacent to Fifteen Mile Creek (on the south side of the

south of the Columbia before 1750 were pushed to the north.[9] Other anthropologists substantially agree that the Snakes wedged themselves between the Cayuses and Mollalahs, while a third group claims that Tenino expansion to the south sent the Mollalahs fleeing westward, after which (sometime between 1810 and 1820) they conducted raids against the Snakes.

Mollalah Indians at the turn of the twentieth century told of civil strife among the Cayuses "in the long ago." After bitter fighting a band of seceders, with families and possessions, moved west from the bunchgrass region of the upper Columbia in search of a new home. Finding all the territory east of the Cascade Mountains occupied by warlike tribes, they moved down to the Willamette Valley and became Mollalahs. Although they made peace with the Indians living there, they harbored hatred for the Cayuse tribesmen who had driven them from their homes. Subsequent generations of Mollalahs, nursed on hatred of Cayuses implanted by their elders, determined to challenge their enemies to a showdown in the Cascades. The result was disastrous for the Mollalahs. In the ensuing conflict their number was reduced by half. An attempt to avenge the defeat likewise failed, upon which the Mollalahs were forced to sue for peace. Just when these events occurred is not known, but a missionary among the Cayuses and Nez Percés in the 1830's and 1840's reported that some three generations earlier a band leaving the Cayuses had crossed the Cascades. From it the Mollalahs descended, retaining Cayuse features "most strikingly."[10]

Columbia River near The Dalles), the Tygh Valley, and the Deschutes. From these locations they raided the Wascopums and other peoples in the vicinity of The Dalles. William Cameron McKay, "Early History of The Dalles," McKay Papers. Ray says the Snakes fought the Umatillas in the eighteenth century, forcing them to take refuge on Blalock Island in the Columbia River. "Tribal Distribution," 391.

[9] Melville Jacobs doubts that there was an immigration of Shahaptians north across the Columbia River within the past two hundred years. "Historic Perspectives in Indian Languages of Oregon and Washington," *Pacific Northwest Quarterly*, XXVIII, 1 (January, 1937), 69.

[10] Ray, "Tribal Distribution," 391–92; S. A. Clarke, *Pioneer Days of Oregon History*, I, 133–37; H. H. Spalding to Superintendent of Indian Affairs, November

According to Cayuse tradition, sometime before 1750 a war party of Cayuses and their neighbors the Umatillas was encamped on the Malheur River, a tributary of the Snake. Spies were dispatched to bluffs overlooking the river to watch for enemy Snakes. What they saw threw them into great consternation: the Snakes appeared to be riding either elk or deer. The spies hurriedly returned to their war chief, Ococtuin, with this intelligence. Perhaps disbelieving their story, the chief sent other warriors to ascertain the reason for what he thought must surely be an illusion. They, too, saw what appeared to be Snakes riding elk or deer. Dumbfounded, the group inched closer to discover that the hoofprints were not split but solid and round. Thoroughly upset by this discovery, Ococtuin abandoned his war plan for one of peace, a wise decision. After arranging a truce with the Snakes, the erstwhile war party returned home with a pair of horses, descendants of Spanish ponies. The Cayuses treated their newly gained treasures with great care, and the following year the mare foaled. Then the Cayuses decided to send out another party, this time to steal more horses from the Snakes—to them a much easier way to increase their herd than breeding.[11]

18, 1850, Microcopy of Records in the National Archives, *Oregon Superintendency of Indian Affairs, 1848–1873*, Microfilm No. 2, Roll 12 (Cited hereafter as *Oregon Superintendency*, Microfilm No. 2, Roll 12). Anthropologist Albert S. Gatschet said in December, 1877, that Mollalah Indians informed him that their ancestors (presumably before their acquisition of firearms) were victims of raids by Cayuse Indians. "The Molale tribe raided by the Cayuses."

[11] William Cameron McKay, "The Origin of the Horse," McKay Papers. In another version of the Cayuses' acquisition of horses, the Shahaptians were said to have acquired them from the Shoshonis, but only after they had given everything they had for a mare and a stallion. When they returned home, the Shahaptians separated the two animals, the Yakimas taking the mare for safekeeping from marauding Snakes. Each year the mare was brought to the Walla Walla Valley to be bred, "so there were many horses." H. M. Painter, "The Coming of the Horse," *Pacific Northwest Quarterly*, XXXVII, 2 (April, 1946), 155–57. The spread of the horse in the Pacific Northwest was charted by Harold E. Driver and William C. Massey, "Comparative Studies of North American Indians," *Transactions of the American Philosophical Society Held at Philadelphia for Promoting Useful Knowledge*, N.S., XLVII (1957), 284–87. The Shoshonis got their horses when the animals spread north from the Spaniards in Mexico. Frank Gilbert Roe, *The Indian and the Horse*, 308. See also Clark Wissler, "The Influence of the Horse in the Development of Plains Culture," *American Anthropologist*, N.S., XVI, 1 (January, 1914), 1–25.

With stolen Snake animals and those produced from their own herds, the Cayuses soon developed into formidable horsemen. As the horse served to strengthen the Cayuses' hunting, warring, and raiding propensities, so did these propensities condition the animal to respond to the needs of its master. Under expert tutelage, it quickly adapted to the encircling maneuver of elk and deer hunts, a task which the Indians had once tediously performed on foot. The horse also enabled the Cayuses to meet the Snakes on more even terms, the resulting conflicts intensifying hostilities between the two peoples. There would be no respite until late in the nineteenth century.

Adding power and opulence to their mobility, the Cayuses broke out of their homeland, driving northward to the Columbia River the peoples standing in their way. For a long time they would dominate the ragtag bands which occupied a twenty-mile belt along the Columbia.[12] Pushing east sometime before 1800, the Cayuses swept the foothill slopes of the Blue Mountains, whose soil, born of rude vestiges of ancient volcanic action, produced fine bunchgrass to nourish their mounts. On they went to Rock and Willow creeks, both Columbia tributaries, and Butter Creek, a tributary of the Umatilla, itself a Columbia tributary. Pressing down the Umatilla, they squeezed its peoples farther downstream. Then they headed north from the Umatilla until they reached the timber-skirted headwaters of the Walla Walla, following that stream down its willow-fringed lower reaches to the home of the Walla Walla Indians, whom they subjugated.[13] Moving still farther north, by the beginning of the nineteenth century they had traveled to the rock-rimmed valley of the Tucannon, a Snake tributary. Here their expansion was checked, possibly because they had found a common boundary with friendly Nez Percés. Crossing the wooded, winter-snow-covered crest of the Blue Mountains, the Cayuses traversed a

---

[12] Thomas R. Garth, "Early Nineteenth Century Tribal Relations in the Columbia Plateau," *Southwestern Journal of Anthropology*, XX, 1 (Spring, 1964), 46.
[13] Berreman, *Tribal Distribution*, 59.

defile (known to white men as The Narrows) and descended abruptly into the valley of the Grande Ronde, a Snake tributary.

In the Grande Ronde the Cayuses discovered a gem. The valley was carpeted with grass, and fish abounded in its streams. Protected by pine, fir, and spruce-timbered mountain walls, the Ronde provided the Cayuses pasture for their horses and necessities of their own. They shared it with the Nez Percés, however, for the latter also had discovered its excellence. Here, too, came peaceful Shoshonean bands from the south to trade and sport with the Cayuses and Nez Percés at annual fairs, usually held in mid-July when the women dug camas roots. These were dried, pounded, and molded into cakes to be stored for winter use. The Snakes brought to trade to the Cayuses goods which they had obtained from peoples to the south and east: elk and buffalo meat, tanned robes, and skin lodges.

The Cayuses served as middlemen in the Grande Ronde entrepôt, choosing here, as elsewhere, to exchange goods rather than produce them. To the Nez Percés and Snakes, they traded dried salmon obtained from tribesmen in the vicinity of The Dalles, where the Columbia swirled between narrow basalt walls to create the Pacific Northwest's greatest river fishery. The Dalles, separating the interior and the coastal environments, was also a division point in the trade of the two regions. Sometimes the Cayuses returned to the Ronde with items ranging from shells to slaves which the Columbia fishermen had secured from coastal peoples. At The Dalles the Cayuses traded what they had received in the Grande Ronde.[14] Thus through the Ronde trade center passed goods from points as far away as the Pacific Ocean on the west and the Great Plains on the east.

For the Cayuses there was another paradise: the lush Walla Walla Valley. Like the Grande Ronde, it amply supplied their

14 Hubert Howe Bancroft, *The Native Races, Vol. I, Wild Tribes,* 274n.; Meredith Gairdner, M.D., "Notes on the Geography of Columbia River," *Journal of the Royal Geographical Society,* XI (1841), 253; Charles Wilkes, *Narrative of the United States Exploring Expedition During the Years 1838, 1839, 1840, 1841, 1842,* IV, 394–95; D. Lee and J. H. Frost, *Ten Years in Oregon,* 163.

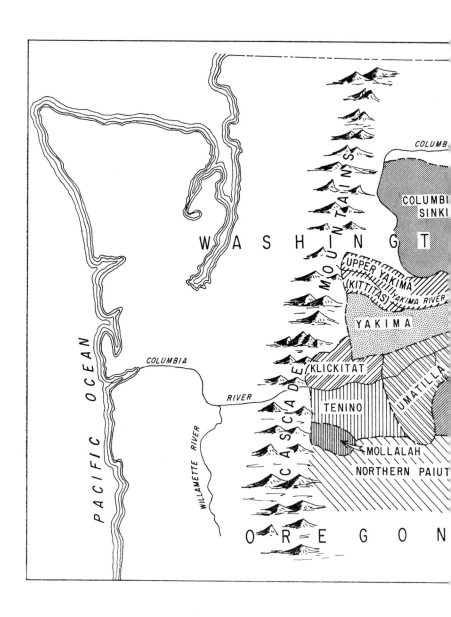

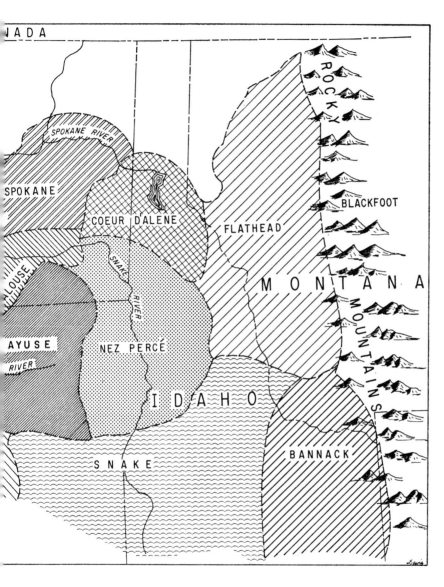

THE CAYUSES AND NEIGHBORING TRIBES IN THE OREGON COUNTRY AT THE
TIME OF WHITE CONTACT, ABOUT 1810

needs, and it too was an entrepôt and concourse of aboriginal travel. Trails from the Rockies and Cascades crossed those from Canada leading south across the Blue Mountains to the Owyhee River, a tributary of the Snake. In the Walla Walla the Cayuses annually met the Nez Percés and other Shahaptian peoples to trade and engage in friendly athletic competition. The valley floor provided excellent footing for horse or foot races and wrestling.

Above all, the two valleys were a meeting ground for the Cayuses and their Nez Percé allies. Since the Cayuses were the first Indians north of the Shoshonean peoples to have horses in large numbers, they supplied them to the Nez Percés and to Salishan peoples farther north.[15] The Nez Percés eventually became more proficient than the Cayuses in the selective breeding of horses, even castrating their stallions. From close economic relations between the two groups there emerged social ties, among them intermarriages ceremonialized in the exchange of horses. One of the most important by-products of the Cayuse–Nez Percé union was Cayuse adoption of the Nez Percé dialect, which was spoken by some four thousand people and was more fluid and considerably less complex than the dialect of the Cayuses.

The Cayuses' alliance with the Nez Percés stood them in good stead in forays against common enemies. Like the Nez Percés, they adopted the Great Plains philosophy of war as their own power grew and as others learned to respect it. Cold, taciturn, and high-tempered, they fought less for territory than for booty and glory. Young Cayuse males soon learned that by bringing home captured women, children, and horses they could raise their status in the eyes of their people. Among the Cayuses, as among peoples of the coast and unlike those of the Great Plains, status and possession were rooted in individuals and family groups rather than bands or tribes.

[15] James A. Teit, "The Salishan Tribes of the Western Plateaus," *Forty-fifth Annual Report of the Bureau of American Ethnology, 1927–1928*, 351.

An integral element of the borrowed Plains philosophy was the incorporation into Cayuse war custom of secret societies and ceremonial preparations for combat. As part of the latter, the young men fasted and purged themselves, swallowing fish oil and shoving willow sticks down their throats to induce vomiting.[16] The purifying sweat bath and ceremonial smoking of the pipe followed. The smoke was accompanied by harangues from the chiefs, who recalled past deeds of glory and exhorted their listeners to perform similar feats. In addressing their people, the chiefs spoke a language reserved for high state occasions, not the baser one of everyday usage.[17] The Cayuses' employment of two tongues may have been adopted from the Nez Percés, since the latter followed that practice and since the Cayuses were beginning to use the Nez Percé dialect. After the harangues came dancing and equestrian feats and maneuvers. Nor did the Cayuses overlook decorating themselves and their horses with paint, feathers, and other trappings.

Behind the ceremonial preparations lay an evolved institutional war machine. By the time of white contact, the Cayuses were composed of three distinct bands, each with a chief and political autonomy.[18] The three chiefs, whose decisions were binding on their people in peacetime, made up the tribal council. Social control was easily maintained, since the Cayuses clung to customs, handed down through generations, which did not conflict with their war posture. Those which did were discarded.

In preparing for war, the selection of chiefs was extremely important. War chiefs achieved their position through ability,

[16] Agnes C. Laut, *The Overland Trail*, 160. The swallowing of willow withes was also practiced by some Cayuses in the spring, to purge their bodies in lieu of a spring tonic. A number of willows were made as pliant as possible, and six or eight held in a row were shoved down the throat into the stomach until the person vomited bile. Andrew D. Pambrun, "The story of his life as he tells it," 179.

[17] Hubert Howe Bancroft, *The Native Races, Vol. III, Myths and Languages*, 625.

[18] For a discussion of political organization see Verne F. Ray, "Native Villages and Groupings of the Columbia Basin," *Pacific Northwest Quarterly*, XXVII, 2 (April, 1936), 113.

good judgment, and courage, having proved themselves in battle. In their hands lay control of a raiding party in enemy territory, a marked contrast to their limited power in their home camps. That sorties were carried out by small numbers of warriors did not minimize the importance of war chiefs in the eyes of their followers. The sight of the chiefs' bear-claw and feather-ornamented wolf headdresses, trailing skin behind, inspired the braves to action.

The Cayuses found adventure by raiding peoples west of the Cascade Mountains. They also ranged as far south as present-day northern California, where they took slaves from the Shasta Indians.[19] Moving into what is now southern Oregon, they took more slaves from the Klamaths and sometimes attacked tribes in the Willamette Valley. One hunting party returning from the Willamette was waylaid between the Cascades of the Columbia River and The Dalles by a party of Chinooks; the Cayuses promptly returned with a war party to even the score.[20] On some raids the Cayuses took their slaves, as well as Columbia River peoples, such as the Walla Wallas, whom they regarded as their inferiors.

Journeys to the country of the Snakes and the Plains tribes often required several days of hard riding over mountainous country. Risks were great. When they had located the enemy, the Cayuses regrouped to plan their attack, usually scheduling it for early morning. At the appointed time, they stealthily approached the unsuspecting camp. Then, with a rush, they shattered the stillness with shrieks. Before the enemy was alive to what was happening, the Cayuses charged, creating bedlam by peppering the camp with serviceberry shafts from their bows. At this point young men who wished to prove themselves on their first raid trailed off to steal horses.

The Cayuses made every effort to aid fellow warriors trapped

19 Garth, "Tribal Relations in the Columbia Plateau," 47.
20 Lee and Frost, *Ten Years in Oregon*, 177.

or wounded by the enemy. There were no women along to mourn the dead, no blankets or skins in which to wrap the bodies, no beads or shells with which to decorate them. There was little opportunity for the fallen to be properly buried with their mounts. When they could, the Cayuses retrieved their dead, burying them in rock-covered holes to prevent detection and desecration by man or beast. It was not practical to return, exhume, and reclothe the bones of the victims in order to comfort their spirits on the long journey to the Happy Hunting Grounds. When the warriors returned home to enumerate the dead, there was much wailing among the people, and the property of the deceased was burned.

On the brighter side for the Cayuses was their booty: horses, goods, and able-bodied women and children. No enemy men here; they had been killed. Tied to pack horses, the captives were led to an uncertain fate at the hands of their masters. Slaves gave the Cayuses increased status. More practically, however, they gathered fuel, helped with the harvest and in the preparation of food, and performed many of the chores assigned to Cayuse women.

White visitors regarded the Cayuse women as slaves because they worked at menial tasks which the haughty men would not perform. These proud warriors believed they could best contribute to the Cayuse economy by providing slaves and goods captured in raids. Devotion to their work notwithstanding, the women sought to beautify themselves with grease, paint, and assorted decorations. Their main garment was a long dress, usually made of tanned antelope or elk skin. During infancy they were subjected to head flattening so that in adulthood they would be attractive to men. Unlike the Chinooks, who used head wedging, the Cayuses bound their infants' heads tightly, with cords passed over pieces of folded hides, until the flattening process was complete. The result was a head with a broad, flat back and the suggestion of an edge around the top. To white observers, their appearance quite naturally seemed monstrous.[21] After the initial contact with white traders, Cayuse women indulged their vanity by tying pieces of mirrors or other shiny objects in their hair.

Cayuse men were equally conscious of their appearance. Increasing wealth and leisure gave them opportunities to decorate their clothing with trappings to complement their athletic physique, which was characterized by high shoulders, flat, long bodies (Cayuse men were often six feet in height), and flat chests. They had broad heads, with not particularly high cheekbones, aquiline noses, and black-brown eyes bordered by thin brows.[22] They paid meticulous attention to the care and decoration of their hair and clothing. Their skin shirts, often decorated with porcupine quills and frequently fringed on the outside seams, reached to the thighs, where they were supported by a waist tie. Fringed skin leggings extended to the upper part of the thigh. Of all their apparel, their tanned skin moccasins would be the last item they would discard in adopting white men's clothing.

With all their pride and desire to perpetuate their race and their valiant protection of one another in times of trouble, the Cayuses, despite the conjurations of their shamans, were mortal men subject to death from accident and disease. They were especially powerless to check infant mortality. Maternity lodges separated Cayuse mothers from their people for a month,[23] but death, many times resulting from the limited nourishment the mothers could provide, often separated them permanently from their offspring. Multiple births were thought to be the work of the Evil One, and children thus born were usually slain.[24] The

21 Clifford Merrill Drury, *First White Women Over the Rockies*, I, 127; Archer Butler Hulbert and Dorothy Printup Hulbert (eds.), *Marcus Whitman, Crusader, Part One, 1802 to 1839*, 274–75.

22 "Report by Chief Trader Samuel Black," Query 45.

23 *Transactions of the Nineteenth Annual Reunion of the Oregon Pioneer Association for 1891*, 100; Henry Rowe Schoolcraft, *Information Respecting the Condition and Prospects of Indian Tribes of the United States*, 655.

24 Charles N. Crewdson, "Christmas for the Hyas Skookum Papoose," *Seattle Post Intelligencer*, December 20, 1903; Lee Moorhouse, "The Umatilla Indian Reservation," *The Coast Alaska and Greater Northwest*, XV, 4 (April, 1908), 243.

death rate was high among medicine men, who killed their fellow practitioners for stealing power.

The Cayuses practiced polygamy to some extent. Those who did so were men of wealth, owners of many horses and other properties, seeking to enhance their status by having several wives. The loss of warriors in combat gave impetus to the practice. Should a Cayuse wife die, her husband could marry her sister. They also practiced sororate, in which a man could also wed his living wife's sister, and levirate, in which at a man's death his brother married the widow.

Countering forces working to diminish Cayuse numbers were other forces tending to keep them in balance. Losses in war were offset by the acquisition of slaves, and the Nez Percés served as a matrimonial reservoir to stabilize the Cayuse population. Moreover, the Cayuses appear to have escaped the ravages of a smallpox epidemic which raced the length of the Columbia River between the coast and the interior in 1782. It wiped out whole bands and halved many more. Cayuse immunity was perhaps more geographical than physiological, however, since they possibly fled to the isolation of the Blue Mountains to avoid contact with victims of the disease. Their population two years before the plague has been estimated at five hundred.[25] Subsequent figures vary widely, but over-all estimates indicate that the Cayuses were not greatly reduced by smallpox.

With a relatively stable population and power, ensconced in a domain stretching from the Snake-Columbia confluence across the vast plateau to the Snake borderlands, the Cayuses were truly an imperial tribe. Their empire received a measure of protection not only from a friendly environment but also from friendly neighbors. On the east were the Nez Percés. On the north were scattered Salishan peoples who, despite occasional raids for Cayuse horses, often went with the Cayuses and the Nez Percés to hunt buffalo on the plains. On the west The Dalles, portal to the Cayuses' heartland, remained under their control by what they

[25] James Mooney, *The Aboriginal Population of America North of Mexico*, 18.

claimed to be the right of ownership. Their practice of exacting tribute, in the form of salmon and other goods, from bands in the area served to give them jurisdiction over that stretch of the Columbia. For years to come they would not let its salmon eaters, teeth worn and eyes blinded by river sand, forget their inferiority.

Had they surveyed their accomplishments at the beginning of the nineteenth century, the Cayuses themselves would have had to pay tribute—to the animal on which they had ridden to power. In contrast to its owner, the cayuse was unprepossessing. Varying in color from black to white, with roans, bays, and other combinations between, it stood twelve to fifteen hands high. It was sure-footed and able to withstand hunger and rough treatment. Its speed and endurance were exceptional.[26] In the early nineteenth century a Cayuse Indian owning fifteen to twenty horses would hardly be considered affluent. Wealthier owners kept up to two thousand for recreation, travel, and trading purposes.[27]

The Cayuses were superb horsemen, a skill they learned rapidly after obtaining their first animals from the Snakes. Breaking colts provided them both enjoyment and challenge. When they lassoed an animal, they choked it down, tied both sets of feet, and threw a wolf or bear skin over its head, leaving it in this condition until it was exhausted and sometimes nearly asphyxiated. Then they loosened its feet. If the animal continued to lunge and tug at the rope, the breakers repeated the process until it became docile.[28] A further refinement in later days was to blindfold the animal after securing its feet. Then came the final act in the breaking process: they saddled the animal with a crude wooden rack and mounted before withdrawing the blinds.[29] The

[26] A. B. Meacham, *Wigwam and War-Path*, 200–201. The cayuse could be loaded to carry up to three hundred pounds. Ben Burgunder, "Recollections of the Inland Empire," *Washington Historical Quarterly*, XVII, 3 (July, 1926), 190–210.

[27] Samuel Parker, *Journal of an Exploring Tour Beyond the Rocky Mountains*, 314.

[28] Charles Grenfell Nicolay, *The Oregon Territory*, 194–95.

[29] E. A. Light, "Incidents of the Early Days," *Tacoma Weekly Ledger*, June 24, 1892; Lucien Williams interview, Gibbon, Oregon, July 17, 1968.

result was usually another serviceable horse and more wealth for its owner. Pride of ownership was revealed in the Cayuses' devotion to trappings—saddles, bridles, stirrups—which, besides being ornate, were utilitarian.

The horse fit the Cayuse way of life—or, perhaps more correctly, the Cayuses fitted their way of life to the horse. In their migrations they depended upon their mounts, which were also excellent pack horses, carrying up to three hundred pounds of gear and supplies, such as lodge mats and robes. Children were tied on gentle animals. And when the Cayuses made camp, the pack horses were turned loose to graze nearby as their owners set up housekeeping.

The cayuse had truly stood its masters in good stead. But the Indians faced a problem which the simple accumulation of horses could not solve. The cayuses had multiplied rapidly, but their owners had not; the deeply ingrained incursive life-style of the Cayuses kept their population small. Raids by hostile Snake Indians were an ever-present danger, but the Cayuses were threatened by another problem that was more gnawing and subtle. Having attained a position of dominance among the various tribes, they began to feel the need of new powers to sustain them—one reason, perhaps, why they contemplated the coming of the white man with little alarm. They had heard that the pale-faced ones had powder and ball, which far surpassed the bow and arrow in their ability to kill. Nor were guns the only magic white men had to offer; they possessed a world of marvelous goods ranging from beads to blankets—admirable means of displaying the wealth and superiority of the Cayuses. Since they had escaped most of the white man's diseases, the Cayuses' apprehension of the perils inherent in his coming may have been blunted. Liquor, the bane of red men, had scarcely reached them from traders operating on the Pacific Coast and east of the Rockies. The lure of the white man's merchandise was strong, however, and the Cayuses had something to offer for it: horses. Like dawn breaking in the east and sweeping over the Blue Mountains in the glorious promise of a new day, there would soon come from the east the palefaced ones, bringing to the Cayuses a different way of life. The imperial horseman waited.

II
Heart of the Beaver

It is one of the ironies of history that great developments in the life of a people have sometimes been the least recorded. Who knows when the first Cayuse returned home proudly carrying an ax, kettle, or gun fabricated in faraway Europe or eastern America? From traders at the end of the eighteenth century, poised to break the isolation of the Trans-Mississippi West, could have come to some Cayuse camp a teasing sprinkle of goods acquired through intertribal exchange. More likely, however, they came on the "pale-winged canoes" of merchants reaping profits from the Pacific maritime trade.

The nature of the first contact between coastal and interior traders and the Cayuses is unknown, but in all probability it was indirect. It is known that at the turn of the nineteenth century the Cayuses moved west to the Willamette Valley over aboriginal trails south of Mount Hood and north to the lower Columbia over an equally ancient trail beneath Mount St. Helens. They could have discovered white men's goods during raids or trading expeditions along the Willamette. The bulk of the western trade in these as in native goods was probably conducted in the vicinity of The Dalles. Likewise, to the east, on the plains, the Cayuses could have encountered white goods filtering west over established Indian trade routes. It is likely that most of the eastern trade was carried out in sheltered intermontane valleys, such as the Grande Ronde.

American explorers Meriwether Lewis and William Clark, who journeyed up the Missouri River, across the Continental Divide, and down the Snake-Columbia river system in 1805, do not mention seeing Cayuse Indians. Not even at The Dalles did they record such a meeting, but small groups of Cayuses could easily have escaped their notice in the late-October bustle of that place. Of the trade Lewis and Clark note:

> We cannot learn precisely the nature of the trade carried on by the Indians with the inhabitants below. But as their knowledge of the whites seems to be very imperfect, and the only articles which they carry to market, such as pounded fish, bear-grass, and roots, cannot be an object of much foreign traffic, their intercourse appears to be an intermediate trade with the natives near the mouth of the Columbia: from them these people obtain in exchange for their fish, roots, and bear-grass, blue and white beads, copper teakettles, brass armbands, some scarlet and blue robes, and a few articles of old European clothing. But their great object is to obtain beads, an article which holds the first place in their ideas of relative value, and to procure which they will sacrifice their last article of clothing or the last mouthful of food. Independently of their fondness for them as an ornament, these beads are the medium of trade, by which they obtain from the Indians still higher up the river, robes, skins, chappeled bread, bear-grass, etc. Those Indians in turn employ them to procure from the Indians in the Rocky mountains bear-grass, pachico, roots, robes, etc.[1]

It is possible that some Cayuses were among the Indians who met the explorers on the Columbia (the "Big River") below its confluence with the Snake (the "Little River"), for in addition to their mountain camps the Cayuses established dwellings along the Columbia, where they mingled with its natives, especially the Walla Wallas and the Umatillas. One of the chiefs, whom Lewis and Clark called Yelleppit, was described as a "handsome well-proportioned man" with a "bold and dignified countenance." Although they associated him with the Walla Wallas, he was perhaps none other than the Cayuse chief Ollicott (Allowcatt). They gave him a medal, a handkerchief, and a string of

---

1 James K. Hosmer (ed.), *History of the Expedition of Captains Lewis and Clark 1804–5–6*, II, 59–60.

wampum and promised to visit him on their homeward journey. True to their word, they came back the following April and were literally a sight for sore eyes, providing as they did eyewater and other medications to the Indians. In return Yelleppit gave them valuable aid, including fish and dogs to eat and horses and canoes to ride. The chief wanted to trade a fine white horse for a kettle but settled for a sword, powder, and some small articles.

Communication between the two groups was effected through a Snake prisoner in the Indian camp and Sacagawea, the Shoshoni woman with the expedition, which facilitated transactions. There was a fiddle-accompanied dance by men of the expedition and another by the Indians collected by Yelleppit, whom Lewis and Clark now saw as "a man of much influence, not only in his own but in the neighbouring nations." The confrontation had been mutually advantageous, and the explorers continued on their way.[2]

On Sunday morning, June 8, 1806, in the Bitterroot Mountains a Nez Percé chief, Cut Nose (named for a lance stroke he had suffered in battle with the Snakes), with twelve warriors entered the Lewis and Clark camp. Two members of the party called themselves Waiilatpus from "a band of Chopunnish [Nez Percés]," but they actually came from a Cayuse band, "which [people] we have not yet seen." The explorers described the latter as consisting of 250 souls living in thirty-three lodges under the "southwest" (Blue?) Mountains on a "small river" (Grande Ronde?) which fell into the "Lewis" (Snake) River above the entrance of the "Kooskooskee" (Clearwater). One of the Cayuses

2 A description of Lewis' and Clark's meeting with the Indian they called Chief Yelleppit is found in *ibid.*, 20, 271–72, 274. The first apparent mention by any white man of Cayuses as such on this stretch of the Columbia River was made by fur trader Alexander Ross in 1811, five years after Lewis and Clark were there. Fur trader David Thompson also passed that stretch of the river in 1811. J. B. Tyrrell, the editor of *David Thompson's Narrative of His Explorations in Western America, 1784–1812*, 350 n., identifies Allowcatt (Ollicott) as Yelleppit, the man Lewis and Clark met. Ross says Cayuse Chief Allowcatt and a Nez Percé chief took precedence over Walla Walla Chief Tumatapum. *Adventures of the First Settlers on the Oregon or Columbia River*, 137–41. The Cayuses' tribal records verify that Allowcatt was their chief.

traded his mount for an expedition horse that was unfit to cross the mountains. To even the unfair exchange, the explorers threw into the bargain a tomahawk they had obtained from a chief living below the Cascades (downriver from The Dalles) of the Columbia River, who had obtained it from a white trader on the coast. The Indians also traded the whites other horses from their bands, which one member of the expedition thought to have been the most numerous he had ever seen in the same space of country.[3]

Remembering President Thomas Jefferson's admonition to treat the natives in "the most friendly and conciliatory manner," the white men ran foot races with their hosts. Then the Indians watched the explorers play prison base, a rough-and-tumble game of capturing and releasing "prisoners" from two opposing teams —a diversion designed to toughen the men for crossing the mountains. The day ended with dancing to tunes sawed out on a fiddle. Two days later the explorers were gone. Pleasant encounters like these prompted Sergeant Patrick Gass of the expedition to write that, unlike the "rascally, thieving set" from the Cascades of the Columbia to the coast, the Indians above that point on the Columbia to the Rockies were "an honest, ingenious and well disposed people."[4]

Very likely the Cayuses, as did other other Indians who encountered Lewis and Clark, told their people of the travelers from the "Land of the Sun's Rising." In time they would learn that the expedition had created an equal stir among white men. For one thing, it guaranteed that the Columbia-Snake river system would become a rich prize in the international fur trade: six years after the Indians visited Lewis and Clark at the con-

3 Hosmer, *Expedition of Captains Lewis and Clark*, II, 327–28, 501; Bernard DeVoto (ed.), *The Journals of Lewis and Clark*, 348–49, 400.

4 Patrick Gass, *Journal of the Voyages and Travels of a Corps of Discovery*, 210–11. Lewis and Clark gave a flag to a Nez Percé chief. Forty-five years later, there was among the Cayuses at the Whitman mission an Indian who was supposed to have taken a flag from Lewis and Clark to plant in the Grande Ronde Valley as a token of peace between Snakes and the Nez Percés, Cayuses, and Walla Wallas. Wilkes, *United States Exploring Expedition*, IV, 394–95.

fluence of the two rivers, they met fur traders there. Contending for it were the Americans, "Boston men," and the British "King George men."

On July 9, 1811, the Indians encountered King George man David Thompson (Koo-Koo-Sint) on his downriver journey of a "Summer Moon" for the North West Company. As Thompson recorded it, the chief, probably Ollicott, met him and

> entered into all our views in a thoughtful manner, pointing out to us their helpless state, and that under their present circumstances they could never hope to be better, for we must continue in the state of our fathers, and our children will be the same, unless you white men will bring us Arms, Arrow shods of iron, axes, knives and many other things which you have and which we very much want.

Thompson informed the chief that his company had armed all the Indians, particularly the "Saleesh and Kootanaes," and that as soon as possible it would do the same for his people. The chief asked Thompson to establish a trading post at the confluence of the Snake and the Columbia, a suggestion pleasing to the Indians, particularly the women, who were much taken with the "Kettles, the Axe, the Awl, and the Needle," as well as blue beads, rings, "and other trifles." The chief wished to obtain weapons from the trader because his people had but few native ones. With white men's weapons they hoped to fight their Snake enemies, who had chased them from their mountain lands to the Columbia River, where they were forced to catch and prepare fish, a task they normally left to lesser river tribes.[5]

A month later some fifteen hundred Cayuses, Walla Wallas, and Nez Percés were encamped along the willow-lined banks of the Walla Walla where it debouched near columned bluffs into the Columbia a dozen miles below the Snake. This time they met traders from Boston man John Jacob Astor's Pacific Fur Company. Rivalry between the Nor'westers and the Astorians had

[5] Tyrrell, *David Thompson's Narrative*, 350–52.

25

been laid aside temporarily in the interest of mutual protection from troublesome Indians at The Dalles. Once that danger spot was passed, Thompson pushed ahead up the Columbia, and the Astorians followed. The Indians invited the Astorians to pass the day with them. All was calm in the Indian camp. Then a large delegation of braves moved in quiet procession toward the visitors' tent. To the Astorians, who had seen the Indians of the lower Columbia, the approaching plateau men were impressive, "generally tall, raw-boned, and well dressed," wearing buffalo robes, white deerskin shirts, and leggings, most of which were decorated with porcupine quills. Their moccasins were trimmed and painted red. To the whites they presented a picture of aboriginal affluence, especially the Cayuses and Nez Percés. The sight of some four thousand horses grazing nearby did little to alter the impression. Particularly eye-catching to the travelers were the guns with which the Cayuses, the Nez Percés, and some of the Walla Wallas were armed.

The warriors moved to within twenty yards of the traders' tent, where each of three chiefs—Tumatapum of the Walla Wallas, Quill-Quills-Tuck-a-Pesten of the Nez Percés, and Ollicott of the Cayuses—delivered harangues in the ancient manner, encouraged by occasional grunts of approval from their people, with Quill-Quills-Tuck-a-Pesten and Ollicott taking precedence over Tumatapum. After the harangues the chiefs and their headmen sat down with the traders to smoke the pipe of peace. At this point the women moved in. Their faces were painted red, and they were clothed in dressed deerskins reaching to their heels, with moccasins and leggings like those of the men and as richly garnished with beads, *higuas*, and other trinkets. Now assembled, the Indians danced and sang in a gesture of peace and friendship; the harmonious mood prevailed the rest of the day. The following day the traders continued up the Columbia to the Snake, where they found a large gathering of Indians, many of whom had followed them.

At the Snake the Astorians found in an Indian camp a British flag which Thompson had left there on his downriver trip to claim British possession north of that point. The chiefs hinted to the surprised and angered Astorians that Thompson had told them the Americans were not to trade above the Snake. The chiefs also said that Thompson had given them presents and that if Astorian leader David Stuart did likewise he could travel wherever he wished. The Indians' insatiable desire for white men's goods had apparently not lessened their ability to play the competition game, which they had learned well in the course of intertribal trading. Of their craving for trade goods, Alexander Ross, who was as careful in observing as in trading, wrote a prophetic description: "They require but little, and the more they get of our manufacture the more unhappy will they be, as the possession of one article naturally creates a desire for another, so that they are never satisfied."[6]

The Stuart party continued upstream to extend its operations in that direction. Soon other Astorians would penetrate the Cayuse heartland. On January 8, 1812, while encamped in the valley of the Umatilla close to the point where it receives McKay Creek (near present-day Pendleton, Oregon), a band of Indians witnessed the arrival of a "fatigued and enfeebled" group of whites from the east led by businessman Wilson Price Hunt. Struggling down the Snake River, across the Powder (a Snake tributary), the Grande Ronde Valley, and the Blue Mountains, the party was nearing the end of a nine-month journey which would take it to Astoria, situated at the mouth of the Columbia. The trip had become more frustrating and fatiguing with every mile, and the expedition had finally splintered in its search for routes and horses to ride over them. John Jacob Astor's plan to test the feasibility of extending a line of trading posts to the Pacific was proving as difficult as the stakes in such a project were high.

The thirty-four mat lodges of "Sciatogas and Toustchipas" (most likely Cayuses and Flatheads) looked inviting to the travel-

---

[6] Ross, *Adventures of the First Settlers*, 130–31.

weary Hunt.[7] Particularly impressive were their buffalo and deer-skin robes. He noted that some Indians had hide-and-mat tipis and that the men wore buckskin shirts and leggings, the women neatly made and ornamented willow-twig caps. In sum, wrote Hunt, they were the "equals [of] that of the best equipped indian tribes." Compared with the expedition's horses, which had been reduced to Pierre Dorion's skeleton steed and one other emaciated animal, the two thousand head ranging the pastures—green now, even in midwinter—gladdened Hunt's heart. So did the Indians' pots and copper kettles, which took precedence over their willow ones, indicating their willingness to trade for these items. When they refused to sell him some highly prized venison,

[7] There has been considerable speculation about the identity of the Sciatogas and Toustchipas. Some say the former were Nez Percés and the latter Kutenais. It seems unlikely that the Sciatogas were Nez Percés, for an early fur man, Alexander Henry, writes of them in his journals as dwelling west of the Nez Percés. Elliott Coues (ed.), *New Light on the Early History of the Greater Northwest: The Manuscript Journals of Alexander Henry, Fur Trader of the Northwest Company, and of David Thompson, Official Geographer and Explorer of the Same Company, 1799–1814* (cited hereafter as *Journals of Alexander Henry*), II, 818–19n. Writes Coues: "Or Sciatogas or Siatogas—that is, the Camass eaters of the N.W. The word is Paiute (Shoshonean); the terminal element *-toga* is the same as the *-tuka* which occurs so frequently in Comanche tribal names, and the *-rika* of various northern Shoshonean designations, as *Yamparika*, Yampa eaters, *Tukuarika*, Sheep eaters, etc. We used to hear a good deal about 'Sciatogas,' but the term was a loose one, indicating several different tribes of northern Paiutes (Shoshonean family), and also including the Cayuses, who are of Waiilatpuan stock. The name has, therefore, lapsed, as one having no exact classificatory sense. Judging from the context, Henry's Scietogas [*sic*] were most likely the Cayuses; but it is impossible to make any exact identification." The geographical location of the Sciatogas as delineated by Astorian Robert Stuart adds weight to their being Cayuses. Writes Stuart: "This nation is about 250 strong, and possess that tract of country bounded on the South east by the Bigflat [the Grande Ronde], on the North by Lewis' [Snake] river, on the West by the Columbia, and on the South by the Walamat, comprising an extent of nearly 100 miles square, intersected by many handsome streams, which are all well stocked with those animals we have come so far in quest of." Kenneth A. Spaulding (ed.), *On the Oregon Trail: Robert Stuart's Journey of Discovery, 1812–1813* (cited hereafter as *Stuart's Journey of Discovery*), 76.
It seems unlikely that the Toustchipas were Kutenais, since that tribe ranged primarily in what is now Canada. Most likely they were those whom Lewis and Clark called Shalees or Ootlashoots, the latter being of the larger grouping Toustchipas, which they called Tushshepahs, or Tushepaws. Hosmer, *Expedition of Captains Lewis and Clark*, II, 345, 506. In the early literature of the West, the word *Shalees* (*Saleesh* or *Salish*) became equated with *Flathead*.

Hunt discovered what other white merchants would find to be a Cayuse hallmark: their shrewd bargaining ability. In his improved state of mind, he seemed to overlook their stinginess and intimated that the venison was hard to come by, the deer being pursued skillfully on horseback, surrounded, and dispatched with bows and arrows with "singular dexterity." Surely he would have mentioned firearms had the Indians possessed them in any quantity. Many Cayuse and Flathead bands had them, but possibly those he met were not privy to the sources of that trade.

Before reaching the Columbia, Hunt learned that the Cayuses trapped beaver, which they traded to white men on the Columbia for tobacco in transactions sealed by big "smokes." The French-Canadians in the expedition, unaware that Stuart's party of Astorians had been on the Columbia, thought that the whites were representatives of the North West Company.

Grateful for the sustenance they provided the expedition, Hunt found no difficulty in evaluating his hosts as "extremely proud" and "the cleanliest indians that I know of," adding: "They do not eat either dogs or horses; nor will they permit the flesh of these animals to be brought into their lodges." The Cayuses were equally pleased with their visitors, particularly after the whites promised to come back with goods to barter for beaver. Hunt reached the Columbia on January 21 and Fort Astoria in mid-February, but the Cayuses waited in vain for his return.[8] War between the United States and Great Britain erupted in 1812, and the following year Fort Astoria was sold to the North West Company.

In July and August another Stuart in Astor's employ, Robert, crossed Cayuse country as he carried reports back to the German-

[8] Information on Hunt's expedition through the Cayuse country may be found in Philip A. Rollins (ed.), *The Discovery of the Oregon Trail*, Appendix A; *Stuart's Journey of Discovery*, 76; Washington Irving, *Astoria*, 310–12; John Bradbury, *Travels in the Interior of America in the Years 1809, 1810, and 1811*, 227–33; T. C. Elliott, *The Earliest Travelers on the Oregon Trail*, 4–15; William Brandon, "Two Thousand Miles from the Counting House: Wilson Price Hunt and the Founding of Astoria," *The American West*, V, 4 (July, 1968), 24–29, 61–63.

born financier. His description of Cayuse-Flathead bands along the route was similar to Hunt's:

This tribe [Sciatoga-Cayuse] as well as the Flatheads (who are reputed to be excellent Indians, about 1,800 warriors, and inhabit that tract of country situate between Lewis' River and the north west branch, or main Columbia, bounded in the rear by the Rocky Mountains) own immense numbers of horses, a great proportion of which run wild in these boundless plains, and are often the red and white man's only dependence for *food*—These two nations are less theivish [*sic*], and much more cleanly, than any of their neighbors; but they are of a haughty and imperious disposition, very impatient of insult and revengeful in the extreme.[9]

In reality the two peoples were not unlike their Snake rivals, belittling fur trading as "only fit for women and slaves," while asserting their independence because "their horses procured them guns and ammunition; the buffaloes provided them with food and clothing; and war gave them renown."[10]

Robert Stuart believed that with proper treatment the Cayuses could be "rendered the best and most useful division on this side of the [Rocky] mountains." Until then, he felt, they would have little reason to trap fur-bearing animals. These he regarded as plentiful throughout the Cayuses' domain, which stretched from the Walla Walla and Umatilla rivers across the Blue Mountains and down equally well-stocked streams in the Grande Ronde, Powder, and Burnt river systems south and east to the Snake borderlands. The Grande Ronde tributaries, wrote Stuart, contained "incredible multitudes of the Furr'd race ... in their bosoms."[11]

Beaver (Pieka) figures prominently in Indian mythology. A persistent (Cayuse?) legend has it that the Nez Percés, Cayuses, and Walla Wallas sprang from pieces of a giant beaver trapped in the Palouse River, whose falls he thrashed out in a retreat up-

---

[9] *Stuart's Journey of Discovery*, 76.
[10] Ross, *Adventures of the First Settlers*, 219.
[11] *Stuart's Journey of Discovery*, 72.

stream from the Snake. Since the Cayuses had sprung from Beaver's heart, they were more energetic, daring, and successful than their neighbors, a testimonial to their stature in aboriginal times.[12] In another legend tracing Cayuse origins to Beaver, the Great Spirit Creator Honeawoat, in response to Cayuse pleas, turned a brave, Takhstspul, into a beaver. With fire stolen from Mount Hood, he swam the Columbia to spit flame into a willow log. Thereafter, willow was used to make fire.[13]

Beaver's importance in the Cayuse genesis gave him no immunity from traps; both he and Otter were caught for their meat and skins. This was not true for Coyote (Talipus), from whose blood, according to another legend among Columbia River tribes, the Cayuses sprang. Coyote must not be harmed, for he was Creator; neither must camp dogs be harmed, because of their supposed relationship with Coyote.[14] The restriction seems not to have been applied to Wolf. White men had no such taboos, although some had feelings about the animals they killed. An old-time trapper in the Rocky Mountains gave this sentimental yet mercantile account of trapping:

> When the beaver are cut [caught] they will twist their foot off. They wont bite it off. They are the most harmless thing in the world. They are just like a little baby. Catch a beaver and touch it and it will just turn up its head; a little one will just turn up and cry like a little baby. I hated to kill them, but says I, "it is $5."[15]

Despite its potential for the fur trade, activity in the region through which the Astorians traveled began haltingly. On February 1, 1814, a party of Cayuses, Walla Wallas, and others visited Fort George (formerly Fort Astoria), asking its traders to come

---

12 Wilkes, *United States Exploring Expedition*, IV, 466–67.

13 Charles Erskine Scott Wood, *A Book of Tales*, 75–80. According to Chinook Indian legendry, Coyote made the Cayuses from the legs of a monster beaver so that they would always be swift runners. F. H. Saylor, "Legendary Lore of the Indians," *Oregon Native Son*, II (May, 1900–April, 1901), 198–201.

14 *Sketches of Mission Life Among the Indians of Oregon*, 47.

15 G. W. Ebberts, "A Trapper's Life in the Rocky Mountains of Oregon from 1829 to 1839," 15.

to their lands, where they said there were many beaver. They made no request, however, for the traders to hunt anything else. In fact the Cayuses and neighboring tribesmen had come to the North West Company's post via the Willamette River, where they had given a company hunter to understand that they wanted no white men and their guns on these ancestral hunting grounds, driving the deer away and making them so wild that they could not be killed with bow and arrow. The traders must have wondered how welcome they would be in Cayuse country when, six weeks later at Fort George, they received word that a Cayuse–Nez Percé war party at the Falls of the Willamette (some twenty miles upstream from its confluence with the Columbia) had killed many Indians, stolen many slaves, and caused general panic.[16]

It appeared that the Nor'westers in the interior trade could look for the same kind of trouble plaguing the Astorians. The key to Astorian success there had lain in the hands of one Donald McKenzie, a former Nor'wester. A man of great size, cunning, and daring, he had character to match that of the land. But, soured on the whole enterprise, partly because Astor had given precedence to Hunt, McKenzie had thrown away the key. In 1812 he broke up a post he had established shortly before in the upper Snake River country. Indian cache robbing and, worse yet, the killing of members of Astorian John Reed's party in the Boise River country during the winter of 1812–13 increased his disillusionment. The result was his initiative in the 1813 sale to the North West Company of Astorian furs and stock on the Columbia and the Thompson (a tributary of the Fraser in present-day Canada).

Not one to fight the Nor'westers, McKenzie rejoined them. In 1816 he returned to the Columbia and the following year reascended the Snake. The North West Company inherited not only its former rival's potential profits but also a number of problems, which had begun on the Palouse River in 1813, when

16 *Journals of Alexander Henry*, II, 818, 827, 853.

Astorian John Clarke hanged an Indian for stealing his silver goblet. This act by one whom Astor had dubbed "the brightest star in the Columbia constellation" did not brighten Nor'wester-Indian relationships and in fact stirred up further trouble by upsetting Indian chiefs throughout the Snake-Columbia country.

The chiefs showed their displeasure in 1814 at a large spring root gathering in the upper Yakima (Kittitas) Valley. To the sprawling noisy camp of Cayuses, Nez Percés, and four other major "warlike tribes" came Alexander Ross, now a Nor'wester, to trade for horses. The chiefs addressed him and his party in this fashion: "These are the men who kill our relations, the people who have caused us to mourn." Aware of the Indians' desire for trade goods—receipt of which, in their system of values, could even the score for a death—Ross met the crisis. Despite constant harassment from the pressing red horde, he gave the Indians a knife, beads, buttons, and rings and then strategically withdrew from their camp, his person and party intact.[17]

That fall the Cayuses moved down to the Columbia-Snake forks to begin the sedentary season, which inclined their normally tall, straight, muscular forms to corpulency. For food they had come to depend increasingly upon such tribes as the Yakimas, to whom they traded furs for salmon, and fisher bands in the vicinity of The Dalles, whose fisheries they claimed.[18] Many times the natives there received rough treatment at the hands of the Cayuses, who were not averse to whipping them when they committed what their overlords deemed some misdemeanor. The Cayuses treated the Columbia-dwelling Walla Wallas somewhat better, but they believed these less robust people to be descended from slaves. The Cayuses felt it beneath their dignity to marry Walla Walla women, although Walla Walla men married Cayuse women.[19] This demeaning attitude toward their neighbors did

[17] Ross, *Adventures of the First Settlers*, 212–14; Alexander Ross, *The Fur Hunters of the Far West*, 22–29.

[18] Lee and Frost, *Ten Years in Oregon*, 177.

[19] Parker, *Journal of an Exploring Tour*, 251; Gairdner, "Notes on the Columbia River," 251–57.

not prevent the Cayuses from obtaining salmon in exchange for horses. In the mountain valleys they depended upon their own skill to trap salmon with various types of barriers their ancestors had devised. One, which they called La Chanash, consisted of a low obstruction placed across a river to catch the leaping fish.[20] In some streams, such as those of the Grande Ronde, they caught salmon in natural shoals with their bare hands.[21]

One day in 1814 a Nor'wester bateau express en route to Fort George tried to slip by the Columbia-Snake forks in midstream to avoid detection by Indians camped there. The latter fired two warning shots to heel the bateau landward. Before the craft reached shore, the Indians jumped into the water and proceeded to beach her high and dry; not until the traders had "smoked themselves drunk" would the Indians allow them to depart. The warning was clear: do not pass this place without first putting ashore. Apparently, however, the Nor'westers did not heed the lesson in Indian protocol. The following June some traders ordered their voyageurs to pole through a rapid before stopping in still water above. They were met by a party of Indians who plunged horseback into the river and grabbed the boats. In the ensuing scuffle two Indians were killed and a third was badly injured. As the three were swept downstream, the traders crossed to the opposite shore before moving to an island for the night. The next day members of the brigade met with an Indian delegation. Ross recorded what happened: "After a three-hour negotiation the whites paid for the two dead bodies, according to Indian custom, and took their leave in peace and safety, and this ended the disagreeable affair."[22]

Unpleasantries did not deter the North West Company management, comfortably situated at Fort William in eastern Canada, from ordering construction of a fort near the two great branches of the Columbia system in 1818. Fort George officials had no

20 "Report of Chief Trader Samuel Black," Query 25.
21 Washington Irving, *The Adventures of Captain Bonneville, U.S.A., in the Rocky Mountains and the Far West*, 339, 342.
22 Ross, *Fur Hunters*, 47.

choice but to acquiesce in the decision—not an easy one because they were much closer to danger than their superiors at Fort William. Nevertheless, wrote Ross, who was assigned to manage the post, "the managers bit their lips and were silent."[23]

The site of the proposed fort, Nez Percés, was marked out "on a level point upon the east bank of the Columbia, forming something like an island in the flood, and by means of a tributary stream, a peninsula at low water." A half-mile upstream from the Columbia's confluence with the Walla Walla, the site lay in a mixed world of stillness and motion. Rugged bluffs, sandy stretches, and wild hills stood silently close by—summer blue, autumn gold, winter white and gray, and spring green. Salmon and sturgeon ruffled the placid Columbia, horses roamed the plain, and wild fowl flew overhead. The Indian warmed himself in his lodge or left it to fish, race, swim, palaver. Now the peace was threatened by white men bent on extracting a profit from the land. True, the Cayuses had wanted a trading post, but what sacredness would the land on which it was to be built hold for the traders? None of the traders' people lay in graves beneath the rock and soil rimming the site. What meaning did natural features have for them, save as helps or hindrances in the pursuit of their trade? To the Indians, each was a story. It had meaning.

The two basalt pillars rising nearly a thousand feet above the Columbia just below the spot where it receives the Walla Walla were known as the Cayuse Girls to Indians in the area. It seems that Coyote, having dispatched his rival, Grasshopper, arrived at a point within a few miles of the Walla Walla, where he fell in love with three Cayuse girls. They were carrying stones into the river to create an artificial rapid in which they could catch salmon. Always the trickster, Coyote watched their efforts from a hiding place; at night he destroyed their work. The girls rebuilt the barrier daily, but Coyote tore it down again each time. On the fourth morning he saw the girls weeping on the bank. When he asked them why they were weeping, they said they were starv-

23 *Ibid.*, 117.

ing for want of fish, which his trickery had denied them. Coyote thereupon proposed to build them a barrier if they would become his wives. Since it was either that or starvation, the maidens consented. A long row of stones projecting into the river fulfilled his promise. For many years Coyote lived happily with the sisters (not an uncommon custom among Cayuse males), but at length he became jealous of them. Using his supernatural powers, he changed two of his wives into basalt pillars, the third into a cavern downstream, and himself into a rock so that he could watch them forever.[24]

The Cayuses and their neighbors were bewildered by the curious assortment of strangers in their land: daring French-Canadians, patient Owyhees from the Sandwich (Hawaiian) Islands, and treacherous Iroquois brought from the East to encourage the Northwest Indians in the fur trade.[25] The last-named were solicitous, too, seeking favors from the builders and payment for logs rafted to the fort. Until these demands were met, there would be no hunting or fishing for the newcomers—and no trade. The whites, however, had by now established a beachhead in a temporary enclosure. Trade began. The workers continued to build.

The Cayuses had made peace with the fur men but not with their perennial enemies the Snakes, a matter apparently of less concern to them than to the traders. Warfare had become a way of life—and death—for the Indians; for the traders it could mean ruin. They knew that only through the friendly disposition of the Snakes could the door be opened to a vast storehouse of furs.

One day the chiefs assembled to palaver with the traders, an occasion on which an astute observer could compare the customs and value systems of the two groups. To a chieftain there could be no better use for a wolfskin than to wear it on his head. Orna-

---

[24] Paul Kane, *Wanderings of an Artist Among the Indians of North America From Canada to Vancouver's Island and Oregon Through the Hudson's Bay Company's Territory and Back Again by Paul Kane*, 185–88.

[25] Richard T. Conn, "The Iroquois in the West," *The Pacific Northwesterner*, IV, 4 (Fall, 1960), 59–63.

mented with bear claws or bird feathers trailing the ground or floating in the breeze when its wearer was on horseback, it crowned him with glory. Equally precious to him was his black-leather girdle, binding his painted shirt and holding his medicine bag, pipe, and other articles. In their proper places were his weapons: lance, scalping knife, bow, quiver of arrows, and the most valuable item obtainable from the white man, a gun. Under him was his favorite horse, his most prized possession, even though he had paid an Indian trader very little for it. He and his people were willing to trade other horses at a reasonable price.[26]

The Indians preferred white horses, with mottled black and white their second choice. The animals' necks were dappled with streams of red and yellow; tails were black and red, clubbed in a knot, and tied short. Head and tail were ornamented, the former with a feather cluster some twenty inches above the ears and the latter with two feather streamers and, as the trade increased, ribbons. In sum, the Indians augmented nature's coloration by painting and otherwise decorating their mounts as they did themselves, creating an illusion of physical unity between man and beast to match what they considered the mystical union between them. At no time was this more apparent than when chiefs and warriors maneuvered their mounts before a battle. Ross described the scene:

> This moment throwing themselves to the right, the next moment to the left side of the horse, twisting and bending their bodies in a thousand different ways. Now in the saddle, out of the saddle, and nothing frequently to be seen but the horses, as if without riders, parrying or evading. . . . So dexterous and nimble were they in changing positions and slipping from side to side that it was in the twinkling of an eye.[27]

One of the important cultural differences between white and

---

26 Nor'wester Ross Cox records the purchase on April 27, 1817, of seven horses "moderately cheap" from a party of "Shyatogoes" and Walla Wallas in the vicinity of Fort Nez Percés. *Adventures on the Columbia River*, II, 168.

27 Ross, *Fur Hunters*, 202–203.

Indian was, of course, language. In communicating with the Indians the traders usually addressed their remarks in French to their Canadian employees, who, through close association with the Indians (including marriage to Indian women), had quickly learned the various native tongues. Standing thus between trader and customer, the Canadians interpreted for both. Perhaps the nearest thing to a universal language employed at trading posts was the flexible Nez Percé dialect, which was undoubtedly understood by the multilingual chiefs. In conveying information to their people, however, Cayuse chiefs used their own distinctive tongue.[28] This system of trader-Indian communication was cumbersome at best, but scarcely more so than the use of Chinook jargon, which worked its way from the lower Columbia to the interior posts. One trader described it as "gibberish, by which we communicate with the Indians . . . a vile compound of English, French, American & the Chenooke dialect . . . such a miserable medium of communication, that very few ideas can be expressed in it."[29]

Another difference in the cultures of traders and Indians was manifested when the latter received word that Walla Walla Chief Tumatapum had returned from warring against the Snakes. They broke off their talks with Ross in favor of a big welcome for the chief. At such homecomings it was customary for the returning warriors to shout and chant as they approached camp, whereupon the old men and women and boys and girls rushed to meet them. In a violent display of vengeance the women pulled the war party's prisoners from their horses, trampled them, tore their hair and flesh—jabbing them with knives, sticks, stones, or any other weapons they could find—then drove them into camp. In the afternoon the camp turned out en masse for a scalp dance. The men, standing some fifteen feet apart, formed two rows, at least a hundred yards long, facing each other. Inside, two rows of

28 "Report of Chief Trader Samuel Black," Query 25; Sir James Douglas Private Papers (First Series), 13.

29 R. G. Large (ed.), *The Journals of William Fraser Tolmie, Physician and Fur Trader*, 210, 221–22.

women faced each other, leaving a five-foot space in the middle. In this area male and female captives were stationed, naked to the waist, holding long poles on which were displayed the scalps of their dead relatives. When the dancing and chanting began, captive and captor alternated to the right and left to the rhythm of a loud drum. The women jeered and subjected the captives to still more torture if they did not "laugh and huzza." Dancing ceased at dusk. The captives were then taken to camp and cared for in friendly fashion, but the next day the cruel routine was repeated. When the ceremonies ended, the captives were no longer regarded as common property. Now slaves, they were placed under their owners' care, after which they were better treated. Yet they were still slaves, and their owners could sell or trade them as they would any other property.[30]

When the council with the traders resumed, Tumatapum, exhilarated by the homecoming ceremonies, remarked: "If we make peace, how shall I employ my young men? They delight in nothing but war, and besides, our enemies, the Snakes, never observe peace." He paused. "Look," he continued, pointing to his slaves, scalps, and arms, "am I to throw all these trophies away? Shall Tum-a-tap-um forget the glory of his forefathers, and become a woman?" The Cayuse war chief Quahat, powerful from the days before the white men came, rose to speak. Like others in the vicinity of Fort Nez Percés, he possessed more authority than many chiefs on the long Columbia, even those of the numerous Nez Percés. He asked: "Will the whites in opening a trade with our enemies promise not to give them guns or balls?" When he had finished his speech, others spoke in the same vein. The traders countered by explaining the prospects for peace and comfort which would follow the trade.[31]

Several meetings were held to discuss this weighty problem. Then one day a messenger notified the traders that the chiefs were of one mind and would present themselves in council to

30 Ross, *Fur Hunters*, 203–205.
31 *Ibid.*, 123.

announce their decision. Soon an entourage of armed and painted chiefs, headmen, and warriors arrived to speak with the white men. There followed a profound silence until the pipe had circled the seated group six times. As the sun dropped behind the hills bordering the west bank of the river, the Indians promised to make peace with the Snakes and gave the traders permission to pass to the Snake country unmolested. They threw their garments on the ground, not merely as a gesture of peace but with the hope of obtaining new clothing from the whites (the Cayuses never allowed ceremony to preclude economic consideration). After another smoke the final seal was put on the treaty.

The Indians may have wondered how permanent the new peace would be; they had made peace with the Snakes before. To himself, but not to them, Ross gloomily evaluated it as "an empty name." Nevertheless, economic necessity demanded that trade be pursued in Snake quarters. In the days ahead their hosts would never let the traders forget that harmony depended no less on the friendly disposition of the Cayuses than on that of the Snakes. For on them, as one trader would put it, depended the success of "business along the Communication."

III
Along the Communication

With a tenuous hope of peace the first Snake expedition set out in September, 1818, under Donald McKenzie: 55 men, 195 horses, 300 beaver traps, and much merchandise. Although it was strong in numbers, all kinds of rumors floated back over the Indian grapevine, hinting of misfortune along the way at the hands of the Snakes. Six months later McKenzie returned, reporting no difficulties from the Snakes but plenty from his Iroquois, who had scattered to take up with native women and live off the land. Discouragement was offset by McKenzie's glowing description of primitive country capped by rich beaver lands at the end of the trail between the Snake and Green rivers.

After a week at Fort Nez Percés, McKenzie went back up the Snake, only to return two months later (his nickname, "Perpetual Motion," was not unwarranted). Other expeditions into the Snake country followed. They were generally successful but always hazardous because of three perils enumerated by Ross: "The Nez Percés behind, the Blackfeet before, the hostile Snakes everywhere around; our people . . . completely surrounded."[1]

The peaceful councils among the Cayuses, their allies, and the fur traders had not altered the whites' plan to build a strong fort. An Indian coming to watch the progress (as many did, some from as far away as The Dalles) would have seen workmen surrounding a hollow square with sawed planks twenty feet long, two and a half feet wide, and six inches thick. A range of four-foot palisades was erected on top to serve as ramparts and provide loopholes,

[1] For an account of the councils with the chiefs and the subsequent opening of the trade, see Ross, *Fur Hunters*, 118–44, 151.

with the whole structure supported by a strong five-foot gallery. Had the visitor some idea of shooting a fire arrow into the fort, his efforts might have been thwarted by reservoirs holding up to two hundred gallons of water. Had he, by special invitation, been permitted to enter the completed fort, he would have passed through an outer gate and then two double doors leading to a twelve-foot-high interior wall with portholes and slip doors beneath two strong wood bastions and a long cannon. With such security it would seem that the Cayuses and their neighbors did not exactly have the run of the place.

The traders usually permitted no more than two or three Indians, and occasionally a few chiefs, to enter the fort at one time. Trade was carried on through an eighteen-inch-square opening in the wall, secured by an iron door behind which was a trading shop. Despite a house erected at the gate strictly for the Indians' use, with fire, tobacco, and a man on duty at all hours, the chiefs viewed the restrictions as a mild affront. "Are the whites afraid of us?" they asked. "If so we will leave our arms outside." "No," said trader Alexander Ross, "but your young men are foolish." The chiefs had to agree. Their trouble-bent young braves might have found their match in the fort's four one- to three-pound pieces of ordnance, ten wallpieces, sixty stands of muskets and bayonets, twenty boarding pikes, and a box of hand grenades. With sturdy palisades like those of basalt nearby, Fort Nez Percés was well named "the Gibraltar of the Columbia," and Ross accurately observed that the trade had "a mixture of the mercantile and the military."[2] Floating over the fort was the Union Jack, symbol of Britain's power and, as Ross put it, her "energy and enterprise, of civilization over barbarism."

The arts of trade and commerce were having little civilizing effect on the "barbarians." They sauntered around the fort, demanding guns, ammunition, flints, and knives on pain of forcing the whites to leave their lands. They scalp-danced, horse-raced,

2 *Ibid.*, 144–46.

gambled, and otherwise idled their time away. They could be seen on every hillock making their toilet, with looking glass in one hand and paintbrush in the other.

To add to the tensions at the fort, problems in the Snake trade had now reached its very doors. A band of Nez Percés returning from an expedition against Snake marauders killed some of them, as well as two members of a fur brigade returning to Fort Nez Percés. In retaliation for their own losses the Snakes trailed the Nez Percés to within three miles of the establishment, killing some stragglers from a Walla Walla camp—one man, four women, and five children—carrying off their scalps, and taking as slaves two young women and a man. In response to this deed some four hundred Cayuse, Nez Percé, and Walla Walla men and women, on foot and horseback, approached the fort—too large a body for its arsenal to match if they became hostile. At the gate they howled, shrieked, cut themselves, and laid the bloated bodies of the Snakes' victims on the ground. Pointing to wounds in his "sister's" body which fort personnel thought resembled arrow wounds, Tumatapum blamed the disaster on the traders for having given balls and guns to the Snakes, all of which could have been a shrewd move to absolve himself of blame for breaking a promise to keep the peace between his people and the Snakes. Knowing better than to question the chief's motives openly, Ross went into the fort, emerged with some red cloth, and laid six inches of it on each body as a token of sympathy. Much lamentation followed; then the mourners moved off to bury their dead.

A brother of one of the women kidnaped by the Snakes pitched his lodge within fifty yards of the fort and began chanting a song —"throwing his body away," as the Indians put it. Then he shot himself in the chest. One of his brothers accused a friendly medicine man sitting at the fort gate of having cast a spell on the wounded man and proceeded to shoot him dead on the spot. Pandemonium ensued: Someone shot the man who had shot the medicine man, and before the chiefs arrived, three more men had been shot. The environs of the fort looked like a battlefield,

43

with five Indians lifeless on the ground and twice as many wounded. Other Indians joining the deadly melee, not knowing what was going on, fired a shot or two at the fort.

The chiefs quickly restored order, and the five bodies were taken away to the Indian camp. Ironically, the attempted-suicide victim survived. The next day the Indians returned to the fort with plenty to talk about and many questions to ask. They indirectly accused the traders of all the troubles and worked themselves up for war against the Snakes. Since such a war would jeopardize the fur trade, fort personnel sought every means to divert them. It took a week of smoking and palaver to calm them down, whereupon the chiefs solemnly promised not to renew hostilities, at least until the fur brigades were gone from the Snake country.

There were signs that the bad relations between the fort tribes and the Snakes might improve. McKenzie and his brigade returned in late spring, 1820, bringing between two and three thousand pelts and two Snake chiefs, the powerful Pee-eye-em and his brother, Amaquiem, of what Ross termed the "Plains-hunting Sherry-dika Snakes." The two had asked to see the Cayuses, exclusive of the Nez Percés, and were afforded protection by the brigade. A welcoming party of Cayuses met the party as it emerged from the Blue Mountains, and all continued peacefully down to the fort. There the Snake envoys and the Cayuses probably laid some sort of groundwork for peace.

Underway at about the same time among the white men were negotiations which would put Fort Nez Percés into the hands of the Hudson's Bay Company in 1821. Snake brigades continued to operate from the fort for a time, but others were launched from more northerly company posts. One such party departing from the Flathead post (near present-day Eddy, Montana) in late 1823 under Ross's leadership learned that Snake-Cayuse peace parleys were about to bear fruit. The following summer on the lower Boise River, Ross heard from Pee-eye-em, who had just completed a two-day journey from the plains, that a peace party from the fort was a short distance away in the camp of Amaketsa, chief of the water-dwelling Snakes, whom Ross called the "War-are-ree-kas" (Warraricas). Accompanied by Pee-eye-em and his warriors, Ross, after a hard ten-mile ride, reached the Warrarica camp at dusk to hold a happy reunion with his far-from-home Cayuse friends.

In rather un-Indian fashion the matter of peace was immediately discussed. Everyone, including Ross, spoke to the question. Pee-eye-em mounted his horse and rode around for some time haranguing the people, who indicated their approval by shouting, "Ho! Ho! Ho!" Thereupon a number of older men conferred and in loud, drawling tones consented to Pee-eye-em's words. There now remained the smoke to conclude the peace. Such ceremonies meant much to Indians, particularly the Snakes, who claimed that they were the first on earth to smoke tobacco.

Pee-eye-em was in charge of arrangements. He seated the Cayuse emissaries and Ross at the back of the lodge. Then eighteen Snake chiefs entered and squeezed down on either side. Across from them, his back to the door, Pee-eye-em sat on his haunches, with Amaketsa on his right and another man on his left, apparently to act as sergeant at arms during the ceremony. The diplomatic circle was now complete. Silence. Pee-eye-em opened a medicine bag, from which he drew a decorated pipe. The bag was not much different from those the Cayuses used in their ceremonies, another indication, perhaps, that the Cayuses and their plateau allies had obtained many of their trappings from Indians to the east on the plains. After a great deal of presmoking ritual, Pee-eye-em took his pipe in both hands, drew three whiffs from it, blew a smoke cloud on its stem, and uttered a prayer. Then, pointing the pipe to the cardinal points of the compass, he blew three puffs of smoke in each direction, followed by more on the stem, signifying that the hatred of war should be buried beneath the earth. Rising, he presented the pipe to one of the Cayuses, whom he directed to touch it with his mouth but not to inhale. He ordered the Cayuse to repeat the process, apparently intend-

45

ing that he understand the seriousness of what was transpiring. Then, putting it to the mouth of the Cayuse a third time, he said: "You may smoke now." After the Cayuse had smoked, Pee-eye-em said to him: "We are brothers."

The pipe was passed around the circle, with the Sherry-dika chief filling and lighting it himself. The tobacco, from a low-growing plant, pounded fine and resembling green tea, must have seemed mild to Ross and to the Cayuses, who were now accustomed to that of the traders. But this was no time to express dissatisfaction with so much as a grimace. Not until after midnight did Pee-eye-em permit the participants to emerge from the stuffy lodge into the fresh air—or air as fresh as air could be in a Warrarica fishing camp on a warm summer night. Ross invited the Cayuses to his camp, promising to escort them out of danger, for he was not completely convinced that Snake treachery might not befall them. Later he learned that his friends had returned to their people in safety.[3] Now, perhaps, trade and the pursuit of other peaceful arts could resume between the Cayuses and their Snake neighbors at fairs like those in the Grande Ronde, where the Cayuses traditionally exchanged their horses for furs, buffalo robes, and skin lodges.

Despite his power, Pee-eye-em could not guarantee that the peace so ceremoniously sealed in smoke might not go up in a puff of the same substance. He had little control over renegade Snake bands, particularly those Ross called the "Ban-at-teels" (Bannacks), which often left their mountain fastness near the lower middle Snake to commit depredations on their enemies. Pee-eye-em had even less control over equally fractious Cayuse and Nez Percé bands, which were likewise free to raid without much tribal restraint.

Although they tried to be hopeful, the fur traders were skeptical of the prospects for peace. When Hudson's Bay Company superintendent George Simpson inspected his firm's establishments west of the Rocky Mountains, he penned at Fort Nez Percés

3 *Ibid.*, 161, 166–67.

on November 3, 1824, an accurate description of the Indians' behavior, observing that they "smoke a Pipe of Peace and part with professions of Friendship but their treaties are no sooner ratified than broken as the moment the conference is over and we turn our backs they are ready to pillage each others Women and Horses and cut each others throats."[4] Simpson's words were borne out the following May, when some Cayuses and Snakes skirmished over horses; a Cayuse was killed, and a Snake chief was severely wounded.[5] More trouble for the Hudson's Bay Company. Yet the chief trader at Fort Nez Percés, John Dease, happily reported on April 7, 1826, that the previous summer he had sent Cayuses and Nez Percés to make peace with the Snakes and thereby cool their mutual hostility. The mission was apparently successful, for the emissaries returned in about six weeks with nearly eight hundred beaver skins.[6] The catch was far below the estimated two thousand beaver of 1824, the most that had ever been brought to the fort. One reason for the low yield may have been what Simpson called "mortality" among the Cayuses during the winter, which prevented them from trading.[7] The malady could have been smallpox, from which the tribes had suffered for fifty years, or it may have been a newly arrived white man's disease, such as measles.

Even when the Cayuses were up and about securing beaver, the economy-minded Simpson thought they and their neighbors exhibited too much independence and too little exertion in the hunts, that they brought in furs only when they felt the need of trade items, being more interested in trappings than trapping. Chief trader John L. Lewes, writing to Simpson from Fort George on April 2, 1822, viewed in a more favorable light the commerce of the Indians, who had "become so much accustomed

---

[4] Frederick Merk (ed.), *Fur Trade and Empire: George Simpson's Journal* (cited hereafter as *Simpson's Journal*), 55.

[5] E. E. Rich (ed.), *Peter Skene Ogden's Snake Country Journals, 1824–25 and 1825–26*, 252.

[6] *Simpson's Journal*, Appendix A, 273.

[7] *Ibid.*, 127.

to the produce of the Civilized world, that they find it necessary to exert themselves to procure their wants and this they know can only be by their hunting the beaver."[8]

Both Simpson and Lewes had evaluated the situation correctly. The Cayuses had truly ambivalent feelings about the trade. They took no great initiative in it and yet felt that only through it could they obtain the goods they needed to strengthen their individual and collective affluence and influence. They had in fact been the first Indians in the vicinity of Fort Nez Percés to trade beaver and horses for guns and ammunition.[9] They showed more interest in caring for and trading horses than furs. The horse trade must have been as lively as that in skins, for we find Simpson complaining about the slaughter of no less than 700 animals in three years' time to supply the needs (mostly food) of the fort. Because of economies made at the fort, such as a skeleton crew, the Indians annually supplied fewer horses.

When Simpson returned to Fort Nez Percés from the lower Columbia in late March, 1825, he did not have to look very far to see more trouble. He found Dease surrounded by some three hundred lodges of Nez Percés, Cayuses, Walla Wallas, and neighboring bands. This in itself was not unusual, but Dease, the "great tea Drinker," as Simpson dubbed him, was in trouble with the Indians. The difficulty apparently stemmed from the disaffection of his interpreter, who, when Dease reprimanded him for "over intimacy with the natives and indiscreet amours both in the Camp and at *Home* [the fort]," had sought to incite the tribes against the establishment. The incident strengthened Simpson's belief that "9 Murders out of 10 Committed on Whites by Indians have arisen through Women."[10]

Simpson later learned through his servant that Dease's interpreter was in league with the Cayuse chief Umtippe (Cut Lip or Split Lip) to massacre the inhabitants of Fort Nez Percés—not a

---

8 *Ibid.*, Appendix A, 176.
9 "Report by Chief Trader Samuel Black," Query 25.
10 *Simpson's Journal*, 127.

difficult undertaking considering the fact that besides Dease there were only eleven other men at the post. The deed was to be done immediately after Dease and his small party left for Fort George with the season's catch. On Sunday, March 27, in an attempt to stave off the rumored attack, Simpson met with three hundred warriors led by nine chiefs: five Cayuses, three Nez Percés, and a Walla Walla. The superintendent gave them about a two-hour speech and some presents, including the customary dram of rum.

The practice of "giving the dram" had grown from Nor'wester days to the point where, at this moment, Simpson could have done nothing else. When they first tried it, the Indians found the rum hard to swallow, but over the years they had developed a taste for it. In fact, so strongly had their thirst increased that in some quarters along the Columbia they received a bottle of rum for every ten skins they brought in. Simpson vowed to end this practice, not in the interest of native sobriety but to cut expenses.

Gifts from the hand of the superintendent included two fathoms of tobacco, three more fathoms for the general use of the camp, and fifty loads of powder and ball. Wrote Simpson:

> The Speech and present were well received, they promised to exert themselves in hunting, to respect the Whites, to protect us while on their Lands and begged me to assure the great Chiefs on the other side of the Water, that they had not two Mouths, one for me, an other for the Camp, that they meant what they said[,] would act up to it and that their hearts were now exactly like those of White Men. Four Hours and many pipes of Tobacco were consumed in this Council, we parted excellent Friends, they proceeded quietly to the Camp with their followers.[11]

In all likelihood Simpson had overrated the danger at Fort Nez Percés. For that matter, he had perhaps also overrated his own peacemaking ability, for he never changed his opinion that the Indians there were "a capricious and treacherous race." He was unhappy with Dease's indulgence, which permitted them

[11] *Ibid.*, 127–28.

more privileges than they had ever before enjoyed at the post. It should be said, however, that the Indians treated Dease as an adopted father. On one occasion in the fall of 1825 he was a special guest at a most unusual event. A chief, after suffering a chain of misfortunes, including the loss of some sons (his bow string had been broken, as he put it), ordered his people to bury him alive. They and, quite naturally, Dease were opposed to it. Always one to allow the Indians their lifeways, however, the trader made no great protest. He received a portion of the chief's legacy: ten of his finest horses. Careful to obey the chief's last request, Dease saw to it that a flag was placed on his grave.[12]

Dease's gesture was heartfelt, but it was also good public relations and certainly in line with company policy to keep Fort Nez Percés operating. The governor and committee in faraway London had urged that the Snake country be exploited before the Americans received it as a result of the inevitable boundary settlement, in which, they believed, the British would be pushed north of the Columbia River.[13] That event was some twenty years off, but consideration of it was already affecting trader-Indian relations at the fort. So eager were the governor and committee to keep the good will of the Indians that in March, 1827, they expressed regret that the new chief trader, Samuel Black, had received orders from his superiors to persevere in moving the fort across the Columbia River to what stood a good chance of becoming British soil. It would have been better, wrote the committee, to have forts on both sides of the river if that was required to keep the Indians happy.

No less interested in harmonious company-Cayuse relations was Simpson. On April 10, 1825, he wrote chief factor Dr. John McLoughlin at Fort Vancouver that "it would be expedient" if trader John Work (whom another trader had dubbed a wanderer "among the Serpents & independent of their venom") took for a

---

12 Peter Skene Ogden [?], *Traits of American Indian Life & Character, By a Fur Trader* (cited hereafter as *Traits of American Indian Life*), 24–27.
13 E. E. Rich (ed.), *Simpson's 1828 Journey to the Columbia*, 50–51.

wife the daughter of a chief of the Cayuse Indians, "the expenses to be defrayed by the Company." Since Work would be a frequent traveler with brigades through Cayuse country, Simpson believed it necessary that "the lady . . . be a passenger on every trip."[14]

The Cayuses were aware of their importance, which by the late 1820's far outweighed their numbers. There had never been many of them in the fort era. They were, in fact, the smallest tribe in the vicinity. In 1829, according to trader Black, there were no more than fifty-four braves. His estimate may not have included scattered Cayuse bands who engaged in very little, if any, trade at Fort Nez Percés. Six years after Black's report, however, the missionary-traveler the Reverend Samuel Parker, in exuberant error, placed Cayuse numbers at two thousand.[15] There is no population breakdown of the three largest Cayuse villages: one under Chief Camaspelo on the headwaters of the Umatilla, another downstream on the Umatilla under two chieftain brothers, Five Crows (Achekaia or Pahkatos) and Young Chief (Tauitau), and a third on the upper Walla Walla under the chieftaincy of the aged Umtippe.

Lesser numbers notwithstanding, the Cayuses continued to display their opulence as though they were the most powerful people on earth. The natural simplicity of their clothing and ornaments, in which, as with their horses, they had always taken great pride, was compromised by trappings and ornaments obtained from the traders. Scarlet cloth joined porcupine quills and human and horse hair to grace the back of deerskin shirts and leggings. To native paints which rendered a black- and white-streaked Cayuse face red, white, or green was added lampblack carried in a small ornamented pouch. With a wooden pin both Cayuse men and women applied the blacking as a beauty mark between the eyelashes and from the outer corner of the eye to

[14] Isaac Burpee, "The Story of John Work," 5; *Simpson's Journal*, Appendix A, 286.
[15] Parker, *Journal of an Exploring Tour*, 314.

the upper part of the ear. A looking glass in a thin wooden frame often replaced talismans around the neck. Pieces of shiny metal in the hair mingled with bead- and quillwork ornaments.[16]

The Cayuse sometimes surrendered to the white man's style by sporting trousers, shirt, and cap, but these were misfits for his body and spirit.[17] He looked best wearing Indian garments from the soles of his moccasined feet to the top of his headdress. To the latter, Black wrote,

> greatest attention is paid. . . . The hair is thought most handsome when it is long and thick. The hair ("part sometimes Borrowed") is usually worn in "two enormous Clubs," one on each side of the head, "some few Nearly to the Heels." Care is taken to cover the forehead with hair, sometimes in the form of "a bunch covered wt the cut ends of Crow Feathers in the form of a Rose wt a Button or Rattle Snakes Rattle &c in the Centre." The "clubs" are formed of "Three plaits matted To the Shoulders from which they are tied to the end wt Slips of Leather & covered or Rolled round wt Slips of the Blackest Fur they Can find generally Otter-Beaver." "When at play &c" the clubs of hair are tied to the crown of the head. Ornaments for the hair are of many different kinds, bead-work or quill-work, pieces of metal, "anything polished sparkling or shining they can pick up."[18]

The Cayuses may not have been unmindful that their importance to the Hudson's Bay Company was beginning to lie not so much in their trading as in their good will. They still controlled the routes through which the fur brigades passed into the Snake country. McLoughlin was widely regarded as a stern disciplinarian of dissident Indians, but he handled the Cayuses with re-

16 "Report by Chief Trader Samuel Black," Query 25.

17 In 1843 a white traveler described a Cayuse chief's clothing as composed of skin breeches, a striped shirt (which he wore over the breeches), and a scarlet coat (gilted off very much in the fashion of the regimentals of a British general), with a headdress composed of a cotton handkerchief thrown loosely over his head, then a cap made of otter skin over the handkerchief, and on the top of the cap, fastened with Indian taste, the long hair of a white horse's tail, which hung in ringlets down the back of his neck. Gustavus Hines, *Wild Life in Oregon*, 166.

18 "Report by Chief Trader Samuel Black," Query 25.

straint. In November, 1830, he promised to fulfill their request for two calves. The animals were to have been dropped off at Fort Nez Percés by a brigade bound upriver to Fort Colville, but it had not been done because it was feared that Snake Indians would steal them. It would be difficult, if not impractical, to ship the calves up the treacherous Columbia, but, in the interest of keeping the Cayuses in good humor, McLoughlin promised to do so. In March, 1832, he wrote Simpson that, although a Cayuse had killed a Fort Nez Percés Indian attached to a Snake brigade, it would be unwise to send a party after him, lest his people defend him and vent their wrath on the company. "If we Kill him," said McLoughlin, "it might be the cause of deranging all our business along the Communication." Perhaps not unimportant in McLoughlin's softening attitude was the realization that he had overreacted in ordering his men to punish coastal Clallam, Clatsop, and Tillamook Indians.[19]

"Business along the Communication," as McLoughlin termed it, was continuing apace as the Hudson's Bay Company sought to take as many furs as it could before the supply was depleted or American trappers moved in. There was even some fear in company circles that the Cayuses were taking furs in the Snake borderlands, lest the treasure be snatched up before the company could get to it.[20]

Because of the crisis nature of the enterprise, the expeditions to the Snake country were well organized and managed. Usually leaving Fort Nez Percés in September, they followed the Walla Walla River and then broke across to and over the Blue Mountains. From there they traversed the Grande Ronde and crossed the divide to Powder River. Shortly before reaching the Snake, the trappers often split up for their season's work. Their harvest gathered, they returned to the fort the following June or July.[21]

[19] Burt Brown Barker (ed.), *Letters of Dr. John McLoughlin Written at Fort Vancouver, 1829–1832*, 173, 258; Dorothy O. Johansen, "McLoughlin and the Indians," *The Beaver*, Outfit 277, No. 1 (June, 1946), p. 20.
[20] Rich, *Peter Skene Ogden's Journals*, 104.
[21] Elliott, *Earliest Travelers*, 14–15.

Until 1831 the key man on the fur-collecting scene was Peter
Skene Ogden. An old-timer from Nor'wester days, he had demonstrated his skill and initiative many times. For example, after
setting out with a large brigade from the Flathead post about
mid-December, 1824, about a year later he took a goodly number
of furs to Fort Nez Percés, despite the fact that nearly half his
men had deserted to a party of trappers from the Rocky Mountain
Fur Company, an American concern. His brigades had to trap
most of their own furs because the Snakes, having no great desire
for white men's goods, brought few to exchange.[22]

Always seeking new fields, Ogden tried to expand the trade
southward to two large lakes, the Great Salt and the Klamath, and
in the fall of 1826 he was in the latter region. In talks with a band
of Klamath Indians near the lower end of the lake, he learned
that Cayuses and Nez Percés had on several occasions—as recently
as that summer—tried to contact them for purposes of war and
trade.[23] The Klamaths knew that a party pushing into their
country would open the way for the Cayuses, but they seemed not
to have feared the prospect, being well armed with bows and
arrows, although deficient in horseflesh. Later, until the 1850's,
Klamath bands raided neighboring Shasta and Rogue River Indians to take prisoners, whom they sold as slaves to the Cayuses
and Nez Percés. Sometimes the Nez Percés came south to pick
up the captives; on other occasions the Klamaths carried them
north to the Columbia over the route traversed by Ogden.[24]

Some of the fur brigades dipped below the Klamath country as
far south as the Sacramento (Bonaventura) River, trapping and
trading with Indians along the way. One such group set out from
Fort Vancouver on August 17, 1832, reaching Fort Nez Percés
nine days later. From there it struck south to the John Day River,
passed Oregon's Malheur Lake, and bore southwest below Mount

22 Rich, *Peter Skene Ogden's Journals*, 263–64.
23 K. G. Davies (ed.), *Peter Skene Ogden's Snake Country Journal, 1826–27*, 33.
24 A. N. Armstrong, *Oregon; Comprising a Brief History and Full Description
of the Territories of Oregon and Washington* (cited hereafter as Armstrong, *History of the Territories*), 114. See also *Sketches of Mission Life*, 69–70.

Shasta to the Sacramento. It was customary for members of interior tribes to join such parties, often swelling their numbers to as many as two hundred. Indian women went along to dress the skins of animals trapped along the way, caring for them until the brigades returned to Fort Vancouver. With their reds and whites (including French-Canadians), mounted on sturdy cayuses, beaver traps slung from the saddles, these colorful caravans probed the American West for furs.[25]

The trapping expeditions depended upon the help of friendly tribes along the way. On September 18, 1832, Cayuses ranging the John Day River country brought fresh meat to the Sacramento-bound brigade. Chief Tauitau's brother, just in from the buffalo plains, informed the whites that the Nez Percés and Flatheads had fought two battles with the Blackfeet. Two days later, the Cayuses reported that two months earlier three Snake Indians had killed a company hunter, one Soteaux, with a knife before he had a chance to fire on them. The unfortunate French-Canadian was with Work's brigade in the land of the Blackfeet, who had killed more of its members.[26]

The Cayuses found it safer to travel to the Snake country with the more numerous Nez Percés or with white trappers than to go there in small groups. In June, 1826, David Douglas, a British botanist known to the Indians as "the Grassman," had to abandon

---

[25] Alice Bay Maloney (ed.), *Fur Brigade to the Bonaventura*, 1–5. Of these brigades, William A. Slacum, agent of the United States, wrote on December 18, 1837, that since 1828 a party of 40 to 50 Canadian trappers and their women, slaves, etc., to the number of 150 to 200, plus 300 horses, had gone out from Vancouver toward the south as far as forty degrees latitude. "These parties," wrote Slacum, "search every stream, and take every beaver skin they find, regardless of the destruction of the young animals: excesses, too, are unquestionably committed by these hunting parties on the Indians; and every small American party (save one) that has passed through the same country has met defeat and death. The parties being much smaller than those of the Hudson Bay Company, the Indians attack them with success; and the Americans hesitate not to charge the subordinate agents of the Hudson Bay Company with instigating the Indians to attack all other parties." *Memorial of William A. Slacum praying compensation for his services in obtaining information in relation to the settlements on the Oregon River*, 3.

[26] For an account of this expedition, see William S. Lewis and Paul C. Phillips, *The Journal of John Work*.

a tour across the Blue Mountains because his Cayuse guide was afraid of the Snakes. By contrast, Douglas observed, the Cayuses did not fear downriver Columbia tribes. At The Dalles a Cayuse chief and three of his men protected the botanist from troublesome Indians. The chief was rewarded with the gift of a shilling, which he suspended from the perforated septum of his nose on a brass wire. It was a seal of friendship.

In the Snake brigade of 1834 were Cayuses, Nez Percés, Chinooks, and other Indians, as well as seventeen French-Canadians. In late July at Fort Hall, on the left bank of the Snake a little above the mouth of the Portneuf, the party met the new fort's promoter, Nathaniel J. Wyeth. The watchful McLoughlin countered this American move by building Fort Boise on the Snake eight miles below the mouth of the Boise. A month after meeting the Hudson's Bay Company group, Wyeth joined fellow American and would-be fur entrepreneur Captain B. L. E. Bonneville in the Grande Ronde. The two worked out a plan to initiate trade with the Cayuses of the Ronde. Wyeth would secure goods for the trade from the brig *May Dacre*, which he was to meet on the lower Columbia. To round out the bargain, the brig would carry Bonneville's furs back to the East.

The two Americans were as impressed with Cayuse furs as were the Hudson's Bay men, one of whom noted that the Indians often had three or four packs of beaver skins to a lodge.[27] The furs that Bonneville saw had been secured less often by Cayuse trapping than by trading with certain "shy and ignorant" Snake bands. To Bonneville the Cayuses appeared needy and eager to trade, since they were poorly supplied with rifles. For a light weapon they were willing to offer a good running horse (but certainly not one of their best). The captain previewed the quality of Cayuse horseflesh at a race in which one of the Cayuses' entries bested two other horses, one Shoshoni and the other American, the winner "scarce drawing a quick breath when all

27 H. S. Lyman, "Reminiscences of F. X. Matthieu," *Oregon Historical Quarterly*, I (March–December, 1900), 100.

was over." Bonneville noted that the Cayuses loved to game and gamble and thought them a "mild, playful, laughing" people, devout, rigidly observing religious ceremonials—all of which augured well for their integrity in the trade.

It was not to be. When Wyeth reached the mouth of the Columbia, he found that lightning had struck the *May Dacre* during her voyage, causing her to miss the salmon season, on which his plans were partly based. Wyeth had written Bonneville: "Your Beaver traded from the Skiuses [Cayuses] is so much seized from the common enemy in trade [the Hudson's Bay Company], so far so good." But Bonneville had not counted on the power of the Hudson's Bay men. Twice at Fort Nez Percés they rebuffed him. The ground was slipping from under the Americans.[28] Two years later the Hudson's Bay Company purchased a visible reminder of Wyeth's dream: Fort Hall. When Wyeth left the mountains, the fur trade was drawing to a close, which may have been no consolation to him for his loss. The beaver were about trapped out as hunters probed ever deeper into mountain defiles for their furs. The building of Fort Hall and Fort Boise had deranged Cayuse trade patterns with the Shoshonis and Nez Percés in the Grande Ronde.[29]

The Hudson's Bay Company victory over its rivals was Pyrrhic. The Cayuses brought fewer and fewer furs each year and demanded more and more for them. When Bonneville departed, the Indians gathered at Fort Nez Percés to insist on a tariff change in their favor. It had been a touchy matter for years. From his headquarters at Fort Vancouver, McLoughlin admonished his

[28] Irving, *Adventures of Captain Bonneville*, 339–41, 340 n., 397–400. Dr. Elijah White, a member of the Methodist mission to Oregon and later U.S. Indian agent, said Bonneville paid the Indians higher prices for furs than did the Hudson's Bay Company. See White's *Ten Years in Oregon*, 174. William H. Gray, with the missionaries sent by the American Board of Commissioners for Foreign Missions, claimed that when Wyeth was in the country, the Hudson's Bay Company increased the tariff on furs and horses but reduced it to normal when Wyeth was driven out of competition. *A History of Oregon, 1792–1849*, 287.

[29] Thomas J. Farnham, *Travels in the Great Western Prairies, the Anahuac and Rocky Mountains, and in the Oregon Territory*, 82.

traders to maintain the schedules, telling Black on March 20, 1830, that "lowering your Tariff besides the absurdity of doing this at your place with our limited means is exactly similar to a man setting fire to his house when a fire is raging in the vicinity to prevent its being burnt by the fire from his neighbours." To Simon McGillivray at Fort Nez Percés he suggested that no guns should be traded for horses if the horses could be obtained by any other means. When chief trader Pierre Pambrun refused to grant a tariff change, the Indians reportedly set upon him and bound him with cords. Either then or on another occasion Pambrun reported that he had been obliged "to fly to his double barrel gun" to protect himself from some Indians in their anger over the rate of exchange.[30]

Obviously the Indians did not understand the economics of the fur trade in a market characterized by a dwindling supply and a dwindling demand. Company officials complained that prices asked by Indians at the forts and in the Snake country were so exorbitant that no furs could be profitably procured in those places.[31] Yet the trade continued, and the beaver pelt continued to be the standard of wealth and the rate of exchange on which trader-Indian commerce was based. With the establishment of the international boundary in 1846, trade was further curtailed. The Cayuses understood politics no better. How, they wondered, could white men in a far-off land draw a line separating countries?

Still the Indians, under the humoring of the traders, brought in some furs and, braving opposition from the Snakes and other enemies, went out on trapping expeditions. They were increasingly on their own now, however, and as late as the 1840's they were ranging into the Shasta and Sacramento areas to obtain blankets, powder, and balls in exchange for beaver pelts and horses. And occasionally the Cayuses crossed the Cascade Moun-

[30] White, *Ten Years in Oregon*, 174; Barker, *Letters of Dr. John McLoughlin*, 100, 121; Reverend Jason Lee to My Dear Nephew, April 25, 1838, Jason Lee Papers.
[31] E. E. Rich (ed.), *Eden Colvile's Letters, 1849–52*, 148.

tains to trade at Fort Nisqually, the Hudson's Bay Company fort on lower Puget Sound.[32]

Cayuse trade continued to be chiefly in horses, which never ceased to be an important measure of their wealth. One white traveler observed that a Cayuse was thought to be poor when he had only fifteen or twenty head.[33] Another noted that Cayuse horses were never used for plowing and when traded brought a blanket and a few articles of merchandise.[34] In the early 1840's Chief Five Crows was reputed to be the richest man in the country, possessing upwards of a thousand horses, cattle, many slaves, and five wives. It was said that he dismissed the wives in order to present himself at the gate of a company fort with "a band of retainers, master, and men all as gay as butterflies" to seek the hand of the daughter of one of the officers. Rebuffed, he reportedly married one of his slaves, causing great scandal among his people.[35]

Five Crows and his fellows were still dependent upon Hudson's Bay Company traders and would remain so until the traders were forced out by the Indian war in 1855. In fact, the company both established and toppled chiefs. Quahat continued to be the leading Cayuse chief until his death about 1831. A special agent for the United States government, Thomas Farnham, out west in 1839, thought that Quahat's brother (whom he did not identify) was "a man of considerable mental powers" but with none of the fire and energy attributed to Quahat, although the Hudson's Bay Company had proclaimed the brother high chief.[36] The powerful Tauitau might have become the company-favored chief had he not led the attack on Pambrun and fallen into disfavor. Since the

---

[32] *The Journal of John Work, January to October, 1835*, 90; "Fort Nisqually Journal of Occurrences, 1833–39."

[33] Farnham, *Travels in the Great Western Prairies*, 82.

[34] Parker, *Journal of an Exploring Tour*, 234.

[35] Sir George Simpson, *Narrative of a Journey Round the World During the Years 1841 and 1842*, I, 164.

[36] Farnham, *Travels in the Great Western Prairies*, 82.

Cayuses wished to maintain relations with the firm, Tauitau's reputation also suffered at their hands. [37] He later regained influence among his people, however, and for many years played an important role in their councils.

The company's influence in chief making and breaking was made possible by its hold over the Indians in the dispensing of goods. It could not, however, fail to take into account tribal customs; traders recognized as chief a man who claimed the position on the basis of inheritance or wealth. The company's bestowal of goods upon a candidate tended to strengthen his position among his people, thus facilitating the trade. American critics doubted the efficacy of the policy, claiming that the most troublesome Indians were made chiefs and bought off to keep them and their followers quiet.[38] In the case of Tauitau, they were quick—and happy—to point out that his fractiousness had backfired against the traders.

Certain aspiring chiefs also had misgivings about the system, as was revealed one day in the early 1840's in an interesting dialogue between chief trader Archibald McKinlay and Tauitau (now also known as Young Chief). The latter wanted a clerk fired. The employee, William Tod, following the established practice of disciplining the Indians, had become involved in a tussle with Watashchenownan (Afraid of the Earth), the son of Walla Walla Chief Peopeomoxmox (Yellow Bird or Yellow Serpent), in which Watashchenownan was badly mauled. Watashchenownan wanted Tod to leave the fort, to which request McKinlay responded: "Are you a chief?" The young Tauitau said: "Oh, I don't know. Ask my people whether I am or not." Said McKinlay: "I don't know whether you are a chief or not, but I know your father was one—and if he had been surrounded by 400 or 500 men, who tried to force him to act against his conscience, would he have

---

37 White, *Ten Years in Oregon*, 174; Gray, *History of Oregon*, 286; Barker, *Letters of Dr. John McLoughlin*, 254–55.

38 Archer Butler Hulbert and Dorothy Printup Hulbert (eds.), *Marcus Whitman, Crusader, Part Two, 1839 to 1843*, 3.

yielded? No! They would not have frightened him, and neither can you frighten me."

The trouble had started when an Indian stole some wood, always a coveted commodity, and for a while the situation was tense. Several hundred Cayuses, Nez Percés, and Walla Wallas gathered at Fort Nez Percés, dispensing with their usual three-circuit ride around it with a musket-firing salute, the change of pattern an ominous sign. Calm was restored, however, and the clerk remained.[39] As if to demonstrate that they held no grudge against the fort, when it burned to the ground in 1843, the Indians gathered under Cayuse leadership to rescue its properties and prevent looting.[40]

Such gestures of Cayuse good will toward the company and the firm's patronage could not halt a decline in Cayuse fortunes. Farnham had observed that in 1839 the Walla Wallas and Upper Chinooks near The Dalles were the only tribes to recognize Cayuse supremacy.[41] Like that of all other Indians in the Northwest, the Cayuses' population had dwindled. Special agent Duflot de Mofras of France put their number at a conservative two hundred in 1841.[42] They were losing on another front, too, for their mother tongue was now giving way (except among the older Cayuses) to the more fluid speech of their more numerous neighbors the Nez Percés.[43]

Could the Cayuses continue to hold a position of prominence? Perhaps, but things would have to change. If the best their Great

[39] "Narrative of a Chief Factor of the Hudson's Bay Company by Archibald McKinlay," 7–13. In a January 23, 1892, letter to Eva Emery Dye, Sarah I. McKinlay, wife of Archibald McKinlay, said the incident had been precipitated "more for play than anything else" and that Tod had been too hasty in reacting to it. Eva Emery Dye Papers. The incident is also recorded in a letter from McKinlay to Elwood Evans dated March 14, 1882. Evans Papers.
[40] Simpson, *Journey Round the World*, 161–62.
[41] Farnham, *Travels in the Great Western Prairies*, 82.
[42] Marguerite Eyer Wilbur (ed.), *Duflot de Mofras' Travels on the Pacific Coast*, 174–75.
[43] Large (ed.), *Journals of William Fraser Tolmie*, 337; P. L. Edwards, *A Sketch of the Oregon Territory; or, Emigrants' Guide* (cited hereafter as Edwards, *Emigrants' Guide*), 8.

Spirit could offer was to confer upon them only Indian knowledge, they believed it necessary to find an additional powerful Supreme Being. In their contacts with traders they had been introduced to the God of a new religion, a new magic. Already Christian emissaries were carrying his message to the West. Soon they would arrive in the Walla Walla Valley, where free traders had settled. The Cayuses would then make a mission, instead of a fort, the center of their hopes.[44] Was the lushness of the valley, compared with the barrenness of Fort Nez Percés' environs, an omen of better days to come, a new magic to give them guns, blankets, and other goods and restore them to power and prestige? They would see.

[44] Fort Walla Walla had changed much since it was built and would change still more in the years ahead. For details, see Thomas R. Garth, "Archeological Excavations at Fort Walla Walla," *Pacific Northwest Quarterly*, XLIII, 1 (January, 1952), 27–36.

IV
A Strange New Thing

As with their introduction to white men's goods, the time and place of the Cayuses' first contact with Christianity is not known. It probably did not occur when they met the Lewis and Clark Expedition, which had no charge to extend religion but only to gather facts, or, as Jefferson expressed it, "better [to] enable those who may endeavour to civilize and instruct them, to adapt their measures to the existing notions and practices of those on whom they are to operate." Perhaps initial Cayuse exposure to Christianity came from traders, particularly Roman Catholic–oriented Iroquois and French-Canadians, brought west in the employ of the North West Fur Company. Scattering as they did among the Northwest Indians, the Iroquois could easily have implanted among them Christian forms and ceremonials.[1] In Hudson's Bay Company days French-Canadian trappers were an important force in the extension of the faith because of their close association with the Indians and their marriages to Indian women.

The personnel at the trading posts were not impervious to the spiritual welfare of their Indian clientele. A traveler observed in 1835 that the traders taught the natives "the first principles of our holy religion; especially in regard to equity, humanity, and morality."[2] Another 1835 traveler wrote that Indians at Fort Walla Walla, the name increasingly used by Americans in referring to Fort Nez Percés, said their prayers under one of its bastions and held services with songs and prayers for about five years.[3] And a missionary observed that the Indians' worship,

1 Conn, "The Iroquois in the West," 59–63.
2 Parker, *Journal of an Exploring Tour*, 132.
3 Gairdner, "Notes on the Columbia River," 257.

established by traders utilizing native customs, consisted of singing a form of prayer, after which their chief gave them a talk.[4]
The sending of Cayuse Halket (named for John Halkett, long-
term member of the Hudson's Bay Company Committee), the son
of Cayuse Chief Willatmotkin, as well as Cayuse Pitt and other
chieftains' sons, to the Anglican mission school at Red River in
the late 1820's and early 1830's indicated that company management was not untouched by the growth of evangelicalism in the
homeland. Returning on furlough in 1833, Cayuse Halket, then
a lad of fourteen years, perhaps told his people of his mission
experiences before resuming his studies at Red River. His people
awaited his return to be their chief and tell them more magic
words, but in vain. His accidental death near the school in early
1837 brought anguish to them—and anger to a few among them
who said that the company had killed him.[5]

Stemming indirectly from the experiment of sending chiefs'
sons to the mission school was the journey of four Indians, Nez
Percés or Flatheads, to St. Louis for the "whiteman's Book of
Heaven." Widely publicized in American circles, the event was
equally well known to Indians awaiting the arrival of missionaries. In the summer of 1834 some Cayuses with a Hudson's Bay
Company brigade near Fort Hall learned that the St. Louis quest
had not been in vain. They met Methodist Jason Lee and his
party (traveling with Wyeth), the first to respond to the Indians'
call, and on Sunday, July 27, attended services conducted by Lee.
Although they did not understand a word he said, they maintained "the most strict and decorous silence," rising and kneeling
when he did.

The Indians had held their own devotions the night before.
The ninety-minute ceremony had included the chief's harangue,
a reminder to his listeners of their obligations to the Great Spirit,
maker of light and darkness—a contrast to the evil workings of

4 *Marcus Whitman, Crusader, Part One,* 281.
5 Thomas E. Jesset, *Chief Spokan Garry, 1811–1892,* 45–46, 57; Clifford Merrill
Drury, *Marcus Whitman, M.D., Pioneer and Martyr,* 184, 192; Dr. William McKay
to Eva Emery Dye, July 14, 1892, Eva Emery Dye Papers.

"the Black Chief" below. Then followed a prayer by the chief, his hands clasped on his breast and his eyes lifted beseechingly toward heaven, with appropriate response from the congregation. The whole company joined in the chief's song, their clasped hands moving rapidly across their breasts, bodies swinging to the rhythm of the chant. He ended it with a swelling, groanlike noise echoed by the people. Despite its embellishment with chants and body rhythms too deeply engrained to be altered, the ceremony revealed no disharmony with Christian beliefs. Had there been, the traders under whose aegis this kind of service had been encouraged would have cared little in their unconcern with theological niceties. John K. Townsend, of the Wyeth party, a scientist and no theologian, wrote of the ceremony: "I think I never was more gratified by any exhibition in my life."[6]

Witnessing a similar service in the Grande Ronde a month later, Captain Bonneville observed that the Cayuses, like the Nez Percés and Flatheads, had strong devotional feelings cultivated by some "resident personages" of the Hudson's Bay Company. Further evidence to him of the trader hand in this phase of Indian life was the Indians' observance of Sundays and cardinal holidays of the Roman Catholic church. And he noticed that, as they had been encouraged to do at the posts, the chiefs, afoot or horseback, exhorted their people to good conduct and right living, to which the latter, at the end of every admonitory sentence, responded in unison with one word, the equivalent of "Amen." Bonneville noted that such rituals, a mixture of aboriginal ceremonies, were often carried on in a large lodge erected for that purpose and that, when they ended, not even Sundays could prevent the Indians from racing horses at full speed or gambling in every corner of the camp. As in white communities, however, Wyeth informed Bonneville, there were among the Indians "religious charlatans," a reference to prophets like those among the Flatheads. By captivating the people with their mysterious knowledge, the seers

---

[6] John K. Townsend, *Narrative of Journey Across the Rocky Mountains, to the Columbia River,* 227–29.

often took command of tribes or split them to establish themselves as independent chiefs or shamans.[7] The two Americans may not have known that the Prophet Dance had perhaps spread from Indian-Christian roots in the Flathead country to the Cayuses and other tribes of the Snake-Columbia river system. In fact, the religious dances and ceremonials which travelers of the time witnessed in that region were perhaps a Christian-compounded form of the Prophet Dance.[8]

One reason prophets held sway over their people was the latter's wish to hear "a strange new thing," which helps to explain the Indians' friendly welcome to white men in their lands. When the Cayuses and Nez Percés of the Hudson's Bay Company brigade met Lee at Fort Hall, they wanted him to remain in their country to teach them the strange new thing. Lee promised that when he established a school they would be welcome to send their children to it to learn of the white man's way of making a living and of his God.[9] To show his gratitude to the missionary, one of the Cayuses gave Lee a horse and guided his party to the Grande Ronde. There several Cayuse chiefs, including the influential Tiloukaikt (Teelonkike), gave the whites additional horses in exchange for presents left over from the party's mountain outfit. The gesture was a symbol of friendship and good will, for no other gifts presented to western travelers were more valuable than horses. The grateful missionaries could easily understand why the Cayuses were "a governing tribe," their superiority acknowledged by others.[10]

Although Lee was diverted from the interior to set up operations in the Willamette Valley, the Cayuses soon gained new

[7] Irving, *Adventures of Captain Bonneville*, 344–45. The writings of travelers in Indian country at this time are replete with accounts of prophets and prophetesses rising among the tribes to pose a threat, not only to Christian missionary efforts, but to the Indian religious establishment as well.

[8] Leslie Spier, *The Prophet Dance of the Northwest and Its Derivatives*, 20, 35.

[9] *Sketches of Mission Life*, 199.

[10] Lee and Frost, *Ten Years in Oregon*, 121–23.

hope for a mission in their own country. At 2:00 P.M. on October 8, 1835, an encampment of some dozen Cayuse lodges, pitched a short distance below Fort Walla Walla, welcomed the Reverend Samuel Parker, on tour for the Calvinist-oriented American Board of Commissioners for Foreign Missions. From his Indian escort, who Parker thought was trying to upstage him with "some new thing," the Cayuses learned that the missionary had come not with goods to trade but with lessons to teach in the worship of God. The protocol-minded Cayuses arranged themselves in a single-file reception line, with chiefs and principal men at the head, next the common men, followed by the women according to rank—wives of chiefs, the old, the younger—and finally the children according to age. The reception was brief but warm. Parker soon departed, asking the Indians to meet him later at the fort, where, with the aid of an interpreter, he promised to tell them about God. They shook hands with him and watched him depart downriver.[11]

The Cayuses and allied tribes were at Fort Walla Walla to meet Parker on May 1, 1836. They seemed to have lost none of their interest in his mission—with the possible exception of one Cayuse chief who disliked what Parker said about polygamy. The chief said that he was too old to change either his ways or his wives and that if it meant going to the place of burning then he would just have to go. Parker happily observed that this attitude did not characterize the Cayuses generally. Of course, among the Cayuses, as in other tribes, there were always more Indians with only one wife than there were with several. Parker spent several days in the vicinity of Fort Walla Walla and, unlike many of those spying out that Canaan of another day, had nothing but favorable things to report of his journey.[12] An interpreter at the fort, John Toupin, later said that in 1835 he, Pambrun, and Parker visited the site of the proposed American Board mission. It was twenty-five miles east of the fort up the Walla Walla Valley at Waiilatpu,

[11] Parker, *Journal of An Exploring Tour*, 134–35.
[12] *Ibid.*

"The Place of the Rye Grass," on the lands of three chiefs: Umtippe, Waptashtakmahl (Red Cloak or Feathercap),[13] and Tiloukaikt. Toupin said that Parker told the Indians that he had come to select a place to build a preaching house, to teach them to live, and to teach school to their children. But it would be a doctor, or medicine man, not he, who would do all this. The doctor, said Parker, would be chief of the place and would come the following spring. According to Toupin (a Roman Catholic and unfriendly to Parker), Parker told the Indians:

> I come to select a place for a mission, but I do not intend to take your lands for nothing. After the doctor is come there will come every year a big ship loaded with goods to be divided among the Indians. Those goods will not be sold but given to you. The missionaries will bring you ploughs and hoes to learn you how to cultivate the land, and they will not sell but will give them to you.[14]

One Cayuse did not wait for missionaries of the American Board to come to him. He was Waileptuleek, who had accompanied the Lee party from Fort Hall to Fort Walla Walla. In July, 1836, he visited Lee's Methodist mission on the east bank of the Willamette sixty miles upstream from its confluence with the Columbia on a rich-bottomed, tree-bordered prairie near present-day Salem, Oregon. Waileptuleek was so pleased with what he saw that he returned home for his family, whom he brought to settle near the mission. He arrived on September 6, the very day that the Reverend Marcus Whitman, M.D., and the Reverend Henry H. Spalding, American Board missionaries (who might have been his teachers had they come earlier), were leaving Fort Walla Walla for Fort Vancouver before setting up the mission at Waiilatpu.[15] Some of Waileptuleek's children at-

---

[13] Nearly thirty years later, Gray claimed that Feathercap was Tiloukaikt. *History of Oregon*, 189. Archibald McKinlay, the trader at Fort Walla Walla, identified him as Waptashtakmahl. *Marcus Whitman, Crusader, Part Two*, 248.

[14] Toupin's statement appears in Secretary of Interior, *Annual Report, 1857–58, House Exec. Doc.* No. 38, 35 Cong., 1 sess., Serial 955, p. 18. Parker does not mention the journey Toupin described. If it did occur, it seems more likely to have been in 1836 on Parker's return to the interior.

tended the Methodist school and appeared to be making progress despite communication in the Chinook jargon, which missionaries, like fur traders, found to be an "imperfect medium of communication." It was in fact a poorer medium for the missionaries than it was for traders, for it had no words to convey basic Christian doctrines, of which the Indians had only a vague notion in the first place.[16]

In February, 1837, Waileptuleek's family fell ill. Two of the children died in quick succession, and a third lay ill with fever. Two years earlier, in midsummer, an Indian had died at the mission from what was diagnosed as consumption. His relatives had come, wailed over his grave, and departed helplessly for home. In August of that same year, the "Intermittent Fever," which had first broken out on the lower Columbia in 1829, "began to shake its burning, freezing subjects" around the mission, causing much sickness, "for which there was no remedy." A hospital to care for the sick was finished in 1840.[17] Even then, as Dr. Elijah White, a former assistant to Lee at the Methodist mission, reported in 1843, the school of no more than thirty scholars could produce little good "among the scattered remnants of the broken tribes of this lower district, who are fast disappearing before the ravages of the most loathsome diseases."[18] In 1842 a white resident of the Willamette had written: "Over this vast region did the dark angel of death move his laden sceptre—the children of the forest knew no remedy and died."[19]

Seeking to escape the dark angel, Waileptuleek fled for his life in a canoe down the Willamette, but as he landed, another member of his family succumbed to the disease. By tragic irony, the strange new thing that Waileptuleek's family had received from

15 Hines, *Wild Life in Oregon*, 22–24; Myron Eells, *History of the Indian Missions on the Pacific Coast*, 21.

16 Lee and Frost, *Ten Years in Oregon*, 126–33.

17 *Ibid.*, 150. There are numerous references to the "Intermittent Fever" of the 1830's. One of the most dramatic accounts of it is in *Traits of American Indian Life*, 69–71.

18 White, *Ten Years in Oregon*, 194.

19 Edwards, *Emigrants' Guide*, 21.

the missionaries was death. To compound it, a girl who had lost two or three members of her family at the Willamette school died two years later at the Waiilatpu mission from a disease "centered in her head" at a time when "light had just begun to dawn upon her soul."[20]

Despite these sad occurrences Lee's influence continued to work in Cayuse country, although indirectly. A Cayuse chief returned to his people with two paintings the missionary had given him. Using them as his text, he preached for several days, directing his remarks to the troublesome Chief Umtippe. The old chief, under exhortation of his fellow tribesmen, finally said that it was enough and that he would henceforth be a good Indian. On another occasion, a white party visiting Waiilatpu met an Indian who had obtained from some whites a large picture of the devil. By showing his people that he was master of the Evil One, he was able to exert considerable influence over them.[21]

"I am done wandering. I know now how white people live and I wish to make a farm, raise cattle, live like white people and want the missionaries to settle in my country." Thus spoke a Cayuse chief who in early September, 1836, accompanied the Whitman-Spalding party from Fort Walla Walla to Fort Vancouver, the sanctuary and outfitting place for western travelers. The chief was aboard when the two missionaries sailed upstream to begin their work among the Cayuse–Nez Percé people.[22] In the first week of October the Cayuses met the two men who had come to Waiilatpu to establish the mission. The meeting was friendly. During the pleasantries the Indians assessed the newcomers: Spalding, rather muscular, and Whitman, "above medium height; of spare habit; peculiar hair, a portion of each being white and dark brown, so that it might be called iron-gray; deep

[20] Transactions Oregon Pioneer Association 1891, 111–12.

[21] Henry H. Spalding to Rev. David Greene, Secretary of the A.B.C.F.M., September 4, 1837, American Board File, Spalding Papers, Vol. 138, Letter 22; Hines, Wild Life in Oregon, 176.

[22] "Spalding's journal while traveling from Fort Vancouver to the Nez Perces country and back," Spalding Papers, Item 204.

blue eyes, and large mouth."[23] Missionaries and Indians met as virtual strangers. The Indians had had but a fleeting glance at their future teachers as the latter passed through the valley from the east on a journey during which they gained information about the Cayuses from travelers and hunters along the way. Both missionary and Indian had something to offer for the success of the venture that was about to be undertaken: the white men their knowledge, words, and hands to help their charges along the way to a new life; the Cayuses their receptiveness, indicated in a speech by one of their chiefs. The setting was ideal: a lush valley protected from extremes of weather. Unlike the Grande Ronde, where Whitman had considered locating, there was less danger here from Snake incursions.

In the mutual exuberance over the possibilities afforded by the land, little attention was paid to the legalities of its occupancy, a matter which would make it a briar patch of contention in years to come. There was much to do. The physical ground had scarcely been broken, but the spiritual ground had. Prospects appeared good. Near the spot where a small creek, called Pasha (or Paska) by the Indians and later Mill Creek by the whites, joined the Walla Walla River, Whitman selected a site for his home, the heart of the mission.

The Cayuse chief at Fort Walla Walla was not the only one who assured the missionaries that he would change his way of life. Nez Percé Chief Rottenbelly (Tackensuatis) vowed to give up his roving ways for the life of a farmer, requesting all the help he could get for himself and his people. The Nez Percés, however, were unhappy that Whitman, as a result of his tour of the Walla Walla Valley, had decided to settle there. A "warm debate" over the location of the mission had flared among Cayuse and Nez Percé women when the missionary party met them at Fort Hall on the way out.[24] The Nez Percés claimed not to have had as much trouble with white men as their Cayuse neighbors, perhaps a

---

23 Gray, *History of Oregon*, 108.
24 Spalding to Greene, September 20, 1836, Spalding Papers, Vol. 138, Letter 27.

veiled intimation that some misfortune might befall Whitman were he to settle among the Cayuses. This opinion was pressed not entirely from sour grapes; like other Indians astride the paths of white commerce, the Cayuses had more opportunity for conflict than did the more peripheral Nez Percés. Nevertheless, the latter had to reconcile themselves to two missions—one for the Cayuses at Waiilatpu and another for themselves at Lapwai, near the confluence of Lapwai Creek and the Clearwater River. And they had to be satisfied with one missionary instead of two. According to Spalding, they must not have felt too bad about it, for with his coming, he wrote, their "joy seemed complete."[25]

William H. Gray, a layman who had come with the Whitman-Spalding party, and two Hawaiians on loan from the Hudson's Bay Company began constructing a 30-by-36-foot frame house with a lean-to, the Whitmans' first living quarters. To the Cayuses it bore only a faint resemblance to the bastioned fort—an invitation, perhaps, for them to enter it without restriction and fear of frowning cannon. Even though the house was no fort, the Cayuses could not understand why its occupants did not trade for furs in order to give them more for their pelts than they were getting at the post. How, they asked, could the missionaries bring them a strange new thing without giving them something tangible?

The few Cayuses who had not gone to hunt buffalo helped with the house building, but it was strange work for them. Women put up the Indians' lodges. Certainly Whitman's wife, Narcissa, did not erect hers. Pregnant, she had remained with the Pambruns at Fort Walla Walla. Her arrival on December 10 and the wait for her baby gave the Cayuses something to talk about during the winter, which was snowier than usual.[26]

The birth of Narcissa's child, a girl, on March 14, 1837, caused an even greater stir among the Cayuses than had the coming of Narcissa to Waiilatpu. Chiefs, headmen, and women daily

[25] Spalding to Greene, February 16, 1837, *ibid.*, Letter 21.
[26] *Marcus Whitman, Crusader, Part One*, 252–57.

thronged the small house to see the curiosity, a strange new thing in their land. On the day after her birth, Chief Tiloukaikt came to see the one he called a Cayuse *temi* ("girl") because she was born on Cayuse *waitis* ("land"). But why, asked the Indians, was she clothed in a dress and lying in bed with her mother and not in a *tecash* ("cradle board") in a maternity lodge? They must have thought it strange, too, that her head was not being restrained for flattening.

With continuing cold weather and no gatherings outside possible, mother and baby went to services in Tauitau's lodge, which, joined with several others of mats and skins, with a central fire, made a suitable meeting place for several people. Morning and evening services had been in vogue in this makeshift long house before the missionaries arrived. Now its occupants received help in their singing from the missionary's wife. It almost made her forget that she was in a primitive land, for the Indians performed well.

There remained the question of how well they would perform in the forthcoming ground-breaking and planting season. No matter how willing their spirit to perform these operations, their flesh was weakened by sickness, primarily inflammation of the lungs. The wife of Chief Umtippe, on whose land the mission stood, was also stricken with the illness. The sick accepted Whitman's ministrations, but many found his medicines of temporary benefit, for they did not take care of themselves and relapsed. When Umtippe's wife showed no improvement, the chief, "a savage creature in his day," told the doctor that if she died, he would kill him. Interpreter Toupin later claimed that he was in the room when the chief said: "Doctor, you have come here to give us bad medicines; you come to kill us, and you steal our lands. You had promised to pay me every year, and you have been here already two years, and have, as yet, given me nothing. You had better go away; if my wife dies, you shall die also."[27] Not wait-

27 Secretary of Interior, *Annual Report, 1857–58*, 19.

ing for his wife to die or for Whitman to leave, Umtippe summoned a well-known Walla Walla *tewat* ("doctor"). After several incantations over the sick woman the *tewat* pronounced her cured, received a horse and blanket for his pay, and departed for home. The woman did recover, enhancing, for a while, the *tewat*'s reputation. A short time later Umtippe fell ill and came to Whitman for aid. Had he not been an influential chief, Whitman might have spurned him for having called a *tewat* to care for his wife. The doctor's medicine helped the chief survive, a fate better than that of a war-chief relative who, sick only six days, died at the hands of the Walla Walla *tewat*. The day the war chief died, Umtippe's younger brother, Isaiachalakis (Wet Wolf), shot the *tewat* dead. All were avenged. From these developments Whitman must have gathered that a doctor in Indian country had little security.[28]

These events brought to light basic cultural differences between the missionaries and their Cayuse flock. To Narcissa Whitman the *tewat* were performing a "species of juggling" and "playing the fool." The practitioners, of course, were following the customs of their way of life; like other Indians, the Cayuses believed that their doctors possessed wonderful faculties of conjuration and supernatural power. Among the Cayuses, as among their Walla Walla neighbors, candidates for medical practice were not always sons or daughters of doctors. When they were eight or ten years old, they went off somewhere alone to await communication with or visitation from their *tamanowas* ("spirit"), which appeared to them in the form of a bear, eagle, coyote, buffalo, or other bird or beast. If they returned without success, they were sent back until, in a dream or trance, they saw their animal spirit. Then they told what they had seen and heard to a shaman, who instructed them to call on their spirit to assist them in every undertaking. But not until manhood (or womanhood) was the

---

[28] *Transactions Oregon Pioneer Association 1891*, 91–96. A good analysis of the missionary-Indian conflict may be found in *Marcus Whitman, Crusader, Part Two*, 1–20.

novitiate initiated into his sacred profession in the medicine dance, in which he imitated his power spirit.

When a medicine man entered the lodge of his patient, who lay on a hide or mat, he approached the sick one making much noise, shouting, clapping his hands, beating his breast. He then sucked and blew on his patient to drive or pull "evil spirit darts" from his body. There was much professional jealousy among practitioners. When Umtippe visited Whitman, he was merely taking a customary route from one doctor to another. Had Whitman been an Indian, he might have suggested that Umtippe's former doctor be killed. Deaths at the hands of medicine men were commonplace, particularly during epidemics, which were becoming more frequent. If a patient died, he was wrapped in hides and blankets. Then followed lamentations, often led by paid women mourners, with the extent of mourning determined somewhat by the status of the deceased. As a final act friends and neighbors presented to the dead one's relatives various gifts, sometimes depositing them in his grave.[29]

Differences between Cayuse and missionary were being revealed in ways other than those pertaining strictly to life and death. For example, Cayuse chiefs noted that Whitman and Spalding each had only one wife. They could not understand this arrangement, for they believed that, as they put it, when there were many wives they all "had more to eat." The missionaries tried to make their wives' work easier. Cayuse women (Mrs. Whitman called them slaves) performed menial tasks. "Why do you take your wife with you to Mr. [Elkanah] Walker's? Why do you not go alone? What do you make so much for her?" These pointed questions were directed to Whitman by Chief Tiloukaikt, Umtippe's successor as chief of the Cayuse band in the Walla Walla Valley. Whitman saw such questions as reflecting a clash not with Cayuse culture but with Cayuse conscience.

[29] Healing and burial practices varied among the tribes. For a general description of these customs among Indians of the Pacific Northwest, see Schoolcraft, *Indian Tribes*, 652; Armstrong, *History of the Territories*, 121–22; *Sketches of Mission Life*, 61–65.

Equally contradictory were the missionary and Cayuse concepts of hospitality. When Mrs. Whitman took a little Indian boy into her home, his relatives, who had abandoned him, believed that such generosity should have been extended to them. The missionary lady did not welcome them into her house, not even to eat or, worse yet, to worship. Why, they asked, could they not look through the windows of the house (which they did— from curiosity, not perversity)? And why, they would ask for many years to come, did the missionaries extend their hospitality to travelers when they did not extend it to the ones they called their children? It was apparent that manners in Cayuse lodges, with no doors to knock on or windows to see through, did not fit those in the white man's "castle."

Closely associated with the contrasting roles of Cayuse women and the white woman in their midst was the two peoples' concepts of work. The Cayuse had long held that workers were inferior people or slaves. Consequently, Indians working for the Whitmans were mainly Walla Wallas, "the Kayuse ladies" being "too proud to be seen usefully employed." When it seemed that their children might do some chore for the missionaries, Cayuse parents became "panic stricken and [made] trouble." The Calvinistic society from which the missionaries came glorified work, and so Whitman extended his plantings (some dozen acres of peas, corn, and potatoes by the spring of 1837) in hopes that the Cayuses would emulate his example and profit by the fruits of his and their labor. It would have been difficult for the men to have profited much from his example, since most of the Indians' farming was done by women and slaves.[30] From a practical standpoint Whitman hoped that results of their toil would obviate their need for seasonal migration. However, the Cayuses found it difficult to discontinue these rounds, so deeply rooted in their way of life.

In deference to their own customs and to those of the mission-

[30] The Whitmans did not mention slavery among the Cayuses, possibly because it was such a sensitive issue in the East.

aries, the Cayuses believed that they could be both huntsmen and farmers. At harvest time (August through November) they were in their village in force, their conical lodges dotting the landscape above the mission and their multicolored horses grazing peacefully on the nearby valley floor—and sometimes not so peacefully in the unharvested gardens. During December and January many Cayuses were off on hunts, some of them as far east as the buffalo plains. During February and March they returned for spring planting, only to leave again at the end of April to dig camas on the slopes of the Blue Mountains and in the Grande Ronde Valley. In the Ronde, as elsewhere, they never abandoned their role as traders, securing from the Snakes even the lodges sheltering them from the weather.[31]

The migrations disturbed the continuity of the mission church and school at a time when the Cayuses were learning the Word in one and English words in the other. The absences also prevented the missionaries from learning the Nez Percé language, in which instruction was held. Wishing to perpetuate their positions of importance, the chiefs wanted the missionaries to instruct them in some new thing, which they vowed to pass on to their people as they traveled around. The missionaries, however, feared that the new thing might suffer in transit at the hands of the chiefs. Whitman feared that, as middlemen between teacher and people, the chiefs were depriving the latter of a formal education. Yet he was not afraid to entrust to a well-coached Indian "rehearser" the responsibility of repeating, line for line, the sermon from his lips. In Whitman's thinking, neither chiefs nor Indians understood the fundamentals of Christianity. When in 1840 he told them that they were not Christians, their proud hearts were pricked to the core, and some of them even threatened to whip him.[32]

[31] For a pattern of these migrations, see *Marcus Whitman, Crusader, Part Two*, 294–301.

[32] *Transactions of the Twenty-First Annual Reunion of the Oregon Pioneer Association for 1893* (cited hereafter as *Transactions Oregon Pioneer Association 1893*), 129–31.

The missionaries tried to hold a tight rein on Cayuse education. Thomas Farnham, a traveler-immigrant who came west with the Peoria party, agreed almost completely with Whitman's teaching methods. His only objection was the use of the Nez Percé language instead of English, which he thought could have given the Indians "treasures which centuries of toil, by a superior race have dug from the mines of intelligence and truth." Of the school session of September 24, Farnham wrote:

> In the afternoon, Dr. Whitman and his lady assembled the Indians for instruction in reading. Forty or fifty children between the ages of seven and eighteen, and several other people gathered on the shady side of the new mission-house at the ringing of a hand-bell, and seated themselves in an orderly manner on wooden benches. The doctor then wrote monosyllables, words, and instructive sentences in the Nez Percés language, on a large blackboard suspended on the wall, and proceeded first to teach the nature and power of the letters in representing the simple sounds of the language, and then the construction of words and their uses in forming sentences expressive of thought. The sentences written during these operations were at last read, syllable by syllable, and word after word, and explained until the sentiments contained in them were comprehended; and it was delightful to notice the undisguised avidity with which these people would devour a new idea. It seemed to produce a thrill of delight that kindled up the countenance and animated the whole frame. A hymn in the Nez Percés language, learned by rote from their teachers, was then sung, and the exercises closed with prayer by Dr. Whitman in the same tongue.[33]

There was progress in the gardens, too. In the spring of 1838 the Cayuses had planted about an acre of potatoes and good-sized fields of corn and peas. The next year there was more cultivation, and neighboring bands of Walla Wallas and Cayuses came for seed to plant in their own lands. Acreages increased, too, as the Indians learned from the doctor the importance of irrigation.

[33] Farnham, *Travels in the Great Western Prairies*, 81–82.

They took water from his ditches until they discovered that they could make their own, for there was water enough for all.[34]

Progress was being made, but there was no evidence that basic differences between Cayuses and missionaries were being resolved. In moments of optimism the latter thought they were and could be more so with increased means and men. Means: fences, plows, hoes, books, iron for mills, stoves, and kettles. Men: mission personnel reinforcements needed because of the mission's central importance in the American Board's Oregon operations. Travelers and immigrants, some coming in wagons ("land canoes") in the summer of 1840, found the mission a convenient stopping place between the East and the Columbia River. Although the missionaries conceived of their station as a haven for weary white travelers, they believed better relations with their flock could be maintained if the whites brought virtues rather than vices. Their virtues were indeed hailed—encouragement like that from Farnham, who rejoiced "that on the barren soil of the Skyuse heart was beginning to bud and blossom and ripen the golden fruits of faith of Jehovah, and hope in an after state." An unwelcome vice was whisky drinking. In 1843, Cayuse chiefs and headmen at the mission, in good American style, took the pledge to refrain from drink, for John Barleycorn, too, was a traveler on the Immigrant Trail.

Protection from Papists (Roman Catholic priests who had recently come to Oregon) was also needed. On November 18, 1838, the Reverends François Norbert Blanchet and Modeste Demers, missionaries for that part of the Diocese of Quebec between the Rockies and the Pacific, en route with a Hudson's Bay Company express from eastern Canada, appeared at the fort. During a twenty-four-hour stay there as guests of its Catholic trader, Pierre Pambrun, the priests performed three baptisms and celebrated one mass. They also received Cayuse and Walla Walla chiefs and their people who had heard of their arrival. In late June, 1839,

[34] *Marcus Whitman, Crusader, Part One,* 291–301; *Marcus Whitman, Crusader, Part Two,* 177–80.

79

Father Demers returned to the fort; there were Canadians to marry, infants to baptize, and Indians to teach—and to tell that the Protestant missionaries (whom they called teachers) had talked too long and baptized too late. One baby baptized in time was the child of Tauitau. The doctor certainly had not ordered the baptism, but since he had less influence over the chief's people in the Umatilla River camps than over those on the Walla Walla, there was nothing he could do. Soon the priests, by illustration, confined the Protestants in flames at the bottom of the Catholic Ladder. It may have been some consolation to the American Board that Spalding went from band to band with a Protestant Ladder showing the Pope leading his followers into hell.[35]

There was no end of Cayuse anxiety either. Were the American Board missionaries, from whom they had expected special magic, reserving it all for themselves? Waptashtakmahl and Isaiachalakis, brothers of Umtippe, now dead, asked questions about the mission located in their midst. Were not the missionaries rich and getting richer? The Whitmans had a new house, and their clothes, worn, washed, and hung out to dry, displayed the missionaries' opulence for all red men to see. Why, asked Tilkanaik,[36] could not horses graze on the point of land between the two streams? After all, it was Cayuse land, and there were no fences on it. And if the horses were eating corn, was that not fruit

35 For information on the coming of the priests, see F. N. Blanchet, *Historical Sketches of the Catholic Church in Oregon During the Past Forty Years, 1838–1878*, 11, 16, 21. See also F. N. Blanchet *et al.*, *Notices and Voyages of the Famed Quebec Mission to the Pacific Northwest*, 18, 30. An article in the *Catholic Sentinel*, July 22, 1875, p. 1, described the Catholic Ladder as "a chronological chart representing the history of religion and the various mysteries of our holy faith in regular order, so that when once the illustrations are explained any number of persons can be made to understand their meaning at once. This became necessary in consequence of the large number of Indians desiring instructions; and as the over worked missionaries could not long remain in one place, the *Ladder* would be left with the chief or head man of the tribe, who would explain it as he had been taught by the missionary. In this way the Catholic faith was rapidly propagated, and the Indians who had never seen a priest could glean some knowledge of the history of our holy faith." See also Theodore J. Hilaire, "Pedagogy in the Wilderness," *Oregon Historical Quarterly*, LXIII (March-December, 1962), 55–60.
36 Not to be confused with Tiloukaikt.

of the earth? And why did Indians have to confine themselves to the Indian house (which Whitman had conceded them)? Why could they not enter the missionaries' rooms, with which it was connected?

Soon the Indians were not merely asking questions but striking blows, with Tilkanaik, in the summer of 1841, delivering a sharp one to Whitman's chest in the continuing wrangle over owner-ship of the mission land. There was another incident in early fall, involving a horse, in which Tiloukaikt struck Whitman and pulled his ears. Three times he threw into the mud the hat from the missionary's head (which, according to phrenological science, "was marked not only by veneration and benevolence, but by combativeness").[37] It was apparent that Whitman had done little to knock the aboriginal edge off Tiloukaikt's behav-ior. He must have realized it when the chief told him in sub-stance: "Doctor, I am mad at you. Before you came, we fought with each other, killed each other, and enjoyed it. You have taught us that it is wrong, and we have in a great measure ceased. So I am mad at you for preventing our doing what we enjoyed."[38]

The age-old migratory habits of the Cayuses were leading them into trouble which Whitman may not have anticipated. One chief, Iatin (Big Belly or Gros Ventre), who had been down to the Willamette settlements, forbade William H. Gray to cut timber without paying for it. Iatin had heard it said in the settlements that when anyone refused to leave white men's lands they were forced off. In 1841, at Tiloukaikt's fishing camp in the Grande Ronde, a half-blood Iroquois, Joe Gray, told the Cayuses that the missionaries were making the Indians miserable and ought to pay for their lands. At Spalding's Lapwai mission, Tom Hill, a Delaware Indian (called a Shawnee by some), told the Cayuses the same thing.

[37] The *Prattsburg* (New York) *News* of January 27, 1898, carried a description of Whitman which, as late as that date and after the fact, was marked by phrenological overtones.
[38] Eells, *History of Indian Missions*, 227–28.

81

In one of their frequent encounters at Fort Walla Walla the Cayuses heard Archibald McKinlay, named chief trader after Pambrun was killed in an accident involving a horse, compare their behavior to that of dogs. Stung by McKinlay's remarks, the proud Cayuses powwowed and moved to Whitman's mission one day in early October, 1841, to begin another round of unpleasantries. Several of them stormed the house. Sakiaph entered with a hammer and Palaistiwat with an ax. Disarmed, the latter came back with a club and the former with a gun. Again the issue was property, and the missionary said he would not yield "a single awl or pin." The trouble broke up, but, wishing to vent their anger, the recalcitrants said that they would go to the fort to see whether McKinlay would still call them dogs. On the next day, Sunday, October 3, many Indians boycotted services at the mission; some broke windows and troubled the animals. At the fort McKinlay took a hard line, backed by his arsenal and threats of reinforcements from chief factor McLoughlin. Helping to save McKinlay's life, perhaps, was his marriage to an Indian woman, whom he had taken to wife in the Hudson's Bay Company's manner of encouraging its men to marry Indian women. Some Cayuses remained adamant for payment in cattle for the missionaries' use of their land, wood, and water, but in a surprise move Tiloukaikt pleaded with the malcontents not to make such extortions by fear. Cayuse Chief Camaspelo from the Umatilla headwaters, arrived on the scene and urged them to say nothing more.[39]

There were no major confrontations between the mission staff and the Cayuses during the winter of 1841–42. There were none with Whitman during the following winter: he was then on his well-known midwinter ride to the East. To him the trip was crucial to the success of the mission, for he felt the urgency of securing support for its perpetuation. Some patriots subsequently believed that he had ridden to save Oregon for the United

39 Accounts of the disturbances are to be found in *Transactions Oregon Pioneer Association 1893*, 140–43. Mrs. McKinlay was the daughter of Peter Skene Ogden. Besides white blood, Flathead and Crow Indian blood also flowed in her veins. Sarah I. McKinlay to Eva Emery Dye, March 20, 1892, Eva Emery Dye Papers.

States, but what had the journey done for his Indian parishioners? To them, as to the whites, it was especially crucial. A persistent rumor among the Indians had it that Whitman was planning to return with fifty men to fight them. If that were to prove true, their warriors vowed to warn tribes from the Rockies to the coast to fall upon the missionaries and kill them in their sleep. White supporters of Whitman, in their zeal to extend American civilization and Christianity to the Indians of the interior Pacific Northwest, may have forgotten one very important point: the success of the mission depended less on them than it did on the Cayuses.

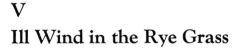

V

Ill Wind in the Rye Grass

In late October, 1842, during Whitman's absence, many Cayuses were sorry to see Mrs. Whitman leave Waiilatpu for the Wascopum mission (organized by Methodists in 1838 at The Dalles) after an Indian attempted to assault her. Many Cayuses were also sorry that the gristmill burned to the ground under mysterious circumstances shortly after she left. By repairing to The Dalles, Mrs. Whitman made no escape from Indians; the Cayuses continued to go there as they had for generations. The previous year a member of Commander Charles Wilkes's United States Navy Pacific exploring expedition had opined that Indians visiting The Dalles were outlaws of their various tribes. Other white visitors made similar observations. Wrote one:

They [the Cayuses and Nez Percés] first announced their approach to the station by firing their guns, by drumming, and by terrific war-songs. They were mounted on horses, strangely decorated. From the head of one streamed the hair of the scalp of a Blackfoot Indian; from another, the hideous scalp of a buffalo—the horns still protruding. Their riders were not less fantastically dressed. All available ornament, and different-colored clothes, were laid under contribution,—the garment, in some instances, trailing to the ground. They came on with furious prancing and reckless disorder, yelling and singing as they came. A part alighted near the mission house, and danced, yelled, and drummed, much doubtless, to *their own* gratification. One of the chiefs then entered the house, to assure the inmates of their peaceful purposes; an assurance not altogether unnecessary . . . after the exhibition of so much

84

of the spirit of war. They only wished to show them, he said, how they prepared for battle.[1]

Boisterous Cayuse–Nez Percé arrivals at The Dalles were almost as frightening to the resident Indians as they were to the whites, for the Cayuses still claimed the fisheries—a little less vigorously now than in former years, but still with enough force to make the local Indians short of fish. The cries of penitents in the Wascopum revivals of 1839 and 1840 sounded much better to missionary ears than the sounds of intruding savages, but as long as the mission remained (until 1847), those sounds never stopped.[2]

On November 20, 1842, snow-capped Mount St. Helens, sixty-five miles northwest of the Wascopum mission and forty-five miles due north of the Columbia River, scattered smoke, blew ashes, and rolled lava. Was the mountain god expressing anger with his children? Or, like a Mount Sinai in the Oregon wilderness, was the mountain saluting an American Moses, Dr. Elijah White, now a government Indian agent to the Oregon country, and his party, then making their way up the Columbia to institute new laws among interior Indians? Or was this Oregon Carmel raining a fiery salute to one bearing the name of the prophet, one who, like him, had come to challenge the heathen prophets of Baal? In many respects White truly deemed himself a nineteenth-century Moses. Of his leadership of the 1842 immigration he boasted: "I question whether since the day when Moses brought the people of Israel out of the land of the Egyptians, to lead them to the promised land, there was a greater undertaking of the sort, resting on the responsibility of a man."[3] Many of his contemporaries, especially those of the American Board of Commissioners

1 *Sketches of Mission Life*, 91–92.
2 *Ibid.* For the founding of The Dalles mission and life there, see Lee and Frost, *Ten Years in Oregon*, 151–213.
3 Elijah White, "Government and the Emigration to Oregon," 19. For an account of Mount St. Helens' volcanic activities, see Kenneth L. Holmes, "Mount St. Helens' Recent Eruptions," *Oregon Historical Quarterly*, LVI (March–December, 1955), 197–210.

for Foreign Missions, would question this claim, not alone out of esteem for the first Moses, but out of the lack of it for one whom Gray's acid pen described as a "notorious blockhead" and a "puff-ball of folly and ignorance."[4]

The laws White presented to the Indians were based to some extent on the commandments given to Moses. Like the biblical statutes, White's, too, were a decalogue—or would have been had the Nez Percés not added an eleventh, a dog-control law. White left enforcement to chiefs elected by the tribes. White's task was an urgent one, for conditions among the Indians, especially the Cayuses, were unsettled. There were rumors that they, the Walla Wallas, and the Nez Percés were about to attack the interior mission stations and the Willamette settlements. Since white emigrants were beginning to enter the Oregon country, it was imperative that the Indians there be disciplined under law.[5]

On December 1 a "few... shy" Indians met White at the Whitman mission. The number was too small to do business, and so the agent moved quickly to the Spalding mission. The meeting there began on the right note with a speech by Five Crows. Not unaware that white man's knowledge enhanced a chief's position, Five Crows had attended school at Lapwai the previous winter, and the missionaries had named him Hezekiah, which sounded much like his Cayuse name, Achekaia. Said Five Crows to White and his party:

> It does not become me to speak first: I am but a youth, as yet, when compared to many of these my fathers; but my feelings urge me to arise and say what I am about to utter in a few words. I am glad the chief has come; I have listened to what has been said; have great hopes that brighter days are before us, because I see all the whites are united in this matter; we have much wanted some thing; hardly knew what; been groping and feeling for it in confusion and darkness. Here it is. Do we see it, and shall we accept?

His audience's answer to the question was apparently affirmative.

[4] Gray, *History of Oregon*, 214, 282.
[5] Elwood Evans, *History of the Pacific Northwest*, I, 234.

His task at Lapwai completed, White moved on to Waiilatpu, where he felt that he had his work cut out for him. Instead of pushing a hard line, he allowed Thomas McKay, long-term Hudson's Bay Company employee, and Cornelius Rogers, both serving as interpreters, open negotiations. Rogers, having despaired of conveying religious concepts to the Indians, had earlier left the employ of Whitman's mission.[6] In council Waptashtakmahl wept "for the first time in his life," but Tauitau, less moved than his fellow chief, said that whites were more to blame than Indians for troubles, alluding to the base conduct of some whites whom the Cayuses had met in the Rockies on buffalo hunts. Many white hunters, traders, and trappers had sold the Indians cards, telling them that they were the "magic book," the Bible. The White party informed the chief that such instances did not apply to "the present cases of difficulty."

Admitted to see Dr. White, Tauitau said that, eight years earlier, as high chief he had attempted to keep his people in line by flogging the young men—and Pierre Pambrun, too, he might have added—and by reproving the middle-aged. But by so doing, he said, he had lost his popularity, being "left alone to say my prayers" and "go to bed, and weep over the follies and wickedness of my people." To demonstrate his grief, he, too, wept before the agent. With these two Cayuses exhibiting such apparent contrition, White thought it timely to reprimand the tribe for its conduct toward the Whitmans. The small group of Cayuses present, likewise apparently contrite, expressed their willingness to accept the Nez Percé laws.[7] Since they did not know how their absent brothers felt, they agreed to meet White again in the spring to reach a better understanding with him. Having done as much as he could, White departed for the Columbia and the settlements. The Cayuses returned to their haunts.[8]

---

[6] Rogers, his wife, and several others were drowned in 1843 when their boat was swept over Willamette Falls. Drury, *Marcus Whitman*, 250.

[7] See Appendix A for a copy of the laws.

[8] White, *Ten Years in Oregon*, 172–200.

White could not return any too soon. Rumors were rife in the settlements that the interior Indians were in an extremely agitated state. And Narcissa Whitman in the middle at The Dalles, lamented: "It is the Kaiuses that cause all the trouble."[9] White's statements had not allayed the Cayuses' fears. They did not object to his laws, but they had gained from him the impression that they would be compelled to adopt them.[10] Angered by such a prospect, some Cayuse chiefs had suggested rushing to the Willamette to cut off its inhabitants with a sudden blow (some young white hotbloods there were suggesting the same treatment for the Indians).[11] Perhaps the young chiefs might have attempted such a move had it not been for the restraining hand of their elders. The Cayuses informed William Geiger, a Whitman employee, that part-time Hudson's Bay Company interpreter Baptiste Dorion, a half-blood, had told them the Americans had designs on them. Upon hearing this, they sent Chief Peopeomoxmox to Fort Vancouver to gain factor John McLoughlin's assurances that the Americans would not attack and that if they did they would get no help from him. McLoughlin's influence served as a formidable restraint, since he was the major source of American credit in Oregon.

White's return trip to the interior was thus needed to calm the Walla Wallas, Cayuses, and Nez Percés, "the only three tribes from which much is to be hoped, or any thing to be feared, in this part of Oregon." He found that the Indians had retained their character. The Cayuses were still "brave, active, tempestuous, and war-like, . . . independent in manner," and often "boisterous, saucy, and troublesome in language and behavior." The more numerous but less affluent Walla Wallas were not much different. The Nez Percés were noble in every white man's book, but in White's thinking they could, through intermarriage and

9 *Transactions Oregon Pioneer Association 1893*, 158–60.
10 Drury, *Marcus Whitman*, 287.
11 In *Wild Life in Oregon*, 147–49, Hines tells of the tension that was building during the interval between White's two missions into the interior.

other contacts with the Cayuses and Walla Wallas, become "contaminated" and cause trouble.[12]

White and a small party set out for the interior on April 29, 1843. The group would have been larger had McLoughlin supported its purpose. To the factor's credit, it should be said that he had perhaps done more than any other individual to keep the Indians peaceful. The delegation reached Waiilatpu on May 9, an auspicious time because Whitman was absent; he opposed forcing the Cayuses to accept the laws. The party saw very few Cayuses, since most of them were camped at the base of the Blue Mountains. Word was sent to the chiefs that the agent wished to see them at the mission. Some came to report that most of their people could not come in very soon because they were in the mountains hunting elk. In the meantime, Waptashtakmahl, decked out in a "fantastical" mixture of Indian and white clothing with a headdress belying his English name, Feathercap, escorted some of the visitors on a tour of Cayuse farms located about a mile from Waiilatpu. There the visitors observed that about sixty Cayuses had planted quarter- to three-acre plots of well-fenced ground to wheat, corn, peas, and potatoes.

Hearing of a large Cayuse and Walla Walla encampment fifty miles away at the headwaters of the Umatilla, the Reverend H. K. W. Perkins of the visiting delegation went to invite them to the council. After riding twenty miles farther than he had anticipated (the Indians had moved), he found Cayuse Chiefs Tauitau and Five Crows and Walla Walla Chief Peopeomoxmox. With the last was his son, Elijah Hedding (Toayahnu), who had spent several years at the Methodist mission school in the Willamette Valley. As White and his party journeyed to the Nez Percé country, the Cayuses gathered at the mission with mixed feelings. Some wanted to meet the Nez Percés and their chief, Ellis, while others wanted the Nez Percés to remain at home.

On Monday, May 22, three hundred mounted Cayuses and Walla Wallas were on the Waiilatpu plain to meet about twice

12 *Ibid.*, 164–66.

that number of Nez Percés. The Cayuses, particularly Tauitau, had worked themselves into a fevered state of excitement, which Henry Spalding was able to cool down with prayers. By the following morning Tauitau was calm enough to bring the meeting to order and hear what White had to say: he had come not to "catch them in a trap as a man would catch a beaver," but to do them good. He said that they would have to do good themselves by laying aside their former practices and prejudices and stopping their quarrels. They would, he said, have to cultivate the land and accept good laws. He outlined what appeared to be a contract between chiefs and Indians—the chiefs setting an example of love, good works, and humility and the people responding with obedience and remembrance of their chiefs in morning and evening prayers.

The Cayuses asked to hear the laws, which were read first in English and then in Nez Percé. In reply to an inquiry, Peopeomoxmox was informed that the laws were recognized by God, which made him happy because now he would not have to go to hell for whipping his people, as some of them had said he would. Tiloukaikt saw no reason to accept the laws just because the Catholic Tauitau wanted them. It was quickly explained to him that the laws were meant to apply equally to Catholic and Protestant. A formerly influential Indian, the Prince, said that he wanted more time to examine the laws, which the agent had brought to the Cayuses "as in a wind," speaking "as to the air." He said that he wanted to know what the whites could offer to the Indians in a more tangible way. Perhaps he was seeking to regain a position of importance through possession of material goods. White replied that he could offer little in a material way because he was neither missionary nor trader. Iatin said that he thought the young braves were not very sympathetic with the laws, since they had so much stolen property in their lodges.

An object lesson in the need for law and order occurred on the first day of the council, when an Indian shot a hole in the head of John the Hawaiian. The victim survived because there had been no ball in the musket. The chiefs captured the Indian who had committed the deed, found him guilty, but delayed sentencing until they received the laws. The chiefs generally spoke in favor of the laws and on the following day, Wednesday, May 24, voted unanimously for them.

It would be wrong to think that the Cayuses had been a people without laws; they had lived under a legal code from earliest times. John K. Townsend noted, for instance, that Cayuse lasciviousness was effectively checked by severe and rigidly enforced self-enacted laws.[13] Samuel Parker observed at about the same time that among the Indians the law was so correctly written on their hearts in conformity to the written law of God that every infraction of the Seventh Commandment was punished with severity.[14] Whitman testified that the mode of worship and system of punishment introduced to the Cayuses by traders had rendered them more civil and little addicted to theft.[15]

The laws White presented for Cayuse approval were those previously adopted by the Nez Percés. The laws were silent on matters of adultery (about which the Cayuses had traditionally strict codes), which had been of so much concern to missionaries, and dealt instead with murder, theft, and property damage, such as burning and other destructive acts. In this context they revealed a deference to white culture. Punishment for anyone willfully taking a life or burning a dwelling was hanging. This must have seemed indeed severe and strange to the Cayuses, whose families punished a murderer in other ways, though often they exacted payment from his people for the life taken. Entering a dwelling (the white man's castle) was illegal, though it had never annoyed the Indians as it had the whites. Whereas many references concerned damage to Indians' livestock, crops, buildings, and fences, the white framers of the laws sought to protect their own highly prized private properties from Indians. Burning of a dwelling

---

[13] Townsend, *Narrative of Journey*, 350.

[14] Parker, *Journal of an Exploring Tour*, 242–43.

[15] T. C. Elliott, "The Coming of the White Women, 1836," *Oregon Historical Quarterly*, XXXVII (March–December, 1936), 87–101, 123.

required forfeiture of life, while the burning of an outbuilding was to be punished by fifty lashes and payment of all damages. The penalty for theft was twofold repayment and a number of lashes based on the value of the items stolen. The punishments seem harsh, but it should be remembered that in that day penalties exacted in the white community for wrongdoing were also harsh. Whipping, administered to recalcitrant Indians, was also practiced in the white community.[16]

Under the laws whites would punish violators of their own race.[17] Since the chiefs were to be enforcers among the Indians, the council next turned its attention to their selection. Despite some opposition from his fellows, Tauitau was nominated and elected to the Cayuse high-chieftaincy. Previously, power among the Cayuses had rested primarily among three chiefs. Now authority and responsibility for tribal wrongdoing were no longer to be diffused among the trio but were to rest with a single high chief. Like Hudson's Bay Company and government officials, White knew that it was much easier to deal with one chief than with many.

The day ended with feasting on a fat ox, which White had purchased at the mission, and a fat hog, which Mrs. Whitman had donated. The Indians were finding domestic animals a good substitute for game, and the next morning, Thursday, May 25, some of them worked out with White an agreement by which they were to receive a cow for each horse they had furnished Oregon-bound Jason Lee nearly a decade before. The Cayuses considered a good horse and a good cow an even trade. Possibly Lee would have felt it an unequal exchange, for he believed Indian horses to be less gentle and fine blooded than American stock. When he accepted the horses, however, he was in no position to bargain.[18]

16 There were also many instances in the Indian community of red men whipped by whites, such as traders and missionaries.

17 Whitman was very critical of this weakness because "of the lack of a law-enforcing agency." Drury, *Marcus Whitman*, 351.

18 The price of a good horse at Waiilatpu in 1841 was twenty dollars. Wilkes,

After the business was concluded, Tauitau announced that since his religion was different from that of the Whitman-influenced Cayuses he could not accept the high-chieftaincy. His brother, Five Crows, was immediately nominated. "Our hearts go toward him with a rush!" the people were reported to have shouted as his qualifications were being presented. Five Crows won the election handily, which pleased the whites, too, for he was popular with both peoples. To show his gratitude, he wept when his victory was announced. With a quick election of sub-chiefs the main business of the four-day council was completed.

Now followed the closing feast. In one of his first official acts Five Crows called the table to order. A blessing was asked, and the crowd, including women and children (not usually present at such state affairs), assaulted the barbecued meat with their fingers, to the accompaniment of clattering teeth and smacking lips. The ox, which one member of White's party said had been grazing peacefully on the prairie three hours earlier, was devoured in twenty minutes. After the feast there followed the traditional pipe-smoking ceremony. Five Crows; Ellis and his fellow Nez Percé chief, Lawyer; Tauitau; and Peopeomoxmox spoke. A session of prayer followed. The Cayuses and Nez Percés were at peace with each other and with the whites. The next morning they came to bid White and his party farewell and to inform them that the Indian who had shot John the Hawaiian had been sentenced to forty lashes on his bare back (he was probably one red man who wished that the Cayuses had not adopted the laws). That evening on the campground, now desolate save for the smoldering fires, a solitary Indian boiled the feet of the ox for his next day's meal.[19]

On Saturday, May 27, White's party, with Mrs. Whitman, left Waiilatpu for the lower country. In their absence the Cayuses

United States Exploring Expedition, IV, 395. The _St. Louis Republican_, September 23, 1844, presented Lee's evaluation of horses.

[19] For information on the Cayuse council, see Hines, _Wild Life in Oregon_, 175–85, and White, _Ten Years in Oregon_, 213–19.

may have been calmed somewhat by the adoption of the laws, but if so, it was only temporarily. They had no assurance that Whitman was not returning from the East with a small army. He was, in fact, at that very moment in the vanguard of a group much larger than the fifty the Cayuses feared he would lead. A thousand members strong, it was composed of American patriots driven by "the finger of God," which never pointed in "a direction contrary to the extension of the glory of the Republic!" It was destined to conquer the Indians as no mere force Whitman was rumored to be bringing could have conquered them.

The diseases which had plagued the Northwest Indians since their initial contact with the whites would work no greater effect on them than the sickness known as Oregon Fever.[20] In the western reaches of the Oregon Immigrant Trail the finger pointed its way up many crossings of the Burnt River (a Snake tributary) and down the Powder, up a ridge and down into the Grande Ronde, thence up a steep pinewood stretch of the Blue Mountains, and down the Umatilla to the Columbia. Some of the "army" continued, as had their predecessors, to break north of the main trail to the mission to rest and replenish supplies (often with dire consequences to the mission's provisions) before continuing on the most arduous leg of their westward journey: down the Columbia to the settlements. In late October, about the time of Whitman's return, the Pathfinder, Captain John C. Frémont, exploring for the United States government, discovered that immigrants stopping at the mission had found the path to it before him.[21]

The Cayuses' apprehension about the white newcomers was

20 *New York Tribune*, February 25, 1845. The number of Oregon-bound immigrants varied from year to year. In the initial migration of 1842, there were from 112 to 137 souls; in 1843, from 875 to 1,000; in 1844, 700; in 1845, 3,000; in 1846, 1,350; in 1847, perhaps because of the recent Anglo-American boundary settlement, 4,000 to 5,000; in 1848, 700, the smaller number attributable, perhaps, to news of the Whitman massacre; in 1849, 400, the smaller number attributable, partially, to migrations to the California gold fields. Joseph Ellison, "The Covered Wagon Centennial," *Washington Historical Quarterly*, XXI, 3 (July, 1930), 176.

21 J. C. Frémont, *Oregon and California*, 249.

offset somewhat by the opportunities to trade with them. It was not uncommon during the immigrant season—late summer and early fall—for the Cayuses to ride along the Immigrant Trail, sometimes as far east as Forts Hall and Boise, to trade their horses for worn-out cattle. Sometimes they exchanged fresh oxen for twice as many jaded ones. Often along the trail the Cayuses, some of them speaking English, bartered fish from late Umatilla River runs and vegetables from late harvests for calicoes, nankeen cloths, and clothing. They continued to trade with immigrants after the latter reached the Willamette Valley. Accustomed to dealing with fur traders, many Cayuses did not know the value of money; for that matter, the realities of frontier economics also forced the whites to barter.[22] While the Cayuses were benefiting from trade in their location on the Immigrant Trail, the Nez Percés, living in an area peripheral to it, were lamenting their lack of such dealings.[23]

Business dealings between Cayuses and travelers in the early 1840's were generally satisfactory to both groups. Some immigrants even complained of the prices Whitman charged them for provisions at the mission. Lansford W. Hastings' statement in his *Emigrants' Guide* (1845) that the Cayuses and their mission brothers were a "villanous and treacherous race of thieves" seems to have been as far off the mark as his proposed route for the Donner party the following year.[24] Naturally, the travelers expected the worst. One company in 1842 remained at the mission only a day because of "verry bad treatment" from the Indians.[25] Since it had reprovisioned there—on "reasonable terms"—and since it was mid-September, the party quickly moved on.

[22] For information on the Cayuse-immigrant trade, see *Transactions Oregon Pioneer Association 1893*, 66–68; Joel Palmer, *Journal of Travels Over the Rocky Mountains, to the Mouth of the Columbia River; Made During the Years 1845 and 1846*, 53–66, 127. Palmer states on p. 27 that in 1846 an ordinary horse brought fourteen dollars, not much more than what it was worth in 1841. It could also be traded for four blankets.

[23] Palmer, *Journal of Travels*, 130.

[24] Lansford W. Hastings, *Narratives of the Trans-Mississippi Frontier*, 59.

[25] Medorem Crawford, *Journal of Medorem Crawford*, 20.

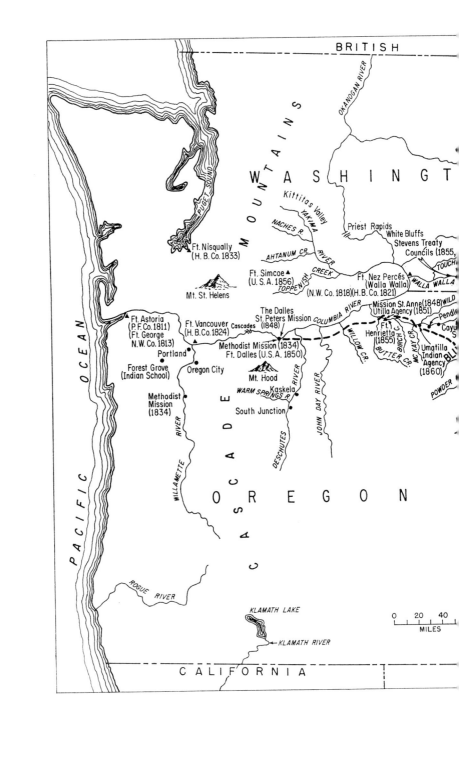

COLUMBIA

Colville (H. B. Co. 1825)

R O C K Y

M O N T A N A

RIVER

LAKE COEUR D'ALENE

Flathead Post (H. B. Co. 1821)

M
O
U
N
T
A
I
N
S

Red Wolf's Crossing

CLEARWATER RIVER

B
I
T
T
E
R
R
O
O
T

Lapwai (Spalding's Mission 1836)

M
O
U
N
T
A
I
N
S

SALMON RIVER

I D A H O

W
Y
O
M
I
N
G

RIVER

Ft. Boise (H. B. Co. 1834)

Ft. Hall (1834)
(H. B. Co. 1836)

SNAKE RIVER

OREGON IMMIGRANT TRAIL (ROAD)

N E V A D A

U T A H

Davis

THE OREGON COUNTRY IN THE NINETEENTH CENTURY

The Cayuses appeared friendly enough to travelers as long as the latter kept moving, particularly on a direct route down the Umatilla to the Columbia. With time, those detouring via the mission became increasingly unwelcome. Perhaps few Cayuses would have guided immigrants there as willingly as did friendly, prayerful Stickus (Istukus) after Whitman was forced to leave his returning party at the Grande Ronde to attend the ailing Spaldings. Whitman thought that the mission Indians had been kind to the 1843 immigrants, but on May 20, 1844, he wrote: "The Indians are very quiet but are solicitous about so many coming into their country." He noted that all the whites had gone to the Willamette Valley but feared that "the Indians will not like either to respect the interest of the whites as they ought nor the whites to forbear with the Indians." The Cayuses were becoming increasingly unhappy because settlers were recouping horses and cattle in the rich bunchgrass pasturage of the Umatilla and Walla Walla valleys. Livestock which the Cayuses had secured from immigrants in trade and which bore American brands was sometimes claimed by unscrupulous whites. That occasionally a few Indians drove off settlers' stock and returned it for a reward did little to diminish ill feeling toward the Cayuses.[26] At the mission virtually everything Whitman did, such as moving cattle and sheep from one place to another, was to the Indians an indication that he was preparing to flee the country to meet the Americans.[27]

The summer of 1844 was quiet on the surface. Some Cayuse and Walla Walla chiefs went to California to trade furs and horses for cattle. Without their restraining hand, a party headed by the son of one of the absent Cayuse chiefs rounded up a group of young men and rode to The Dalles, where they forced the Indians living there to give them horses, dried salmon, blankets, and other goods. The chief's son proudly rode back to the mission

[26] G. J. Tucker, "Pilot Rock Emigrant Road, 1861 and 1862."
[27] Marcus Whitman to Mrs. Alice Loomis, May 20, 1844, Letter P-A, 231:8, Bancroft Library; Spalding to Greene, October 17, 1845, Spalding Papers, Vol. 248, Letter 130.

98

with his tribute, just as his forebears had returned to their camps from such ventures for generations. He called at Whitman's home, but the missionary told him that he did not "shake hands with robbers." The answer was curt, but Whitman had had his fill of Cayuse raids on The Dalles. On another occasion a young Cayuse shot a Wascopum chief (aiming his shot through a slit in a lodge) because the Wascopum had tried to recover his property.

On the night he returned, the marauding son of the absent chief went to bed as usual, but about midnight he roused his wife to get him something to eat. She gave him some dried buffalo meat. While eating it, he fell dead, perhaps having choked on it. Whitman's medicine was thought to be the cause of his death.[28] Six years earlier, mission personnel had put emetics in melons to discourage the Cayuses from stealing them, and Indian dogs had been killed by poisoned bait put out for wolves. These incidents had only increased the Indians' fear that Whitman, like a vengeful medicine man, was trying to kill them. Nor were they pleased that because of sickness, short supplies, and a snow-covered trail across the Blue Mountains, some of the 1844 immigrants had taken up all available space in the mission houses, even occupying rooms the Indians had been forbidden to enter. All of this was further proof to them that the missionaries were more concerned with their white brothers than they were with the Indians.

That winter another young Indian died. Elijah Hedding, member of a party of Walla Wallas, Cayuses, and other interior tribesmen who went to California on a trading mission, was shot by an American at Sutter's Fort on the Sacramento in a dispute over horses. A witness to the murder, the victim's father, Peopeomoxmox, quickly gathered members of the expedition who, abandoning their properties, hurried home over snowy mountain trails. To show that he did not seek revenge, in the spring of 1845 he invited the Whitmans to a feast at which, in a speech, he implied that the old superstition of taking the life of a medicine man, such

---

[28] The account of the young chief is found in *Transactions of the Twelfth Annual Re-Union of the Oregon Pioneer Association for 1884*, 35.

99

as Whitman, had never entered his mind. If that thought had not occurred to him, it soon would.

In early May a party of twenty to thirty chiefs and braves of the Cayuse, Walla Walla, and Nez Percé tribes conferred with Whitman, Spalding, and other mission personnel. The Indian party had come as a sort of board of inquiry to consider whether Whitman was worthy of death. Chief interrogator was Peopeomoxmox. Since his murdered son had been a mission student and a preacher of sorts, would it not be equitable to exact the life of another preacher, namely Whitman? Moreover, had not the doctor extended hospitality to some Americans who had killed two Snake Indians (Snake enmity with the Cayuses and Walla Wallas notwithstanding)? To Peopeomoxmox the discussion of Whitman's fate may have been academic, but among his people and the Cayuses, killing medicine men for failing to cure patients, for stealing one's power, or for just evening a score was anything but academic. A white trader claimed that during a five-year stay at Fort Walla Walla the Cayuses and Walla Wallas living near there had shot seven medicine men that he knew of and probably more than three times that number altogether. The always practical McLoughlin had taken into account "their manner of thinking" in this regard, tending to defer to God rather than to the company in meting out punishment.[29]

But why had Peopeomoxmox raised the question at all? Perhaps when he realized the ineffectiveness of White's system of punishment for whites who killed Indians, the chief had acceded to tribal pressure to consider reversion to the old ways of handling such matters. When the meeting with Whitman and Spalding ended, the Indians rode off, warning the missionaries that they would not personally harm them but that their young men might. They then went to Fort Walla Walla, where Peopeomoxmox bitterly protested the death of his son and the two Snakes. He was finally calmed down and given presents.[30] That fall several Cayuse

29 *Ibid.*, 35.

and Nez Percé headmen peacefully traded horses for cattle in the Willamette Valley.[31]

An American traveler witnessing events at the fort warned prospective settlers to group themselves in companies of no less than thirty well-armed men; if they did not, he said, their westward journey might be terminated before they reached the Willamette. [32] Word had already spread to the immigrants that in their travel plans they had best take into account the threatening mood of the Cayuses and Walla Wallas. At Fort Boise in 1845, mountain man Joe Meek arranged to guide an immigrant party over a hazardous route up the Malheur River and across intervening ridges to the Deschutes and The Dalles in order to give agitated tribesmen a wide berth.[33] If one group (later named the Joel Palmer party for one of its members who subsequently figured prominently in Oregon affairs) that late summer expected trouble from the Cayuses in the Grande Ronde, it received instead a surprise lecture from "old Chief Aliquot," who chastised them for playing the un-Christian game of cards. Convicted by the chief's words, Palmer wrote that he "inwardly resolved to abandon card playing forever."[34]

In 1845, because he feared that the Cayuses might harm the whites, Whitman rode south from Spalding's mission to the Powder River to warn a ninety-wagon company that a large party of Cayuses and Walla Wallas was heading its way across the Blue Mountains. When the Indian vanguard entered the camp armed with guns, swords, quivers, and bows, Whitman told one of the chiefs that the Boston men would send people to defend the travelers, that shiploads of soldiers and guns would come to kill all the Indians who molested the Great Father's people on their

30 Overton Johnson and William H. Winter, *Route Across the Rocky Mountains,* 109–15.
31 Spalding to Greene, October 17, 1845, Spalding Papers, Vol. 248, Letter 130.
32 Johnson and Winter, *Route Across the Rocky Mountains,* 145.
33 For the story of this trail, see Keith Clark and Lowell Tiller, *Terrible Trail: The Meek Cutoff, 1845.*
34 Palmer, *Journal of Travels,* 54.

way to the distant valley. The Indians were nonplused at finding the doctor with the company. A Cayuse chief broke the awkwardness of the confrontation by pledging, with a smoke, to aid the Great Father. The Walla Walla chief laid his bow and quiver on the ground, as did twelve of his followers, and smoked the pipe. Still fearing treachery, the whites held the Walla Walla chief at gunpoint to prevent him from returning to his men. When he tried to leave, Whitman was reported to have said, "Move and my man shoot you like a dog." The chief remained motionless for the rest of the night and was disarmed shortly after sunrise by arriving Nez Percés. Whitman's actions and his service in guiding the immigrants to The Dalles won their gratitude, but he had done nothing to please the Cayuses and Walla Wallas. With them, not the immigrants, he would have to live, and that proved to be an increasingly difficult task. Tauitau threatened the missionary's life, causing Whitman to write Elkanah Walker on November 20, 1845, "I am so nervous that I cannot govern my hand, so that you will excuse me."[35]

The summer of 1846 passed quietly in Cayuse country, as summers generally did. In early fall, however, some whites arrived at Waiilatpu just as the Indians were returning from their summer rounds, increasing tensions between the two races. Meanwhile, several hundred miles southwest, a Cayuse–Nez Percé band raided a defenseless Indian village, killing the men and many of the women and children and taking the rest as slaves.[36]

In view of such incidents, it is not surprising that the fear of invasion by northern Indians was felt as far south as California. Word was out there in early September, 1846, that one thousand Walla Wallas (a designation Californians applied to several tribes, including the Cayuses), armed by the Hudson's Bay Company, had returned under Peopeomoxmox to avenge the death of his

[35] Sarah J. Cummins, *Autobiography and Reminiscences of Sarah J. Cummins, Touchet, Wash.*, 37–42; Clifford Merrill Drury, "Marcus Whitman—A Reappraisal," *The Record*, XXXI (1970), 41.
[36] Spalding to Greene, February 3, 1847, Spalding Papers, Vol. 248, Letter 134.

son. The whites rushed to Sutter's Fort, claiming to have seen the Indians' advance party approaching to attack the fort and, if they failed in that, to drive off all the cattle in the Sacramento Valley. Settlers braced for the expected attack. The twelve dilapidated pieces of artillery with which the fort was to be defended were readied, and men were sent out to scout the situation. On September 12, United States Navy Lieutenant Joseph Warren Revere and twenty-five men arrived from Sonoma. The next day it was ascertained that the invaders consisted of a small party of men, women, and children.

When Peopeomoxmox and his band arrived, the chief said that he had no hostile intentions, adding that the forty men, women, and children who were with him (many of whom were sick in their camp, pitched where the Feather River enters the Sacramento) had come only to hunt and trade for cattle. Yet he repeated what he had said when his son was killed and what he was reported to have said as he began his California journey: that "the blood of my slaughtered son calls for vengeance," which he might have tried to seek had he not found, to his surprise, so many Boston men in California. Adhering to Revere's suggestion, Peopeomoxmox visited the grave of his son and remained on friendly terms with the Americans during the winter. Ten of the Indians joined John C. Frémont's California Battalion and participated in the fighting which accompanied the annexation of California to the United States.[37]

A son of Peopeomoxmox who arrived home ahead of the Walla Walla–Cayuse California expedition broke the news that it had not only failed to avenge the death of his brother but that upwards of thirty of its members had died of illness. As he announced the deaths, victim by victim, in the old manner, a great

---

37 Edwin Bryant, *What I saw in California*, 273–74; Joseph Warren Revere, *Naval Duty in California*, 125–31. See also Robert Fleming Heizer, "Walla Walla Indian Expeditions to the Sacramento Valley," *California Historical Quarterly*, XXI, 1 (March, 1942), 1–7, and John Adam Hussey and George Walcott Ames, Jr., "California Preparations to Meet the Walla Walla Invasion, 1846," in the same issue of *California Historical Quarterly*, 9–17.

howl went up from the people, and the women loosened their hair in grief. Runners carried the bad news to all the camps, throwing them into great consternation.[38] The turmoil had no chance to cool before the fall tide of white immigrants rolled in, the largest of the 1840's. To add to the Indians' woes, the immigrants brought measles with them. The Indians took Whitman's medicine, along with some treatments he did not prescribe, such as the sweat bath and cold-water plunge. In the lodges a grim four-act drama was enacted: fever, breaking out, dysentery, death. Lumping the California deaths with these, the Indians blamed them on white people in general and on Whitman, their high chief, who had allowed the disease to come, in particular. One, according to a story told later, made himself sick to test Whitman, saying that if the doctor's medicine killed him everyone would know what had killed the others. The experiment proved fatal— proof enough![39]

In their usual manner the French-Canadians, eastern Indians, and others kept the pot boiling, pouring into it the poison of suspicion as deadly as that of the disease itself. Joe Lewis, like Tom Hill an eastern import, was a leader in the agitation. So was Nicholas Finlay, a former Hudson's Bay Company employee who had taken a Cayuse wife.[40] In his lodge were rehearsed all the old stories of whites uncorking bottles to release disease germs to kill the Indians so that they could take their land, tales of how he and others had overheard the Whitmans plotting to poison the Indians, and other fabrications which had been making the rounds since a smallpox epidemic of a decade before. If these statements were false, asked the Indians, why was it that so many of their people had died and not the whites? The only immunity they understood was immunity from Americans.

Where could they go for help? The magic from American Board missionaries had failed them. Perhaps there would be

---

[38] Kane, *Wanderings of an Artist*, 196–97.
[39] Curtis, *North American Indian*, VIII, 81.
[40] Drury, *Marcus Whitman*, 387.

assistance from the Black Robes. Since the first priests arrived on the Columbia in the late 1830's, a few Cayuses had turned from Whitman to them for new hope. One Indian instrumental in diverting the Cayuses was a young man named Pierre, who in 1842 went to the Roman Catholic Mission of St. Paul in the Willamette Valley. When he returned, he baptized children and adults in danger of dying and was careful to say his prayers.[41] Tauitau had also been instrumental in leading his people away from Whitman. Now, with many of them dying, he was more certain than ever that the fathers had greater medicine than the doctor. His hopes of finding a strange new thing at Boston man Whitman's mission were shattered in a blast of disenchantment. Even King George Fort Walla Walla had more to offer: blankets, coats, knives, and tobacco. To the chief this was the kind of medicine to cure Indian ills. Yet he had never forgot that the Black Robes had baptized his son, and, obedient to their instructions, he had led his people in prayers of the church.[42] He had also appealed to the fathers to open a mission on his lands, some of which, plus a house (built for him by employees of the Hudson's Bay Company as a reward for his good behavior), he offered to give them to establish it. With even greater vision the Reverend Augustin Magloire Blanchet (brother of François Norbert Blanchet), bishop of Walla Walla, sought to unite Tauitau's people with those of two other chiefs, Tiloukaikt and Iatin, to rebuild the religiously divided Cayuse house. The bishop was convinced of the success of his plan by reason of many Cayuse complaints about Whitman, whose days in the field he believed to be numbered.[43]

On September 5, 1846, Bishop Blanchet and a missionary party

[41] Blanchet et al., Notices and Voyages, 172–73.

[42] Hines, Wild Life in Oregon, 169–70.

[43] Sister Letitia Mary Lyons, Francis Norbert Blanchet and the Founding of the Oregon Missions, 1838–1848, 181–82. McKinlay, in a letter to Elwood Evans dated August 2, 1880, maintained that Dr. John McLoughlin deprecated the conduct of priests "in meddling with the Indians attached to the stations already established by the American Board," wishing them to use their influence only north of the lower Columbia River. Evans Papers.

consisting of the Reverend Pascal Ricard, O.M.I., superintendent of the Oregon Oblate mission and two scholastics were welcomed to Fort Walla Walla by chief trader William McBean, who was "Polished and a good Catholic." On September 23, Whitman arrived at the fort from The Dalles, whose mission he had just acquired for his board to block a Catholic mission there. Standing before him in the flesh were those whose coming he had increasingly feared. He would have agreed with Ricard (though for different reasons) that "of a sudden all the devils of hell seemed to league themselves against us." Now more than at any other time in the mission field Whitman feared for his own safety. There is also evidence that he had come to believe that Oregon belonged to his fellow Americans, whose increased numbers there would preserve it—and perhaps his life as well.[44]

The bishop awaited Tauitau's return from a hunting trip as Whitman simmered and blamed the chief for inviting the missionaries. On October 26, Tauitau appeared to say that he was eager to have the priests and that the bishop was welcome to the house and to as much land as he wanted. The priests must have been happy to see him, for earlier, when McBean had escorted the bishop to the house, a Cayuse guarding it had refused to turn it over to the cleric. Some of the Catholics were piqued by this action, first at Whitman, whom they believed to have been the cause of the lockout, and also at Tauitau, whose absence on a buffalo hunt had produced the awkward situation. Tauitau suggested that the Cayuse mission be established in the fertile, centrally located lands of Tiloukaikt's village near Waiilatpu. This seemed a good possibility, since Tauitau, through his wife, claimed ownership of Tiloukaikt's land. But how did Tiloukaikt feel about the proposal? Perhaps not very receptive. He had always told Whitman that the land (in the Chinookan-like concept of Cayuse family ownership) was his, not the missionary's or the tribe's.

Two weeks later Bishop Blanchet met with Tiloukaikt, Cam-

[44] Drury, "Marcus Whitman—A Reappraisal," 45–46.

aspelo, Tamsucky (a Cayuse headman), and other Cayuses. Following Indian custom, each chief spoke in turn. According to Thomas McKay, who attended the meeting, Tamsucky reiterated his belief, shared by most of the chiefs present, that Whitman had robbed and poisoned the Cayuses. This statement drew a rebuke from the bishop.[45] Tiloukaikt spoke last. He had questions for the bishop. Had the Pope sent the missionaries? Had he sent them to ask for lands? Who would maintain the missionaries and would they give presents to the Indians, plow their lands, and help them build houses and feed and clothe their children? The bishop said that he had come not to take lands but to save souls but that some land was necessary for Indian and missionary support. He said that he would make no presents and would neither plow nor build for them nor feed or clothe their children. But, he said, if he employed them, he would pay them for their work.

When the bishop ended his speech, the young men retired from the room, and Tiloukaikt said that he would not oppose the wishes of Tauitau. He asked Blanchet to send someone to his lands to select a site; the bishop agreed. Four days later the Reverend Jean Baptiste Abraham Brouillet, who had arrived at the fort a month after the missionary delegation, went to Tiloukaikt's village to look over the site. However, word came from Tiloukaikt that no land was available other than that on which Whitman's mission stood. Brouillet, as had Blanchet, disclaimed any intent of taking the property. Believing it urgent to enfold the Cayuses, many of whom were dying that very moment, Brouillet hurried to Tauitau's village to tell him that the bishop would establish his residence in the 18-by-30-foot house prepared by Tauitau and would take lands there. On November 10, Brouillet returned to the fort, and on the next day, again wasting no time, he set out to put the house in order for the bishop. He returned to the fort on the twenty-sixth to announce that all was in readiness. About evening on the twenty-seventh, Blanchet, Brouillet,

[45] Jacques Rousseau, M.S.R.C. (ed.), *Caravane vers l'Oregon*, 227; Secretary of Interior, *Annual Report, 1857–58*, 21–22.

and a Mr. LeClair arrived at the house. The long-sought Roman Catholic mission for the Cayuses had been established on the Umatilla River. The Catholics named it Mission St. Anne.[46]

With the founding of Mission St. Anne, it appeared that two arms of Christianity were to compete for the salvation of Cayuse souls. But death from measles—grim, unrelenting, and swift, unleashed by "all the devils of hell"—threatened to intervene.

On the day the Catholic mission was established, Whitman, in response to calls from Indians, went to the Umatilla to minister to the sick. He did not stay long in this place he could no longer claim as his own. As he took his leave, he was warned by the faithful Stickus that his life was in danger, and an elderly woman seized the reins of his horse and uttered a similar warning. But, perhaps thinking less of himself than of others, he hurried home to treat the sick at his own mission, his guests and his Waiilatpu flock, free riders of the plateau now unhorsed by disease. As he rode, the Grim Reaper was girding himself to bring death, not only by measles but also by murder, as he sharpened his scythe and prepared to ride a pale horse through the Place of the Rye Grass.

[46] For the story of Mission St. Anne, see William Lyle Davis, "Mission St. Anne of the Cayuse Indians, 1847–1848."

Courtesy G. Matthews Collection

These wild horses are descended from the cayuses of the Cayuse
Indians.

The two basalt columns at the mouth of the Walla Walla River were known as "Rocks of the Kye-use Girls." From an 1847 sketch by Paul Kane.

Fort Nez Percés in 1818.

The Whitman mission at Waiilatpu in 1845 as seen by William Henry Jackson. *Left foreground,* the mansion house; *left background,* the mill; *center,* the blacksmith shop; *right,* the mission house.

Walla Walla Chief Peopeomoxmox in 1847. From a painting by Paul Kane.

Mountain Man Joe Meek, first U.S. marshal of Oregon Territory.

Cayuse Chief Tiloukaikt, who owned the land on which the Whitman mission was built. From a painting by Paul Kane.

Tomahas buried his tomahawk in the skull of Dr. Marcus Whitman on November 29, 1847. From a painting by Paul Kane, based on a sketch Kane made in 1847 a few months before the Whitman massacre.

VI
Ride a Pale Horse

It was Monday morning, November 29, 1847. A cold mist settled over the Place of the Rye Grass. Its tree-lined creeks had surrendered burnished gold to late-autumn gray, and the sun's rays no longer burst over the Blue Mountains into the valley. Daylight revealed winterlike hues, a fit setting for the business of this day. An Indian came early to report the death of a child. Burial followed swiftly, for contagion precluded Indian as well as Christian preburial mourning. Only a few Indians attended the services. Shortly after noon, three white men began butchering beef. Blanketed Indians sat on a pile of fence rails, watching and perhaps remembering another butchering time when Dr. Whitman had smeared the blood of a steer on a Catholic Ladder, warning that Cayuse country would soon be bathed in blood.[1] This day that prophecy was to be fulfilled.

There were strange contrasts this day: white men butchering, grinding at the mill, tapping a hammer in the mission house to lay a floor; the buzzing of students at the school, reopened after illness and now called into afternoon session; continued sickness in the mission buildings and in Cayuse lodges. In the lodges it was the last day to nurse sick bodies before the Grim Reaper arrived, and the last day also to nurse a decade of accumulated suspicions and grievances ready to burst into violence.

After the child's funeral an Indian wearing a green cap entered a room occupied by Mrs. L. W. Saunders, the wife of a teacher. Whitman, apprehensive, was there, too. Mrs. Saunders offered the Indian a chair. He sat a few minutes, went to the next room, re-

[1] Davis, "Mission St. Anne," 195–96.

turned. The doctor left. The Indian with the green cap left. About two o'clock in the afternoon some Indians came to the mission house seeking medicine. There was a knock on the door leading from the dining room to the kitchen. Mrs. Whitman answered and then called her husband. The doctor opened the door. An Indian tried to enter the room, but Whitman blocked his way. The doctor then went to the closet under the stairs for medicine and returned to the kitchen to find that Tiloukaikt and another Cayuse, Tomahas, had entered the room. Whitman talked with Tiloukaikt, possibly about deaths that day in the lodges. While Tiloukaikt diverted Whitman in conversation, Tomahas struck him with a tomahawk. Attempting to escape, the doctor staggered outside and fell to the ground. A convalescing youth, John Sager, who was winding twine in the kitchen, reached for a pistol, but the Indians shot him dead. A Cayuse named Klokamas took the dead lad's straw hat, and Indian women plundered the pantry. Joe Lewis searched for clothing. An Indian entered the room of an immigrant tailor, Isaac Gilliland, who was sitting on a table, sewing; twelve hours later he died from his wounds.

When they heard gunfire, the Indians watching the butchering dropped their blankets and attacked with guns and tomahawks. One of the butchers, immigrant Jacob Hoffman, fought back with an ax, dodging repeated Indian thrusts in a retreat to a corner of the mission house where horsemen with lances cut him down. The Indians wounded another immigrant, Nathan Kimball, in the arm. The following day, disguised as an Indian, he went to the creek for water. The Indians shot him and left his body near a fence. The third butcher, immigrant W. D. Canfield, escaped to the blackmith shop and fled to Spalding's mission after dark. The Indians chased Andrew Rodgers, the man hired to teach the mission's white children, struck him on the head, and shot him in the arm. Several Indians also chased immigrant Peter D. Hall, who slid down the side of a house and ran to the willows to escape to Fort Walla Walla, after which he reportedly drowned as he fled to the Willamette Valley. Some Indians killed miller Walter Marsh and held L. W. Saunders, the teacher, while another Indian attempted to shoot him as he tried to escape the school to reach his wife in the mission house. He failed and lay dead halfway to his destination. At some point in the tragic scuffle old Tenino Chief Beardy (also known as Sue) arrived on the scene and in a loud voice vainly tried to dissuade the Indians from their slaughter.

Narcissa Whitman called to Lewis outside the mission house, asking if he had instigated the trouble. Just then a young Indian named Frank Escaloom, standing on the schoolhouse steps, shot Mrs. Whitman in the left arm. She fell screaming to the floor. Attackers began beating down the doors to enter the mission house living room. Succeeding, they rushed toward the door leading to the stairway, intending to go upstairs to find those who had fled there. A gun barrel, detached from its works and held by Rodgers, protruded from the stairs, slowing them down. At this point, Tamsucky came in to tell those upstairs that the Indians were going to burn the house, that he was friendly, and that they would be spared and should all go to Nicholas Finlay's lodge. The whites and Indians parleyed. Then, threatened by the gun barrel, Tamsucky gingerly climbed the stairs, having convinced Mrs. Whitman of his sincerity.

The adults decided to go downstairs first. There the weakened Mrs. Whitman lay on the settee. Rodgers took one end, and Lewis came in to take the other. The Indians outside crowded up to the north door, and as Rodgers emerged, they shot him down. Lewis dropped the settee, stepped back, and began firing. One bullet crashed into Mrs. Whitman's cheek and another into her body. An Indian tipped the settee, dumping Mrs. Whitman's body into the mud, and another lifted her by the hair and struck her face with his leather quirt, all to the accompaniment of moans from the dying Rodgers. Though Whitman had always been afraid that one day the Indians would kill him, his wife had never feared for her own life. Lewis found a boy (the slain John Sager's brother, Francis) hiding in the rafters of the schoolhouse and allegedly killed him. Before day's end there were more mutilations of the dead, though no scalpings.

A week later the Indians added to the massacre by killing two sick white immigrants, Crockett Bewley and Amos Sales. Deprived of Whitman's care, two sick children, Louise Sager and Helen Meek, died within a fortnight.

Flaunting both the laws of Moses and those of Elijah White with tomahawk and gun, the disillusioned Cayuses had slain their teachers. The martyrdom of the Whitmans gave rise to a futile controversy over the culpability of the Hudson's Bay Company and the Roman Catholic church. But that was of no direct concern to the Cayuses. A small group of malcontents had wreaked vengeance on those from whom they had expected bold magic but had received bad medicine. By one Indian estimate nearly two hundred of their people had died in the plague.[2] In the exhilaration over their vengeance for these deaths, the killers may have failed to foresee that white men would seek from them a retribution of their own.[3]

[2] Drury, *Marcus Whitman*, 394.
[3] Oscar Canfield, a child of nine at the time, later recalled that "about forty" Indians took part in the mass murder. William S. Lewis (ed.), "Oscar Canfield's Pioneer Reminiscences," *Washington Historical Quarterly*, VIII, 4 (October, 1917), 251–56. As might be expected, there are numerous accounts of the massacre, many of them conflicting. For a carefully written one, see Drury, *Marcus Whitman*, 390–411. William Fraser Tolmie, of the Hudson's Bay Company, in a letter to Elwood Evans dated December 26, 1878, told him that at the time of the measles outbreak the Indians wanted to wipe out not only the Americans but also the British. Evans Papers.

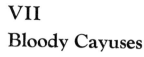

VII
Bloody Cayuses

The Waiilatpu killers danced in cele-
bration. When the drumbeats and
shrieks at last died down, the wind rose
and then stilled, and a cold fog blotted
out the stars.[1] At dawn a cluster of
Indians on the hill east of the mission
chanted a mournful death song, the
same one heard on the Umatilla the night of the killing when
Stickus' two wives sang it from foreknowledge of the event. At
the blood-spattered mission the fiendish yells and savagery of the
previous day had given way to the groans and sobs of the survivors, horror-struck by the mutilated bodies of dear ones lying
about. Spared the sight were those who had fled to the safety of
Fort Walla Walla.

The killers returned to the mission on Tuesday, November 30,
1847, with captive white women and children. To them the
whites were slaves, no different from those taken in earlier times.
The Indians ordered them to prepare breakfast and forced some
of the women to cook and taste other meals for them as an insurance against poison. Several days later the convalescing Amos
Sales told his captors that he would soon be able to work for them,
but death at their hands spared him from becoming their slave.[2]
As the killers reveled in their ancestral practice, other Cayuses
stood by, powerless to stop them. On the day of the massacre two
of Whitman's Cayuse herdsmen and other friendly Indians had
taken some of the white children to safety, pleading with the wild

[1] Frank T. Gilbert, *Historic Sketches of Walla Walla, Whitman, Columbia and
Garfield Counties, Washington Territory,* 120.
[2] Matilda J. Sager Delaney, *A Survivor's Recollections of the Whitman Massacre,*
20, 23.

ones to spare the others. Another had hidden Nathan Kimball, but not well enough, for he, too, became a victim.

On Tuesday evening Father Brouillet, in from the Umatilla, entered Tiloukaikt's camp near the mission. Even if the Indians had not told him what had happened, he could have sensed as much by the charged atmosphere of the place, which for the second night was the scene of excited dancing. The next day Brouillet buried the Protestant bodies in a common grave. With uninvited Edward—Tiloukaikt's son and also one of the killers —the priest left the mission to return to the Umatilla. Three miles out the two met Spalding coming from the Umatilla, where Stickus had warned the missionary that the Cayuses had "decreed against" the Americans. As Brouillet and Spalding met, Edward raced back to Waiilatpu to inform his fellows of Spalding's approach. Since the Cayuses had marked the missionary for extinction, those of Tiloukaikt's camp wasted no time in riding out to capture him. Arriving at the place where preacher and priest had met, they found that Spalding had fled, bypassing Waiilatpu, where his daughter was a captive. A heavy fog helped prevent his pursuers from finding him and he eventually returned home to Lapwai.[3]

In December the Indians forced several captive women to become their wives.[4] Artist John Mix Stanley, approaching Waiilatpu when informed of the massacre, wrote that one Cayuse killer, Shumahiecu (Painted Shirt), had taken from the captive women a wife, "a young and beautiful girl of fourteen." In order to "gain her quiet submission to his wishes," he had threatened to kill her mother and sisters. Concluding his report of the episode, Stanley wrote: "Thus in the power of savages, in a new and wild country remote from civilization and all hope of restoration, she yielded herself to one whose hands were yet red with the blood of an elder brother."[5]

3 Secretary of Interior, *Annual Report, 1857–58*, 38–39.
4 Hubert Howe Bancroft, *History of Oregon, Vol. I, 1834–1848*, 662.
5 Secretary of Interior, *Annual Report, 1854–55*, Sen. Exec. Doc. No. 1, 33 Cong., 2 sess., Serial 746, p. 427.

One of the captives, Mrs. Nathan Kimball, was forced to live with the Indian who had shot her husband. Another, Esther Lorinda Bewley, was taken to the Umatilla, where Five Crows forced her to spend each night in his lodge, thereby fulfilling his long-standing dream of having a white woman. During the day she was under the protective custody of Bishop Blanchet at neighboring Mission St. Anne. There was later considerable controversy in white circles about whether Five Crows, a Spalding convert, was protecting Miss Bewley as a Christian gentleman or a lustful savage. In a deposition Miss Bewley claimed the latter, stating that she was dragged nightly from the helpless bishop to the chief's lodge.[6]

Although some white Protestants thought Blanchet had aided and abetted the Indians in the massacre, he had not. When he learned of it, he summoned Five Crows, Tauitau, and other Cayuses to tell them how grieved he was over the atrocious act, expressing hope that the women and children would be spared until they could be sent to the Willamette. The Indians responded by promising to care for the captives. It was apparent that Five Crows thought he was doing his part. Aware that the Waiilatpu Cayuses were angry because Brouillet had warned Spalding, Blanchet feared retaliation from their fellow tribesmen on the Umatilla, which might explain why he did not intervene in behalf of Esther Bewley. A force far stronger than his fear of priests caused Five Crows eventually to relinquish her: his fear of soldiers.[7]

On the Umatilla the Cayuse mood was one less of vengeance than of despair. On the Willamette the mood of the Oregon provisional government was one of alarm as the governor, George Abernethy, informed the legislature of the massacre. He had been told of the tragedy through a messenger sent from Fort Vancouver by chief factor James Douglas, who had learned of it from Wil-

[6] Secretary of Interior, *Annual Report, 1870–71*, Sen. Exec. Doc. No. 37, 41 Cong., 3 sess., Serial 1440, pp. 34–37; *Transactions Oregon Pioneer Association 1893*, 96.
[7] Secretary of Interior, *Annual Report, 1870–71*, 36.

liam McBean. The Cayuses were as unaware of the message that was sent as they were of the Oregonians' reaction to it. On December 8, the day Abernethy gave the news to the legislature, that body authorized the formation of a company of riflemen, "not to exceed" fifty men, to protect citizens at the outpost of white settlement at The Dalles. Forty-six men responded to the call. On December 9 they were on their way. On December 10 a bill was passed in the legislature authorizing the raising of five hundred mounted volunteer riflemen. The governor issued the first of two proclamations for volunteers. One hundred came out. On Christmas Day the second proclamation was issued for raising the balance of the authorized riflemen.[8]

White hotbloods in the Willamette Valley would have agreed with Camaspelo, who, with other chiefs, visited Bishop Blanchet on December 18 to tell him the Cayuses were doomed to die. So full of despair was Camaspelo that he favored killing the horses and leaving the country.[9] By this time news of the massacre had spread throughout the Indian country, although some Cayuses later said they knew nothing of it for two weeks. When the Nez Percés learned of the affair, they were greatly troubled. On December 16 two of them had arrived on the Umatilla with a letter from Spalding, asking for help in getting his family and himself out of Lapwai and assuring the Cayuses that peace-seeking Americans would not come to their country in retaliation. Since Spalding could not have guaranteed that the killers would go unpunished, it would appear that he sent the message to calm the Cayuses until he could leave. Recent events had given him ample reason to fear for his life.

In their December 18 meeting with Blanchet the chiefs asked him to tell Governor Abernethy not to send an army but to come himself in the spring and hold council with them. The bishop replied that he could not accede to their wish until he knew the

8 Secretary of War, *Annual Report, 1889–90, Sen. Exec. Doc. No. 6, 51 Cong., 1 sess., Serial 2678, p. 2; Bancroft, *History of Oregon, Vol. I, 1834–1848, 670–71.

9 Secretary of Interior, *Annual Report, 1857–58, 43.

disposition of all their people. With Camaspelo's help he arranged for the Cayuses to meet at Mission St. Anne in two days.[10] In the meantime he cautioned Camaspelo that the longer his people delayed in coming to an understanding among themselves about who was responsible for the massacre the more difficult it would be to make any arrangement for a settlement. The problem of pinpointing responsibility threw the Cayuses into much confusion, as did the merits of discussing it with officials of the provisional government.[11]

On December 20, Tauitau, Five Crows, Camaspelo, and Tiloukaikt (who came from his Waiilatpu camp) met in council with Brouillet, LeClair, and Godfroi Rousseau, of the Catholic mission. Brouillet expressed pleasure at the chiefs' desire to avoid war. He told them the Nez Percés wanted him to tell Governor Abernethy not to send troops and had proposed that the government be requested to send up "two or three great men" to make peace. When they arrived, Brouillet explained, the captives would be released, and no more harm would be done to the Americans until it was known what the governor would do. Brouillet said that he was unable to respond to the Nez Percé suggestion until he knew how the Cayuse chiefs felt about it and asked them to tell him.

The first to speak was Camaspelo. He said that he approved of seeking Abernethy's help in preventing retaliation against them.

Tiloukaikt spoke next—for two hours. He said that before the whites came to his country the Cayuses were at war constantly, with blood "continually seen." But, he added, after white men came with the Word of God, which forbade killing, the Cayuses lived in peace. Then, revealing his belief in the Cayuse custom of evening the score, he said that he hoped that the many Cayuse deaths at the hands of white men would make the whites forget

[10] Davis, "Mission St. Anne," 203.
[11] Curtis, *North American Indian*, VIII, 82; Rousseau, *Caravane vers l'Oregon*, 232.

the slaughter of their brothers—by his own hand, he might have added.

Tiloukaitkt's son, Edward, bearing a bloody Catholic Ladder, repeated Whitman's warning that as long as priests were among them there would be no peace.[12] Edward reinforced the ideas presented by his father, speaking of the many Cayuse deaths and alluding to Joe Lewis' statement that the Whitmans had poisoned the Indians. That Andrew Rodgers, a massacre victim, had "attested" to that fact was "proof" enough.

Five Crows and Tauitau added little to the conversations, but they did approve six proposals drawn up for presentation to the governor. These included a request that the Americans not go to war with the Cayuses; that the Indians forget the murders committed against them; that the death of Elijah Hedding in California be put out of mind; that the government send to them a peace commission of two or three members, upon whose arrival they would free the captives; that Cayuses not harm Americans before the arrival of the commission; and finally that Americans travel no more in Cayuse country because the young men might harm them. Tiloukaikt, Camaspelo, Tauitau, and Five Crows signed the document, and Bishop Blanchet personally presented to Governor Abernethy the Cayuses' request that a delegation be sent to them to talk peace.[13]

To the proposals Blanchet appended a letter stating that the massacre had occurred because of the Cayuses' "anxious desire of self preservation"[14] and that they now wanted to forget the past and live in peace, despite the fact that many Indians in the area would join them should they become involved in a war with the whites. The bishop reported that he had told the chiefs that they could expedite matters by giving up the "American girls" in their

12 Secretary of Interior, *Annual Report, 1857–58*, 43–45.
13 *Ibid.* See Appendix B for the text of the Cayuse letter to the governor; Rousseau, *Caravane vers l'Oregon*, 227.
14 Davis, "Mission St. Anne," 206.

possession. All had agreed except Five Crows, who resisted pleas from the others to relinquish his "wife."[15]

The chiefs soon received another summons to a council, this one to be held at Fort Walla Walla on December 23 with the Hudson's Bay Company's Peter Skene Ogden, who had come up from Fort Vancouver to gain the release of the white prisoners. Aware of the Cayuses' temperament from long association with them in the fur trade, he was fearful lest they kill the remaining captives. Tauitau, Tiloukaikt, and a dozen of their men proceeded to the fort, convening there at 9:30 A.M. on the appointed day. Two Nez Percés and Peopeomoxmox were also there to hear Ogden request release of the captives. Speaking directly to the point, as company traders were wont to do with the Indians, Ogden blamed the chiefs for not restraining their young men and preventing them from committing murder. He may have gained their confidence by assuring them that, in line with established policy, he was acting for the company, not in behalf of the Americans, having left Fort Vancouver before the Willamette settlers knew of his journey. In true trader fashion he drove a sharp bargain, telling them that he could offer them nothing for their captives, whom they had hoped to retain to guarantee Cayuse security.[16] The chiefs pondered Ogden's warning that refusal to release the whites might very well push the Americans into a war against them.

In addressing the chiefs, Ogden was not unmindful that war would seriously damage company business. He cited the harmonious relations that had existed between the Indians and his firm, adding assurances that if they did not harm company men it would stay on friendly terms with them. His word strengthened their belief that it was not the British whom they must fear but

15 *Ibid.*
16 "Chief Factors P. S. Ogden and James Douglas to Sir George Simpson. Fort Vancouver, March 16, 1848," in "Notes and Documents: Whitman Material in the Hudson's Bay Company Archives," *Pacific Northwest Quarterly*, XXXIII, 1 (January, 1942), 63.

the Americans. In a letter to George Simpson, Ogden expressed his belief that the Americans would obtain the Oregon country "by blood or total annihilation."[17]

Employing the same trait for shrewd bargaining which characterized Cayuse trade at the fort, Tiloukaikt and Tauitau offered to release the captives—for a price. Sensing Ogden's concern, they must have thought that with a little pressure they could get him to appease them with an exchange of gifts for an assurance of peace. Not all the chiefs appeared as mercenary as Tiloukaikt and Tauitau, however. John Mix Stanley related how Shumah-iecu movingly told Ogden of his attachment to his white wife and how, as a great warrior possessing many horses and cattle, he had offered them all to her with the promise that if she did not choose to live with his people he would abandon them to make his home in white men's country.[18]

The Cayuses' persistence paid off. In exchange for their prisoners Ogden promised them fifty blankets, fifty shirts, ten guns, ten fathoms of tobacco, ten handkerchiefs, and one hundred rounds of ball and powder. Surely the chiefs must have known that had there been no lives at stake they would have never won a trading bout so handily. Fulfilling their end of the bargain, they delivered forty-six prisoners to Fort Walla Walla to join the five Americans who had already fled there. The chiefs might have delivered them less readily had they known that Major Henry A. G. Lee, appointed by Governor Abernethy as one of the commissioners to treat with friendly interior Indians and commanding the advance volunteer rifle regiment, had arrived at The Dalles on Christmas Eve.[19]

On New Year's Day, 1848, Spalding arrived at the fort with a

17 *Ibid.* Americans were angry because Ogden, while passing up the Columbia, had dispensed ammunition to Indians at the Deschutes River. For him to have forgone this traditional service might have aroused the Indians' suspicions, frustrating his plan to rescue the hostages. McKinlay to Evans, March 28, 1899. Evans Papers.

18 Secretary of Interior, *Annual Report, 1854–55*, 427.

19 Bancroft, *History of Oregon, Vol. I, 1834–1848*, 683; Secretary of Interior, *Annual Report, 1857–58*, 47.

delegation of fifty Nez Percés and ten whites who had been held, perhaps in the protective custody of those tribesmen.[20] The following day the whites set out by boat with Ogden for the Willamette Valley. There his action was described as "the legitimate offspring of a noble, generous and manly heart." The party left shortly after noon, only hours before fifty armed Cayuses rode up to the fort to kill the missionary. Had the Cayuses not received intelligence of the rifle regiment at The Dalles before the whites' departure, they would soon have learned of it from other Cayuses, Teninos, or runners dispatched to area tribes.

The Americans had sent their own "runners"—to the commander of American forces in California seeking his help.[21] Preparations were also under way to send Joe Meek, whose daughter had sickened and died after the massacre, to Washington, D.C., to seek help from the United States government. Appeals for aid were also sent to the commander of a United States naval squadron in the Pacific and to the American consul in the Hawaiian Islands.[22]

In their traditional browbeating fashion the Cayuses warned the Deschutes Teninos and the Wascopums (Chinookan peoples at The Dalles) to join in a united front against the Americans or suffer Cayuse wrath. Under this pressure two Tenino bands, one under Welaptulket and the other under old Beardy, and a few Wascopums joined the Cayuses.[23] On January 8, twenty-three Indians, eight of them Cayuses, ran off a herd of immigrant cattle at The Dalles. The military volunteers discovered the stock two miles east of Fort Lee (established at The Dalles). Two men pursued the Indian raiders, followed by Lee and five or six men on horseback and later still others to a total of seventeen men. They finally engaged the Indians in a two-hour skirmish, which

[20] H. K. Hines, *An Illustrated History of the State of Washington*, 73.

[21] Rosetta W. Hewitt, "Joseph L. Meek," *Washington Historical Quarterly*, XX, 3 (July, 1929), 199–200.

[22] Robert Carlton Clark, "Military History of Oregon, 1849–59," *Oregon Historical Quarterly*, XXXVI (March–December, 1935), 18.

[23] Sarah Hunt Steeves, *Book of Remembrance of Marion County, Oregon, Pioneers, 1840–1860*, 160.

ended with three Indians dead and one wounded but with the Indians garnering some three hundred head of immigrant cattle.[24]

The next day a detachment was sent out to bring in, for his own protection, Seletsa, the friendly Tenino brother of Beardy. Seletsa probably came in willingly, since he had been robbed by the Cayuses for refusing to join them. The volunteers also captured sixty Indian horses. On January 23 an advance party of fifty Oregon volunteers under Colonel Cornelius Gilliam reached The Dalles and set up camp; Gilliam promptly named the post Fort Wascopam.[25] Three companies of volunteers, close behind Gilliam, arrived at The Dalles and camped. Three other companies were organizing to follow, and more were being raised. The total volunteers, shy of the five hundred authorized, would arrive at The Dalles before Gilliam started east from there. The presence of so many troops did not deter hostile Indians from infiltrating the area to harass friendly tribesmen and the soldiers. Some of the hostiles drove the whites' horses to a hillside, tied ropes to the animals' feet to make it appear they had strayed, and then waited on the other side of the hill for the whites to retrieve them. When the whites appeared, the Indians killed two of them.

Near a small creek thirty-five miles up the Deschutes River from The Dalles, some retreating mountain-bound Teninos and Cayuses made a hasty camp in a deep cut on the east side of the river. On January 29 they rode out to meet Major Lee and twenty scouts, who had seen the dust kicked up by their horses. Lee and his men charged, killing a brave and capturing two women and a number of horses. Finding themselves in the thick of more Indians than their small force could handle, the whites hastily retreated to the shelter of some rocks and bushes in a ravine. The place offered less protection than they wished, for the Indians,

24 Evans, *History of the Pacific Northwest,* I, 279.
25 When the rifle regiment arrived, it set up Fort Lee. When Gilliam and his volunteers came, a larger post, Fort Wascopam, was established. Bancroft, in his *History of Oregon, Vol. I, 1834–1848,* 701, says that Colonel Gilliam arrived at The Dalles on January 24.

employing the most ancient of tactics and weapons, rolled stones down on them until dark. One man straggled back to camp with an arrow in his hip.[26]

The next morning the Indians met Colonel Gilliam and 130 volunteers a quarter-mile away. Armed with rifles and bows, the red men deployed in a line atop a bluff, separated from the oncoming troops by a deep ravine on the sides of Meek's Cutoff (from the Immigrant Road, formerly the Immigrant Trail). The approaching volunteers halted, whereupon the Indians, as was their custom, hurled insults at them for a while and then began firing. In the din the tribesmen failed to hear Lieutenant T. C. Shaw give his Company B troops battle orders, urging them to move out and take some Indian scalps.[27] As the command set out on foot across the ravine, the Indians continued firing but overshooting their mark—a reflection less on their marksmanship than on the accuracy of their cumbersome muzzle-loading weapons. In a style more savage than civilized, the volunteers came on, whooping and perhaps causing some discomfiture among the Indians, who probably did not expect such noises from their foes. Just as the two forces were about to engage in hand-to-hand combat, the outnumbered Indians retreated. A small party on fast horses pursued them, but the red men escaped.

The soldiers sent back to The Dalles for provisions. In the meantime the Indians hastily fled their camp, about two miles away, leaving behind dried salmon, roots, and potatoes.[28] In their haste they also abandoned property taken from immigrants, as well as forty horses and four head of cattle. The soldiers burned the camp,[29] though some of them later denied doing so. The In-

[26] Bancroft, *History of Oregon, Vol. I., 1838–1848*, 701–704; Evans, *History of the Pacific Northwest*, II, 337.

[27] Steeves, *Book of Remembrance*, 159–61.

[28] *Ibid.*, 162.

[29] Some sources say Gilliam did not permit the camp to be burned. In *History of the Pacific Northwest*, II, 337, Evans states that no tent or skin home was destroyed because of "Colonel Gilliam's character, his great sympathy for the fallen, weak and helpless." But anyone familiar with the colonel's character knows that he favored killing the Indians and destroying all their property. That the camp

dians themselves said that in retaliation for the deed they put the torch to buildings at Whitman's mission[30] and braced for vengeance in kind by erecting fortifications at the old mill, eighteen miles away. From the skirmish emerged a footnote tinged with not a little irony: Perrin Whitman, nephew of the doctor, claimed to have killed a chief and another Indian.

After more brushes the main body of Indians moved out, some to the west to enlist help from the Willamette Indians. Among those contacted were the Cayuses' ancient neighbors the Mollalahs. With the Klamaths and Modocs of present-day southern Oregon, the Mollalahs frightened settlers unnerved by the absence of so many of their men in the interior fighting the hostile Indians. Cayuse spies reportedly tried unsuccessfully to persuade the Mollalahs to bury the hatchet and join the Klamaths in harassing the whites.

Some of the hostile Indians continued east to join a large group of Indians moving west from Cayuse country to meet the Americans, and a group of Cayuses went north to the Columbia to warn fellow tribesmen that whites were coming to make war. One of the plotters of the massacre, Nicholas Finlay, hurried to the Spokanes to solicit their aid; it was refused. In mid-February two Yakimas brought word to The Dalles that although the Cayuses had asked them to fight they would not do so because they had no quarrel with the whites, especially those who kept off their lands. The Cayuses were attempting to form a grand alliance against the whites, and in their eagerness they may have encouraged rumors that Americans were killing priests, Hudson's Bay Company personnel, and French-Canadians on French Prairie in the Willamette Valley.

The result of the Cayuses' diligence in recruiting became evi-

was destroyed is attested to by the soldiers. Secretary of War, *Annual Report, 1889–90*, 5. See also A. E. Garrison, *Life and Labour of Rev. A. E. Garrison: Forty Years in Oregon*, 54.

[30] Superintendent Anson Dart's report regarding claims of Indian-destroyed property, Manuscript 57/276, Envelope 6E, Walker Papers.

dent in February when some Nez Percés, Walla Wallas, Umatillas, and most of the Palouses, who lived along the Palouse River, a Snake tributary, came over to their side. Thus strengthened, the Cayuses set out to confront the soldiers under Colonel Gilliam, who had left The Dalles on February 15, heading west up the Immigrant Road. Before his departure, however, Beardy, wishing none of the treatment the Cayuses had doled out to his brother, sent two men to the colonel to sue for peace. They were given flags to take to their chief. Gilliam, whose disposition was to fight, would have preferred to kill the chief and any other Indian he met. He was restrained from doing so by three peace commissioners, Major Lee, mountain man Robert Newell, and Joel Palmer, sent to tell the Cayuses there would be peace if the Whitman murderers were surrendered.[31]

The commissioners left The Dalles on February 14, wishing to proceed ahead of the troops in order to confer freely with the Indians, as Governor Abernethy had intended, for they knew full well that Colonel Gilliam opposed their mission. They succeeded in outdistancing the troops, but the next day, to their disappointment, the volunteers caught up with them. Traveling awkwardly together into Indian country under orders of the provisional government were two groups with different objectives: the commissioners, under administrative appointment, charged with preventing a coalition of Cayuses and other Indians, and the volunteers, under legislative authorization, charged with capturing the Whitman murderers. It appeared that Abernethy was trying to hold out both the carrot and the stick, the former to Indians not yet directly involved in hostilities and the latter to their belliger-

---

[31] *Oregon Spectator*, April 6, 1848, pp. 2–3; G. W. Hunt, *A History of the Hunt Family From the Norman Conquest, 1066, A.D., to the Year 1890*, 33. One participant, inflamed by the passion of the time, believed the commissioners were under the influence of the Hudson's Bay Company. That firm, he wrote on August 10, 1849, "held the cords of vengeance for the purpose of letting these murderers have time to run off their stock, women and children, and these alone knew our horses were not fleet enough to take them." Typescript copy in Clarence B. Bagley, "Miscellaneous Selections of Historical Writings, 1843–1932."

ent brothers.[32] However, the provisional government had not expected the commissioners and the volunteers to appear together. While the commissioners were camped on the Deschutes River, several Tenino bands agreed to come in and talk peace. A number of less peacefully inclined Indians, camped near the upper John Day crossing, fled with ground caches of food before the troop reached that point on February 18.[33] The volunteers moved deeper into Indian country to make contact with the hostile Indians. Staying out of combat range, Indian scouts kept the troops under constant surveillance as they moved from their camp near the John Day crossing to Willow Creek, where they would remain until February 23.

A party of twelve Indians accompanied Beardy east along the trail behind the troops as the latter decamped. When they reached the Americans, they held council with the commissioners, and the chief agreed to bring in cattle and horses stolen from whites at The Dalles. If this was not assurance enough of his good faith, Beardy said, he was willing to go to war against the Cayuses.[34] Even Tenino Chief Welaptulket extended a peace feeler by sending a horse along as a present to Thomas McKay (son of Astorian Alexander McKay), captain of a company of French-Canadians.[35] To demonstrate their peaceful intentions, the Indians had brought with them a flag that had been given to Beardy.

Meanwhile, another flag was being delivered by the Nez Percé Elijah to William McBean at Fort Walla Walla. The commissioners had sent him there to spread the word that they were on their way to meet with the Indians. Elijah also carried a message from Spalding to the Nez Percés, asking them to remain at peace. He had apparently passed through the hostile Indians' lines without arousing suspicion that his mission was detrimental to their cause.

32 Priscilla Knuth, editor, *Oregon Historical Quarterly* to authors, August 21, 1969.
33 Dorothy O. Johansen (ed.), *Robert Newell's Memoranda*, 107.
34 *Ibid.*, 108.
35 Bancroft, *History of Oregon*, Vol. I, 1834–1848, 709.

The Indians continued their surveillance of the troops, now moving deeper into the interior. On February 23 the volunteers reached Wells Springs on the Immigrant Road (about fifteen miles south of present-day Boardman, Oregon). They knew that they were being watched because they had found telltale horse signs. By now the Cayuses had mobilized their forces, and repercussions were felt at Mission St. Anne, which Brouillet was forced to close. Shortly after he and LeClair abandoned it on February 20, the Indians burned it down.

The main body of hostile Indians, now 418 strong, moved west to make their stand.[36] Accompanying them were a hundred women and old men who had come to see the slaughter of the whites.[37] To keep their people in a warlike mood, the chiefs harangued in the ancient manner, reminding them that Elijah Hedding's killers had never been caught, a fact which rankled the Cayuses no end. Ironically, Hedding's father, Peopeomoxmox, had participated in neither the massacre nor the present fighting. Accused by the Cayuses of being afraid of the whites, he replied: "I am not afraid of the whites, nor am I afraid of Cayuses. I defy your whole band. I will plant my three lodges on the border of my territory at the mouth of the Touchet [a Walla Walla tributary], and there I will meet you if you dare to attack me." True to his word, he moved his camp there and remained for a time.[38] But this was neither the time nor the place for neutrals. If the Walla Walla chief would not avenge the death of his son, young Cayuse braves would.

[36] *Newell's Memoranda*, 120n.; *Oregon Spectator*, March 23, 1848, p. 2.
[37] Clinton A. Snowden, *History of Washington: The Rise and Progress of an American State*, II, 353.
[38] Secretary of Interior, *Annual Report, 1854–55*, 431; J. F. Santee, "Pio-Pio-Mox-Mox," *Oregon Historical Quarterly*, XXXIV (March–December, 1933), 170.

VIII
The Cayuse War

February 24, 1848, was bright and warm for a winter day. The volunteers, under the watchful eyes of hostile scouts, moved toward a place called Sand Hollow, eight miles east of Wells Springs on the Immigrant Road. A familiar terrain of rugged cuts and washes at the hollow afforded the Indians excellent cover should they need it. About noon, war painted and feathered, on equally decorated horses much fresher than those of the troops, the warriors rode to meet their foes, making hostile gestures as they went. The three commissioners, carrying a white flag, rode out ahead of the companies to meet them. The Indians warned them to keep away and wheeled their horses in closer. The gallery of women and old men watched from a safe distance. A volunteer recalled the presence of another audience, made up of northern tribesmen—Coeur d'Alenes, Flatheads, and Pend Oreilles—summoned to war by the Cayuses, who had told them that whites in Oregon had killed all Catholics and Hudson's Bay Company men, including Thomas McKay. But, said the soldier, when the northern Indians met the commissioners and saw McKay very much alive, and when they learned that the volunteers had come to punish the Cayuse killers, an old Flathead chief withheld his men from the engagement.[1]

The warriors aligned themselves about four feet apart in a hunting-style maneuver encircling the command, rode to within gun range of the soldiers, backed off, and came on again at full speed. With a defiant yell and brandishing their weapons, they

---

1 W. W. Walter, "Reminiscences of a Forty-Niner," Manuscript 1741, Holland Library, Washington State University, Pullman, 4.

broke into a second circle within the first, shouting, "We will beat the Americans to death with clubs, and then proceed to the Willamette and take the women, and all their property."[2] Five Crows and Grey Eagle shouted encouragement to their men, telling them that, like their mother, the earth, they would let no harm befall them and that the enemy would never reach their Cayuse homeland, the Umatilla River. According to some white accounts, Grey Eagle, a shaman, summoned his guardian spirit and encouraged his warriors by boasting that he would swallow all the bullets the Americans could fire at him. At the same time Five Crows, not to be outdone, boasted that bullets could not hurt him.[3]

Spurred on by these words from their chiefs, the Indians formed to the right of the volunteers as the latter began to divide into north and south wings. To prove their claims, Grey Eagle and Five Crows rushed headlong toward the troops. One, probably Grey Eagle, shot a dog which ran out from among the soldiers; this unexpected incident helped ignite the skirmish. Convinced of his invulnerability, Grey Eagle rode to within close range of the troops. A shot in the head from McKay's rifle felled the chief, and another from the captain's gun struck Five Crows in the arm. McKay, whom William H. Gray called "the most reliable half-native servant the [Hudson's Bay] company ever had,"[4] personally knew many of the Indians against whom he was fighting—and he knew their weaknesses. So did Baptiste Dorion, another half-blood with the troops. As Grey Eagle rose to a sitting position, his gun still smoking, Dorion ran out and stomped the shaman's proud face.[5] Supreme irony! It was Dorion who in 1841 had circulated among the Cayuses rumors that "the Americans were coming to make war upon them and take their country."[6]

2 Bancroft, *History of Oregon, Vol. I, 1834–1848*, 710.
3 Charles N. Crewdson, "How We Got Oregon," clipping in the [Clarence B.] Bagley Scrapbook, No. 6, p. 57.
4 Gray, *History of Oregon*, 282.
5 *Transactions of the Twenty-Seventh Annual Reunion of the Oregon Pioneer Association for 1899*, 68.
6 *Newell's Memoranda*, 94.

The wounding of their chiefs threw the Indians into confusion, and they fell back. Five Crows shouted to them to continue the fight, whereupon they regrouped and reloaded their rifles. Twenty minutes later they charged again, firing all the way.[7] Returning the fire, the volunteers maneuvered to protect their supply train until they could reach a favorable spot to form a defensive corral. The Indians attacked repeatedly, their fusees throwing balls farther than the soldiers' weapons (each man had brought his own). Twice in the engagement the volunteers fired their long-barreled nine-pound cannon, dragged along on the rear wheels of an immigrant wagon.[8] Never had the Indians heard such noises as those that came from the "big medicine" gun. Neither of its two bursts was lethal, but they may have frightened the Indians more than the troops realized.

The Indians fell back, skirmishing, changed tactics, sent a knot of braves to decoy a soldier detachment protecting the supply wagons, and maneuvered to outflank the volunteers. To counter this move, Captain H. J. G. Maxon, Fourth Company, pulled his men from the right flank to protect his exposed left.[9] After the company had been deployed, the Indians surrounded the men, giving them a good fight and disabling eight of them.[10]

In the meantime, another group of warriors rode in a V formation to penetrate the gap in the volunteers' line. The soldiers succeeded in closing the gap and drove them off. The Indians withdrew some distance, dismounted, and crawled to the top of a ridge to fire from the high grass. The volunteers charged them in lines two deep, whooping at the top of their lungs. The Indians retreated, seeking shelter among the buttes of Butter Creek, eight or nine miles from the spot where the skirmish had begun.

It was nearly sundown. The Battle of Sand Hollow had lasted

[7] In his *History of the Pacific Northwest*, II, 338, Evans mistakenly says that Five Crows was killed.
[8] Steeves, *Book of Remembrance*, 163.
[9] T. A. Wood, "The Cayuse War," *Oregon Native Son*, II (May, 1900–April, 1901), 33.
[10] Hines, *Illustrated History of Washington*, 197.

three hours.[11] In the safety of the buttes the Indians assessed the day's combat. It had been indecisive, a disappointment to both the combatants and the Indian spectators nearby. The warriors who had ridden out seeking a glorious victory had suffered heavy losses. Eight were dead, some with horse reins tied to their wrists;[12] all but two bodies had been retrieved. One victim was Welaptulket's brother, a fact which perhaps set the chief to thinking about returning stolen immigrant property and suing for peace.

Resting, the Cayuses had time to ponder not only their strategy but also their fate. The outcome of the day's fighting would hinder their attempts to stir a general Indian uprising.[13] They had already received word that the Colvilles, who lived just below the Canadian border and were suffering from dysentery and measles, were opposed to joining the hostile cause. And the influential Peopeomoxmox had not wavered from his isolation.[14] Neither had the Yakimas, Spokanes, Flatheads, or most of the Nez Percés. Most discouraging to the Cayuses, however, was the dissidence within their own ranks. On the evening of the skirmish, several members of their party, including Nicholas Finlay and his two brothers, went to the commissioners, who were camped with the volunteers at a waterless spot a few miles from the scene of action, and made peace. The next day, as the soldiers moved east, other Indians approached the commissioners, only to be told to wait for them until the command reached water.[15] Commissioners and command found water but no Indians on Butter Creek about nine miles west of the lower crossing of the Umatilla on the Immigrant Road (near present-day Echo, Oregon). They went on, arriving at the Umatilla late that evening.

11 The Battle of Sand Hollow has also been called the Battle of Dry Plains. Secretary of War, *Annual Report, 1889–90*, 8–9.

12 Walter, "Reminiscences," 4.

13 Clarence B. Bagley, "The Cayuse or First Indian War in the Northwest," *Washington Historical Quarterly*, I, 1 (October, 1906), 44.

14 *Oregon Spectator*, March 23, 1848, p. 2.

15 *Newell's Memoranda*, 109.

At this point the hostile Indians captured the volunteers' runner, Elijah, and the message he was carrying from McBean to the commissioners. A Nez Percé deputation bearing a white flag was permitted inside the volunteers' lines, a move which Colonel Gilliam thought was a ruse to allow the Indians time to put more distance between themselves and the soldiers. The commissioners finally persuaded the colonel that the Nez Percés, acting in good faith, truly wanted peace.[16]

During the night of February 25 the Indians drove their stock across the Umatilla not far ahead of the soldiers. The next day they swarmed the hillsides, keeping an eye on the troops as they crossed the Umatilla—which Grey Eagle and Five Crows had vowed the soldiers would never do. The main body of hostile Indians veered north toward the Walla Walla Valley. During the day a number of them, including Stickus, came to seek an audience with the commissioners, who told the Indians to meet them at Waiilatpu. Five Crows told his warriors that if he died they were to fight the Americans without end; should he live, he said, he would fight with them.

On February 27 most of the Indians moved farther north. A few sentries remained behind to check on the volunteers' progress as they, too, turned north toward the Walla Walla. Some Indians trailed off toward the Blue Mountains, while others rode in to join those moving toward the Walla Walla.[17] At Fort Walla Walla on the twenty-eighth, Peopeomoxmox met the troops, who by then had swung around to that point. He said that he wanted peace and, to prove it, gave the soldiers beef from his own herd, undoubtedly fearing that his participation in the conflict had jeopardized not only the rest of his cattle but, more important, his rumored two thousand horses. A few miles below Waiilatpu the hostile Indians from the Umatilla, trailing dust visible for twenty miles, reached Tamsucky's camp to continue the fray.

[16] T. C. Elliott, "'Doctor' Robert Newell: Pioneer," *Oregon Historical Quarterly*, IX (March–December, 1908), 116–18.
[17] Steeves, *Book of Remembrance*, 164; *Newell's Memoranda*, 109–10.

Aware that the main body of troops was only a short distance from the fort, the Indians at Waiilatpu wasted no time regrouping their forces and moving northeast to camp on the Touchet River, about eighteen miles above the old mission.

The volunteers, also with little time to waste, were on the move on March 1, riding from the fort up the Walla Walla about eleven miles to the camp of Peopeomoxmox. Light snowfall that day settled the dust raised by Cayuse horses, but this would not have hindered the scouts as they watched their pursuers from vantage points in the hills. At the mission the soldiers found the disinterred bodies of the massacre victims, chewed by wolves and surrounded by charred and scattered papers, books, pieces of iron, and other debris which at one time had been buildings, fences, wagons, and other properties.[18]

Stickus left the Cayuse camp to parley with the commissioners and the volunteers' officers. Unnerved by this move, the Cayuses dispatched runners to the Nez Percés to prevent them from siding with the troops, since the Cayuses had apparently learned that the Nez Percés were to meet the commissioners at Waiilatpu for the express purpose of preventing a Cayuse–Nez Percé alliance. William Craig, mountain man and resident among the Nez Percés before the massacre, now with the volunteers, left three days later, on March 5, to gather them for the Waiilatpu council.

The volunteers began building fortifications from the burned-out ruins of all the buildings except the gristmill, which the Cayuses had not fired. They also brought in a band of horses and a few cattle belonging to the Indians. On March 4, Joe Meek, who had traveled upriver with the troops, left for Washington, D.C., carrying messages and a memorial from the provisional government asking the United States to extend its jurisdiction over the Oregon country. He depended on his Hudson's Bay Company disguise—a red belt and a Canadian cap—to protect him from Indian attack.

18 *Newell's Memoranda*, 110; Thomas R. Garth, "Waiilatpu after the Massacre," *Pacific Northwest Quarterly*, XXXVIII, 4 (October, 1947), 315.

A few Nez Percés and Peopeomoxmox came into the volunteers' camp to talk. Wanting to fight instead, Colonel Gilliam refused to speak to them and stormed off.[19] By contrast, the commissioners hoped to avoid violence by meeting with the red men. The Indians could not have failed to notice the division between the commissioners and the soldiers. The Nez Percés, Walla Wallas, and other friendly Indians riding into the valley may have thought that the soldiers were disregarding the commissioners' efforts when they saw the former constructing a military post (to be named Fort Waters for Major James Waters of the command) and a stockade with materials from the gutted Waiilatpu buildings. They noted that the soldiers expected trouble. Why else would they be converting the fire-blackened mission into a hospital and living quarters?[20]

March 6 dawned cloudy. More cattle were driven in. About noon Craig arrived with 250 Nez Percés, Camaspelo, and a few other Cayuses. In a move designed to put the visitors in a good mood, they were given an American flag. The next morning Gilliam formally opened the council,[21] perhaps reluctantly, since he sought action rather than words. After the traditional pipe smoking, the commissioners spoke, explaining why they and the troops had come to Indian country—namely, to capture only those responsible for the Waiilatpu murders.

The Nez Percé chiefs were quick to point out to the Americans that, unlike their Cayuse neighbors, they had not killed their missionary and had told the Cayuses to surrender the killers. Messages from Governor Abernethy and Spalding were read, urging them to form no coalition with the Cayuses. Old Joseph (Tuekakas), chief of a Nez Percé band in the Wallowa Valley of northeastern Oregon, speaking, as he put it, "for all the Cayuses present,"[22] said that he did not want his children wounded, al-

19 *Newell's Memoranda*, 111.
20 Garth, "Waiilatpu after the Massacre," 315; Walter, "Reminiscences," 4.
21 Bancroft, *History of Oregon, Vol. I, 1834–1848*, 721.
22 Frances Fuller Victor, *The Early Indian Wars of Oregon*, 182.

though his brother (Five Crows, his maternal half-brother) had been. He concluded his remarks by promising not to protect the Cayuse murderers. Other Nez Percé headmen spoke, followed by Camaspelo. Said the Cayuse chief:

> My people seem to have two hearts—I have but one. My heart is as the Nez Perces. I have had nothing to do with the murders. Tam Suckie came to me to get my consent to the murder, before it was committed. I refused. I pointed to my sick child, and told him my heart was there, and not on murder. He went back and told his friends he had obtained my consent—it was false. I did not give my consent to the murder, neither will I protect or defend the murderers.[23]

Camaspelo didn't explain, however, why he hadn't warned Whitman, who had ridden forty miles to attend the sick child. And although he asserted that some Cayuses wouldn't hide the murderers, he didn't explain why he had made no agreement to bring them in.

The assembled Indians heard Commissioner Palmer say that should they unite and kill the Americans more of his countrymen would come to avenge their deaths. Because of their "bad hearts," which had killed the Americans in massacre and war, said Palmer, the Indians had forfeited their lands. They got no better word from Newell, who said: "What have the Cayuses made, what have they lost? Everything, nothing left but a name. All the property they have took in a short time will be gone, only one thing left, that is a name, 'The Bloody Cayuses.' They never will lose that."[24]

The day after the council, March 8, the Cayuses received a delegation of Nez Percés who had been permitted to meet with them and attempt to persuade them to yield the murderers. Most of the guilty were in Cayuse camps that very moment, but their people were determined not to hand them over. That Camaspelo and Tauitau had come out for peace may have stiffened the

---

23 *Oregon Spectator*, April 20, 1848, p. 1.
24 *Ibid.*, April 6, 1848, p. 3.

resistance of the murderers' protectors. Accompanied by two Cayuses and a Nez Percé and carrying a flag, Stickus left the Cayuse camp to confer with the Americans. The old chief's reception by Gilliam, who had now moved his volunteers three miles closer to the hostile Indians, was as cool as the weather.[25] The colonel refused to have anything to do with Stickus, believing that the Cayuses, whatever the chief might think, would never capture Tamsucky and would never urge Tauitau to gather his people in. In exchange for "five murderers" Gilliam offered to take the troublesome Joe Lewis, evidently considering it a reasonable exchange. The offer undermined the position of the commissioners, who had maintained all along that the Cayuses should turn over all the guilty Indians to protect themselves from white recrimination.

Frustrated by the colonel's bargaining and inflexibility, Commissioners Newell and Palmer returned to the Willamette. As they journeyed west, Stickus and his party went east to the Cayuses with news of the troops' deployment. The Cayuses broke camp and hurried to their old Tucannon tribal boundary line. As they did, Tauitau separated his people from their trouble-bent brothers, who trailed to the mouth of the Tucannon to join their Palouse allies. With such influential tribesmen as Tauitau breaking away, perhaps the commissioners' efforts had not been in vain. Their attempt to use the Nez Percés to influence the Cayuses might also be paying off.

The volunteers continued their march on the Nez Percé Trail in search of their quarry. On March 10, Craig was officially appointed agent for the Nez Percés. The next day Stickus and two Cayuses, again bearing an American flag and leading two horses (one stolen from whites on the Umatilla), set out to meet the troops. He told Gilliam that he had persuaded Joe Lewis to come with him but that the hostile Indians had rescued Lewis. Although he could not deliver Lewis, Stickus said that he would bring Whitman's stolen property and meet the colonel at the

25 Bancroft, *History of Oregon*, Vol. I, *1834–1848*, 720–22.

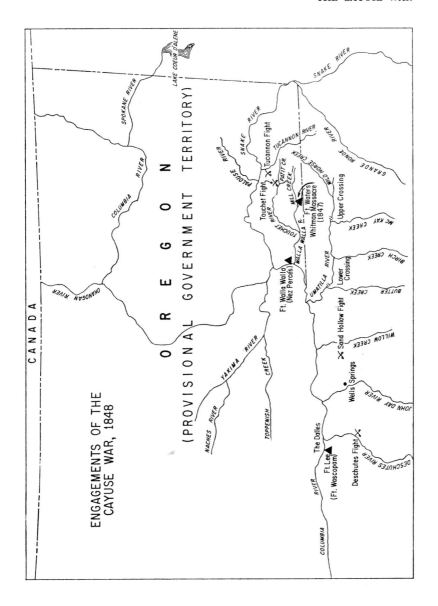

ENGAGEMENTS OF THE
CAYUSE WAR, 1848

crossing of the Touchet (near present-day Waitsburg, Washington), some twenty miles from Waiilatpu.[26]

When the volunteers reached the crossing the next day, March 12, Stickus did indeed meet them with more than forty head of cattle, about the same number of sheep, a few horses, fifty-six dollars in cash, and two thousand dollars' worth of other property, mostly clothing. Hostile Indians who had camped there the night before had already hurried off in different directions. Tamsucky went to the east, halting near Red Wolf's Crossing (present-day Alpowa, Washington). Tiloukaikt took the main body of Cayuses, along with some Palouses and a few Walla Wallas, Umatillas, and Nez Percés, to the mouth of the Tucannon, thirty miles north.[27]

They did not know that Gilliam had decided to pursue them by night march on the thirteenth.[28] Reaching a small spring near the Tucannon, the colonel received a message from Tauitau, camped a short distance upstream, professing friendship and declaring his intention to forsake his hostile brothers. The latter were unaware of the proximity of the troops, who had moved down the Tucannon to make camp before daybreak, March 14, near a large Indian encampment on the south bank of the Snake. The Indians there planned to swim their stock and ferry themselves across the river that day. At dawn an unarmed old man walking along the hill above the Tucannon's mouth was overtaken by the Americans. He quickly placed a hand on his head and the other over his heart, saying that the camp belonged to Peopeomoxmox and the murderers were gone. But, he added, it was their stock which grazed on the hillside. To the volunteers there appeared to be thousands of head, much of the herd belonging to Tiloukaikt. The old man advised the troops that their only recourse was to take possession of the murderers' stock.[29]

Four hundred Indians (mostly Palouses now that the Cayuses had divided) looked up to see Gilliam's command riding boldly

26 *Ibid.*, 722.
27 *Ibid.*; *Oregon Spectator*, April 6, 1848, p. 3.
28 Bancroft, *History of Oregon, Vol. I, 1834–1848*, 723.
29 *Ibid.*

into their camp. Although armed, the Palouses professed friendship. The soldiers were ordered to hold their fire.[30] The Indians succeeded in convincing the troops that the murderers were north across the Snake and that all the Indians on the south bank were friendly. Yet at that very moment, unknown to the soldiers, the murderers were within gun range, and others were not much farther away in Palouse country.

Unable to round up the murderers, Gilliam ordered his men to collect enemy horses, after which the troops turned and rode for the Touchet River. When the command withdrew, the Cayuses at once began to swim cattle across the Snake to outwit the Americans. After the troops and their four hundred captured horses and cows had gone about a mile, the Cayuses rode in to join ranks with the Palouses and turn on their pursuers. Thus began an all-day running fight in which warriors of the two tribes initiated minor skirmishes, fell back, and charged again and again.[31]

As in the previous encounters, the Indians exchanged verbal insults with the troops throughout the day. To understand what the warriors were saying, the soldiers utilized the services of Mungo Antoine Ansure, of Captain McKay's company.[32] Moving out between the lines, Mungo told the volunteers that the Indians were calling them cowards and then called out to the Indians that the soldiers would fight when they reached the Touchet. In the course of the skirmishing the interpreter's horse was shot from under him. Along the way the Indians swore to kill him and made a run to cut off three men dropping back to protect him. As the trio sped toward their company, one was shot in the leg with an arrow and fell from his horse, shouting that he had been killed. With prodding from his comrades he regained his horse and, with

[30] *Oregon Spectator*, April 6, 1848, p. 2. One of the troops in a company that had fallen to the left near the river fired at an Indian in a canoe crossing the Snake and killed him. H. A. G. Lee, "An Account of the Tactics of Col. Gilliam's party on March 11–12 [1848] in the Cayuse War," 5.

[31] Bancroft, *History of Oregon, Vol. I, 1834–1848*, 723.

[32] In *History of the Pacific Northwest*, I, 287, Evans lists Mungo as a member of McKay's company. It is not known whether this is the Mungo Mevway who lived at the Whitman mission and would have been twenty-one years old in 1848. Drury, *Marcus Whitman*, 217.

their help, escaped.[33] Concerning this incident, historian Elwood Evans wrote of an Indian "who was about to finish the killing of Mungo" when he was shot by a soldier who fell from his horse, feigning an injury.[34]

The Indians persisted in annoying the command, which by nightfall had retreated to a creek a few miles from the Touchet crossing, where they made camp, hoping for a respite from harassment.[35] The men were tired, hungry, cold, and wet, for it had rained that day. They carried two of their wounded on litters[36] and dared not start fires lest they become targets for the Indians, who took pot shots at them throughout the night. Gilliam thought that if he turned the captured stock loose their owners might cease firing, take their mounts, and leave. He was wrong. The Indians correctly surmised that the stock was being turned loose because of the troops' weakened position.

The Indians resumed the chase the next morning when the troops took to a hilltop. Again threats and insults flew back and forth between the two sides. To ensure that their remarks were being understood, the volunteers again sent Mungo out between the lines. The Indians knew that they must keep the soldiers from fording the swift Touchet. Within two miles of the ford they sped ahead of the latter to gain the thick brush cover at the river, at which point a fierce, hour-long battle ensued. The Indians failed to win because they resorted to tactics used in fighting other tribes: each man fighting for himself, relying more on noise and threats than on careful marksmanship. They prevented the soldiers from carrying their wounded across the river until a detachment came up to help those already at the task. A group of Indians about thirty feet away was routed in the fracas. A bullet struck an Indian, and as the man who had fired the shot was reloading, the Indian rolled over; another soldier shot him. An Indian sprang from the bushes, firing. Nathan Olney (later a

33 Walter, "Reminiscences," 5.
34 Evans, History of the Pacific Northwest, II, 373.
35 Steeves, Books of Remembrance, 166.
36 Walter, "Reminiscences," 5–6.

prominent figure in Indian affairs in the Oregon country) reportedly rushed up, grappled with the warrior, and pounded him with a club until it broke. They then fought with their fists until Olney finally killed the Indian with a knife.[37] The *Spectator*, an Oregon City newspaper, published a glowing account of the battle, as penned by Captain Maxon:

> The history of Savage warfare contains few instances of greater Indian prowess and daring, than the scene which followed. The struggle for the ford was obstinate for some time, the fire of the combatants mingling together evinced the obstinancy of the combat. And here I must say had it not been for the bold and decided stand of a few young men at the most vulnerable point—the army must [might] have sustained a heavy loss in crossing the stream, perhaps been thrown into confusion and cut to pieces. In an hour, the sound of our rifles had hushed. The long battle was ended. We were all over the river alive, and but 9 or 10 wounded, none mortally. It was not so with our enemy. The deafening roar of their musketry which had been expounding in our ears for 30 hours had died away—their shrill war whoop was changed to the melancholy death song—while a number of their lifeless brothers who lay on the field, heard not their mournful elegy.[38]

The Indians carried off their dead and wounded to the accompaniment of the groans of the dying and the death chant of the survivors.[39] The Cayuses considered making one more stand, but they retired instead, perhaps because so few of the other tribes had joined them. The Yakimas and Spokanes had kept their distance, as had most of the Nez Percés. The latter had, in fact, barred the Cayuses from coming into their country, although some of them attended a Cayuse feast after the Touchet fight. The Cayuses, of course, had succeeded in holding their Palouse allies, some Umatillas, and perhaps fewer Walla Wallas, whose chief, Peopeomoxmox, had his own private war going—largely

---

[37] *Illustrated History of Lane County, Oregon*, 162.
[38] *Oregon Spectator*, April 6, 1848, p. 2.
[39] Sources vary with regard to the number of Indians killed and wounded. One says six were killed and thirty wounded. *Transactions Oregon Pioneer Association 1893*, 102. In "The Cayuse War," 45, Bagley says four were killed and fourteen wounded, as does Mrs. Victor, *Early Indian Wars of Oregon*, 189.

one of barbed words rather than arrows—against the Oregon provisional government's legislature. In December, 1847, that body, believing that every gun in Indian hands was pointed at whites, had approved an act "to prevent the introduction of Firearms among the Indians."[40] The old chief resented the act because his people depended upon guns for sustenance.

Failure to secure and retain allies and even large numbers of their own people had hurt the Cayuses deeply. A student of the Pacific Northwest Indian wars, Frances Fuller Victor, affirms that by 1849 the Cayuses were so reduced in numbers that they could not have waged war without help from neighboring tribes.[41] A superintendent of the Oregon Methodist mission said that if the Cayuses had succeeded in drawing Walla Wallas and Nez Percés into hostilities against the whites the latter would have been involved in "a most serious and embarrassing" war.[42] Instead, by failing to draw upon the large reservoir of interior warriors save the Palouses, the Cayuses failed to give the whites any substantial opposition.

The Cayuses were now in a precarious position. Realizing the danger, Tiloukaikt hid out among the Palouses. His sons, along with Tamsucky and Joe Lewis, left Nez Percé Red Wolf's camp for Fort Boise.[43] The hostile Indians who had not participated in the murders were also in a dangerous situation, seeking to keep their distance from both the whites and the murderers. Some of them joined the Palouses, while others fled to the upper Burnt River; Five Crows went to the Wallowa Valley to nurse his wounds in the company of Nez Percé Chief Old Joseph. In the best position were the friendly Indians, who had remained in the Walla Walla Valley. They went to Fort Waters to claim

40 *Laws of a General and Local Nature passed by the Legislative Committee and Legislative Assembly, 1843–49*, 48.
41 Frances Fuller Victor, "The First Oregon Cavalry," *Oregon Historical Quarterly*, III (March–December, 1902), 123.
42 Robert Moulton Gathke (ed.), "Documentary: The Letters of the Rev. William M. Roberts, Third Superintendent of the Oregon Mission," *Oregon Historical Quarterly*, XXI (March–December, 1920), 37.
43 *Oregon Spectator*, June 15, 1848, p. 2.

their stock. They and other peaceful Indians were told to wear white flour-sack rags around their head for identification.[44]

On March 20 all but 150 of the volunteers left Fort Waters for The Dalles. Those who remained began renovating the Whitman mission buildings. Twenty thousand board feet of lumber piled at the sawmill were used in the project. The gristmill was put in repair to grind Indian wheat found in a cache.

In their work the soldiers sought to erase the scars of death and pillage at The Place of the Rye Grass. But their saws and hammers could never eradicate memories which the events there had etched deep into the minds of both Indians and whites. As if disease and massacre were not tragedy enough, the Cayuse War had robbed the tribe of many young men. The soldiers had also suffered losses, though fewer in number. One of the soldiers who would never again see the green of the Willamette Valley was Colonel Gilliam, who was accidentally shot to death. What did the balance sheet show? The peace commissioners had failed to induce the Cayuses to deliver the murderers so that they, as a people, might escape white wrath. If the volunteers had sought to kill some Indians, it may be said that they succeeded.[45]

War's end found the Cayuses divided. Days of continual chase had forced them to abandon caches of food, and they were hungry. They had lost more than five hundred horses. One could write truly of them: "The Cayuses as a people were financially ruined. Their prestige as a nation was gone, their leaders went into exile."[46] Huddled around their scattered campfires in silent fear, they knew that the white man had neither spoken his last word nor fired his last shot.

[44] William Minthorn interview, Thornhollow, Oregon, July 16, 1968.

[45] On February 25, 1851, the legislature of Oregon Territory sent a memorial to the U.S. House and Senate praying for an appropriation to pay debts incurred by the provisional government. The petitioners asserted that expenses of the Cayuse War should be borne by the nation at large, since it was "a war fought in self-defence for the United States by the people of this Territory." *Memorial of the Legislature of Oregon praying an appropriation for the payment of expenses incurred by the Provisional Government of Oregon in the Cayuse War. Sen. Misc. Doc. No. 29, 31 Cong., 2 sess., Serial 592, 1851, pp. 1–3.

[46] Wood, "Cayuse War," 35; "A Veteran of the War of '48," *Oregonian* (Portland), June 26, 1921.

IX

Wanted for Murder

The spring of 1848 was a dark one for the battered Cayuses. In their Walla Walla heartland the soldiers were still entrenched at Fort Waters, where they held Tenino Chief Welaptulket prisoner, although, true to his promise, he had returned stolen immigrant property to Fort Walla Walla.[1] In contrast to his integrity, the soldiers had reneged on their promise to accept him on friendly terms. His incarceration served to warn the Cayuses that the soldiers were still in a punitive mood. In their despair the Cayuses turned to thoughts of peace, at least to the extent of disengaging themselves from the hostile Indians, though not to the extent of searching out the murderers. Hanging over them was the threat of the white man's vengeance. Even less discriminating than his guns were the white man's other weapons, the most powerful being the diseases with which the Cayuses had become tragically acquainted. During the winter measles had claimed sixty Nez Percés alone in the Blue Mountains. Against disease the Indian was unable to hold his own; with guns he had a fighting chance, but with the recent ban on firearms it appeared that he would not have even those. Walla Walla Peopeomoxmox was still seething because, he said, the ban placed him on a level with the murderers.[2] Even the threat of the ban had resulted in neutrality among the Spokanes and Yakimas. It must have been with much consternation that the Yakimas received word from Captain Maxon in late March or early April that "the Americans and Hudson Bay Company people are the same as one, and you will

1 *Oregon Spectator*, June 1, 1848, p. 2.
2 *Ibid.*, April 20, 1848, p. 2.

get no more ammunition until the war is at a close."³ Like the
Yakimas, the Nez Percés, wanting ever more guns, were careful
not to initiate a course of action that would jeopardize their
weapons. They felt that, if anything should be banned, it ought
to be Cayuses. By practicing this philosophy on their Cayuse
neighbors, they forced some of them east of the Rockies to find
sustenance on the buffalo plains.⁴

While they tried to limit the Indians' supply of guns and ammunition, whites in the Willamette Valley sought more military
aid. They held to the idea of forcing out the Cayuses and defend-
ing their own lands from a possible though apparently highly
improbable Cayuse invasion. They appealed to higher authorities
for troops and a warship.⁵ They also continued administrative
policies calculated to keep pressure on the Indians. Henry A. G.
Lee, who succeeded Joel Palmer as superintendent of Indian
affairs, traveled to Fort Waters to replace the late Colonel Gilliam
as commander of the volunteers. With Governor Abernethy's
blessing, Lee, now a colonel, pursued a policy of treating all
Indians as enemies should they be found armed in Cayuse coun-
try.⁶ Whether the Indians were aware of this policy is not known,
although they had known that Lee was coming their way.

Lee had barely arrived at Fort Waters on May 9 when he re-
linquished his command to Major Waters. Troops at the fort
preferred this change of command because they perhaps felt that
as peace commissioner Lee had been too easy on the Indians.
Shortly the new superintendent held a promised council with
those Indians who were beginning to separate from the hostiles:
some Nez Percé chiefs, along with Peopeomoxmox, Tauitau,
Otter Skin, Stickus, and Camaspelo. He told them that the mili-

³ Ibid.
⁴ Bancroft, History of Oregon, Vol. I, 1834–1848, 729.
⁵ J. M. Shively, postmaster, Astoria, Oregon Territory to Colonel R. B. Mason,
April 15, 1848; C. E. Pickett to Mason, May 6, 1848. Microcopy of Records in the
National Archives, The 10th Military Department, 1846–1851, Microfilm No. 210,
Roll 3.
⁶ Bancroft, History of Oregon, Vol. I, 1834–1848, 730.

tary would hold the country until the murderers were punished, the stolen property returned, and the destroyed property paid for. Only then would the soldiers go home. The chiefs were in a difficult situation: if they attempted to deliver the murderers, there could be war among their people; if they did not do so, there would be war with the whites.

With second thoughts about his recent hostile words, Peopeo-moxmox, along with a weary Tauitau, promised to follow the wishes of the superintendent. Lee may not have been impressed by the sincerity of Peopeomoxmox, believing that he and his followers had returned to the Umatilla only to tend the murderers' stock. And what about the wily Tiloukaikt and his band of hostiles, the object of the military search? Since the March wars he had chosen to remain on the right bank of the Snake River, finding temporary advantage behind that natural moat. There he was among his most faithful allies, the Palouses. The lush reaches of the lower Columbia Plateau were greening now with spring grass, providing plenty of food for his stock. Also important was the fact that he was a safe distance from Fort Waters and yet near enough to be apprised of plans initiated there to trap him. Very likely he had been informed of such plans by certain Palouse chiefs who offered to ferry troops from the mouth of the Tucannon across the Snake where it receives the Palouse from the north. When Waters' command reached that point on May 19, no Palouses were there to meet it. They had perhaps delayed their appearance to give Tiloukaikt and his people time to move up the Snake to more remote areas in the Clearwater country. On the following day seven Palouses came to the river to ferry the troops across. Strong winds delayed them for a day, giving Tiloukaikt more time to flee farther up the Snake.

Across the Snake, Waters' command secured the services of an Indian guide, who was warned that he had better lead it to Tiloukaikt's camp. The troops could ill afford to linger, for delays had already given Tiloukaikt time to put distance between

146

himself and both Waters' command and that of Major Lee, which consisted of 121 men proceeding east toward the Snake to Red Wolf's Crossing. On the eighteenth Lee and Waters had divided their forces to form the jaws of a trap that would ensnare the elusive refugee.[7]

Movement was just as difficult for Tiloukaikt and his following as it was for the troops, for he had stock to move and, more important, women, children, and old people. These difficulties notwithstanding, he succeeded in maintaining a safe distance between himself and his pursuers. In their haste the refugees could neither harvest nor store their customary spring root crops, and the men had to forgo their own activities, even the rounding up of their horses.

On May 22 a delegation of Spokanes, sent by their American Board missionaries, Elkanah Walker and Cushing Eells, met Waters to offer their services, specifically to drive down to him thirty head of Tiloukaikt's cattle. These arrived the next day. The Spokanes also brought with them two spies claiming to be Nez Percés, who reported that Tiloukaikt had fled to the mountains along the Snake, leaving part of his stock in the care of some of his men.

As Major Joseph Magone, of Waters' command, and a hundred volunteers proceeded to gather Tiloukaikt's animals, they surprised an Indian on a hill. He fled at the sight of the troops. The troublesome Baptiste Dorion and eight others in the lead deemed his flight sufficient cause to chase him downhill to the river. When they saw the volunteers, two Indians on the bank jumped into a canoe but were shot and killed as they paddled toward the opposite shore. In their thirst for blood the pursuers had not observed the formality of first identifying their targets.

Beardy was camped nearby with his people. The old chief declared that there were no murderers in the vicinity. Tiloukaikt had left, he told Magone. His men had ferried across the river two soldiers en route to Waters' camp with a message from Lee,

[7] Victor, *Early Indian Wars of Oregon,* 209–11.

and he had captured some of Tiloukaikt's abandoned stock. Leaving a detachment to guard the Indians and their stock, Magone rode farther upriver for the captured stock. Along the way he met Nez Percé Chief Richard, recently appointed to succeed Ellis, who had died. Richard assured Magone that Tiloukaikt and his people had indeed left the area. Meanwhile, in Magone's absence, four or five of his men left Beardy's camp, crossed the Snake on a raft, and shot two Indians. The troops also shot another Indian who claimed as his own the cattle they had rounded up.[8]

The Nez Percés near the mouth of the Clearwater were visited on May 21 by Lee and his men, who had crossed the Snake at Red Wolf's the day before. The Nez Percés told Lee that Tiloukaikt had departed two days earlier (on the nineteenth) and was in the vicinity of Lapwai, although some of his stock was below. Promising to take Lee to Tiloukaikt's camp, an Indian escorted the officer and his men to Lapwai, where they arrived late in the day. Lee was no stranger there, nor was he to its Nez Percés.[9] Many of them remembered him from the winter of 1843–44, when he had served with Spalding, teaching at the mission. For several days the Nez Percés came to listen to this man, one of the three great men come to deal with the Cayuses and now superintendent of Indian affairs. They heard him say that the business of the military was to punish the Cayuses, but since it had failed to do so, it had the privilege of seizing their property. The Nez Percés in turn informed Lee of the movements of the murderers, who had fled east, and helped him round up 118 of their horses and 42 of their cattle. One of the horses was given to Tenino Chief Seletsa, since the Cayuses had stolen one of his.

Before leaving Lapwai, Lee's command offered the Nez Percés several hundred dollars' worth of enticing merchandise for apprehending the murderers or any two of their leaders. Half the sum was to be paid for any one of the murderers, and a quarter of it for the capture and delivery of certain Indians less guilty of

8 *Oregon Spectator*, July 27, 1848, p. 4.
9 *Ibid.*

148

the crime. Those most responsible were listed as Tiloukaikt, Tamsucky, Tomahas, Joe Lewis, and Edward, son of Tiloukaikt. Cited as less responsible were Llou-Llou, Pips, Frank Escaloom, Quiamashouskin, Estools, Showshow, Pahosh, and Cupup-Cupup, "or any other engaged in the massacre."[10]

Unaware of the reward, Peopeomoxmox learned in mid-June that two of the murderers were near the point where the Yakima River joins the Columbia. He ordered his men to find them, tie them up, and hang them. One was captured and hanged, but the other escaped. Lee's command, with the help of Peopeomoxmox and his men, pursued the escapee, Thomas (Tomahas?), who Lee said had killed an American at the Waiilatpu gristmill.[11]

On their departure from Lapwai the troops learned that Tiloukaikt and his people were in the hills seeking food for themselves and their salvaged livestock. Tiloukaikt undoubtedly gave much thought to what he would do next. To move east across the Rocky Mountains to the Great Plains would be dangerous because of the Blackfeet. To go south to the land of the Snakes would be equally dangerous. To trail north to the Spokanes and their Salishan neighbors would be futile, considering their neutrality. Closer to home there was always the chance that the Nez Percés would throw their full resources behind the government in its search for the murderers. Confronted with these frustrating alternatives, Tiloukaikt chose to keep his hostile following in the mountains, avoiding any movement toward trouble.

If Tiloukaikt planned no momentous change of tactics, the soldiers were beginning to reappraise their own. Having tested

[10] Victor, *Early Indian Wars of Oregon*, 212–14. See also "Documents Pertaining to the Whitman Massacre and Trial of the Cayuse," Manuscript 318, Oregon Historical Society. This is an official document naming the principal murderers and their accomplices. It seems unlikely that, since they prepared it in the field, the troops had the list of names before they began their campaign. It also seems unlikely that the Indians would have had anything to do with accepting such a proposal if indeed they had not played some responsible part in the massacre. See Appendix C for details of the reward. See also *Oregon Spectator*, July 13, 1848, p. 1.

[11] *Oregon Spectator*, June 29, 1848, p. 3, and July 13, 1848, p. 1. The victim to whom Lee was referring was Walter Marsh.

the idea that if they remained in Cayuse country the Indians would yield the murderers, they now began to believe that Tiloukaikt and the others would remain in hiding until the soldiers were gone. A factor in the change of thought was the expectation of very little help from the Nez Percés because of their traditional ties with the Cayuses. Yet the provisional government did not completely abandon the interior to the Indians. When Waters, now a colonel, departed for the settlement on June 8, he left Captain William Martin in charge of fifty-five men.[12]

Since the government had not been able to check the Indians with bullets and rifles, it now sought to do so with bans and rulings. First had come the ban on guns and powder; now there was one on Roman Catholic and Protestant missionaries. When Bishop Blanchet reached The Dalles on June 10, Lee forbade him to advance farther into the interior. There was to be no more missionary activity among Indians east of the Cascade Mountains until well-organized and disciplined troops under the command of United States officers had been sent there.[13] Disregarding Lee's order, the zealous Blanchet and his helpers returned to minister to the Cayuses in their migrations. The bishop felt compelled to keep his flock together and to return to it those errant souls who believed the priests' power had failed the Indians in their time of trouble.

On July 9, Tauitau met Brouillet, hoping that he could take the missionary back to his camp. Unable to accede to the chief's wishes, Brouillet gave him instructions about preparation of the mission. This failed to satisfy the chief. "We were to unite all upon the lands around our Blackrobes to learn the words of the Chief on High and listen to His counsel," Tauitau lamented. "But now there is no one to encourage us to do good. We will go on straying here and there and we will be very unfortunate." Rousseau of the Catholic mission also thought the situation unfortunate, especially since the Cayuses already had "a touch of

12 Bancroft, *History of Oregon, Vol. I, 1834–1848,* 736.
13 *Oregon Spectator,* July 13, 1848, p. 1.

civilization."[14] Although prospects looked dim, the priests remained in the country.

American Board missionaries were unable to return to the scene of their former labors, although a group of peaceful Cayuses attempted to follow the teachings of the martyred Whitman, thus perpetuating between them and their Catholic brothers a schism that continued for years.

In contrast to the bans affecting Indian welfare, few were imposed on the military. Remaining to guard the Walla Walla Valley during summer months, when the green of their own Willamette Valley beckoned them, Lee and Waters authorized their men to claim Cayuse lands. This was good news to the troops, who had been casting covetous eyes on the valley ever since they had arrived. Why not claim the land, they asked, as a reward for their military effort, especially since they had little to show for it in the form of Cayuse prisoners and booty? Their people in the Willamette, more crowded now by nearly a decade of immigration, were also beginning to see possibilities of settlement in the interior. Commented the editor of the *Oregon Spectator*: "That country would have been much settled before now, but for the efforts made by the lamented Dr. Whitman, on behalf of the Cayuses, to prevent it."[15]

Soldiers and citizens alike benefited from a proclamation issued by Lee after consultation with Governor Abernethy to make it official. The document stated that, "in consideration of the barbarous and insufferable conduct of the Cayuse Indians," their land had now been "forfeited by them, and [was] justly subject to be occupied and held by American citizens."[16] Cayuse memories were not so short that they had forgotten Lee's promise, made as a peace commissioner, that he had not come to take their land.

---

[14] Alvin M. Josephy, Jr., *The Nez Perce Indians and the Opening of the Northwest*, 281. See also Rousseau, *Caravane vers l'Oregon*, 233, 242–43.

[15] *Oregon Spectator*, July 13, 1848, p. 2.

[16] *Ibid.*, p. 1.

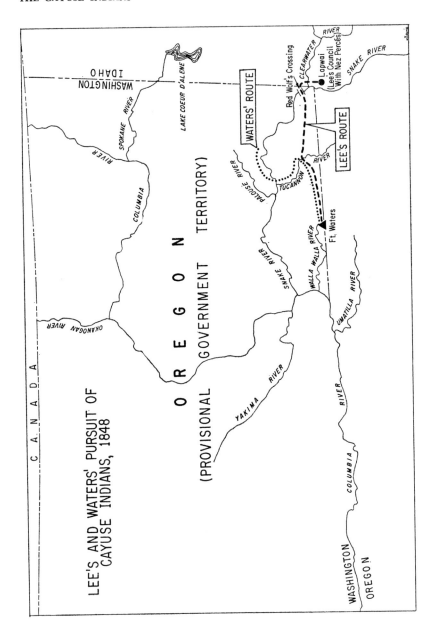

LEE'S AND WATERS' PURSUIT OF CAYUSE INDIANS, 1848

After the last members of the Fort Waters garrison left for home to receive their discharges, a few of the wandering Cayuses returned to the valley. During the summer they remained quiet, as did their brothers elsewhere. The editor of the *Spectator* happily reported on October 12 that the "present immigration" of 177 wagons, a much smaller number than usual, perhaps because of uneasiness over the massacre, had traveled unharmed over the Immigrant Road and had arrived safely in the Willamette.[17]

As the Cayuses returned to the scene of the massacre, the effects of that event were being felt in far-off Washington, D.C. The deed itself and Joe Meek's arrival there further hastened organization of Oregon as a United States territory. The absence of federal jurisdiction, even after Oregon had become American territory as a result of the Anglo-American boundary settlement of 1846, had served to give the provisional government independence in peace and war. Lee's proclamation forfeiting Cayuse lands was typical of the free-wheeling action of that temporary government. Having fought the Indians without the aid of federal troops, who were engaged in the Mexican War, it now believed itself entitled to some sort of reward for its effort. Oregon Territory was finally established on August 14, 1848, by an act of Congress, although the provisional government continued to operate until territorial officers were appointed.[18] United States jurisdiction became effective on March 3, 1849, when the Oregon territorial government took over.[19]

When he arrived in March, 1849, from the Mexican War, the new governor, Joseph Lane, found plenty of problems to occupy his attention. In April he held council with interior Indians at The Dalles to establish friendly relations, a move designed to protect immigrants from attack as they journeyed from The Dal-

[17] *Ibid.*, October 12, 1848, p. 2.
[18] Frederick V. Holman, "A Brief History of the Oregon Provisional Government and What Caused Its Formation," *Oregon Historical Quarterly*, XIII (March–December, 1912), 137.
[19] *Transactions of the Third Annual Re-Union of the Oregon Pioneer Association*, 71.

les down the Columbia River. He also hoped to keep the Indians from forming an alliance with the hunted Cayuses.

In his first message to the territorial legislature, delivered on May 7, 1850, Governor Lane spoke of conditions in the interior:

> The Cayuse nation remains unpunished for the Massacre at Waiilatpue; but the whole tribe will be held responsible, until those, whoever they may be, concerned in that melancholy and horrible affair, are given up for punishment. A fine Regiment of troops [the Mounted Riflemen], commanded by officers who have distinguished themselves in the service of their country, are *en route* for Oregon, and may be expected to arrive by the middle of September. It will then be in the power of the Government, to make this tribe accountable for their wrong-doings, and I can assure you, that our Government will not suffer the guilty to go unpunished.[20]

Most Oregonians agreed, even those who had gone to the gold fields of California. Many of them had carried south with them a hatred of Indians engendered by the Cayuse War. Shocking indeed to gold seekers from more refined regions of the world were the actions of those raw Oregon frontiersmen, who indulged their hatred of red men "freely by shooting the Indians on every favorable occasion."[21]

Along with many of their number in California, and still apprehensive of Cayuse incursions, Willamette citizens looked forward to the arrival of the rifle regiment from Fort Leavenworth (Kansas). The federal troops reached the Umatilla River at 9:00 A.M. on September 11, 1849, and found the countryside at peace.[22] A number of Cayuses came out of their mat-and-brush lodges to meet them, showing no signs of hostility. Small boys

[20] Priscilla Knuth and Charles M. Gates, "Oregon Territory in 1849–1850," *Pacific Northwest Quarterly*, XL, 1 (January, 1949), 11–12.

[21] Georgia Willis Read and Ruth Gaines (eds.), *Gold Rush*, II, 1073.

[22] Clark, "Military History of Oregon, 1849–59," 21–22; Raymond W. Settle (ed.), *The March of the Mounted Riflemen*, 226, 229. The regiment's Pacific Northwest expedition was authorized in May, 1846, but the unit was diverted to the Mexican War.

were keeping watch on "droves of horses" in the hills while their mothers tended garden plots. Yet the regiment saw ample evidence—in graves on the Umatilla and decayed buildings at The Dalles—of the violence that had swept the country only a few months before.

Certainly the appearance of the troops brought no joy to the Cayuses. If they feared destruction, they might have found comfort in the words of former Commissioner Robert Newell that "to exterminate the Indians will cost more than to outlive him by scientific display of superior nobleness of character and intellect."[23]

With the Mounted Riflemen safely at Fort Vancouver in October, 1849, preceded by the arrival of two companies of the First Artillery by sea around Cape Horn, Governor Lane had leverage to persuade the Cayuses to deliver the murderers—considerably more than he had enjoyed in the spring. "I carried on negotiations with the Cayuses in 1849 in a friendly manner," he said later, "with the hope of getting them to surrender up the principal actors in the murder of Dr. Whitman, his wife and many others at Waiilatpu, without war. But told them that war upon them would be certain if they did not deliver up the guilty."[24] Lane was not certain at that time what effect his words would have upon the Cayuses, whom he described to the secretary of war as a "haughty, proud and over-bearing people," eight hundred in number, two hundred of whom were braves, "well-armed," and, through fear, "on amicable terms with the whites."[25]

The governor could expect support from the Hudson's Bay Company, which wished to keep peace among the tribes in order to stabilize its business, already plagued by dwindling fur

[23] *Newell's Memoranda*, 95.

[24] Myron Eells, "Indian War History Errors," *Oregon Native Son*, II, 3 (July–August, 1900), 124.

[25] Lane to Secretary of War, October [1849], Microcopy of Records in the National Archives, *Oregon Superintendency of Indian Affairs, 1848–1873*, Letter Book A:10, Microfilm No. M-2, Roll 3 (cited hereafter as *Oregon Superintendency, A:10, Roll 3*).

harvests. Lane also received backing from several interior chiefs,[26] some of whom told him that their people looked on the freedom of the guilty Cayuses as "a license for the most atrocious outrage."[27] And an increasing number of Cayuses, Walla Wallas, Nez Percés, and even Palouses who had earlier sympathized with the murderers were becoming interested in capturing them. In late October, 1849, Timothy and several other Nez Percés persuaded Tauitau to come out openly on their side after acquainting him with Lane's intentions. When they learned that William McBean at Fort Walla Walla had already informed the chief of the governor's words, however, the Nez Percés decided to convey Lane's message to Peopeomoxmox and his fellow Walla Walla chief, Pierre.[28] Murderer Tomahas, desperate now like an animal trapped in a hunters' circle, would have killed Timothy had not McBean intervened. The trader even feared for his own life at the hands of the outlaws.[29]

Before the governor's message reached the remaining Nez Percés,[30] one of their chiefs, Tomootsom, and twenty of his men decided to attack the murderers in the belief that they had killed the Cayuse Tintinemetsa (Willouskin) and stolen his horses. The Nez Percé party went as far as Waiilatpu, where it found Tintinemetsa very much alive.[31] The murderers, aware of Nez Percé designs on them and becoming more desperate all the time, prepared to retreat deeper into the mountains with their families. The Nez Percés sought McBean's advice on whether to chase them. He told them to lose no time in making the pursuit, for he knew that if the hostiles escaped the whites would hold the entire Cayuse tribe responsible.[32]

26 Lane to Young Chief [Weatenatenamy], November 9, 1849, *ibid.*
27 Lane to Secretary of War, October, 1849, *ibid.*
28 McBean to Craig, October 22, 1849, *Oregon Superintendency*, Microfilm No. 2, Roll 12.
29 *Ibid.*
30 Lane to McBean, November 10, 1849, *Oregon Superintendency*, A:10, Roll 3.
31 McBean to Lane, January 6, 1850, *Oregon Superintendency*, Microfilm No. 2, Roll 12.
32 *Ibid.*

Tomootsom and his twenty men seem to have led the chase, but they were joined by sixty Cayuses under Tauitau, plus Pierre and five Walla Wallas. Peopeomoxmox changed his mind and did not go. At Fort Walla Walla, McBean expected an attack by the murderers, who, he feared, might have learned that he had encouraged their capture. Pierre, camped near the fort, gave the trader some protection, but Peopeomoxmox would not go near the place.

In spite of the intense cold, the ill-clad pursuers, mounted on poor horses, rode into deep snow after the fugitives, who were moving their families and livestock still farther into the mountains. Three days out, at about sundown, the Indian posse overtook them at the headwaters of the John Day River,[33] first capturing their livestock and then confronting them as they hid behind makeshift fortifications. A Nez Percé, Hoot Hooshe, shot and killed Tamsucky. Pierre and an Indian named Chappylie shot Cayuse Shumkain. Four others were captured: Tamsucky's son, the slayer of Crockett Bewley; Cayuse Tlocoomots, co-killer of some of the Waiilatpu ill; Cayuse Eyoweahnish, attacker of a sick man pulled from a mission bed; and Cayuse Kiamasumpkin (Panther's Coat), one of Mrs. Whitman's assailants.

At the suggestion of the posse, the women, children, and old people were separated from the other fugitives. Surrounded, the murderers exchanged shots with their pursuers, wounding Hotomashoo, a Walla Walla. Making their escape were Tomahas, slayer of Dr. Whitman; Tiloukaikt, present when Tomahas killed the doctor; Estonish, who killed some members of the mission household; Isaiachalakis, who shot at Mrs. Whitman and killed other whites; and Snake Tsooyoohah, who killed an American near Fort Boise.[34]

Only partly successful in their attempt to capture the murderers, the Indians returned to Tauitau's camp on the Umatilla

[33] H. O. Lang (ed.), *History of the Willamette Valley*, 317–18.
[34] McBean to Lane, January 6, 1850; Red Wolf to Lane, January 5, 1850, *Oregon Superintendency*, Microfilm No. 2, Roll 12.

to discuss further action and divide the property taken from the fugitives. A deep undercurrent of dissension developed because the Nez Percés felt that the Cayuses had cheated them in the distribution of the spoils.

In December, Tauitau attended a meeting called by McBean at Fort Walla Walla to explain a message from Lane. Upon learning that the governor could offer no peace to the Cayuses until their murderous fellow tribesmen had been apprehended, Tauitau expressed willingness to pursue them and asked the Nez Percés to choose the time. The latter were slow to respond. To demonstrate his sincerity, Tauitau furnished the Americans all the horses they wanted. Eager to return to his Umatilla home, he left the meeting after designating Camaspelo to act in his place. The Nez Percés said that their hearts had not changed, that they would not toss the governor's words aside. Their chief, Looking Glass, suggested that the posse ride out again in two months to resume the search, but Camaspelo objected that the delay would give the murderers a chance to escape, suggesting instead that the pursuers secure fresh horses, provisions, and warm clothing and set out immediately.[35] Camaspelo's craving for action may have stemmed from his desire to finish the business and remove the government bee from the Cayuse bonnet.

The matter of resuming the search rested for a while, but discussion of the identity of the uncaptured murderers continued. There was much talk among the Cayuses and the Nez Percés about whether all the accused were actually guilty. The Nez Percés deemed guilty anyone who was in hiding. The Cayuses disagreed. Meanwhile, the subjects of their debate had circled around, stolen horses from their fellow Cayuses, and fled again. A Cayuse party gave chase but the snowless, frozen ground revealed no tracks. The fugitives had not gone far when Tauitau offered the Nez Percés some captured horses again requesting them to join his people immediately in the chase. The Nez Percés refused,

35 McBean to Lane, January 6, 1850, *ibid.*

so strained had relations between the two peoples become over identity of the murderers.[36]

The new year, 1850, found the Indians quiet—usually an omen of ill feeling among the tribes. Nez Percé Red Wolf went to Fort Walla Walla in January, requesting that McBean ask the governor to give him a flag. In a letter to Lane, written for him by McBean, the Nez Percé thanked the governor for "laws and instructions" he had sent.[37] McBean also told Lane that the Nez Percés, as they had been requested to do, had rid the area of the murderers. In a letter dated January 5, he assured the governor for Red Wolf that should any of the fugitives return to Nez Percé country they would be killed. Smarting because his people had received no spoils from their pursuit of the fleeing killers, Red Wolf informed Lane: "We consider the Cayuse accountable for the murderers as they have all their property and a part of the murderers in their village."[38] Concluding with an explanation of tribal disposition of war booty, he said that the Nez Percés would not help the Cayuses unless the latter promised to "divide the property[,] for it has been our rules [that] property taken in war belonged to them that took it."[39]

Stripped of property and without sufficient food, some of the murderers turned and rode back toward Tauitau's camp to surrender. The chief decoyed the others in, [40] catching the wiliest of them: Tiloukaikt and Tomahas. In an attempt to capture the murderers, a Cayuse received a wound in the face which disfigured him so badly that he was thereafter called Cut Mouth John.[41] In later years he was well known to whites because of both his disfigurement and his continued friendship with them.

Tauitau visited Fort Walla Walla throughout the winter,

[36] Ibid.
[37] Ibid.
[38] Red Wolf to Lane, January 5, 1850, ibid.
[39] Ibid.
[40] McBean to Lane, February 7, 1850, ibid.
[41] Lang, History of the Willamette Valley, 318. Cut Mouth John is identified by A. J. Splawn in Ka-mi-akin: Last Hero of the Yakimas, 48, as a Wasco (Wascopum) Indian.

159

promising McBean that he would draw the remaining fugitives to his camp and denying, in spite of Nez Percé assertions to the contrary, that his nephew Moath was an outlaw. McBean was certain from Tauitau's attitude that during the previous autumn, had the French-Canadian Narcisse Raymond not spoken to the Indians in such a way as to discourage the relinquishing of their captives, the chief would have killed them long before McBean advised the governor to dispatch a force to rout them. The trader cautioned Tauitau against freeing those he held. In his continuing ill humor against the Nez Percés, Tauitau said that the captured Tomahas was of that tribe, a relative of Chief Looking Glass. There may have been some truth in this assertion, since many Cayuses were related to Nez Percés.[42]

It is unlikely that Governor Lane knew of Raymond's statement to the Cayuses about holding their wrongdoing fellows, because on January 25 he wrote Tauitau a letter, delivered by Raymond, in which he reminded the chief of an earlier (November) letter saying that the Cayuse nation could have peace with the government [only] viz the surrender of the murderers of Dr. Whitman, family and others for trial and punishment. He warned Tauitau that the murderers must be given up; if they were not, he said, the Cayuse Nation would be destroyed. Softening, Lane assured the chief that he did not want that to happen, that he wanted to be a friend and protector of the Cayuses, but that he could not do so until the murderers were given up. At the end of the letter the governor informed Tauitau that the Nez Percés would assist in capturing the murderers, who must be closely watched lest they escape permanently.[43]

Governor Lane was not unmindful of tensions between the Cayuses and the Nez Percés, for on January 28 he warned the latter not to make war "against the good and friendly Cayuses." Moreover, "I do not want you to hurt the innocent," he cau-

---

42 McBean to Lane, February 7, 1850, *Oregon Superintendency*, Microfilm No. 2, Roll 12.
43 Lane to Young Chief, January 25, 1850, *Oregon Superintendency*, A:10, Roll 3.

tioned, because "our laws protect the innocent and punish the guilty." In a February 7 letter to the governor McBean suggested that Lane send someone to pick up the prisoners held by Tauitau. No time should be lost in doing so, warned McBean, "else they may possibly escape," adding that "I have cautioned Young Chief [Tauitau] against their possibility of doing same."[44] When Lane received McBean's letter some two weeks later, he instructed Brevet Major J. Samuel Hatheway, who had arrived on the transport *Massachusetts* with two companies of artillery, that, since "the principal proportion of the murderers" were prisoners of Tauitau, he should proceed to the chief's village to bring them in. By incarcerating the "principal proportion of the murderers," Lane thought he could write a new chapter in Cayuse-white relations. As he put it, "The only barrier to a permanent peace with the Cayuses" would thus be removed.[45] What he was really saying was that peace had been secured on the terms of the whites, whom he represented. The weary Cayuses had no other choice but to accept it.

[44] Lane to Nez Perce Chiefs, January 28, 1850, *ibid.*; McBean to Lane, February 7, 1850, *Oregon Superintendency*, Microfilm No. 2, Roll 12.
[45] Lane to Major John Samuel Hathaway [Hatheway] [n.d], *Oregon Superintendency*, A:10, Roll 3.

X
Cords of Vengeance

In early April, 1850, Governor Lane proceeded to The Dalles to bring in five murderers being held there.[1] With a military escort for protection he returned toward Oregon City with three of them, the other two in custody following.[2] Taken downriver were Tilou-kaikt, Kiamasumpkin, Tomahas, Isaiachalakis, and Klokamas. How the decision to deliver only five prisoners was reached is not known. The Cayuses implied that there could have been no more than five because all the others responsible for the Whitman killings were dead. Also unknown is whether any of those Tau-itau had held before the delivery were killed. Nor is it known whether any were freed as having had no part in the atrocity. It may have been that several of those who were rounded up were released, since it was the Cayuses' prerogative to bind them over or release them, regardless of whether or not the Nez Percés found them guilty. On May 27, Lane happily reported to the secretary of war that the five he had brought in were the only murderers supposed to have been alive.[3] He seems to have had no concern about the disposition of the other captives; he had his five prisoners, and that was what mattered.

As the prisoners traveled toward the white settlements, a member of their military escort asked them why they had surrendered. Retaining his Cayuse pride and refusing food, one snapped: "What hearts have you to offer to eat with me, whose hands are red with your brother's blood?" Replying further to the question

1 *Oregon Spectator*, April 18, 1850, p. 2.
2 *Ibid.*, May 2, 1850, p. 2.
3 Lane to Secretary of War, May 27, 1850, *Oregon Superintendency*, A:10, Roll 3.

why he had given himself up, he said: "Did not your missionaries teach us that Christ died to save his people? So die we to save our people."[4]

The Reverend François Norbert Blanchet, now archbishop of Oregon City, maintained that the five Indians had come in only to confer with the whites.[5] Others also said that those whom Tauitau had turned over to the authorities were innocent but that when they came to talk they found themselves prisoners of the Americans. Another claim held that they had surrendered in lieu of the murderers so that the Cayuses could have peace. The evidence supports none of these viewpoints. Nothing in the official records shows that Lane had any kind of agreement to parley with five members of the tribe about the murders; he had negotiated only with Tauitau. The five were, in fact, delivered by the Cayuses, whose pursuit of them is well documented.[6]

It would not have been in character for the five Cayuses to declare their guilt when first apprehended if they had been innocent. Even though their fellow tribesmen declared that they had committed the Waiilatpu murders, they would have felt no responsibility or guilt for having done so. Under the goading of such malcontents as Joe Lewis, they believed such an act justifiable in retaliation for Indian deaths at the hands of white men.[7]

At Oregon City the captives were bound over to Joe Meek, now first United States marshal of Oregon Territory, and taken from the mainland across a guarded bridge to Abernethy Island, in the

---

[4] Hubert Howe Bancroft, *History of Oregon, Vol. II, 1848–1883,* 95.
[5] *Ibid.,* 94n.
[6] The Cayuses later admitted that the men hanged at Oregon City committed the murders and accompanying depredations and that it was therefore unjust to hold the tribe responsible for their actions. Manuscript 57/276, Envelope 6E, Walker Papers.
[7] Joe Lewis, who escaped with two of Tiloukaikt's sons, killed one of them, the other escaping. Lewis had told the Cayuses he would bring ammunition from the Mormons around Salt Lake City to help them in their fight. He had also told them they must continue to fight the Americans. His murderous career came to a close when he was shot and killed in what is today southern Idaho as he attempted to rob an express. Lang, *History of the Willamette Valley,* 317; *Oregon Spectator,* April 20, 1848, p. 2.

middle of the Falls of the Willamette. They would perhaps have understood little of the complicated pretrial legal maneuvering. They were, however, aware of the need for defense counsel and offered fifty horses for that service.[8] A true bill was returned on May 13 and filed on May 21, indicting each of the five for the murder of Dr. Whitman.[9] A number of separate indictments were issued: all five were indicted for the death of Dr. Whitman, Mrs. Whitman, Sager, Rodgers, Hoffman, and Saunders; Klokamas and Isaiachalakis, for the death of Gilliland; and Tomahas, for the death of Emmon Stevens.[10]

The indictment was read to the prisoners and interpreted for them by the counsel for their defense: Knitzing Pritchett (then secretary of the territory), Major Robert B. Reynolds (Runnels), and Thomas Claiborne. A copy of the indictment was furnished the Indians, as was a list of the petit jury members. The court ruled that from the time they were handed the indictment the Indians had two days to make a plea. On the next day, May 22, the court convened at 9:00 A.M., at which time defense counsel filed a "plea in bar of jurisdiction," claiming that at the time of the alleged felony the accused belonged to the Cayuse Nation, which, being west of the Rocky Mountains, was outside the limits of Indian country as defined by act of Congress in 1834. The replication was that trade and intercourse with Indian tribes to preserve peace on the frontiers was set out in law by act of Congress on June 30, 1846, whereby all territory south of the Forty-ninth Parallel belonged to the United States and that, since Waiilatpu was in Cayuse territory, the five were subject not to United States laws but to the "laws and usage of said Cayuse nation."[11] Judge O. C. Pratt rejected the plea.

8 Bancroft, *History of Oregon*, Vol. II, *1848–1883*, 94.
9 See Appendix D for a copy of the indictment.
10 "Whitman Massacre Records of the trial of the Whitman murderers," Envelope 37, Holland Library. One of the indictments in this group of papers accuses Tomahas of killing Emmon Stevens. The name was either incorrect or that of someone Tomahas had killed somewhere else.
11 The plea is found in "Whitman Massacre Records." During his term as judge, Pratt bought up claims from soldiers who served in the Cayuse War. Sidney Teiser,

After defense counsel entered its exceptions to the ruling, it was asked what further plea it had. "Not guilty" was the reply. Next, counsel petitioned for a change of venue, asserting that the accused could not receive a fair and impartial trial in Oregon because many of the territory's "most respectable citizens" had threatened the five with death if they were acquitted and because "respectable and influential citizens" had used their "powerful influence to inflame the public mind" against them. Counsel believed it mandatory that the trial be shifted from the hostile atmosphere of Clackamas County to Clark County, across the Columbia River. Judge Pratt rejected the petition. The fate of the accused would be decided in the Indian-fearing Willamette Valley.

The jury was impaneled and sworn. Witnesses for the prosecution, which was conducted by District Attorney Amory Holbrook, were called singly into court and examined.

Testimony: Mrs. Eliza Hall states that measles prevails at the mission among the Indians to whom Whitman administers medicines and many die. At a distance of a hundred yards she sees Tiloukaikt strike the prostrate Whitman with a hatchet; Whitman is only six feet from the mission house. Indians attack a man by name of Hoffman; Hoffman falls. Witness starts for mission house. Several Indians are between her and the house. She helps carry Whitman into another room. She helps place Mrs. Whitman on a settee in the mission house. Tamsucky comes in and tells her that she must go home. The witness goes about thirty yards, hears gunfire, and sees Mr. Rodgers throw up his hands.

Next called is Mrs. Esther Lorinda (Bewley) Chapman. She testifies that she is at the mission, upstairs in bed; she hears angry words below in the kitchen, thinks she hears the voice of Tiloukaikt, and hears gunfire. The witness comes downstairs and sees persons bringing Whitman, a cut across his face, from the kitchen into the house. As she begins to leave with Mr. Rodgers and Mrs.

"First Associate Justice of Oregon Territory: O. C. Pratt," *Oregon Historical Quarterly*, XLIX (March–December, 1948), 177.

Whitman, they are both killed. Later, the witness helps carry Mrs. Whitman into the yard. She sees Tamsucky there. Joe Lewis has a gun. Two persons are killed by the natives.

Josiah Osborne is called. He says that Whitman has given medicine to Indians and whites, that the Indians know that whites die as they do, and that Whitman is anxious about his safety, speaking of it particularly in 1845. The witness does not know whether the doctor is aware of the immediate danger. Osborne, too, lies ill in the doctor's house. He hears gunfire, goes to the door, and sees the wounded Kimball running. Osborne retreats inside and sees Tomahas pursuing Mr. Saunders. Under the floor with his family, he hears "murder going on."[12]

After the prosecution witnesses had testified, an article in the *Oregon Spectator*[13] stated that Tiloukaikt admitted striking Whitman with his hatchet, as attested by Mrs. Hall; that Tomahas admitted shooting Whitman; and that Klokamas (the smallest of the five) admitted helping kill Sager. Kiamasumpkin was reported as being present but not participating in the affair. These so-called confessions were carried all over the country to a citizenry stunned by news of the slaughter, yet relieved to learn that the killers had confessed. Publications in England and France also carried stories about the outrage which had snuffed out a Protestant community in far-off Oregon.

The defense now presented its case, which seems to have been based on the assertion that not only did the accused not murder Whitman but that the killings were justified on grounds that the missionary was killing the Indians. Dr. John McLoughlin, the first witness called, testified that as early as 1840 and 1841 he had warned Whitman of danger. The former Hudson's Bay Company factor also corroborated others' testimony that the Cayuses killed their medicine men for failing to cure patients.

Stickus testified next, telling how, on the day before the mas-

12 "Whitman Massacre Records"; *Oregon Spectator*, May 30, 1850.
13 *Oregon Spectator*, May 30, 1850, p. 2.

sacre at his Umatilla lodge, he had warned the departing mission-ary to be careful because "bad Indians" would kill him.

Last on the stand for the defense was the Reverend Henry H. Spalding, who testified that he was in Stickus' lodge with the doctor and, like him, was warned of impending disaster.[14]

In desperation Tiloukaikt swore that an Indian in Cayuse country, one Quisham, would testify that Whitman had given medicine to the Indians, after which many of them died. Fast-moving frontier justice did not take time to bring Quisham into court to testify.[15] Neither did it take into account tribal custom, consideration of which in an age more enlightened by anthro-pological findings might have been weighed carefully.

Major Reynolds opened summary arguments for the defense, and then Claiborne led off for it. Marshal Meek said that Clai-borne "foamed and ranted like he was acting a play in some theatre," with gestures so powerful they smashed two tumblers of water which Judge Pratt had ordered filled for him.[16] Pritchett, "a man having brains," spoke for forty-five minutes in summa-rizing the defense's case.

District Attorney Holbrook closed the prosecution's final arguments, reported the Spectator, with "a neat, condensed, and forcible presentation of the whole subject."[17] On Friday, May 24, when court reconvened, the prisoners were brought to the bar. In a seventy-minute talk, Judge Pratt instructed the jury regard-ing the law and the testimony. He overruled a motion by the defense for arrest in judgment of the court. He also denied a request for a new trial.

Court reconvened at 4:00 P.M. to receive the jury's verdict. The prisoners were found guilty as charged, and Pratt sentenced them to be hanged on Monday, June 3, at 2:00 P.M. He said to the condemned:

14 "Whitman Massacre Records."
15 Ibid.
16 Frances Fuller Victor, The River of the West, 495.
17 Oregon Spectator, May 30, 1850, p. 3.

You, Telokite, Tomahas, Clakomas, Isiaasheluckas and Kiama-sumkin, having been duly convicted by the finding and verdict of the Jury, of the crime of wilful murder as alleged in the indictment, are therefore each adjudged to suffer death by hanging, and you and each of you are ordered and adjudged to be taken from hence to a place of security and confinement, and there kept until Monday the 3d day of June A.D. 1850, and on that day at the hour of two o'clock in the afternoon, be taken by the Marshal of the District of Oregon, to the gallows or place of execution to be erected in Oregon City, and there by him be hung by the neck, until you are dead.

And may God in His Infinite Grace have mercy on your souls.[18]

The editor of the *Spectator* added his own judgment to that of Pratt by saying: "It is a happy day for Oregon when the administration of Justice is reposed in hands so firm and fearless."[19] Three of the condemned, Meek said, "were filled with horror and consternation that they could not conceal."

The court proceedings, witnessed by crowds ranging in size from two hundred to three hundred persons in the five-hundred-soul river boom town, were "orderly, quiet and solemn." "Free Cayuses" roamed the streets, and Spalding used his spare time to converse with them and the white citizens. Claiborne disputed the clergyman's right (during the trial, presumably) to talk with the Indians, the upshot of which, the *Spectator* reported, was that Claiborne abused the clergyman "in language at once severe, profane, and improper." He later apologized.[20]

In grief and fear the free Cayuses fled Oregon City,[21] which was pressed in as closely by rock bluffs as the condemned Indians were trapped by its people. A group of whites attempted to obtain acquittal of the five defendants, but Governor Lane, who might have pardoned them, had departed for California immediately after the trial, leaving Secretary Pritchett as acting governor.

18 *Ibid.*
19 *Oregon Spectator*, May 30, 1850, p. 3.
20 *Ibid.*
21 *Catholic Sentinel*, April 20, 1872, p. 2.

Pritchett refused to grant a reprieve as petitioned by some citizens, giving as his reason his uncertainty whether the governor was yet out of the territory. He carried in his pocket the death warrant signed by Lane.[22]

Since the petitioners could not save the lives of the condemned, Archbishop Blanchet sought to save their souls. They had refused to see Spalding. Aided by Father August Veyret, Blanchet brought a Catholic Ladder to aid in their instruction. Twice daily for eight days Veyret visited the doomed Indians. True to their proud and haughty tradition, they did not flinch in confinement. During this time Meek spoke with them many times. To him they gave only one explanation for their crime: their fear of Whitman and other whites who would take their lands and, by superior numbers, crowd the Indians off the face of the earth. According to Meek, Kiamasumpkin declared his innocence to the very last.[23] The archbishop had prepared, not only for Kiamasumpkin but the others as well, statements of innocence, some of which they signed the day before their execution.

In Blanchet's declarations Tiloukaikt maintained that all the Indians who had committed the crimes were dead, two of them his sons; that he had foreknowledge of the event because Tamsucky had told him of it; that he had made no statement of confession to the marshal; and that it was not true that the priests had encouraged the Indians to kill Whitman. Kiamasumpkin asserted that he was not at Waiilatpu at the time of the massacre; Klokamas, that he was present but, like Tiloukaikt, blameless and that the ten murderers were all dead; Isaiachalakis, like the others, that ten, all dead, had done the deed, which in no way had been instigated by Catholics.[24]

Many people crowded into Oregon City on June 3 to witness the hangings.[25] The *New York Tribune*, a continent away from

22 *Ibid.*
23 Victor, *River of the West,* 494.
24 *Catholic Sentinel,* April 27, 1872, p. 2.
25 Victor, *River of the West,* 496.

169

the site, noted that "an election and a hanging match took place at Oregon City. The town was full of men and women, the former coming to see how the election resulted, and the latter to see how the Indians were hung."[26]

A scaffold had been constructed south of Dr. McLoughlin's house, along with a platform of "six or seven" steps. At 9:00 A.M. the five condemned men were baptized by the archbishop and given the sacrament of confirmation. At 2:00 P.M. the prisoners were brought forth by a squad of soldiers. As they ascended the scaffold, they heard words of consolation and encouragement and prayers for the dying.[27] Meek arranged them in order for the drop. Kiamasumpkin reportedly begged the marshal to kill him with a knife.[28] As their hands were bound, Tiloukaikt, with great energy, refused to submit. When a crucifix was held before him, he calmed and then tried to address the crowd, but his words were incoherent. Meek "soon put an end to his entreaties by cutting the rope which held the drop, with my tomahawk." Continued the marshal, "As I said, 'The Lord have mercy on your souls,' the trap fell, and the five Cayuse hung in the air."[29]

As he gave the last blessings and words of exhortation, Veyret was reported to have said: "Now then, children of God! Onward, onward to heaven! O Lord Jesus, into thy hands I command [sic] my spirit, have mercy on my soul."[30] He then fell to his knees, praying for the condemned Cayuses.

Three died instantly. Two struggled, Tomahas the longest. Said Meek: "It was he [Tomahas] who was cruel to my little girl at the time of the massacre; so I just put my foot on the knot to tighten it, and he got quiet."[31]

26 *New York Tribune*, August 21, 1850.

27 *Catholic Sentinel*, April 20, 1872.

28 Victor, *River of the West*, 496.

29 *Ibid.* Historian Elwood Evans says Meek did indeed utter the words attributed to him, plus two more, "I can't," not recorded in Mrs. Victor's *River of the West*, 496. See Evans' *History of the Pacific Northwest*, II, 585.

30 In the *Catholic Sentinel*, April 20, 1872, p. 2, in an article by "An Observer," the writer says that it was Blanchet who uttered the last words. See also Victor, *Early Indian Wars of Oregon*, 251.

31 Victor, *River of the West*, 496.

Thirty-five minutes later the Indians' bodies were taken down and buried. The aloof *New York Tribune* commented more than two months later: "Much doubt was felt as to the policy of hanging them, but the *popularity* of doing so was undeniable. . . . They were hanged, greatly to the satisfaction of the ladies who had traveled so far to witness the spectacle."[32] And in 1879 a contributor to an eastern publication wrote an epitaph for Oregon City:

> The little nasty town . . . was the scene of a self-immolation as great as any of which we read in history, and there were not three persons there who appreciated it. The accursed town is, we hear, still nastier than ever, and the intelligent jury—no man of whom dared to have a word of pity or admiration for those poor Indians— with the spectators of that horrid scene, are either dead and damned, or they are sunk in the oblivion that is the fate of those who are born without souls.[33]

[32] *New York Tribune*, August 21, 1850.
[33] Helen Hunt Jackson includes this quotation from the November 1, 1879, issue of *Army and Navy Journal* in a section of *A Century of Dishonor* entitled "Sequel to the Walla Walla Massacre," 407–10.

XI
Pent-up Tempest

Willamette-bound travelers on the Immigrant Road during the summer of 1850 rolled through Cayuse country fearing reprisals for what their fellow countrymen had done to the five tribesmen in Oregon City, but there was no trouble from the Cayuses. A few of the Indians even trailed the wagons out of the Grande Ronde, showing no signs of hostility while others rode up merely to look them over, taking nothing of value from the whites. Still suffering deprivations of the recent war, some Cayuses begged food from the travelers, though one, displaying fierce pride, told the Henry J. Coke immigrant party in October that his people were very rich and needed nothing because they had plenty of cattle, corn, and potatoes. When they wanted money, cloth, blankets, or paint, he said, they bartered horses for these items at Walla Walla or in the Willamette Valley.[1] In contrast, a Cayuse chief showed papers to white travelers to prove his innocence in the Whitman massacres. One traveler in the 1851 migration found the Indians friendly and settled on the Umatilla River.[2]

Assaying the Willamette-bound traffic, the Indians feared that whites moving from that valley to the interior would increase now that the Cayuses had been punished by war and hanging. Early on the morning of June 20, 1851, eight Cayuse chiefs and their attendants arrived at a spot three miles up the Walla Walla from Waiilatpu to meet with Anson Dart, the new Oregon super-

[1] Henry J. Coke, *A Ride Over the Rocky Mountains to Oregon and California*, 293. Some Oregonians wanted the Cayuses to pay the whites' war claims.
[2] This was Henri Chase, who the following year moved to the Nez Percé country.

intendent of Indian affairs,[3] and two interpreters, the Reverend Elkanah Walker and Perrin Whitman.

Dart described the Cayuses, numbering 126, as "a proud, haughty race, but very superstitious,"[4] perhaps gaining some impression of their nature from their avoidance of the "haunted" mission site, with grass grown high and trails untrod.

Dart's presence indicated that the white man was continuing to shift from guns to words in his Indian policy. An act of Congress of June 5, 1850, had provided for commissioners to negotiate treaties for Indian land west of the Cascade Mountains and to move its owners east of those mountains. It had also provided for extending laws and regulating trade with Oregon Indians west of the Rocky Mountains and created a superintendency of Indian affairs in Oregon, separating the superintendent's duties from those of the governor.[5] Not only did the Indians of eastern Oregon wish western Indians to keep off their lands but the westerners did not want to move east of the mountains. Consequently, the treaties were never ratified. An act of Congress of February 27, 1851, abolished the offices of treaty commissioners, assigning their duties to the superintendent of Indian affairs.[6]

The tribes east of the Cascade Mountains had every reason to be apprehensive. In their June 5 council with Dart at The Dalles, the Indians of that area appeared upset by rumors that the whites would drive them from their country. Dart tried to assure them that such would not happen, a theme he reiterated in all his talks with interior Indians during a journey which ultimately took him to a Nez Percé council on June 27. Apparently, however, he did not tell the Cayuses about the Donation Land Act of September, 1850, granting 320 acres of the public domain to single

[3] The office was created by an act of June 5, 1850. C. F. Coan, "The First Stage of the Federal Indian Policy in the Pacific Northwest, 1849–1852," *Oregon Historical Quarterly*, XXII (March–December, 1921), 57.

[4] Report of Anson Dart, September, 1851, *Oregon Superintendency*, Microfilm No. 2, Roll 11.

[5] Coan, "First Stage of the Federal Indian Policy," 54.

[6] *Ibid.*, 55.

persons settling in Oregon before December 1, 1851, and 640 acres to married couples, to be granted in fee simple on actual residence of four years.[7]

In their June 20 meeting with Dart the Cayuses exhibited the same conciliatory attitude they had shown white travelers on the Immigrant Road. They appeared pleased that the United States had chosen to deal with them despite the misdeeds of some of their fellow tribesmen. And to demonstrate to Dart that they regarded his visit as friendly, they consented to the erection of an agency house in their country. The superintendent, in turn, promised them fair treatment in the future.[8] On the other hand, Walker, who had been forced from his Spokane mission by the Cayuse War, questioned Cayuse sincerity, particularly when his party arrived at Waiilatpu to find no chiefs there to meet them. When the Indians did appear, he softened his attitude somewhat, thinking them friendly only "so far as appearances are concerned but ... Indians & Cayuses at that."[9] Although "rusty in the language," the missionary held worship services with the Cayuses, among many of whom he noticed defection to the priests. This disturbed him because missionaries of his own denomination had been unable to return to the interior since the Cayuse War, while the Catholic priests simply disregarded the missionary ban. The Reverend Toussaint Mesplié, of St. Peters Mission at The Dalles, conducted irregular services among the Cayuses. But the priest found that the services had to be conducted in the Cayuses' own country, for when they came to The Dalles, it was to trade, not to worship.

Perhaps the most specific result of Dart's visit was his negotiation with the Cayuses for the establishment of an agency among

[7] Section 10 of the Pre-emption Act of September 4, 1841, was extended to include Oregon on July 17, 1854. Provision was made to except from pre-emption lands held in reserve by the government or lands to which Indian title had not been extinguished. Secretary of Interior, *Annual Report*, 1857–58, 4.

[8] Bancroft, *History of Oregon, Vol. II, 1848–1883*, 214.

[9] Walker to Wife and Family, June 22, 1851, Manuscript 57/276, Envelope 9, Walker Papers.

them. The fact that there was more timber on the Umatilla than on the Walla Walla made the former a focal point of Cayuse-government relations just as Waiilatpu had been the center of missionary endeavor and before that Fort Walla Walla had been the center of trade. Not that there were no religious or mercantile activities on the Umatilla. It continued to be the center of Catholic visitation, as it had been before the Cayuse War. As for commerce, white merchants considered the environs of the proposed Indian agency a desirable location for trading posts because of its location on the Immigrant Road. On July 23, 1851, A. F. Royer was licensed to trade on the Umatilla,[10] and the government soon received other applications to trade there.

For giving the government permission to build the agency house, the Cayuses expected something in return. In late 1850 they had requested a sawmill,[11] some of them wanting its lumber to build houses like those of Whitman and the traders. Most Cayuses, however, still wished to live in their traditional lodges. The commissioner of Indian affairs, theorizing that the Indians had only one choice, "early civilization or gradual extinction,"[12] saw the withholding of the sawmill as a lever with which to pry the Cayuses into accepting on their lands the Indians of western Oregon, a move that would protect the latter from the Willamette settlers, who wanted them out of the valley. He, therefore, advised Dart to postpone the matter for the time being.[13]

There was no delay in establishing the agency, which the government needed to keep the Cayuses and other tribes at peace

[10] *Oregon Superintendency*, Microfilm No. 2, Roll 12.
[11] Dart to Commissioner of Indian Affairs, November 6, 1850, Microcopy of Records in the National Archives, *Oregon Superintendency of Indian Affairs, 1848–1873*, Letter Book B:10, Microfilm No. M-2, Roll 3 (cited hereafter as *Oregon Superintendency*, B:10, Roll 3).
[12] Coan, "First Stage of the Federal Indian Policy," 57. Robert Newell, appointed by Lane as subagent of Indian affairs in Oregon Territory east of the Cascade Mountains and south of the Columbia River, recommended in a report dated August 10, 1849, that an agency be located on the Umatilla on the Immigrant Road, there being no grass or wood on the Walla Walla.
[13] Commissioner of Indian Affairs Luke Lea to Dart, January 14, 1851, *Oregon Superintendency*, Microfilm No. 2, Roll 12.

among themselves and with white settlers. Dart had written to a John McFarland at Lower Crossing (on the Umatilla), near the site of the proposed agency, to proceed with the erection of the buildings on cottonwood-lined shores (opposite present-day Echo, Oregon)[14] where the Immigrant Road turned west to the John Day River. The distance west of the Blue Mountains was some sixty miles; the distance south of Fort Walla Walla, some twenty-five miles.

The main building of the agency, at that time called Utilla, was an 18-by-20-foot frame structure. Some of its lumber came from Whitman's old sawmill twenty miles away. The total cost was $3,635.39.[15] Later, near the building, a stone-lined well was dug and a rail fence built. Watching the white man erect the house, the Cayuses perhaps wondered how many similar structures his fellow countrymen would build in the Indian country, for by now they had probably learned of the Donation Land Act, which had sacrificed their land to white settlement. The commissioner of Indian affairs in far-off Washington, D.C., was not unmindful of their fears when he wrote:

The principle of recognising and respecting the usufruct right of the Indians to the lands occupied by them, has not been so strictly adhered to in the case of the tribes in the Territories of Oregon and Washington. When a territorial government was first provided for Oregon, which then embraced the present Territory of Washington, strong inducements were held out to our people to emigrate and settle there, without the usual arrangements being made, in advance, for the extinguishment of the title of the Indians who occupied and claimed the lands. Intruded upon, ousted of their homes and possessions without any compensation, and deprived, in most cases, of their accustomed means of support, without any arrangement having been made to enable them to establish and maintain themselves in other locations, it is not a matter of surprise that they have committed many depredations upon our citizens, and been exasperated to frequent acts of hostility.[16]

14 *Umatilla Indian Reservation Then and Now*, 1.
15 J. W. Reese, "The Exciting Story of Fort Henrietta," 4.

176

With an agency building, there would naturally follow white men to occupy it. The Cayuses opposed Dart's plan to appoint Henry H. Spalding their agent,[17] and so in his stead came Elias Wampole, who arrived in Oregon in June, 1851, and reached the Umatilla in September. For a time after his arrival he communicated with the Cayuses through Chief Garry of the Spokanes. He then reported to Dart that the Cayuse chiefs had been in to see him and had gone away satisfied.

It is interesting to note that in his reports Wampole complained of "evils growing out of the squatting traders,"[18] especially since, before reaching the agency, he had refused to license "a Jew" at The Dalles to trade in Indian country unless he took Wampole in as a partner—without the agent furnishing any capital. Quickly formed, the partnership was as quickly dissolved when the trader paid Wampole $250, secured by a bill of sale for some twelve or fourteen head of cattle. In October, Dart charged Wampole with permitting four traders to enter the country on condition that each of them furnish him a good horse. Under pressure from his superiors the agent tried to pass off the proposition as a joke,[19] but he later accepted the horses. Before being relieved of his duties in 1852, Wampole traded to the Indians certain goods obtained from Royer.

To keep on good terms with his Indian clients, Wampole allowed them to stay on the premises day and night and eat at his table. On December 18, 1851, Otter Skin and his men ate with the agent in what he called their "Christmas visit." Among other chiefs enjoying Wampole's hospitality in January and February, 1852, were Camaspelo, Stickus, and Tauitau. On one occasion Tauitau received from the hospitable agent a "britannia mug." Other gifts stimulated the Cayuses to seek even more gratuities.

---

[16] *Annual Report of the Commissioner of Indian Affairs, 1858*, 7.
[17] Dart to Spaulding [Spalding], October 14, 1850, *Oregon Superintendency*, A:10, Roll 3.
[18] Wampole to Dart, September 17, 1851, *Oregon Superintendency*, B:10, Roll 3.
[19] Dart to Commissioner, October 21, 1851, *Oregon Superintendency*, B:10, Roll 3.

According to Wampole's reports, these included muslins to bury their dead and words "of kindness and consolation to the living."[20] The condolences were not expressed in the Chinook tongue, although one of Wampole's expense vouchers was for the services of a linguist in that dialect, who Dart said "could not speak one word."[21]

A white visitor who shared Wampole's table was the Reverend Eugene Casimir Chirouse, O.M.I. (ordained at Fort Walla Walla on January 2, 1848), who was making a mid-February trip to the interior. In March he was encouraged to re-establish Mission St. Anne on the Umatilla, in part by Dart's freedom from sectarian bias, which placed no obstacles in the priest's way. However, he did not minister there as a resident priest until May 7.[22]

One of Chirouse's major concerns was to protect his flock from white incursions, which he knew augured nothing but trouble. As on other Indian frontiers of the American West, cattlemen spilled into Cayuse country. Among those arriving in 1852 were Lloyd Brooke (Brook), George Bomford (Bumford), and Rufus Ingalls. The last was soon replaced by John Noble and a silent but later well-known partner, Ulysses S. Grant, an officer at Vancouver Barracks.[23] In 1853 these men were licensed to establish a trading shop.

As cattlemen entered Cayuse country, wagonloads of immigrants in large trains, such as those of 1852, continued to pass through to the settled Willamette Valley. One Cayuse chief was reported in an eastern newspaper as wanting at least one settler to remain and become his neighbor. According to the story, the unnamed chief, owner of two thousand horses, offered six hundred of them to a white American to settle in his country, marry his daughter, and teach his people to farm. He was reported to

20 Wampole to Acting Superintendent of Indian Affairs for Oregon, Dubois, December 30, 1850 [1851], Oregon Superintendency, Microfilm No. 2, Roll 12.
21 Dart to Lea, September 3, 1852, Oregon Superintendency, B:10, Roll 3.
22 Sister Mary Louise, O.P. [Nellie Sullivan], "Eugene Casimir Chirouse, O.M.I., and the Indians of Washington." See also Catholic Sentinel, March 25, 1851.
23 Click Relander, Strangers on the Land, 40.

have received many letters from American men, who may have wished less for the daughter's hand than for her father's land. Yet one traveler said that Cayuse women possessed a beauty which could have served as "a passport to the best American society."[24]

With increased movement over the Immigrant Road came more friction between the Cayuses and the white settlers, explorers, and soldiers. The Cayuses' memories of soldiers were never pleasant; whenever they saw one, they assumed he had come to fight, thus perpetuating the mutual ill feeling. Believing that their lands would soon be taken, the Cayuses sought to even the score by stealing the whites' stock, taking their prizes at two places on the Immigrant Road: at the foot of the Blue Mountains and at Butter Creek, west of the agency. They offered to "find" immigrant stock for a fee—five dollars for the return of two or three steers run off at night. Lacking ransom money, some immigrant families were forced to abandon their livestock. It was no consolation to them that they suffered more depredations from the Snakes than from the Cayuses.

Joel Palmer, who replaced Dart as Oregon superintendent of Indian affairs on March 17, 1853,[25] received a letter from one H. Smith, who complained that Utilla Agency had been "a curse from having an incompetent speculating trading shop" which purchased stolen white stock from the Indians, encouraging them "to steal with impunity" from practically every wagon train to the point where they had "ruined" many immigrant families.[26] Some of the grievances to which Smith referred had been directed to Major Benjamin Alvord, commanding a garrison of army regulars at The Dalles. The immigrants said that they had received no satisfaction from him.

The Cayuses were unhappy with the cattlemen. During the winter and spring of 1852–53 they held councils with the Nez

---

[24] Orange Jacobs, *Memoirs of Orange Jacobs Written by Himself*, 58–59; Abigail J. Duniway, *Captain Gray's Company*, 160.
[25] C. F. Coan, "The Adoption of the Reservation Policy in the Pacific Northwest, 1853–1855," *Oregon Historical Quarterly*, XXIII (March–December, 1922), 1.
[26] H. Smith to Palmer, May 3, 1853, *Oregon Superintendency*, B:10, Roll 3.

Percés, Walla Wallas, and Umatillas to discuss plans for ridding themselves of the intruders.[27] Adding urgency to the situation was their definite awareness by now of the Donation Land Act, opening to settlement interior lands which had been practically closed since the Cayuse War.

The military was well aware of the impending showdown between Indians and whites. On February 23, 1853, Colonel B. L. E. Bonneville prophesied that during the forthcoming summer the Indians would oppose with force white occupation of their Walla Walla lands.[28] At The Dalles on July 17, Major Alvord expressed a similar belief: that if settlement was attempted as planned war would likely result, this time with the Cayuses receiving help from their powerful Yakima neighbors, as well as from the dreaded Klickitats, dwelling between the Yakimas and the Columbia River. These two peoples, cringing at the prospect of a white invasion, had appealed to the warlike coastal Nisquallies to join them in eliminating the white scourge. Yakima Chief Kamiakin, who condemned the Cayuses for their recent war, now offered to lead an Indian coalition against the invaders.

With Yakimas in attendance several feasts were held in Cayuse country to plan extermination of the whites. At one given by the Nez Percés, nearly forty head of cattle were killed to feed the assemblage.[29] Those present supported a plan to recruit all the Indians from the coast to the Rockies. At similar councils plans were advanced to assemble representatives from all tribes on the right bank of the Columbia at Mool Mool (Bubbling Water), in the lower Yakima country (where Fort Simcoe was established in 1856). Invited to other war councils were tribes on the Columbia's left bank, ranging from downriver Chinooks to the Blackfeet on the east. Because he wished to avoid trouble, the Reverend Charles Pandosy, O.M.I., laboring on the Ahtanum River in Yakima country, did not inform military authorities about the

27 Secretary of Interior, *Annual Report, 1857–58*, 10.
28 Coan, "Adoption of the Reservation Policy," 9.
29 Secretary of Interior, *Annual Report, 1857–58*, 10.

Indian gatherings, even after visiting Cayuse country in the spring.[30] However, he did tell Mesplié, at The Dalles, of conditions. "Yes," he wrote, "the clouds are gathering upon all hands. ... The Tempest is pent up ready to burst." He added, *"The cause of this war is that the Americans are going to seize their lands."*[31]

Demonstrating that their threat was not mere campfire talk, the Indians began to husband their precious supplies of ammunition.[32] Where the Hudson's Bay Company had long been the major source of Cayuse guns and ammunition, the Indians could now acquire them from a proliferation of independent traders. (Besides guns, powder, lead, and bullets, they continued to purchase those items traditionally striking their fancy: green and blue blankets, looking glasses, kettles, vermilion, scarlet cloth, pipes, tobacco, and other items.[33]) Providing another source of Cayuse arms were the immigrants, who traded them for horses and melons and vegetables from Indian gardens along the Umatilla. The Cayuses may also have obtained weapons from the Mormons, as well as from the Catholic priests; in the summer of 1847 a Lieutenant Rogers had reported to Governor Abernethy that he had confiscated a quantity of guns and ammunition from priests at The Dalles. Although the clerics had intended that the Indians use these supplies to provide themselves with game, many people, particularly in the Protestant community, felt that they were helping the Indians rid the country of Americans.[34]

30 *Ibid.*

31 Pandozy [Pandosy] to Mesplié, April 17, 1853. Microcopy of Records in the National Archives, *Oregon Superintendency of Indian Affairs, 1848–1880, 1858–1859*, Microfilm No. 234, Roll 611.

32 This fact became known to the whites when B. F. Shaw, special Indian agent, wrote Governor Isaac I. Stevens, on February 10, 1856: "There is no doubt they had been preparing for war for two years as they had great amount of ammunition on hand." Microcopy of Records in the National Archives, *Washington Superintendency of Indian Affairs, 1853–1874*, Microfilm No. 5, Roll 20.

33 Invoice Trade Goods, February 23, 1853, *Oregon Superintendency*, Microfilm No. 2, Roll 13.

34 William H. Gray, *The Moral and Religious Aspect of the Indian Question*, 16–17.

The Cayuses warmed to a planned war against the Americans by venting their wrath on passing immigrants.[35] In the meantime they continued to hold secret meetings in various places to plan the extermination of their foes. Kamiakin's emissaries were well received in Cayuse country.[36] An indication of how widespread were the invitations to join his cause were those extended to tribes of the Willamette and Umpqua valleys of Oregon.[37] It is not known whether Kamiakin and his allies talked to the Snakes, but the latter committed more than their usual number of depredations during the 1854 immigration. The threat of impending war with the whites caused several tribes to forget old animosities, but it was too weak to prevent the Snakes from forgetting theirs as they rode out to steal and kill many Cayuse horses and cattle during the cold winter of 1852–53.[38]

The Cayuses did not leave it to Kamiakin alone to spread the war cry. They sent runners to tribes as far north as the Canadian border and above and as far south as the Oregon-California border and below, where many ancient enemies lived. They also dispatched messengers east to the Rockies to secure help from former enemies in that direction. Agent Joel Palmer on the Umatilla expected such distant tribes as the Klamaths, the Rogue Rivers, and the Shastas to seek help from the Cayuses in their own antiwhite campaign in the Rogue River country of southern Oregon.[39] The Cayuses, however, probably had little enthusiasm for fighting other Indians' battles. Even the common front which the northern interior tribes were forging was developing cracks. In the spring of 1853, for instance, the Cayuses and Walla Wallas

35 Pambrun, "Story of his life," 137. The Indian agent at Utilla reported that up to October 22, 1853, the immigration past that place in that year totaled 6,449 persons. *Weekly Oregonian*, October 22, 1853, p. 2.

36 The Snakes, aided by Mormons, were premature in beginning their depredations in 1854 by attacking immigrants. *Ibid.*

37 Snowden, *History of Washington*, III, 296–97.

38 L. G. Torrence to Dart, February 1, 1853, *Oregon Superintendency*, Microfilm No. 2, Roll 13.

39 Palmer to Thos. R. Williams, August 26, 1853, *Oregon Superintendency*, B:10, Roll 3.

engaged in a boundary dispute, a source of great concern to Palmer, who told the commissioner of Indian affairs that "the interposition of the government to adjust the difficulty may be called for at early day."[40]

Palmer could testify from experience that intertribal machinations made it difficult for Indian agents to perform their tasks. One who was particularly affected was Philip Thompson, sent to administer Utilla Agency until the government appointee arrived. The Cayuses expected presents from him; when he told them he had none, they threatened to claim the agency house as their own. Reminding him of promises made by Dart and Wampole, they freely roamed the premises. More than once Thompson drove them from his sleeping quarters and kitchen. Dart had asked the commissioner of Indian affairs how to solve the problem. "Almost every day," he said, "some chiefs or head men come to make enquiries or to transact some business, and expect to be furnished with food while here."[41] Thompson blamed Luke Torrence, former special agent at Utilla, for such Cayuse informality when in fact it had begun with Wampole. During the winter of 1852–53, Torrence had kept a man busy gathering fuel to warm a continual houseful of Cayuses and neighboring tribesmen.[42]

Sometime before September, 1853, Tauitau made his last visit to the agency house. In October his relatives held a potlatch to mourn his death, which occurred in buffalo country on September 3.[43] Tauitau had kept the peace, engineered the capture of the Whitman killers, and protected his people from hostilities. Quite unlike him was a possible candidate for the now-vacant chieftaincy, Five Crows, a leader of the hostile Cayuses. Their activity was of great concern to special agent Thomas Williams. In July, 1853, he informed Palmer that Major Alvord had received a

[40] Palmer to Commissioner of Indian Affairs George Manypenny, May 24, 1853, *Oregon Superintendency*, B:10, Roll 3.
[41] Dart to Lea, November 25, 1852, *Oregon Superintendency*, B:10, Roll 3.
[42] Torrence to Dart, February 1, 1853, *Oregon Superintendency*, Microfilm No 2, Roll 13.
[43] *Oregon Spectator*, October 6, 1853, p. 2.

"confidential communication" from a friend stating that the Yakimas had sought to unite with the Cayuses and other Indians against the whites but that the attempt "was unsuccessful and the matter blew over without damages."[44] The informant was wrong. Without Tauitau's restraining hand, the alliance was forged.

The feast honoring Tauitau also served as an occasion for the Cayuses to select a new head chief. Weatenatenamy, Tauitau's nephew, was favored by most Cayuses, although there was no public announcement concerning the matter because it had not been completely settled.[45] Accustomed to having the chief trader at Fort Walla Walla pick their head chiefs, the Cayuses now asked the government's long-haired "New Chief," Robert R. Thompson, to choose one for them.[46] When he arrived at the Umatilla on October 6, Thompson was invited to the potlatch and was thus aware of the politicking palaver concerning the selection of a new chief.

The Cayuses had difficulty in communicating with Thompson because there was no interpreter.[47] He declined the invitation to choose their chief, saying that it was their responsibility, not his. In the middle of the discussions he was invited to Fort Walla Walla by chief trader Andrew D. Pambrun, son of the late Pierre Pambrun, for what purpose he did not know until he arrived, accompanied by several Cayuse chiefs. A number of Indian leaders had convened a council there to select Tauitau's successor.

Unfamiliar with the American policy of permitting the tribes to choose their leaders, the Indians listened to Pambrun, who said that since they had been unable to settle on a chief Five Crows should be named. Thompson immediately objected. He

44 Williams to Palmer, July 13, 1853, *Oregon Superintendency*, B:10, Roll 3.
45 R. R. Thompson to Palmer, October 25, 1853, *Oregon Superintendency*, Microfilm No. 2, Roll 13.
46 Thompson later became a partner with John C. Ainsworth and S. G. Reed in the Oregon Steamship and Navigation Company. Elkanah Walker was commissioned May 19, 1852, to serve as Indian agent but refused to work among the Cayuses and was assigned elsewhere.
47 Thompson to Palmer, October 25, 1853, and Thompson to Palmer, March 21, 1854, *Oregon Superintendency*, Microfilm No. 2, Roll 13.

and Pambrun knew that Five Crows was "especially obnoxious" to Americans.[48] Pambrun responded by telling the Indians in essence that what he had said was true and that humanity demanded (as company personnel had always believed it did) the selection of a new chief. As he sought to challenge Pambrun's words, Thompson was warned not to say anything prejudicial to the company, but he would not agree to this. When he was finally invited to speak, he told the Cayuses that since Pambrun was not authorized to choose their chief they should disregard his remarks.

After he returned to the agency, Thompson wrote Palmer that he deemed it "the first importance that the influence of this foreign Company with the Indians within the Territory be broken up, that the Indians may fully realize that they are under the influence of Americans and not British control."[49] The agent had perhaps been nettled by the circulation among the Cayuses of inflammatory remarks made to them by former "French" employees of the company, now settlers, that the American government intended to take their lands without their consent.[50] Their talk tended to keep alive the deep-seated anti-American, pro-British feeling among the Indians. Agitation by French-Canadians and mixed bloods was prompted not only on behalf of the Indians but in their own interests as well; like the Indians, they feared American encroachment on their Walla Walla farms. That is not to say that the mixed bloods and the Indians always saw eye to eye, for occasionally they tangled. In one instance the agent asked them to suspend certain operations in the valley until a satisfactory arrangement could be worked out with their Indian neighbors.[51]

Thompson wrote Pambrun that the Cayuses and the Nez Percés would now look to him for guidance in selecting a chief

48 Pambrun had returned to the area in 1850.
49 Thompson to Palmer, October 21, 1853, *Oregon Superintendency*, B:10, Roll 3.
50 *Ibid.*
51 *Ibid.*

as they had once sought it from the company.[52] He knew that the Cayuses, like the Nez Percés and the Walla Wallas, were governed by an aristocracy of wealth based on the number of horses owned and that in such a case they could readily select their own chief.[53] He warned the trader that the United States government expected cessation of outside interference which tended to violate federal statutes. American displeasure with British interference was carried over Pambrun's head to chief factor Ogden at Vancouver, who assured Palmer that Pambrun would be informed that he had, as Ogden put it, "nothing whatever to do with the political affairs of the natives."[54]

Palmer advised Thompson that the Hudson's Bay Company could be expected to compete for the Indian trade but that it was wrong for the company to exert political influence over the Indians, particularly in the choice of a chief and specifically Five Crows, who could "be regarded in no other light than an enemy to the people and government of the United States." The superintendent recalled the chief's conduct at the time of the massacre, when he "sent for and forced one of the young girls" to stay in his lodge and "submit to his brutal lust." Palmer also recalled that Five Crows had counseled for continuance of the Cayuse War and had opposed surrender of the murderers and that, in contrast to his unfriendliness to Americans, he had been a favorite of the chief traders at Fort Walla Walla, where all decisions concerning him favored the Hudson's Bay Company over the U.S. government and its people. In his concluding remarks, Palmer opined that "these considerations constitute a strong and justifiable reason for your interference to prevent, the selection of this notorious Indian as the principal chief of the Cayuses."[55] This sugges-

52 Thompson to Pambrun, October 21, 1853, *ibid.*
53 R. R. Thompson, Annual Report [n.d.; 1854?], Microcopy of Records in the National Archives, *Oregon Superintendency of Indian Affairs, 1848–1873*, Letter Book C:10, Microfilm No. M-2, Roll 4. (cited hereafter as *Oregon Superintendency*, C:10, Roll 4).
54 Ogden to Palmer, February 6, 1854, *ibid.*
55 Palmer to Manypenny, December 15, 1853, *ibid.*

tion of interference in Indian politics may have set poorly with Thompson, who believed in the Indians' freedom in such matters.

Regardless of who might become their chief, most Cayuses were bound by one resolve: to protect themselves from a white influx. The slightest white stirring in their country aroused their suspicion, especially if the whites were soldiers. In July, 1853, Lieutenant Rufus Saxton and a party composed of two officers, two civilians, eighteen soldiers,[56] twenty-three packers, three herders, two cooks, and a guide were camped on the Umatilla River. Alarmed by their presence, the Cayuses dispatched a delegation to determine whether, as they had heard, the troops intended to make war on them and take their horses. Saxton said that he had come on a mission of peace to all Indians and promptly invited their chief to his camp for a talk. An unidentified chief departed for the parley, but a wagon he had obtained from some immigrants broke down, delaying his smoke with the officer.[57] The chief may have been Weatenatenamy, who was finally chosen head chief to replace his uncle, Tauitau. He took the latter's English name, Young Chief, as well as his position.

Saxton's immediate mission was to carry supplies to Isaac I. Stevens, coming west to assume his duties as governor of recently organized Washington Territory.[58] The thirty-five-year-old, politically ambitious Stevens was directing survey teams searching for a northern transcontinental railroad passage to complete work begun that summer by Captain George McClellan. Along the way Stevens learned from some Coeur d'Alene Indians that, during the summer, thirty wagons had traversed the country from Fort Walla Walla through the Yakima Valley and the rugged Cascade Mountains to the coast. The presence of Stevens and his party in the Walla Walla Valley gave its Indian residents additional worries, as did still another member of the railroad

[56] *Reports of Explorations and Surveys, to Ascertain the Most Practicable and Economical Route For a Railroad From the Mississippi River to the Pacific Ocean 1853-5*, XII, 108.
[57] *Ibid.*, I, 253.
[58] Washington Territory was created March 2, 1853.

survey force, A. W. Tinkham. Although they may not have understood the precise nature of Tinkham's work, the Cayuses probably surmised that in some way it presaged the coming of more white men. It did, and the Cayuses would not have long to wait.

XII
Speak Straight

While the engineers surveyed Cayuse lands, government officials sought ways to secure them. Joel Palmer wrote Isaac I. Stevens on January 16, 1854: "I have recommended in my letters to the Indian Department the early extinguishment of Indian titles to all lands belonging to these three tribes [Cayuses, Walla Wallas, and Nez Percés], lying within this Territory as a measure important to the preservation of peace." Palmer also suggested early purchase of a strip of land on each side of the Immigrant Road and no change in the management of the tribes until Congress acted.[1] Meanwhile, Stevens, now well established as governor of Washington Territory, was expressing to the commissioner of Indian affairs his belief that the best policy was to pay Indians for their lands and place them on reservations. In a message to the legislature on Februray 28, 1854, he urged that a memorial be sent to Congress requesting that treaties be made with Indians of Washington and Oregon territories. "The Indian title has not been extinguished east of the Cascade Mountains," he wrote. "Under the land law of Congress, it is impossible to secure titles to land, and thus the growth of towns and villages is obstructed, as well as the development of the resources of the Territories."[2]

The tribes of eastern Oregon and Washington territories would have been blind not to see that the hand now writing treaties with tribes west of the Cascade Mountains was about to point the finger at them. The Cayuses were so angry and bent on

[1] Palmer to Stevens, January 16, 1854. *Washington Superintendency*, Microfilm No. 5, Roll 23.
[2] Coan, "Adoption of the Reservation Policy," 13.

189

war to resist such transactions that they would have resisted imple-
mentation of Palmer's suggestion to the Utilla agent that "persua-
sive measures alone are left us by which to control the Indians and
preserve peace." The method Palmer had in mind was to show
them clearly and forcibly the consequences of their failure to
negotiate.[3] Not the least reason why he was interested in negotiations with the Cayuses was that their territory was divided. A
small segment of the Utilla Agency's jurisdiction lay above the
Forty-sixth Parallel, which divided Oregon and Washington
territories, while the remainder was situated in upper middle
Oregon.

On July 20, 1854, Robert R. Thompson reported from the
agency that the only remedy for the unsatisfactory conditions in
the interior was for the government to extinguish the Indians'
title to their land and place them on reservations.[4] At the same
time Palmer recommended the adoption of laws to govern the
Indians, along with provisions for schools, missionaries, and
agricultural instruction. His suggestions later became the basis
of Indian policy in Oregon and Washington territories. On July
31, acting in accordance with Palmer's and Thompson's recom-
mendations. Congress authorized treaty making in order to
purchase Indian lands; the tribesmen would be placed on reservations.

The government's plans strengthened the Indians' resolve to
exterminate the whites. Powwows became bigger and their participants more agitated. Most Pacific Northwest tribes were represented at an all-Indian council in the Grande Ronde on Cayuse
soil the summer of 1854 to discuss a course of action against the
Americans. Even the Shoshonis were present, although during

[3] Palmer to Manypenny, December 15, 1853, *Oregon Superintendency*, C:10,
Roll 4.

[4] Coan, "Adoption of the Reservation Policy," 7. Palmer recommended to the
commissioner of Indian affairs on June 23, 1853, that Indian lands be purchased
and that the Indians be placed on reservations, a marked departure from Dart's
policy of permitting the Indians to mingle with the whites if they were unwilling
to move east of the mountains, under which conditions they would have been
exterminated.

the summer the Cayuses had fought some of their bands. Whatever intertribal power plays may have taken place in the Ronde,
Yakima Chief Kamiakin emerged as moderator, calling for the
establishment of an Indian confederacy to oppose the whites.[5]
    Not all Cayuses were bent on war. Stickus held out against it,
maintaining that the Indians were too weak for such an undertaking. He knew from experience that there were advantages in
being friendly with the whites. In May he had gone to the agency
seeking presents from Thompson in return for promises he
claimed Palmer had made to him during the Cayuse War.[6]
    The anticipated white overtures came in early 1855 when the
Cayuses and other eastern Cascade Mountains tribes were visited
by James Doty, Governor Stevens' secretary, to ascertain their
feelings about selling their lands.[7] Doty thought that they wanted
to sell, but he must have gained that impression by talking only
to the headmen of those bands favoring treaty making with the
government. In reality, the major Cayuse factions were opposed
to it, believing the feather on an arrow to be mightier than that on
a pen.[8] The aggressive Stevens informed Doty by letter on January
18, 1855, that his duty as secretary was to operate among the
Yakimas, Walla Wallas, Cayuses, and Nez Percés; to prepare for
the Blackfoot council; and to make way for treaties to place the

    [5] Josephy, Nez Perce Indians, 312. In a letter dated January 7, 1857, George Gibbs
told James G. Swan, a Washington Territory coastal resident, that during the summer of 1854 a council was held in the Grande Ronde, that several tribes were
represented there, and that the question of war and peace was discussed. Gibbs
said Kamiakin did not attend, sending his brother Sklome (Skloom) instead as his
representative. James G. Swan, The Northwest Coast, 426. For an account of the
council, see Splawn, Ka-mi-akin, 25–26.
    [6] Thompson to Palmer, May 22, 1854, Oregon Superintendency, C:10, Roll 4.
    [7] Secretary of War, Annual Report, 1855–56, Sen. Exec. Doc. No. 66, 34 Cong., 1
sess., Serial 822, p. 24.
    [8] Lawyer the Nez Percé was especially conciliatory to meeting in council. Peopeo-
moxmox was not so favorably inclined, but after several conferences with Doty, he
agreed on March 26, 1855, that it would be better to sell his lands at that time for
a fair price and a reservation than to be continually quarreling with white men and
end up with nothing. See Stevens to Doty, January 18, 1855, Washington Superintendency, Microfilm No. 5, Roll 1. Doty to Stevens, March 26, 1855, ibid., Roll 23.

Indians on reservations so that their country could be opened to white settlement.

Stevens had no definite plans concerning when to hold council with Indians east of the Cascade Mountains and those near the Rockies. For that matter, he had no assurance that they would meet him at all, especially after receiving a March 26 letter from Doty informing him that the Cayuses and Walla Wallas had "assumed to dictate" to immigrants where and when the whites should settle in their country. Doty urged the governor to treat with the Walla Wallas and Cayuses of the Walla Walla Valley before the summer immigration passed through, particularly since it struck him "as an important consideration" that most Indian disturbances there arose from white encroachment. He said further that, although Peopeomoxmox was willing to meet Stevens near the holdings of the Brooke, Bomford and Noble firm in the valley, a council should be held in early May at William Craig's at Lapwai. Should Palmer attend it, opined Doty, joint treaties for Oregon and Washington could be effected at the same time.[9]

On April 1, Doty and A. J. Bolon, a subagent, persuaded Kamiakin to participate in a council, but it was the Yakima chief who chose the meeting place: the old Indian grounds on Mill Creek, six miles above Waiilatpu in the Walla Walla Valley.[10] Eventually representatives of all tribes concerned agreed to meet there with Stevens and Palmer. The council was set for May 29, 1855.

Turning away from Stevens' hoped-for treaty settlement,[11] the tribes, save those preferring words to weapons, agreed to take the warpath against the whites and the civilization for which they stood. As council time neared, the actions of certain Cayuses

[9] Doty to Stevens, March 26, 1855, *Washington Superintendency*, Microfilm No. 5, Roll 23.

[10] Charles Marvin Gates (ed.), *Messages of the Governors of the Territory of Washington to the Legislative Assembly, 1854–1889*, 24.

[11] Stevens to Doty, April 10, 1855, *Washington Superintendency*, Microfilm No. 5, Roll 1.

indicated that they would not meet graciously. As a preview to upsetting the proposed treaty making, five of them rode the countryside, entering settlers' homes and breaking down stock pens.[12]

If the Cayuses had little contact with Doty in the Walla Walla to arrange for the council, it was because most of them had gone to the root grounds. Thompson was assigned the responsibility of gathering them in, a difficult task since he did not know how many Cayuses he was looking for. In 1854 they had refused to tell him their number, claiming that one time Dr. Whitman had conducted a census, after which many of them died.[13]

In response to a message received at the root grounds, two Cayuse chiefs came to the agency to talk with Thompson. He spoke of their participation in the forthcoming gathering in "general terms," as he put it, careful not to tell them the whites wished to purchase their land. Had he done so, they would have refused to attend at all. He wrote Palmer:

> I know very well their sentiments in regard to parting with what they call their lands, which is, that they will never consent to part with them. I am informed that they say, Why should we want a few goods in exchange for our lands, we have plenty of cattle and horses to exchange for such things as we want. We love our country —it is composed of the bones of our people, and we will not part with it. . . . Yet I am not without hope that we may succeed with them, through the Walla Wallas and Nez Perces. . . . You need not be surprised if you should hear of difficulty with the Cayuses before the assembling of the council, as there is a party of five young men who seem bent on doing mischief.[14]

Two of the troublemakers were sons of Tauitau and Tamsucky. The five, Thompson reported, acted "defiant and insolent . . . as if they wished to provoke difficulty." They went to Brooke's farm and ran in front of the oxen with which he was plowing,

12 Stevens to Manypenny, June 12, 1858, *ibid.*
13 Thompson to Palmer, May 22, 1854, *Oregon Superintendency*, C:10, Roll 4.
14 Thompson to Palmer [n.d.], Microcopy of Records in the National Archives, *Oregon Superintendency of Indian Affairs, 1848–1873*, Letter Book D:10, Microfilm No. M-2, Roll 5 (cited hereafter as *Oregon Superintendency*, D:10, Roll 5).

flinging their blankets in front of the animals and causing them to run. That night, stripped to their breechcloths, they paid him another visit, this time pulling him out of bed. Their actions quite naturally put the other scattered whites on the defensive. Thompson talked with the Cayuse head chief, who was likewise on the defensive, asserting that perhaps the whites had provoked the trouble because the Indians had suffered many indignities at their hands and the whites had only laughed.[15]

Doty spoke to Peopeomoxmox about the "turbulent conduct" of the young Cayuses. The Walla Walla chief, regarded as cooperative, could have done little to curb their misconduct by talking with their elders, although he was influential among both his own people and the Umatillas, who probably would have sided with him had a division developed between them and the Cayuses.

Actions like those of the five Cayuses put the whites in a cautious mood as treaty negotiations neared. Making Stevens even edgier was word that the Cayuses, Walla Wallas, and Yakimas planned to attend the council with hostile intentions. The governor also received a warning from the Reverend Pascal Ricard, now superior of the Catholic mission in the Yakima and Cayuse country.[16]

En route to the Walla Walla Valley, Governor Stevens stopped at The Dalles to request a military escort from Major Gabriel J. Rains, now commanding the garrison there. The major was not convinced of the necessity to provide it, an indication of the differing views of army and territorial personnel concerning the conduct of affairs in Indian country. Nevertheless, he sent along Brevet Lieutenant Archibald Gracie and a party of thirty-seven troops and guides, one of whom was Cut Mouth John. Along the way the detachment added a corporal and nine privates who had been on the Umatilla pursuing some Indian murderers,

15 *Ibid.*
16 Isaac I. Stevens, *Speech of Hon. Isaac I. Stevens, Delegate From Washington Territory, on the Washington and Oregon War Claims Delivered in the House of Representatives of the United States, May 31, 1858,* 4 (cited hereafter as Stevens, *Speech*).

bringing the number of soldiers to forty-seven.[17] Stevens regarded them as a police force to check potential violence from the Cayuses, who he felt might have to be treated as conquered people.[18]

Some of the troops tarried to visit the Cayuses and enter their lodges along the Umatilla River. Lieutenant Lawrence Kip wrote that although they were notoriously the most unfriendly tribe to whites among all Indians of the region, they cordially received their visitors.[19] As the soldiers traded pleasantries with the Indians, Stevens sent word to Doty that if Peopeomoxmox did not object to the presence of a company of territorial regulars the Cayuses should be incorporated with the Walla Wallas under Peopeomoxmox. That way, he explained, "the Cayuses if treated as a conquered people will not be considered as holding lands, but finally as a band of Walla Wallas in the Tribe with whom we may associate them."[20] Such a suggestion would have filled Cayuses with instant fury, not just because of the treacherous nature of it but because they believed themselves superior to the Walla Wallas.

Doty had shielded from the Cayuses the purpose of the council. Yet, they learned of it through the Indian grapevine in the Yakima country, where, on April 3, Doty had stated his intent to purchase all land belonging to the Indians and remove them to reservations.[21] The Cayuse chiefs freely expressed their apprehensions to Thompson, who, like Doty, told them nothing. Five Crows told Thompson in April that his uncle had advised him "to guard his country with a jealous eye—that they should keep a strict watch on whites when they came into it."[22] The chief conceded

---

[17] Granville Owen Haller, "Indian War of 1855–56," 9, manuscript in Haller Papers. See also Lawrence Kip, *The Indian Council at Walla Walla, May and June, 1855*, 9.

[18] Stevens to Doty, May 20, 1855, *Washington Superintendency*, Microfilm No. 5, Roll 1.

[19] Kip, *Indian Council at Walla Walla*, 10.

[20] Stevens to Doty, May 20, 1855, *Washington Superintendency*, Microfilm, No. 5, Roll 1.

[21] James Doty, "Journal of operations of Governor Isaac Ingalls Stevens."

[22] Thompson to Palmer, April 14, 1855, *Oregon Superintendency*, D:10, Roll 5.

that whites knew more than Indians when it came to laws and general subjects but that Indians knew enough for their own good. Neither, he said, did they want to change the sky and earth and the things surrounding them, for they loved their country, which gave them birth and nourished them and gathered them up when they died. In short, they wanted to be left alone.[23]

A short time earlier, following a dispute between Five Crows and a white man over the ownership of a horse, the chief had explained to Thompson the workings of Indian law—particularly the old Cayuse custom of seeking vengeance by obtaining satisfaction from tribes or families rather than from individuals. In reporting the matter, Thompson wrote: "The laws and customs of their forefathers as handed down to them from generation to generation, are viewed with a sacredness bordering on devotion, and are maintained with a zeal and tenacity truly astonishing." As a loyal American, he added: "When [therefore] we see them discarding their own [laws] and adopting those of the white man, we may indeed hope that the chambers of their understandings have been opened and that the efforts of the philanthropic have not been altogether in vain."[24]

In late May word spread that the Cayuses, Walla Wallas, and Yakimas were determined to make no treaty. Some 300 Cayuses, 120 of them warrior age, and a band of more than 150 Walla Wallas approached the treaty grounds on May 26 without their chief, who arrived with some of his people two days later. Gaily dressed, whooping and shouting, they circled the 2,500-man camp three times in their fashion, making no attempt to disguise their hostility and eyeing the white troops, who had arrived on the twenty-third. Weatenatenamy, Five Crows, Umhowlish, Howlish Wampo, Stickus, and Camaspelo rode up to Stevens' and Palmer's tent, where they were invited to dismount. They did so and shook

23 R. R. Thompson, Annual Report, August 14, 1855, Microcopy of Records in the National Archives, *Oregon Superintendency of Indian Affairs, 1848–1873*, Letter Book F:10, Microfilm No. M-2, Roll 7.
    24 *Ibid.*

hands, but "in no cordial manner." When invited to smoke, they declined, saying that they had not come that day to talk.[25]

The treaty commissioners were as disheartened by this response as they were by word received later that the Cayuses would combine with others to make no deal with them. As council time neared, the Cayuses suggested to their allies the immediate killing of Stevens, Palmer, and their military escort.[26] Stevens ordered the American flag, a symbol of power, raised at the white campsite and never pulled down. On Monday, May 28, when the Yakimas entered the grounds, the Cayuses summoned several tribal leaders to an urgent meeting. Whatever their strategy may have been, it is known only that they planned to make no deal with the Americans for their country. That day Peopeomoxmox told the whites that he, Weatenatenamy, Lawyer, and Kamiakin would do all the talking at the big council—an indication that the tribes had engaged in more than social chatter at their pre-council meetings.[27]

On the day Peopeomoxmox made his announcement (Monday), a private meeting between the commissioners and the Cayuses and Walla Wallas was held, with the Reverend Joseph Menetrey, S. J., Pandosy, and Chirouse in attendance. The commissioners, wondering what the disposition of the Cayuses and Peopeomoxmox might be,[28] had decided that the best way to find out was to confer with them. They found the Cayuses extremely unfriendly.

On Tuesday, May 29, the council formally opened. Stevens gave a short speech after the various auxiliaries and interpreters had been sworn in. By then it had begun to rain, and the meeting was adjourned until the next day, a delay not in the least annoying to the Indians; the Americans felt they had no time to lose. By this time there were on the grounds some five thousand Indian men, women, and children from tribes as far distant as the Canadian border, including, besides the principals, some five hundred

25 Doty, "Journal of operations."
26 Haller, "Indian War of 1855–56."
27 Josephy, *Nez Perce Indians*, 317.
28 Doty, "Journal of operations."

Palouses, Umatillas, Klickitats, and others. Stevens learned more about Cayuse independence when a Cayuse chief spurned an offer of two oxen for a feast, asserting that he, like Kamiakin, had plenty of cattle.[29]

Of the meeting held on Wednesday, May 30, Lieutenant Kip wrote:

> It was a striking scene. Directly in front of Governor Stevens' tent, a small arbor had been erected, in which, at a table, sat several of his party taking notes of everything said. In front of the arbor on a bench sat Governor Stevens and General Palmer, and before them, in the open air, in concentric semi-circles, were ranged the Indians, the chiefs in the front ranks, in order of their dignity, while the background was filled with women and children. The Indians sat on the grounds. . . . There were probably 1,000 present at a time.[30]

The council got under way. Palmer spoke, and then Stevens, who told his audience that during the previous year he had gone to see "the Great Father" in Washington, D.C., and that while he was there he had told him the Indians had been good and that he, the Great Father, should do something for his red children. Stevens dwelt at some length on what the President had done for Indians east of the Rocky Mountains. Said the governor: "We want you and ourselves to agree upon tracts of land where you shall live; in those tracts of land we want each man who will work to have his own land, his own horses, his own cattle, and his home for himself and his children."[31] Then he told the Indians that he wanted them to have schools, mills, shops, teachers, doctors, lawyers, and many other things. "Now," he said, "we want you to agree with us to such a state of things: You to have your tract with all these things; the rest to be the Great Father's for his white children."[32] Stevens spoke further. A white critic has written of

[29] Snowden, *History of Washington*, III, 298.
[30] Kip, *Indian Council at Walla Walla*, 15.
[31] Josephy, *Nez Perce Indians*, 319.
[32] *Ibid.*

Stevens' spiel: "The transparency of the speeches of Governor Stevens and Superintendent Palmer is so obvious that it is a wonder the commissioners could not realize the ease with which the Indians saw through what they were saying."[33] The governor's red critics were ready made. None of them, especially the Cayuses, were impressed by his humanitarian concern for the red man, for the promised gifts and ideas of progress, such as a transcontinental railroad, a potential route to the Pacific for which he had surveyed.

On Thursday, May 31, Stevens reiterated that he wanted the Indians to have many gifts. Among other things he promised to end the Blackfoot menace to western tribes in their buffalo hunting—hunting which would have been wiped out by the kind of progress he was advocating. Palmer spoke at least one encouraging word: the Indians must be protected from bad white men who at that very moment were scheming "to get your horses." That evening, Weatenatenamy consented to dine with Stevens and Palmer. Later he sent word to them that the Indians did not wish to meet in council the next day, preferring to feast and game as they were doing at the moment. The commissioners reluctantly deferred to their request.[34] In reality the various headmen were seeking a respite to consider their responses to Stevens' proposals. They held serious discussions concerning the commissioners' talk, but there was some social visiting by whites in Indian lodges and some reciprocal calls by the Indians, "who pay little regard to visiting hours," going into the whites' quarters very early in the morning.[35]

On Saturday, June 2, sensing a toughening Indian response to his words and those of Stevens, Palmer discarded his statement that he did not wish to frighten them and warned the Indians that white settlers were entering their country "like grasshoppers on the plains." No one could halt them, he said, any more than

---

[33] *Ibid.*, 318.
[34] Doty, "Journal of operations."
[35] Kip, *Indian Council at Walla Walla*, 16.

the flow of the Columbia River could be stopped. He urged them to choose immediately the lands they wanted. Stevens asked the Indians to reply. "We are tired," said Five Crows. Palmer said that the whites had nothing more to say.

The Cayuses had planned that Weatenatenamy should speak for them, but Five Crows felt compelled to dwell at some length on the theme that the Indians did not wish to become farmers and disturb the earth. With some anger Peopeomoxmox told the commissioners:

> We have not seen in a true light the object of your speeches . . . you have spoken in a round about way. Speak straight. I have ears to hear you, and here is my heart. . . . You have spoken in a manner partly tending to evil. Speak plain to us.[36]

Several others spoke, the last a Cayuse whose remarks were "unfavorable to the reception of the treaty."[37]

Cayuse anger carried over into plotting sessions that night. The object was to massacre the whites on the council grounds and capture the military garrison at The Dalles. The Yakimas and Walla Wallas were nearly convinced that they should join the Cayuses in such an action.[38] The Nez Percé representative, Lawyer, was not at the meeting, but his spies brought him word of the Cayuse plot.[39] Fearing for Stevens' life, he went to warn the governor about midnight, offering to return with some of his people to pitch a lodge near Stevens' camp. This he did.[40]

On Monday, June 4, Lawyer was the first Indian to speak. Wishing to offend no one, he said: "There are a good many men here who wish to speak. Let them speak."[41] Other Indians did so,

---

36 Josephy, *Nez Perce Indians*, 322.
37 Kip, *Indian Council at Walla Walla*, 16.
38 Josephy, *Nez Perce Indians*, 322.
39 Helen Addison Howard, *Saga of Chief Joseph*, 50.
40 Such a move by Lawyer would undoubtedly have caused a rift between the Cayuses and Nez Percés. One writer suggests that since Stevens did not mention Lawyer's telling him any such story, it is possible the move was prompted solely by a Cayuse–Nez Percé split. Josephy, *Nez Perce Indians*, 323.
41 *Ibid.*

Stickus of past grievances and Peopeomoxmox most pertinently: "You [commissioners] have spoken for lands generally. You have not spoken of any particular ones."[42] Forced to specifics, Stevens laid some plans before the Indians, namely, that he planned to create two reservations, one on Nez Percé lands and the other on those of the Yakimas. He proposed sending the Cayuses with the Walla Wallas, the Umatillas and Spokanes to live with the Nez Percés, and most other tribes to live with the Yakimas. The Indians shied away from the idea as if it were the plague, and their opposition was just as contagious. The commissioners wearied of their delaying talk of the "next moon."

On Tuesday, June 5, Stevens elaborated on his reservation proposals, explaining payments for ceded lands. That night the Cayuses were openly antagonistic. When Lieutenants Kip and Gracie made their rounds of the Cayuse camp, as they had done frequently, several young braves tried to block their advance. When the officers reined their mounts past them, the Indians backed down. The whites had called the bluff, but, since they feared an outbreak of hostilities, they had little to gloat about.

On Wednesday, June 6, Stevens admonished the chiefs to make known their acceptance or rejection of the terms offered.[43]

On Thursday, June 7, the Indians, evincing no haste to accede to the governor's request for a quick decision, engaged in repetitious talk as Stevens kept repeating: "Let us have your hearts straight out." From Lawyer he got a long-winded speech and, finally, an expression of approval of the treaty proposal. Then the angry but temper-holding Weatenatenamy presented a lengthy argument against selling Indian lands. Even Stickus, the white man's friend, opposed abandoning Cayuse country to move in with Nez Percés. Kamiakin refused to speak. Said Palmer:

> The hearts of the Nez Perces and ours are one. The Cayuses, the Walla Wallas, and the other tribes say they do not understand us. ... How long will these people remain blind? We come to try to

42 *Ibid.*
43 Doty, "Journal of operations."

open their eyes. They refuse the light. . . . I have come a long way. We ask you to go but a short distance. We do not come to steal your land. We pay you more than it is worth. There is the Umatilla Valley that affords a little good land between two streams and all around it, is a parched up plain. What is it worth to you, what is it worth to us? Not half what we have offered you for it.[44]

The council wore on. Indian tempers flared. Finally Howlish Wampo declared that he would not leave his land for that of the Nez Percés, and as for Palmer's words, they were crooked. Five Crows said that although his people had once been as one with the Nez Percés, they were now divided. Under pressure of such bitter feelings the Indians that night felt the need of reaching some sort of agreement among themselves. What tactics they discussed is not known, but their strategy changed the next day in council. On the basis of subsequent events it may be assumed that the Indians were secretly preparing to drive the Americans from their country and therefore decided to yield and sign the treaty, which would be valueless if they carried out their plan.

On Friday, June 8, Weatenatenamy said that the Cayuses could not understand why the governor had given them no voice in choosing a homeland, adding that he wanted to talk about the matter. A short time later Palmer revealed that on the previous night Stevens had made plans for three reservations, the third for the Cayuses, Walla Wallas, and Umatillas in their homelands.[45] Palmer also promised that homes would be built for the chiefs on this reservation, as on the other two, and that salaries would be paid chiefs and others. The Indians, he assured, would receive all the promised gifts, such as schools and farm supplies, and, more important, plenty of time to move to the reservations when the Great Father approved the treaty.

The promise of a reservation encompassing their homeland eased the Cayuses' tensions somewhat, as did word that they would be separated from the more numerous Nez Percés—pos-

[44] Kip, *Indian Council at Walla Walla*, 18, 21.
[45] *Ibid.*

sible insurance against further loss of their tribal identity. Only Kamiakin held out. Then, as if on cue, Looking Glass, an anti-reservationist, created more confusion in the council. War painted and dangling a Blackfoot scalp, he scolded his people for what they had done, telling them to go home to their lodges.[46]

Saturday, June 9, the council met after Stevens had talked privately with Kamiakin and Peopeomoxmox; they agreed to sign. According to Doty: "the Chief [Kamiakin] said he saw that we had brought presents, to give to the Indians, but for himself he did not wish to take any of the presents now. When the Treaty had been approved by the President, and the Indians moved out of their Reservation, then he would accept his share of the goods."[47] Kamiakin apparently feared that accepting gifts for signing the treaty, even token ones, would make it more binding.

When the talks began, Stevens at first ignored Looking Glass to read the three treaties. Presently he called on the Nez Percé chief to speak. Looking Glass, goaded by Weatenatenamy, said that he did not order white men around and that they in turn should not order his people around. "I am going to talk straight," he said. "I am not like those people who hang their heads and say nothing." He was obviously referring to Lawyer. Running his finger along a map, Lawyer said that he wanted a reservation which included all lands the Nez Percé owned at the time. After the meeting Peopeomoxmox and Kamiakin signed.

At the council as an interpreter was William Cameron McKay (son of trader-interpreter Thomas McKay), stockman and later physician to the Cayuses. He witnessed Kamiakin's signing:

... when the Indians hesitated, the Governor said to tell the chief, "if they dont sign this treaty, they will walk in blood knee deep." To illustrate, Mam-ia-kin [Kamiakin] was about the last to sign by making his cross. When he returned to his seat, his lips were covered with blood, having bitten them with suppressed rage. Father Chaurause [Chirouse] the Catholic Priest was standing by me at

[46] Josephy, *Nez Perce Indians,* 328.
[47] Doty, "Journal of operations."

the time, and he drew my attention to the blood, remarking, "I am afraid we will all be murdered before we leave these grounds."[48]

On Monday, June 11, Stevens called on Lawyer, his favorite Nez Percé chief, to keep the word for his people. The governor requested no more speeches. "This will be the last day of the council," he said.[49] At Stevens' urging, Lawyer signed his treaty, followed by Looking Glass, then Old Joseph and the others. The Cayuses signed their treaty last, seeing, Doty said, "that they stood alone."[50]

The council was over. The Indians held "a great scalp dance" in which 150 women took part and then broke camp. Stevens moved east to the Blackfoot country. The Cayuses were angered and frustrated that they had signed away their lands. Like horses, they, too, were to be corralled on a reservation.[51] Because of the treachery from the white man's mouth which would send them there, they vowed to take his blood to avenge that on the lips of Kamiakin.

48 William Cameron McKay affidavit in McKay Papers.
49 Josephy, *Nez Perce Indians*, 331.
50 Doty, "Journal of operations."
51 See Appendix E for a copy of the treaty, listing the boundaries of land ceded and the new reservation.

We-ah - Te-nä- tee-ma-ny
called "the young Chief"
Head chief of the cayuses

Cayuse Chief Weatenatenamy (Young Chief), sketched
by Gustavus Sohon at the Walla Walla treaty council in
1855.

Five Crows (pasht loholski)
or She-ca-yah

Chief of the Cayuses

Cayuse Chief Five Crows, sketched by Gustavus Sohon at
the Walla Walla treaty council in 1855.

Cayuse War Chief Umhowlish, sketched by Gustavus
Sohon at the Walla Walla treaty council in 1855.

Pewpew mox - mox.
Head Chief of the Walla-Walla Indians

Walla Walla Chief Peopeomoxmox, sketched by Gustavus
Sohon at the Walla Walla treaty council in 1855.

Indian agent Nathan Olney fought in the Cayuse War in 1848 and tried to keep the Cayuses out of trouble in 1855.

Joseph Lane, first governor of Oregon Territory.

West Point graduate Isaac I. Stevens was the first governor of
Washington Territory.

Dr. William Cameron McKay was the grandson of fur trader
Alexander McKay. His father, Thomas, fought in the Cayuse
War; his mother was a Chinook Indian.

XIII
Rumblings of War

Seven months after the Walla Walla council treaties were signed, Governor Stevens happily told the Washington Territorial Legislature that he had never seen "such expressions of joy and thankfulness" exhibited to a greater degree among the Indians. Other whites represented that those attending the council—Kamiakin, Peopeomoxmox, Weatenatenamy, Stickus, and Lawyer—had been personally satisfied with its results.[1] These observations indicate a misjudgment of the Indians' true feelings about the council, just as their feelings had been misjudged before it convened. At the council Chirouse and Pandosy, their fingers on the Indians' emotional pulse, warned the treaty makers that trouble was brewing among the red men. Such warnings apparently went unheeded.[2]

Those more familiar with the Indians knew that their chiefs had been forced to sign a piece of paper with bad words written on it. Wrote Dr. William Cameron McKay: "I was familiar with the chiefs and head men of these tribes. They have frequently told me they were opposed to the treaty. . . . They contended with earnestness the treaty was forced upon them by the commissioners."[3] The Reverend Joseph Joset, S.J., ministering to the Coeur d'Alenes to the north, said:

When late Gov Stevens of Wash[ington] Territory went with several gentlemen to make treaties with the Cayuses, Yakamas, Wallawallas and Nez Perces, somebody to prevail on them to sell

[1] Gates, *Messages of the Governors*, 24.
[2] Sister Mary Louise, "Eugene Casimir Chirouse," 27.
[3] William Cameron McKay affidavit in McKay Papers.

their lands, said: "Any how the lands we will have" hearing which the chiefs agreed to make a mock treaty. in order to gain time and prepare for war.[4]

Shortly after the treaty signing, Five Crows, as might have been expected, became one of five chiefs from various tribes to propose war.[5] All summer long he and other Indians talked of the bad bargain they had made at Walla Walla. Outwardly, all appeared quiet in Cayuse country as the Indians tended their Umatilla gardens and went about their summer business. Some Cayuses even cooperated with white men. In July, 1855, Umhowlish and some of his men, with Nez Percés acting as guides, accompanied agent Robert R. Thompson, Captain Olney, and a detachment of troops under Major Granville O. Haller on an expedition from The Dalles to the Snake country. On August 20, 1854, a band of Bannack Shoshonis had murdered a number of immigrants twenty miles from Fort Boise; the party was on its way to punish those responsible for the deed.[6] Umhowlish, whom Haller called the "war Chief of the Cayuses," saw in the occasion an opportunity to seek revenge against his enemies for their continuing raids against his people.

On September 7 in the Grande Ronde, as the expedition prepared to penetrate the Snake country, Haller conferred with Cayuse Chief Weatenatenamy and Nez Percé Old Chief Joseph. He had heard that they were likewise eager to punish their Shoshoni enemies. He asked them to join him but was informed that "they had no such intrutions [sic]." In the Ronde, Haller met Walla Walla Chief Peopeomoxmox, Umatilla Chief Winampsnoot, and Cayuse Chief Stickus, all of whom he entertained with lemon sirup. Peopeomoxmox asked for whisky, finding the lemon sirup "very good Woman's drink."[7] The five rounds of musket

---

4 Joseph Joset, "LXVII A. Account of the Con. Ind[ian] war '58."
5 Granville Owen Haller, "Diary 1856," Entry July 1, 1856, Haller Papers.
6 Granville Owen Haller, "Correspondence from Hdqtrs Winnas Exped. 1855," Entry July 31, 1855, Haller Papers.
7 Granville Owen Haller, "Haller, G. O. Diary 1855," Haller Papers.

cartridges Haller gave them would have found their targets more surely when the drinking was over.

After the libations the members of the expedition moved into Snake country, but there is no record that they found the killers. The scouts, however, discovered an Indian cache which included items stolen from the ill-fated immigrant party. Haller turned them over to their discoverers. The command, at least, returned home safely amid reports that the Snakes had wiped it out.[8] Rumor had it that the Blackfeet had also killed Stevens and his party.

There were as yet no reports of wrongdoing among the Cayuses and other Indians who had attended the Walla Walla council, but the tranquility did not last long. In early September, Qualchan, son of Yakima Chief Owhi, and five other Yakimas killed eight miners along the Yakima River for indiscretion against the Indians, particularly women, and for trespassing on Yakima lands. Hearing of the killing, subagent Bolon left The Dalles in September to investigate. He threatened the Indians with occupation of their lands by government troops to protect the whites.[9] As he was returning to The Dalles, the Yakimas killed him.[10] In retaliation Major Haller was dispatched from The Dalles with 104 men and a howitzer. On October 5, near the Toppenish River (a Yakima tributary), 1,500 braves met his men[11] and soundly trounced them in a two-day battle, sending them reeling back to The Dalles. Participating were elements of nearly every interior tribe, including warriors from the camps of Weatenatenamy and Five Crows. Walla Walla Peopeomoxmox was also reported to have taken part.[12]

[8] Secretary of Interior, *Annual Report, 1855–56, Sen. Exec. Doc.* No. 1, 34 Cong., 1 sess., Serial 810, p. 513.

[9] Secretary of War, *Annual Report, 1855–56,* 54.

[10] Lucullus Virgil McWhorter, *Tragedy of the Wahk-shum.* In this account the Indians tell of Bolon's death.

[11] Secretary of War, *Annual Report, 1855–56,* 54; Reese, "The Exciting Story of Fort Henrietta," 1.

[12] Granville Owen Haller, "Genesis of Oregon-Washington Indian War 1855–6"; Pandosy to Haller [n.d.], Haller Papers.

News of the victory thrilled a thousand Indian camps, around whose fires the warriors danced, vowing to give the same treatment to any soldier entering their country. The Cayuses and other tribes received new bids from the Yakimas to join them in all-out conflict against the whites. Cayuse chiefs responding to the call were Weatenatenamy, Wiecat, Five Crows, Wattastuartite, and, reportedly, Umhowlish.[13] Among the Umatillas were Winampsnoot and Tahkintashukanstowish (Stomish).

Not the least surprised by the Indians' action was agent Thompson. He had been told by Charles McKay (who in turn had been informed by Five Crows) that there was no danger of the Cayuses' allying with the Yakimas in war; Thompson had promptly passed this information on to Superintendent Palmer.[14] Intelligent men in the military and in Indian affairs knew that the roots of the war lay deeper than the killing of a few miners. While some erroneously believed the recent treaty to have been the source of Indian unrest, most knew that its real cause stemmed from the white man's wish to take and hold Indian land. Many Americans blamed the Hudson's Bay Company for selling the Indians arms and ammunition in defiance of an American law forbidding such sales.[15] They were not so quick to point out that some of their fellow countrymen were guilty of the same offense.

The Cayuses remained on generally favorable terms with the company, but former trader Andrew D. Pambrun sensed a new belligerence among them. When Weatenatenamy permitted him to build a house in the Walla Walla Valley, two men he put to work hewing logs for it were harassed daily by three or four Indians, who eventually drove them away. Pambrun sent for Weatenatenamy to talk about the incident, after which the aggravation ceased. Passing Pambrun's house near sundown one day, Weatenatenamy spied the white man. Pambrun asked why he was traveling so late in the day.

13 B. F. Shaw to Stevens, Februray 10, 1856, *Washington Superintendency*, Microfilm No. 5, Roll 20.
14 Thompson to Palmer, October 14, 1855, *Oregon Superintendency*, D:10, Roll 5.
15 Coan, "Adoption of the Reservation Policy," 25–26.

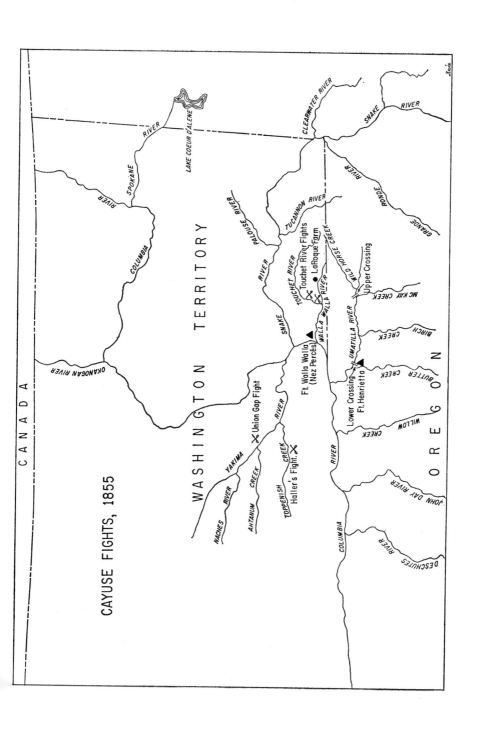

CAYUSE FIGHTS, 1855

"We are like coyotes," replied Weatenatenamy. "We travel night or day."

"But why travel at night?" asked Pambrun, who was acquainted with the Indians' habits well enough to know that by sundown they had usually settled down.

The chief replied, "You will find out soon enough."[16] Pambrun sensed that something was afoot, but his employee Al Talmon, who was married to a Cayuse and knew of her people's belligerence, did not inform Pambrun of impending trouble. Not until Indian agent Nathan Olney came up from The Dalles did he learn the true state of affairs.

Olney went to the Walla Walla Valley to dissuade the Indians there from joining the hostile Yakimas and to warn white residents to clear the area immediately, in case the Indians became hostile. He tried to confer with Peopeomoxmox, but the old chief refused to see him; a hundred warriors in his camp danced around some American scalps. When the agent visited the Cayuses, they told him that they were unhappy with the treaty provision that the Walla Wallas were to locate with them on a reservation. The region was "too small to afford farming and grazing for that number of people and their stock."[17] The ill feeling of the Cayuses toward the Walla Wallas might have been more intense had Peopeomoxmox and the Umatillas not been across the Columbia at the mouth of the Yakima planning war against an enemy common to all of them. The Cayuses and Walla Wallas had more important things to do at the moment than to fight each other or any of their allies in the late Cayuse War—the Palouses were gathering at the mouth of the Palouse River. "The Volcano is about ready to break forth," wrote Olney to Palmer on October 12, 1855.[18]

Olney thought he could keep a lid on the bubbling caldron by telling the Cayuses that there would be no further settlement of

16 Pambrun, "Story of his life," 138.
17 Olney to Palmer, October 18, 1855; Palmer to Manypenny, October 25, 1855, *Oregon Superintendency*, D:10, Roll 5.
18 Olney to Palmer, October 12, 1855, *ibid.*

their country until they could meet with the superintendent again with a view toward changing their proposed reservation boundaries to exclude the Walla Wallas. He knew as well as the Cayuses that he had only made a promise; they had heard promises before. Talking too big and too late, the agent was forced to resign himself to the inevitable war. On October 11 the new Oregon territorial governor, George L. Curry, issued a call for volunteers as the Indians concentrated their forces "rapidly and as secretly as possible."[19] At Olney's insistence, chief trader James Sinclair hurriedly abandoned Fort Walla Walla, leaving its property—except ammunition, which the trader ordered dumped into the Columbia River—in the care of the Walla Walla Pierre. Sinclair and his wife had to abandon their Donation Land Act claim, situated about three miles from present-day Walla Walla. Valley settlers had to leave behind six hundred head of fine breeding cattle from Canada and various company posts, plus thirty horses.[20] A company employee, Hezekiah Van Dorn, was also forced to flee.

In its flight the firm of Brooke, Bomford and Noble left behind large herds of stock and improvements, not only at Waiilatpu but also on the Touchet River. When Olney insisted that Pambrun depart, the latter made arrangements for others in the area to leave: the families of a Mr. Ritter and a Mr. Moar, as well as that of a Mr. Clark, who was in the mountains making shingles. Most Walla Walla Valley whites left in a group for protection. M. G. Arnold, a cattleman in the Umatilla Valley since 1852, and G. A. La Grand, who lived near Utilla Agency, were forced to flee. On McKay Creek, Stickus warned Henri M. Chase, Lloyd Brooke, and P. M. LaFountain (Leframbaine) of the impending trouble. "Saddle your horses," the old chief cried, "and go quickly as you can as there are bad men in our camp who intend to way lay you."[21] Nearly a decade earlier, he had given a similar warning to his friend Dr. Whitman.

19 *Ibid.*
20 John McBean affidavit in McKay Papers.
21 H. M. Chase to McKay, May 3, 1887, McKay Papers.

Dr. McKay, who lived on McKay Creek near what is now Pendleton, Oregon, was visiting the Colville mines near the Canadian border. As he was returning home, Howlish Wampo warned him at Waiilatpu that the whites had evacuated the area and that he had better escape to The Dalles. Howlish Wampo sent his brother, Watshtamena, to escort McKay to his ranch to prevent the Indians from killing him. Stickus also warned McKay to leave, as he had a Mr. Whitney at McKay's. When McKay reached his home, Stickus again came to tell him that it was unsafe for him and his herder, Victor Truitt (Tribit, also Trevitt), to remain any longer. Cayuse scouts failed to discover McKay in the hills and hollows as he made his escape.[22] Why had Stickus warned him? Possibly out of respect for services he had rendered in refereeing troubles between Indians and immigrants. But why had he warned the white families? Possibly out of respect to the memory of his teacher, Dr. Whitman.

The only persons remaining safely in the Walla Walla Valley were French-Canadian former employees of the Hudson's Bay Company married to Indian women. To demonstrate their loyalty to their red in-laws and to ensure continued residence among them, they circulated rumors that encouraged the Indians in their hostility, just as some of them had done at the time of the Whitman massacre.

With the Cayuses now becoming more aroused, one of the French-Canadians, Narcisse Raymond, was hired by Brooke, Bomford and Noble to drive its herd of 375 grown cattle, yearlings, and calves to The Dalles.[23] Apprised of the move, some young Cayuses proposed to their chief, Five Crows, that they steal the herd. He is reported to have tried to dissuade them,[24] but, exhibiting the characteristic impulsiveness of youth, they disregarded his words and ran off most of the herd. Raymond arrived at The Dalles with only eighty head of cattle.[25]

22 John McBean affidavit in McKay Papers.
23 Hezekiah Van Dorn affidavit in McKay Papers.
24 Thompson to Palmer, November 19, 1855, Oregon Superintendency, D:10, Roll 5.

Raymond had also been asked to separate friendly Cayuses from their hostile brothers, a recommendation put forth by Olney, who wanted them taken to the Grande Ronde. Olney also suggested that Thompson remove himself—which the agent had already done—to The Dalles. Olney had asked Raymond to collect the friendly Indians in the vicinity of the Catholic mission in the Walla Walla Valley, but, not wishing to antagonize hostile Indians among his wife's people, Raymond had no desire to ride herd on the nonhostile Cayuses.[26] One of them, The Hunchback, turned out to be not so friendly, reportedly driving off what their fleeing white owners later estimated to be five thousand head of cattle and horses.[27] Most of the friendly Indians, however, did not participate in ransacking and burning white property. On the other hand, some French-Canadians and mixed bloods were not averse to taking whatever the fleeing settlers left behind.

In midautumn six Cayuses went to The Dalles, ostensibly to trade, declaring that they knew nothing of what the Indians were doing, but the white men there had reason to believe that they were up to something. After Haller's defeat Major Rains had begun assembling 335 regulars, three howitzers, a unit of regulars from Fort Steilacoom on Puget Sound, 19 dragoons, mounted volunteers from Oregon, and two other citizen companies—a force of more than 700 men. Their mission was to march to the Yakima country and punish the hostile Indians.

As the group moved toward the Yakima country, Indian scouts warned the Indians in its way that it was far bigger than Haller's command. Consequently, the Yakimas and their allies, including the Cayuse Yatiniawitz (Poor Crane),[28] prepared to escape the advancing troops and join other Cayuses, Umatillas, and Walla Wallas on the plateau. It was reported that Peopeomoxmox and

[25] *Ibid.*; Hezekiah Van Dorn, affidavit in McKay Papers.
[26] Thompson to Palmer, November 10, 1855, *Oregon Superintendency*, D:10, Roll 5.
[27] John McBean affidavit in McKay Papers.
[28] Charles Erskine Scott Wood, "Famous Indians: Portraits of Some Indian Chiefs," *Century Magazine*, O.S., XLVI, 3 (July, 1893), 445.

his forces would cut off Governor Stevens' party in that direction as it returned from the Blackfoot council.[29] In a battle at Union Gap in the Yakima country Rains and his motley army were successful in dislodging the enemy, driving many of them eastward across the Columbia, some toward the Spokane country to an unwelcome reception from neutral tribes in that area.

Superintendent Palmer must have had poor intelligence concerning Cayuse movement in the war zone, for he wrote General Jonathan Wool, commander of the Department of the Pacific, headquartered at Benicia, California, that he was "satisfied that the Cayuses, as a tribe, are desirous of maintaining peace, and that there must be on the part of the whites a departure from the principles of justice, and a violation of rights secured this tribe by the treaty, before they will become a hostile party in this war."[30] Palmer, of course, may have been referring to the friendly Cayuses. If this was the case, he was talking about perhaps less than 20 per cent of the tribe. Governor Stevens, Palmer's fellow commissioner at the Walla Walla council, admitted to the Washington Territorial Legislature in January, 1856, that the war had been plotted "for at least two or three years."[31]

At the very moment that Palmer was ascribing good intentions to the Cayuses, they were pursuing a course prompted by different ones. Many of them crossed the Columbia with Peopeomoxmox to pillage Fort Walla Walla and ride off with a share of its stores, leaving unwanted items lying about. There is evidence that the Cayuses burned Fort Waters and the sawmill and gristmill at Waiilatpu, as well as the sawmill at Mill Creek.[32] They were innocent, however, of burning the agency buildings on the Umatilla; that act was committed by Teninos en route to join the hostile Cayuses. They vainly sought Cayuse help in an attack at

29 *Message of the Governor of Washington Territory*, 63.
30 *Special Report of the Secretary of War, 1855–56*, Sen. Exec. Doc. No. 26, 34 Cong., 1 sess., Serial 819, p. 36.
31 Hazard Stevens, "The Pioneers and Patriotism," *Washington Historical Quarterly*, VIII, 3 (July, 1917), 174.
32 Garth, "Waiilatpu after the Massacre," 318 .

The Dalles, but the Cayuses were too busy tending their own front to engage in such an operation. Without Cayuse support, Tenino Chief Stockwhitley and his men were forced to remain in Cayuse country because alone they could neither fend off the white man nor storm his fortifications at The Dalles.

On the evening of November 18, Major Mark A. Chinn and 150 Oregon Mounted Volunteers arrived on the Umatilla at the site of the abandoned agency.³³ They might have come better armed had their commander, Colonel James W. Nesmith, been more successful in obtaining weapons from General Wool. Distrustful of the meritless objectives of the troops, Wool had been loath to extend them arms, which he feared would be used only to convulse the interior with more warfare. The day following their arrival, the troops began building a fort bearing a very unmilitary name, Henrietta, but appropriate, perhaps, since that was the name of Major Haller's wife. She had given the command its supply wagon.

While the fort was under construction, word came from Raymond (then in Cayuse country) via The Dalles that Peopeomoxmox had gone on a rampage.³⁴ Major Chinn dispatched some men to reconnoiter the surrounding area. They saw fresh tracks but no Indians, but brought in an Indian horse. On the evening of November 19 some Indians up the Umatilla met four scouts from the fort and promptly fired on them. The scouts returned the fire and chased the Indians into a larger body of their fellows; all escaped. The same Indians came upon some Hudson's Bay Company men en route to Fort Colville. Facing certain danger in that direction, the whites returned to Fort Henrietta. There over

³³ Chinn, a lawyer and former member of the Oregon Provisional Legislature, led companies under Captains Davis Layton and Orlando Humason.
³⁴ Colonel Nesmith immediately dispatched a company of volunteers under Captain L. B. Munson and on November 22 sent additional troops: two more companies from The Dalles, one under Captain Alfred B. Wilson and the other under Captain Narcisse Cornoyer, together with Donnell's. Reese, "The Exciting Story of Fort Henrietta," 3. It is possible that the packer was B. F. Dowell, whose train was captured by Indians on Wild Horse Creek. Dowell to McKay, August 7, 1889, McKay Papers.

the next few days the command cut and trimmed logs into nine-foot lengths, placing them endwise in a two-foot trench to make a 7-foot-high stockade enclosing a one-hundred-foot square. At two angles they began building blockhouses of cottonwood logs, constructed two rail corrals—one for horses and the other for cattle —and completed and filled a subterranean ammunition magazine.[35]

The Indians could now expect more detachments to ride out from the stronghold. On November 20 one band north of the fort was set upon by troops and chased to within eight miles of Fort Walla Walla. That same day an officer and eighteen men rode to Upper Crossing (of the Umatilla) on the Immigrant Road (near present-day Pendleton, Oregon), where they reported going to Dr. McKay's home at 11:00 P.M. They found it and other buildings ablaze and vainly attempted to extinguish the house fire.[36] They said they saw many Indian tracks but no Indians. Although the volunteers inferred that the Indians had set the house afire, Palmer later indicated that the troops were charged with having done so.[37]

On November 21 or 22 a large Indian force rode to a spot within one-and-a-half miles of Fort Henrietta and in a clear strip made a design in the sand. Indian dogs aroused a guard at his post near a large stone formation, known as Picket Rock, a mile east of the fort. The guard told the troops what the Indians had done. When the troops rode out, they discovered a large circle enclosing five smaller circles and a heart. In the smaller circles were twigs: four in each of two circles, three in one, and two in each of the others. In the center of the large circle was a single twig. Other troops, mountaineers, and Indian fighters called to study the design interpreted it as a message from Peopeomoxmox announc-

35 Reese, "The Exciting Story of Fort Henrietta," 5.

36 Ibid., 6.

37 Palmer to Manypenny, January 8, 1856, Microcopy of Records in the National Archives, Oregon Superintendency of Indian Affairs, 1848–1873, Letter Book E:10, Microfilm No. M-2, Roll 6 (cited hereafter as Oregon Superintendency, E:10, Roll 6).

ing that four hundred Cayuses, four hundred Yakimas, three hundred Klickitats, two hundred Teninos, and two hundred Palouses, all of one mind, were allied under his leadership.[38] The Indians lighted signal fires around the fort and kept it under surveillance, often moving undetected to within a hundred yards of it. Thus they kept surrounding tribes informed of the volunteers' movements.

Unknown to the Indians, the troops had nearly mutinied because they were restrained from making full-scale raids to harass the Indians and round up their stock.[39] On November 27 a party of volunteers rode to within three miles of Fort Walla Walla, where Indians on rocky heights nearby almost surrounded them; they finally escaped. When they did not return to Fort Henrietta within a reasonable time, a search party was dispatched. Its members saw about thirty Indians, who gave them no real trouble, before they returned to the fort without having sighted the missing group. That evening a second party was dispatched to look for the still-missing men, who did not return until the following morning. Despite the hide-and-seek nature of these sorties, the troops were undoubtedly pleased that they had been able to harass the Indians and capture seventeen horses.

On the night of November 28, signal fires blazed from the hilltops, perhaps warning the hostile Indians that reinforcements were approaching.[40] Heading the unit that reached the fort the next day was "hawk-nosed, heavy-set" Colonel James K. Kelly, who assumed Chinn's command.[41] Accompanying his party were Nathan Olney and six Tenino guides.

December 2 was a day of blinding snow followed by rain. After the arrival of Captain Charles Bennett and his command from

[38] Reese, "The Exciting Story of Fort Henrietta," 7.
[39] Ibid., 9.
[40] Ibid., 10.
[41] After the Indian wars, Kelly served as United States senator from Oregon and chief justice of the Oregon Supreme Court. He had been prevented from assuming command at Fort Henrietta because he was needed in the territorial legislature to make a quorum.

The Dalles, Colonel Kelly and most of his troops departed to make a surprise attack on the Indians. They rode through a cold night rain to Fort Walla Walla, found it deserted, and pressed up the Walla Walla River, where the main body of hostile Cayuses and their allies were gathered under Peopeomoxmox.

In their all-out effort to run down the Indians, the volunteers had left Fort Henrietta exposed. Taking advantage of their absence, the Indians raided the poorly defended post on the evening of December 4, killing a horse guard, Private William Andrews. As trophies they took his scalp and the skin of his bearded face. Indian scouting parties also made off with a pack string en route to the Walla Walla Valley. Not until the next day did Captains Thomas Cornelius and A. J. Hembree and their troops reach the Walla Walla.[42]

As he neared the valley, Colonel Kelly may not have known that the chief he sought to capture, Peopeomoxmox, had been involved in all kinds of intertribal maneuvers to strengthen the hostile group he commanded. The Nez Percés had sent him word through Lawyer and Red Wolf that they would not join him in war,[43] and Old Joseph had told him to mend his ways. He received a better response from Weatenatenamy, the Cayuse warrior. At the same time Five Crows and Camaspelo continued pressing Old Joseph to join the hostile cause with what must have been enticing words, since many Nez Percé headmen were reported as coming "within a hair's breadth of entering the war."[44] The Indians' overtures failed to dislodge Tintinemetsa and others from their neutrality.

Through the heat of the discussions Peopeomoxmox remained the chief of the hostile Indians, a position he had declared for himself when he blocked roads leading through the Walla Walla Valley to Nez Percé country.[45] Five Crows might have risen to

---

42 Later in December, Cornelius, a sergeant in the Cayuse War, was elected commander of the Oregon Mounted Volunteers, replacing Colonel Nesmith, who resigned.
43 Olney to Palmer, November 22, 1855, *Oregon Superintendency*, D:10, Roll 5.
44 Josephy, *Nez Perce Indians*, 355.

leadership of the warring bands, but he now lacked the aggressiveness to do so. Weatenatenamy was too young and inexperienced to challenge Peopeomoxmox.

On December 4 scouts from the hostile camp skirmished with Kelly's command as it moved up the Walla Walla Valley. The next day, near nightfall, the troops reached a point within three or four miles of the main hostile camp on the Touchet some twelve miles above its confluence with the Walla Walla.[46] Outnumbered four to one, Peopeomoxmox and fifty braves, carrying a white flag, rode out to meet Kelly. The Indians halted before the soldiers. When asked the meaning of their appearance, the old chief replied, "Peace."[47] The volunteers told him that he could either go back and fight or come with them. Accompanied by a four-man guard, Peopeomoxmox rode over to the soldiers, who disarmed him and his guard and placed them in custody. Governor Stevens later asserted that Peopeomoxmox surrendered only as a delaying tactic to permit his people to escape the advancing troops.[48]

Their leader in enemy hands, the Indians hastily abandoned camp before dawn on December 6, leaving fires burning and many unpacked provisions scattered about, some of which they had taken from abandoned Fort Walla Walla. When the troops and their prisoners entered the camp, Peopeomoxmox offered to pay for the goods his people had taken, whereupon the troops helped themselves to flour, corn, peas, wheat, sugar, coffee, pork, and anything else they could lay hands on.[49]

The hostile Indians kept watch along the horizon as the troops moved to the mouth of the Touchet, there to join a detachment of nearly fifty men returning from a search for the enemy. At this point on December 7 some three hundred Indians turned on the volunteers in an all-day engagement. Failing to dislodge them,

[45] Doty, "Journal of operations."
[46] Santee, "Pio-Pio-Mox-Mox," 173.
[47] Olney to Palmer, December 8, 1855, *Oregon Superintendency*, D:10, Roll 5.
[48] Stevens, *Speech*, 9.
[49] Palmer to Manypenny, January 8, 1856, *Oregon Superintendency*, E:10, Roll 6.

they pulled back to the east, firing at their pursuers. As the fighting shifted to a spot near the farm of a man named LaRoque, a couple of miles west of Waiilatpu, volunteers' fleet horses moved out ahead of the main body. The Indians barricaded themselves, held off their attackers for a time, but retreated as Captains Alfred Wilson and Bennett moved up with their units. Some of the Indians, barricaded in LaRoque's cabin, maintained harassing fire.[50] As his detachment charged the cabin, Bennett was struck by a bullet and collapsed. Another volunteer was also hit, but the Indians were dislodged.

Now an attempt was made to bind Peopeomoxmox and the men with him. One of the Indians, unable to bear such indignity, drew his knife to resist. For this impulsive gesture, he, Peopeomoxmox, and the others were shot down. Then, General Wool reported to the assistant adjutant general in New York, the volunteers took from the chief's head "some twenty scalps, cut off his ears and hands, and sent them as trophies to their friends in Oregon."[51] Before the campaign was over, a volunteer claimed to have scalped another Indian, boasting, "I had made a good Indian of him."[52]

The chief's scalp could be said to be Exhibit A in the continuing argument between General Wool and the volunteers over the conduct of the war. A spokesman for the latter, Governor Stevens, after interviewing friendly Cayuses about the slaying, reported to Wool that "Pee-pee-mox-mox was slain fairly . . . not entrapped by a flag of truce." The governor concluded his remarks on the affair with the conscience-salving statement that he reprobated "the indignities subsequently committed upon his [the chief's] person."[53] To Secretary of War Jefferson Davis he

50 The LaRoque cabin was built in 1824. B. C. Payette (ed.), *Captain John Mullan*, 266. The cabin was torn down in 1912. Clem Bergevin interview, Walla Walla, Washington, July 19, 1968. Other free trappers and their Indian wives, mostly Flatheads, lived in the vicinity. A settlement, called Frenchtown, later sprang up near there.

51 Secretary of War, *Annual Report, 1855–56*, 58.

52 Fred Lockley, *Oregon's Yesterdays*, 182.

53 Secretary of War, *Annual Report, 1855–56*, 40.

justified the chief's death on the grounds that Peopeomoxmox had endeavored to ambush the volunteers.[54] After investigating reports of the death, Superintendent Palmer wrote:

> No attempt I am told was made by them to escape till it was attempted to bind them. Thus, the chief and four of his men were put to death. . . . Many contradictory reports are current as to the manner of the death of these Indians, and the official report does not explain, nor are its statements in relation to this subject based upon actual observation. The officers are of course compelled to receive the statements of those entrusted with their keeping.[55]

The next morning, December 8, the Indians, now reinforced by a hundred Palouses, resumed the battle before the volunteers had finished breakfast. About five hundred Indians fought fiercely until darkness settled over nearly fifty of their dead, almost half of whom the whites found. Stunned by a bullet wound in the head, Cayuse Red Elk feigned death for two days and then crawled to his comrades,[56] who had mortally wounded eight volunteers.

Two days later, confronted by two companies of reinforcements from Fort Henrietta, the Indians withdrew. The troops moved to a spot two miles above Waiilatpu and built a fort. The Cayuses safely crossed the Snake River to encamp with their Palouse allies, remaining two weeks and sending spies into the Walla Walla Valley to keep an eye on the soldiers' movements. Some friendly Cayuses were in winter camp three miles above the treaty grounds on Mill Creek and nine miles above Kelly's camp. Twenty-five French-Canadians were also in the valley.

The hostile Cayuses went daily to the camp of the friendly Indians, using "every exertion both pursuasion [sic] and threats" to get them to join the hostile cause, but with little success.[57]

---

54 *Ibid.*, 6.

55 Palmer to Manypenny, January 8, 1856. *Oregon Superintendency*, E:10, Roll 6.

56 "A Story of Oregon," *Colliers Weekly*, June 29, 1912, p. 9.

57 Truitt to Palmer, December 18, 1855, *Oregon Superintendency*, Microfilm No. 2, Roll 13.

Headquartered there was Truitt, assigned by Olney as special agent to the friendly Cayuses, Umatillas, and Walla Wallas. In a report, presumably to Superintendent Palmer, Truitt recommended as deserving of protection certain Cayuse chiefs—Howlish Wampo, Tintinemetsa, Stickus, Twelhantemany, Catulpee, Cheanumkun, and Latasee—and Pierre of the Walla Wallas. According to Truitt, they had been threatened with "their destruction" by the soldiers should they harbor the hostile Indians.[58] When he chose Truitt, Palmer bypassed John McBean, whom he described as "the son of the notorious McBean who had charge of the fort [Walla Walla] at the time of the Whitman massacre."[59] Olney hired McBean anyway. Nor did Palmer approve of Raymond for special agent, although the French-Canadian still acted in a local capacity.

Homeward bound from treaty making in the Blackfoot country, Governor Stevens arrived in the Walla Walla Valley by way of Lapwai with nearly seventy armed Nez Percés.[60] He reported seeing no hostiles. The Nez Percés told him things were livelier in the vicinity of their home camp and complained that the Cayuses and Walla Wallas would not allow friendly Nez Percés to traverse the valley en route to The Dalles to trade. Before Stevens concluded a council he had set up in the Walla Walla Valley, the Nez Percés learned that Peopeomoxmox was dead.

On December 16, as Stevens traveled down the Snake near Red Wolf's camp, a Nez Percé in his party saw a strange Indian brought into camp. It proved to be the son of Umhowlish. He said that his father and another man and some women were camped four miles away. Umhowlish had fled there during the last day of the battle, the son said, and had not participated in it. Stevens did not believe the story and sent the Indian back to his father with the following message: "If Ume-how-lish would come in and deliver himself up to the Governor as an unconditional prisoner, he

58 *Ibid.*
59 Palmer to Manypenny, January 8, 1856, *Oregon Superintendency*, E:10, Roll 6.
60 Palmer to Olney, December 12, 1855, *Oregon Superintendency*, D:10, Roll 5.

should have a trial by the White mans [*sic*] law on reaching the settlements, and an opportunity to prove wither [*sic*] or not he was engaged in the War."[61] Umhowlish went to Stevens' camp, insisting that he had done no wrong and expressing fear of being tried by white man's law. Unmoved, the governor took him prisoner.

Stevens' action demonstrated the persistence with which he was pursuing his goal of pacifying the interior and subjecting the Indians to the white American civilization he represented. Did he sincerely believe that such a policy would remain unchallenged by those against whom it was directed?

[61] Doty, "Journal of operations."

XIV
The Volcano Erupts

The northern tribes Governor Stevens visited in his program of pacification and subjection—such as the Spokanes and the Coeur d'Alenes—disliked what he said, but not enough to engage in a war. Most Nez Percés remained friendly, as attested to by the escort they provided him to the Walla Walla. He integrated the Nez Percé guard escort at Lapwai into the militia, just as he activated the Spokane Invincibles to protect himself and his party on the way home. On December 20 he reached Mill Creek, where he found a hundred friendly Cayuses encamped with Howlish Wampo, Stickus, Tintinemetsa, and Pierre with a few Walla Wallas. He made camp near the mission site but on Christmas Eve moved upstream four miles to a more sheltered spot with a supply of wood—a vital necessity because temperatures were dipping to nearly thirty degrees below zero at night. With the Cayuses at Waiilatpu were Captain Narcisse A. Cornoyer, special agent Victor Truitt, and about twenty-five French-Canadians. They may be said to have been more frightened than friendly, since they were under pressure to join the hostile Indians and threatened by the soldiers if they did. The troops did more than make threats; they took pot shots at the Cayuses without bothering to determine whether they were friendly or hostile.

The friendly Indians had Stevens as their neighbor until the last of the month. On December 29 he called them into council to say: "It is best for all those who did not fight to come in and show that they were friendly. Here are Stick-as, How-lish-wam-poo and others that you know—they staid [stayed]. We regard those who staid as friendly and those who ran away as enemies, and they will have to show that they were friendly." Cut Finger (a Cayuse?), responded: "It is the news of the troops coming that made the Cayuse run." Stevens replied that those not joining the friendly Indians would be considered hostile and then praised Stickus and Howlish Wampo for remaining at peace in the valley.

In assessing the recent engagements, Looking Glass said that it had been Cayuse lies about the whites which had made the Cayuses flee and fight. At this point Stickus rose to defend his people, blaming Kamiakin for sending runners to entice them onto the warpath, which had taken them in the wrong direction. He said his relatives were sick and had been left to die, that many had died, and that his son-in-law was not among the hostile Indians but was in buffalo country with Tahwat-tus-son, who likewise was innocent of any fighting. Stickus asserted that he had not come to tell lies, for people who did so were poor.[1]

The Cayuses said that they had come to the council to learn whether they could move to Looking Glass's country, as he said they could. The Nez Percé replied that those with bad words could not come but that, since those at the council were good, they could do so. Expressing his fear of the soldiers, Stickus said he would be only too happy to leave. The Nez Percé Spotted Eagle said that he was glad to hear the Cayuses talk thus, that it looked as if they wished to live and do right when they spoke of joining his people.

The meeting continued the next day. Revealing no other plans for the friendly Cayuses, Stevens said that it was impossible for him to comply with their request to move to the Nez Percé country and that he would leave them an agent and a place to live in the Walla Walla Valley. The governor then departed, taking Umhowlish prisoner. He ordered the Nez Percés mustered out of service and told William Craig, now a lieutenant colonel, to take whatever action was necessary against hostile Indians in Nez Percé country.[2] He also activated a military company of

[1] Doty, "Journal of operations."
[2] Ibid.

ten white men living in the Walla Walla Valley; under the command of Thomas Cornelius, now a colonel, they were to watch over the friendly Indians.

In January, 1856, the friendly Indians at Waiilatpu were visited by Father Chirouse, and what the priest saw led him to believe they were in unsafe hands. On January 15 he wrote to Father Mesplié at The Dalles:

> The volunteers are without discipline, without order, and similar to madmen. Menaced with death every day, the inhabitants of the country, and the Indians who have so nobly followed the order of Mr. Palmer to remain faithful friends of the Americans, have already disposed of their provisions.
>
> To-day these same volunteers are not yet satisfied with rapine and injustice, and wish to take away the small remnant of animals and provisions left. Every day they run off the horses and cattle of the friendly Indians. . . .
>
> I call upon the justice of men, and particularly upon General Wool. Let him send us fifty regular troops, at least, to protect us and the friendly Indians, and stop the grand combination of savages.[3]

Chirouse feared that under such unfavorable surroundings the friendly Indians would join the hostile ones to make even grander the "grand combination" of which he wrote.

When he received a copy of Chirouse's letter, Superintendent Palmer sent it on to General Wool with the comment that the picture of the volunteers "may be strongly drawn, but unfortunately for the character and reputation of our Troops I fear it is too true." He added:

> I am of opinion that nothing short of the immediate occupancy of that Country by regular U.S. Troops can save these Tribes from a participation in this war—the result of which would be to deluge the Country in blood and cast a stain of reproach upon our national reputation, as it is within our power to prevent it and restore our Country to a state of peace and quietude.[4]

3 Secretary of Interior, *Annual Report, 1856–57, House Exec. Doc.* No. 1, 34 Cong., 3 sess., Serial 893, p. 746.
4 Palmer to Wool, January 27, 1856, *Oregon Superintendency*, E:10, Roll 6.

Palmer, in whose jurisdiction lay the reservation established for the Cayuses, wanted to colonize them there. He asked Wool for a hundred troops to proceed at once to the Cayuse country to assist agents in establishing an Indian encampment on the reservation (on the Umatilla at Upper Crossing near the old camps of Five Crows and Tauitau). The superintendent believed it useless to establish the encampment without help from the military arm of the federal government.

In the Walla Walla Valley, Stevens met special agent B. F. Shaw, now a colonel in the Washington Territorial Militia, placed him in command of an organized district, and directed him to fortify the grounds, if necessary, should the Oregon Mounted Volunteers be disbanded. The militia, raised by Acting Governor Charles H. Mason, was to be deployed in the Spokane country to meet Stevens and ensure his safety on his return from the Blackfoot council. General Wool delayed its march by refusing to outfit it, believing reports that the governor was in danger were greatly exaggerated. This, of course, further aggravated the ill feeling between Stevens and Wool. Stevens preferred charges against Wool, calling for an investigation of the general, who he claimed was willing "to play the part of the dog in the manger, neither to act himself nor to let others act."[5]

The hostile Cayuses did not know of Stevens' elaborate plans for their pursuit and demise, even to the barging of supplies up the Columbia River for delivery to the Walla Walla Valley. Neither would they have known of his plan to deploy a thousand troops (five hundred volunteers and five hundred regulars) to drive them northward to the Canadian border.[6] Some of them had already headed in that direction. After Peopeomoxmox died, Palouse Chief Tilcoax offered the Cayuses a haven in his country —and also horses.[7] Kamiakin accorded the affluent and crafty Tilcoax equal rank for help he might give in harassing the whites.

[5] Secretary of War, *Annual Report, 1855–56*, 9.
[6] *Ibid.*, 12–13.
[7] Doty, "Journal of operations."

In the territorial capital, Olympia, Stevens urged Army Colonel George Wright, commanding the Columbia River District, and Major Gabriel J. Rains to dispatch troops to the interior. They refused, citing the "stringent orders" of General Wool. The basic difference between Stevens and Wool was crystallizing around the fact that Wool, although he was not underestimating difficulties with the Indians, preferred to overawe them with the mere presence of troops. Stevens, on the other hand, was anxious to defeat them—shooting first and asking questions later—under the guise of protecting whites. The governor had elaborate plans for securing the interior.[8]

After assessing the situation, Wool wrote that when Oregon Governor George L. Curry dispatched the volunteers to the interior "something had to be done." A fight with the Indians, he said, no matter whether friend or enemy, "was indispensable to excite the sympathy of the nation, and especially Congress, or the propriety of paying contributions, so profusely levied on the people of Oregon might be questioned."[9] Both Stevens and Curry requested Wool's dismissal.

The Cayuses had a friend in General Wool. On February 12, 1856, he informed Stevens that they were daily "menaced with death by Governor Curry's volunteers" and that, when he (Wool) had instructed Colonel Wright (with four or five companies, three howitzers, and a six-pounder, but no volunteers) to take possession of the Walla Walla country, he had charged him with protecting the friendly Indians from depredations by the volunteers. Further, Wool wrote, if Curry's volunteers had not already driven friendly Cayuses and Nez Percés into the ranks of hostile tribes, he hoped the governor would be able to bring the Indians of the region to terms, the butchery of Peopeomoxmox notwithstanding.[10]

Stevens kept up his fight on two fronts, one against General

8 Secretary of War, *Annual Report, 1855–56*, 9–14.
9 *Ibid.*, 57.
10 *Ibid.*, 38.

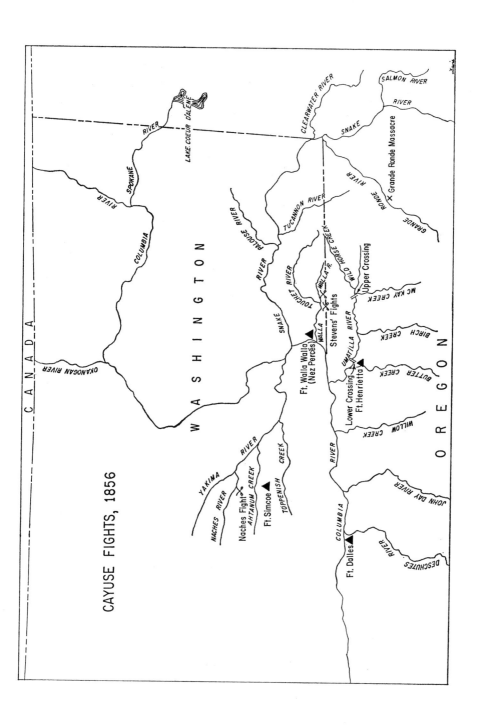

CAYUSE FIGHTS, 1856

Wool and the other against the Indians. He wanted to attack the Indians in late winter, but Wool would not begin operations until spring. This late start, Stevens believed, would render the whole industrial community "ruined" and "paralyzed" with fear and fields untilled. Wool, on the other hand, viewed the industrial community as a source of matériel to be used in waging a crusade against the Indians at the expense of Congress, which would have to foot the bill.[11]

Early in January, 1856, a large number of hostile Cayuses moved in with Nez Percé relatives before Stevens could catch them in his planned invasion of Indian country. The Cayuse hotbloods hounded their hosts to declare hostility toward the whites. At the same time, from their camps among the Palouses some Cayuses drifted down the Snake toward its junction with the Columbia. Others joined the Palouses at the mouth of the Palouse River after being rebuffed by Nez Percé chiefs, such as Looking Glass, who told them to "go and stand their trial."[12] Among the Nez Percés angered by Cayuse pressure were Three Feathers and Eagle from the Light, who wished to purge themselves of their belligerent neighbors because some of their own people had been fired upon by whites who could not tell the two tribes apart.

Bands of hostile Cayuses rode the countryside, spying for their people. One such party discovered Colonel James K. Kelly and seventeen men heading east, by way of Upper Crossing, over melting snows to the Walla Walla Valley. Near the crossing the Indians captured nine horses, among them Kelly's fine riding horse. As one of the soldiers rode back to Fort Henrietta to get more mounts, the others set out with all they had—Indian horses.[13] The colonel described his substitute mount as a "chuckle-headed Indian pony with no form or size; only a mean cayuse." However, one of his men defended the horse, which

11 *Ibid.*, 26.
12 Craig to B. F. Shaw, January 30, 1856, *Washington Superintendency*, Microfilm No. 5, Roll 21.
13 Reese, "The Exciting Story of Fort Henrietta," 13.

started to buck as the party reached the Walla Walla encampment: "If the question of avoirdupois comes in, the pony must have some credit. He must have been something of a 'hoss,' if he was only a cayuse, to handle the colonel's 'heavy weight' so easily."[14]

Chased from their garden spots, root grounds, and fisheries and robbed of their food caches, some of the Cayuses desperately began to seek a way out of the war. Craig wrote Stevens that on January 25 five hostile Indians, four of them Cayuses, came to his house and told him that they wanted peace. The agent advised them to turn themselves in. Not all of them did; to have done so would have meant certain death.[15]

A severe blow to the Cayuses was the winter death of many horses, driven from their usual valley pastures.[16] Some of the weakened animals drowned as their fleeing owners attempted to swim them across rivers; others were abandoned in the Nez Percé country. Stevens had told the Nez Percés to divide such horses among themselves, and so the Cayuses were forced to raid for mounts, as well as for food to fill their empty stomachs. While they were among the Nez Percés they tried to recruit allies.[17] The need for horses was great, however, and in an attempt to replenish their supply, the Cayuses turned to the volunteers. It was said that an Indian party rode to Fort Henrietta about midnight on February 15, found only twelve men guarding the post, and promptly captured three hundred horses. The animals later turned up at The Dalles in the possession of several whites who were planning to drive them to California.[18] The question was,

14 *Ibid.* Kelly was returning from a legislative council session. Colonel Cornelius, who assumed command of the volunteers at Walla Walla when Kelly left, continued in that capacity.

15 Craig to Stevens [n.d.], 1856, *Washington Superintendency*, Microfilm No. 5, Roll 21.

16 *Annual Report of the Commissioner of Indian Affairs*, 1856, 206.

17 Craig to Stevens, February 10, 1856; Craig to Stevens [n.d.], 1856, *Washington Superintendency*, Microfilm No. 5, Roll 21.

18 Andrew D. Pambrun, who returned to the interior in 1856, tells of a band of horses, supposedly stolen by Indians, that was shipped to California. Pambrun, "Story of his life," 142.

How did the whites obtain them? When a white man's horses were stolen, the Indians usually got the blame. In such cases, of course, there was always the possibility that the Indians had sold the stolen horses to unscrupulous whites.

Whatever the identity of the thieves, Fort Henrietta was left horseless until more could be driven in. "Vengeance on the whole Indian race" was sworn by the troops. "Talk is talk," they said, "but it takes work to get horses in this country."[19] Even Governor Curry wondered why horses were lost at the fort from time to time. He was concerned because the animals were to have been used in a campaign by a Fort Henrietta–bound battalion of four hundred recruits.

The Indians needed all the horses they could get to continue their raids against the soldiers. In February they captured thirteen wagonloads of supplies, including ammunition en route from the Umatilla to the Walla Walla Valley. In mid-March a band of Indian raiders met a party of whites out looking for cattle, killed one of them, and took all their horses.[20] Colonel Cornelius kept close watch on his mounts and ordered his camp moved to a site near the Catholic mission to provide better grass and water. Logs from a cottonwood grove were used to build a corral. Two nights later Indians on a nearby bluff showered the volunteers with bullets.

Early spring found the Cayuses and their allies again pressed by the volunteers. Fearing this pressure would send the Indians north into the plateau and his lands, Chief Garry of the Spokanes wrote to his friend Governor Stevens requesting a military detachment to protect his people.[21] In mid-March, Oregon troops moved to the Palouse country, seizing Indian stock and shooting Indians. In an engagement near the mouth of the Tucannon the volunteers killed nine braves. Toward the end of the month the soldiers veered west, endeavoring to trap Cayuses and two Tenino

19 Reese, "The Exciting Story of Fort Henrietta," 14.
20 Pambrun, "Story of his life,"145.
21 Secretary of War, *Annual Report, 1855–56*, 43.

bands which had separated from their Palouse allies. The Tenino band under Stockwhitley remained with the hostile Cayuses, and the other went with Kamiakin.[22]

After the hard winter of 1855–56 more Cayuses rode to the Nez Percé country with expressions of peace; others went only to replenish their supply of horses so that they could continue the war. In the Nez Percé camps friendly Cayuses maintained communication with the hostile Indians. Had the Cayuses been sent to the more isolated proposed Warm Springs Reservation in interior Oregon Territory south of The Dalles, as Palmer had suggested to the commissioner of Indian affairs,[23] they would have had much more difficulty communicating with their hostile fellow tribesmen. That the area was the home of their ancestors would have made little difference to them. Several bands of Wascopums, scheduled for removal to Warm Springs in March, did not want to go without military protection, fearing that free-roaming hostile Cayuses could raid them more easily there than at The Dalles.

To keep hostile Cayuses and Nez Percés apart, Craig organized a volunteer company of white settlers and Indians. They succeeded in capturing a hostile Palouse named Umetaquitat. Craig tried him and, on the Indian's confession of guilt, ordered him hanged the next day.[24] About March 12, Cornelius and his Walla Walla–based volunteers moved out after the hostile Indians, who kept him under surveillance. When he crossed the Snake, other Indians who had moved west crossed over to the Columbia's right bank. When the volunteers approached, still others went north to the Spokane country to remain until the command had crossed the Columbia near the mouth of the Snake, at which time they returned to the Palouse.

Umhowlish attended a large council held in Nez Percé country in March with a friendly message from Colonel Wright. As the

[22] *Annual Report of the Commissioner of Indian Affairs, 1856*, 206, 210.
[23] *Ibid.*, 197.
[24] Craig to Stevens, March 22, 1856, *Washington Superintendency*, Microfilm No. 5, Roll 21.

Indians listened to him, they knew that even if the soldiers wanted peace there would be none because Craig's rough treatment of hostile Cayuses would cause them to fight on.[25] Captain Henri M. Chase, commanding Craig's volunteers, appeared after learning that five lodges of hostile Cayuses and the head chief were camped on the right bank of the Snake below Red Wolf's. However, someone warned the Indians. Four lodges made good their escape; four men and a number of women and horses were captured. Umhowlish left the Nez Percé camp in search of them, finally running them down in the Spokane country. Among the refugees there he found Five Crows and Camaspelo, who had fled when Cornelius moved north across the Snake. Continuing to play the role of peacemaker, Umhowlish repeated his message of friendship, which the two spurned, doubting the validity of any offer from whites. Moreover, they said, they were not yet tired of fighting.[26]

On March 22, 1856, Craig wrote Stevens: "I understand that some of the war party have gone into that country and Indian report says that [Angus] McDonald [Hudson's Bay Company chief trader at Fort Colville] sent some tobacco to the Cayuse chief and invited him to come to Fort Colville. Gary was the bearer of the message."[27] Craig investigated the report about McDonald. The trader said he had not been in touch with Weatenatenamy, the Cayuse chief in question, but had, through a man named Henry Shuttleworth, sent an inquiry to Five Crows to determine whether the trail was open for the company. Five Crows said it was, an indication that the company still held a favored position among the Cayuses; it had not wanted to take their land.[28]

When Five Crows and Camaspelo said that they were not yet tired of fighting, they were expressing a view shared by Indians over a wide area of the interior. In one Yakima-led attack on the

25 Craig to Stevens [n.d.], 1856, ibid.
26 Ibid.
27 Craig to Stevens, March 22, 1856, ibid.
28 McDonald to Craig, May 13, 1856, ibid.

Cascades of the Columbia, James Sinclair, the last trader at Fort Walla Walla, was killed. He had failed to receive immunity from Indian trouble such as the Hudson's Bay Company traders enjoyed. As a result of the raid, the local agent confiscated the Indians' firearms. Former Utilla Agency chief Robert R. Thompson described such actions as coming from a "desperate set of men . . . awaiting a plea to justify them in the slightest degree . . . [to] pounce upon these defenceless Indians and massacre them, without regard to justice, humanity, age, sex, or anything else."[29]

Meanwhile, the military quickened its efforts to catch the hostiles. When the detachment of volunteers under Cornelius reached the Columbia near the mouth of the Snake, the party divided, some of it returning to the Walla Walla Valley and the rest going with Cornelius across the Columbia to search up the Yakima River. There a brief skirmish was fought, and the volunteers returned to The Dalles, where there was much evidence that the army had also resumed its campaign against the hostiles: Colonel Wright had arrived with eight companies of the Ninth U.S. Infantry and had set up his headquarters.

Early on the morning of April 20, sixty Indians raided the vicinity of Fort Henrietta, killing and scalping a horse guard, Private Lot Hollinger, and driving off his horses. They headed south to the headwaters of Butter Creek, outwitting the soldiers at the fort, who thought they would drive the stolen stock north across the Columbia River. From the fort, now strengthened by two companies of Kelly's command, which reached there on April 16, troops took to the raiders' trail, pursuing them for several days. The retreating Indians moved to the comparative safety of the Columbia right bank.[30]

As spring softened in the upcountry, so did Five Crows and Weatenatenamy, who began to weary of their flight. In a letter to Stevens, Garry said the two, "acting for the tribe," wanted peace. The Spokane chief also said he thought it would be all

[29] *Annual Report of the Commissioner of Indian Affairs, 1856*, 211.
[30] Reese, "The Exciting Story of Fort Henrietta," 16–17.

right to make a peace with the Cayuses and not with the Yakimas. Stevens, however, did not view the situation in the same light. In a communication to the commissioner of Indian affairs, he called Five Crows one of the "most vindictive enemies of the whites, and one of the original instigators of the war." Wrote Stevens: "In my mind his presence there [in the Spokane country] is indicative as much, or even more, that the Spokanes are ready to join in the war, as that the Cayuses are desirous of peace."[31]

A party of seventy Cayuses, Spokanes, and other Indians went to Red Wolf's Crossing looking for horses for the Spokanes to ride, but it was reported that "they talked very saucy."[32] There followed a heated exchange between them and Looking Glass, who warned them not to come among his Nez Percés. The Cayuses explained that they had received word from Craig, who, on orders from Stevens, had requested them to come in and talk, which they said they would do some other time, when the governor was not so far away.

Keeping the governor away was his quarrel with General Wool, which had now spilled into the camps of the Cayuses, who repeatedly told the Nez Percés that Colonel Wright, one of Wool's soldiers, wanted peace but that Stevens' order to keep Cayuses out of Nez Percé country was causing all the trouble. Now some Nez Percés began to question Stevens' action in preventing the Cayuses from returning to Nez Percé lands contrary to the wishes of the government. Craig told them that the governor wanted to keep the Cayuses away and that "he alone must be obeyed."[33] The whole affair caused much bitter feeling among the Indians.

In late April, Colonel Wright and a detachment of 350 men left The Dalles for the Yakima country on a peacemaking expedition. On May 11 he was greeted by 1,200 to 1,500 warriors in a skirmish south of the Naches River, a Yakima tributary. The

31 *Annual Report of the Commissioner of Indian Affairs, 1856,* 189.
32 Craig to Stevens, May 27, 1856, *Washington Superintendency*, Microfilm No. 5, Roll 21.
33 Craig to Stevens [n.d.], 1856, *ibid.*

colonel sent for reinforcements to meet "the confederated tribes," which included warriors from the coast and elements of all hostile tribes east of the Cascade Mountains. After the battle Kamiakin left on a reinforcement-seeking tour of his own among the Spokanes, Coeur d'Alenes, and Nez Percés. He succeeded in recruiting a few braves among those tribes, as well as some Okanogans and Colvilles who had come down to join the Cayuses and Palouses.

Kamiakin sent word to all the Indians that he wished the Nez Percés to meet him in council "at the Kamash [camas] Ground." The meeting was held, but Kamiakin was not present. Two of his brothers were, however, and they apparently worked out a new approach to dislodge the Nez Percés from their neutrality. The two Yakimas said that their friends in Wright's camp had told them that the whites intended to wage an indiscriminate war on all the Indians throughout the country, that the whites wanted to keep the Indians divided so that it would be easier to kill them all, and that if the Indians were going to die anyway they had better take to the warpath.

After the council the Cayuses were again reported passing through Nez Percé country and "talking very saucy."[34] Some of them were on their way to the Snake country to solicit aid from their enemies. One Snake party joined them, but another, after doing so, betrayed them. Accompanying a large group of Cayuses, Walla Wallas, Umatillas, and Teninos into the Grande Ronde, the Snakes suddenly fell upon a camp of Cayuses and a few Umatillas. Stung by deceit, the outnumbered Cayuses fought fiercely, but some of them were killed. The others, including the Umatillas, escaped, abandoning their old, young, and crippled. A band of Cayuses camped some distance away with some Walla Wallas learned of the disaster too late to render help. A few gave chase but failed to free the captives after a desultory fight.

Besieged with enticements by Yakima and other hostile emissaries, the Nez Percés felt strongly disposed to join the warring

[34] *Ibid.*

237

ones. Aware of their disposition, Colonel Shaw and a volunteer force—sent to the Yakima by Stevens but not wanted there by Wright—headed toward the Walla Walla Valley, where he found some Oregon Mounted Volunteers. Because of the alarming news from the Nez Percé country, Stevens dispatched another column to the Walla Walla on June 22. A detachment from that command was turned south to the Umatilla to help the Oregon volunteers, who had become embroiled with hostile bands between John Day and Snake rivers. The rest of the command reached the Walla Walla on June 9 and joined Shaw's men.

In July the situation became so acute that packers bringing supplies to volunteers in Nez Percé country gathered twenty-five hundred agitated Indians to talk things over. Causing this state of affairs were "excitable tales" raised and circulated by the Cayuses who were present.[35] A number of Nez Percé chiefs angrily refused to permit any more pack trains to enter their country. Stopped in its tracks, one train returned to Shaw's Walla Walla camp, whereupon the colonel promptly sent a message to Craig demanding an explanation of the demonstrations.

Matters became so precarious that Stevens decided to call a second Walla Walla council. Although many Nez Percés had gone to the hunting and fishing grounds before Craig left for the council on August 28, he had ordered them to return when the meeting convened. The Cayuses had gone to their root grounds. Meanwhile, Shaw's men were impatient for action. He thought that a scout of the Grande Ronde would give them a chance to blow off steam—and perhaps scald a few Indians. Why he chose a spot so far away is not clear—unless it was suggested by Captain John, a Nez Percé friend of Lawyer and Stevens, who acted as guide.

In July some old men, a few young ones, women, children, and a few Walla Walla families camped in the Grande Ronde about eight miles southeast of present-day Elgin, Oregon, to harvest roots. As they were going about their duties early on the morning

35 *Ibid.*

238

of the seventeenth, mounted men from Shaw's command burst upon them, throwing them into a panic. They hurriedly began tossing their gear together for a hasty retreat. The young men rode out to meet the troops, while the other Indians sought to get their families moving. Captain John rode up to speak with the young Cayuses. After a heated exchange of words the Cayuses shouted to one another to shoot him. (According to Shaw's report, the Indians had approached them dangling a white man's scalp on a pole.) Shaw formed his men in line for battle; the guide wheeled and rode back to the volunteers, who then charged. Some families fled in confusion to the brush along the Grande Ronde River, while others ran downstream. Thinking that the Indians were setting up an ambush in the thicket, Shaw split his command, one detachment to cross the river near the Indian camp, the other to march downstream to hold a ford there. The Indians were no match for the soldiers. Old men, women, and children were shot down as they ran for cover. In Shaw's words, "The charge was vigorous and so well sustained that they were broken, dispersed and slain before us."[36]

Shaw showed no mercy. His troops killed a number of Indians running downstream to the ford. Those fortunate enough to escape across the river fled to rocky canyons leading toward the Powder River and then scattered. The fighting lasted until about 1:00 P.M.[37] The detachment which had crossed the river at the campsite fired on another knot of Indians and continued to shoot at them throughout the day. The greater part of the detachment then became separated from the main body, who had ridden back to the camp to destroy the Indians' goods: 150 horseloads of camas, dried beef, flour, coffee, sugar, lodges, ammunition, tools, and assorted other gear. The troops also captured about two hundred horses, most of which they shot.[38]

In the vicinity of the first attack, Shaw's men counted twenty-

[36] William Compton Brown, *The Indian Side of the Story*, 161.
[37] "Autobiography of P. H. Roundtree," in *Told by the Pioneers: Reminiscences of Pioneer Life in Washington*, II, 98.
[38] Brown, *Indian Side of the Story*, 162–63.

seven dead Indians, whose strewed skeletons lay exposed for years. The colonel estimated that his command had killed forty Indians and wounded many more; five whites were killed and four wounded. The volunteers rode back to Walla Walla in separate groups to report their victory. General Wool saw it differently. To him it was the last "strike" of the Washington Territorial Volunteer Army raised by Stevens. "Unfortunately for the glory of this achievement," Wool wrote, "it has been reported that 'the whole object was to plunder the Indians of their horses and cattle, and provoke a prolongation of the war.' "[39]

As Shaw's men returned, a young Walla Walla chief named Homily, seeking to avenge the Grande Ronde massacre, selected ten Walla Wallas and two Cayuses to plunder the volunteers' pack train. The Indians crawled to within a few yards of it, whereupon the whites stole away, after tying their horses to the packs as decoys. With the whites in flight and the troops safely on their way home, the Indians moved in, took the horses and packs, and fled to the mountains. In the packs they discovered two kegs of whisky; Homily emptied one on the ground but permitted his men to drink from the other. The volunteers apparently did not intend to let the Indians go unpunished for the deed; the following morning they tried to even the score again in a brief skirmish.[40]

The volcano which Nathan Olney had said was "about ready to break forth" on October 12, 1855, was about to erupt again. Never in their peaceful history with the whites had the Nez Percés shown such hostility. To keep the volcano from erupting, General Wool issued the following order on August 2, 1856:

No emigrants or other whites, except the Hudson's Bay Company, or persons having ceded rights from the Indian, will be

[39] General John E. Wool, "General description of the military department of the Pacific," 59–60. The number of volunteers killed is taken from Brown, *Indian Side of the Story*, 165. Another account states that three volunteers were killed and three wounded. Seymour Dunbar and Paul G. Phillips (eds.), *The Journals and Letters of Major John Owen, Pioneer of the Northwest, 1850–1871*, I, 138.
[40] Pambrun, "Story of his life," 147–48.

permitted to settle or remain in the Indian country, or on land not ceded by treaty, confirmed by the Senate, and approved by the President of the United States. These orders are not, however, to apply to miners engaged in collecting gold at the Colville mines. The miners will, however, be notified that, should they interfere with the Indians or their squaws, they will be punished and sent out of the country.[41]

By issuing the order, Wool hoped to make the Cascade Mountains a wall separating land-hungry coastal settlers from Indian lands in the interior.

Governor Stevens believed that by holding a council with the Indians he could obviate the need for such a wall. He would go to Walla Walla to placate them in council. He had gone there a year earlier in hope; he would now go in apprehension. On his first trip he had sought to confine the Indians in peace; he would now seek to restrain them from war.

[41] Secretary of War, *Annual Report, 1856–57*, *Sen. Exec. Doc.* No. 5, 34 Cong., 3 sess., Serial 876, p. 169.

XV
Broken Power

The Cayuses, Walla Wallas, and Teninos, "with unconcealed hostility," began to arrive on August 30, 1856, in the valley of the Walla Walla. The Spokanes and Coeur d'Alenes refused Governor Stevens' invitation to attend the council. To taunt Colonel Shaw's men, now returning from the Grande Ronde, a number of Indians rode in mounted on stolen pack mules and wearing clothes belonging to the volunteers. Interpreter-guide Andrew D. Pambrun noted that "under the circumstances we hid our chagrin with smiles," which the Indians regarded as insincere but nevertheless "smiled in turn with apparent satisfaction."[1]

The Nez Percés were the first to enter the council grounds. The little iron cannon firing a welcome to them "could not stand such a pressure and on the third discharge flew into a thousand pieces, but singlurly [sic], tho' surrounded by a large crowd, not a man was hurt."[2] An ominous beginning. Would the council also blow up? Walla Walla Chief Homily said he was unsure of the nature of the council, which in truth was ill-defined. But an explanation from Pambrun seemingly caused him to express willingness to cooperate in the discussions, despite his remark that, although not whipped, he pitied the old and the crippled, who, on crutches, were unable to escape the soldiers. "I sometimes thought of drowning them all and keep on fighting," he lamented.[3] Stevens apparently indicated that the reason for holding the council was

1 Pambrun, "Story of his life," 148.
2 *Ibid.*
3 *Ibid.*

to "restrain the doubtful and wavering [Nez Percés] from active hostility."[4]

The hostile Cayuses, Umatillas, and Teninos did not move onto the council grounds until the day before the first session. They fired the grass to deny fodder to Stevens' mounts[5] and added insult to injury by denying the governor the formality of proper salutation and by coming "armed to the teeth"[6] in defiance of his request that they come unarmed. That night as the volunteers were watching a Nez Percé dance, they were ordered away from it by their superiors. A white man on the council grounds, Dr. Burns, who knew Chief Stockwhitley followed the Tenino to his lodge. When he arrived there, the chief's people demanded to know what the "white dogs" were doing in their camp. As the doctor chewed on a piece of venison, the angry Indians, guns concealed beneath blankets, circulated through the lodge, eyeing the unwelcome visitor.

Later that night, as Stockwhitley, another Indian, Pambrun, and Burns were riding to the whites' camp, their mounts became fouled in a rope strung in front of some Cayuse lodges to catch night prowlers. Instantly the four were surrounded by a group of Indians demanding their lives. Of these belligerents the most "fierce and persistent" was the Cayuse brave Tarkan. As he argued with Stockwhitley, Pambrun dismounted, cut the rope, and rode up to Tarkan, holding (as he told it) his pistol to the Cayuse's head, calling him a bad dog, and threatening to kill him should he say another word. Tarkan checked his tongue and temper but resumed the heated dialogue with Stockwhitley the following morning. The Tenino challenged the Cayuse and his men to a fight. "You are cowards and you want to kill these two white men," he taunted, "because they are alone in my camp. You hired me and my men to fight for you. You promised me gold and

4 Hazard Stevens, The Life of Isaac Ingalls Stevens, II, 203.
5 Wright to Robert Selden Garnett, October 1, 1856, Fort Dalles Papers.
6 Life of Isaac Ingalls Stevens, II, 219.

silver and cows and horses, from first to last you lied, and now I have more ammunition than you have, and I challenge you to fight me tomorrow."[7] Ordering his men to keep their arms ready, Stockwhitley rode to the doctor's camp, the white men following. It might be presumed that his strong words to protect the whites were uttered in exchange for their promise of strong drink, for Burns and chief seated themselves on either side of an alcohol can, from which they drank before Pambrun took it away.

When he opened the council on Thursday, September 11, Stevens lectured the Indians on the justice of the treaties they had signed the year before on those very grounds and spoke of the treachery of the Indians who had murdered white men and then gone to war. The governor's opening remarks revealed that his own hostility was no less than that of his listeners, since he had apparently changed very little the views he had expressed to the Washington Territorial Legislature in January:

> The spirit of prosecuting this war should be, to accomplish a lasting peace,—not to make treaties, but to punish their violation. . . . It was a pleasant feeling that actuated me on my mission, in making these treaties, to think I was doing something to civilize, and render the condition of the Indian happier; . . . I am opposed to any treaties; I shall oppose any treaties with these hostile bands. I will protest against any and all treaties made with them;—nothing but death is a mete punishment for their perfidy—their lives only should pay the forfeit. A friendly Nez-Perce informed me that in the Cayuse tribe, nineteen ill-disposed persons caused all the trouble. Could these be punished, the tribe could be governed. These turbulent persons should be seized and put to death. The tribes now at war must submit unconditionally to the justice, mercy, and leniency of our government. The guilty ones should suffer, and the remainder placed upon reservations, under the eye of the military.[8]

In contrast to the manner in which the legislators received that

7 Pambrun, "Story of his life," 150.
8 Gates, *Messages of the Governors*, 27.

speech, the Indians on the first day of council cold-shouldered the man who had delivered it. They knew that his initial words— namely, that he had labored for their good—came from a forked tongue. On the second day of the council, September 12, the governor further lectured his audience on the treaties they had signed, giving his views on the war and how it could be ended. When asked to express their feelings, none of the headmen wished to speak. Finally, Peeps, a hostile Cayuse, said that there was no need to hurry. Kamiakin was coming, he said, and they wanted to wait for him before making a move. Camaspelo endorsed a Tenino chief who said that the Indians were determined to have and hold their own country. Nez Percé Eagle from the Light reminded Stevens of a certain Nez Percé whom the volunteers had hanged the previous winter. Stevens said that he knew nothing of it but would investigate. With no further progress the council adjourned.

That night the Cayuses, half the Nez Percés, and other hostiles danced until dawn. On the thirteenth, Stevens responded to the inquiry concerning the hanged Nez Percé by saying that he was a spy. A Nez Percé, Speaking Owl, then changed the subject: "Will you give us back our lands?" he asked. "That is what we all want to hear about; that is what troubles us. I ask plainly to have a plain answer."[9] Stevens ignored Speaking Owl's request and, as at the first Walla Walla council, called instead on the friendly Chief Lawyer. In a stormy speech Lawyer called on the Nez Percés to stand by the treaty they had signed the year before, but his tribal antagonists, Old Joseph and Red Wolf, said that they had not understood the treaty and did not intend to give their lands away.

Realizing that he was getting nowhere and alarmed by word that Kamiakin and another Yakima chief, Owhi, were camped nearby, Stevens sent an urgent message to Colonel Edward J. Steptoe and his army regulars, encamped some four miles below the council grounds. He warned the colonel that "one half of the

[9] *Life of Isaac Ingalls Stevens*, II, 216.

Nez Perces and all the other tribes, except a very few persons, are unmistakably hostile in feeling" and that "the Cuyuses [*sic*], the Walla Wallas, and other hostiles were so when they came in. Hence the requisition I made upon you for troops."

The governor was obviously worried. "I particularly desire you to be present to-day," he said, "if your duties will permit, and I will also state that I think a company of your troops is essential to the security of my camp."[10] Should trouble erupt, Stevens believed, his own Nez Percé and sixty-nine-man Washington Territorial Militia guard under Colonel B. F. Shaw could not cope with it. Stevens was stunned to receive a message from Steptoe inviting him to move to the army camp and declaring that on orders from General Wool he could not dispatch regulars to the governor.

Smarting from the rebuff, Stevens moved his camp near that of Steptoe on Sunday, September 14. Along the way he met Kamiakin, Owhi, and Owhi's son, Qualchan, who had camped the night before on the Touchet River. Sending his volunteer and Nez Percé guard up the roadway on Mill Creek, Stevens and a small party took to back trails to watch the Indians. As they did so, Kamiakin and his warriors kept watch on them. Kamiakin and his men, some 350 strong, then moved up, making a "fine show" dressed in their war gear, spread out over perhaps three hundred yards, and riding abreast to within a few hundred yards of the governor. Pambrun rode out to meet them. As he did so, his hair-rope bridle became dislodged from his horse, causing the animal to stampede through the Indians' ranks, wheel, and repeat its headlong flight. The Indians considered this unexpected act one of bravado on the part of the interpreter. Pambrun, however, was only too happy to let another man, George Montour, a French-Canadian trader, settler, and interpreter, approach them. Sensing the attitude of the whites to be one of friendship, Kamiakin dropped his guard and gestured as if to shake the governor's

10 *Ibid.*, 215–16.

hand. When Pambrun warned the governor that this would give the hostile Indians time to mingle with the white teamsters and stampede their animals, Stevens refused, saying that he was in a hurry to get to camp. There, he said, the Indians could come and shake hands. Before Stevens could encamp, however, the Indians rode ahead to preempt the site, a brushy area near water.[11]

The hostile Indians who had been at the council when it opened were notified on Monday, September 15, to move to the new location to continue the parley. When the talks resumed on Tuesday, an Indian sent by his fellows to walk daily within a few steps of Stevens' arbor "office" was challenged and ordered to leave on pain of death if he returned. He promptly abandoned his surveillance. It is not known whether he told the Indians that Stevens was visiting Steptoe's camp to drink bourbon, which Pambrun said "kept the Governor half shot."[12] Perhaps the governor wanted to ease the pain of both a ruptured hernia and ruptured relations with the Indians. Pambrun later observed that had the walking spy taken the "very desirable" scalp of the "Long Haired Chief" he would have been the envy of the entire Indian nation.

In the vicinity at the time of the stalemated sessions, rounding up horses the Cayuses had stolen, was Chief Quiltenenock (whom Stevens called Quiltomee) of the Columbia Sinkiuses, who lived north of the Yakima country. He was destined against his will to remove his people to the proposed Yakima Reservation, although he had not signed the treaty. Unlike the whites, Quiltenenock and most other Indians believed that treaties signed by chiefs of individual bands did not bind other bands. He sought an audience with the governor, just as he had sought one with Colonel Wright, to rectify Kamiakin's misdeed in signing away Sinkiuse lands.[13] Nettled by these old bones dug up from the 1855 council, the governor brushed off the chief, called a halt to the talks, and

---

[11] Pambrun, "Story of his life," 151.
[12] Ibid.
[13] Brown, Indian Side of the Story, 169–74.

told the Indians: "Follow your hearts; those who wish to go into the war go."[14]

The council ended inconclusively on Wednesday, September 17, 1856. Stevens had called the 1855 meeting "most satisfactory." He did not so describe this one. The governor had repeatedly insisted that everything the whites did was justifiable, to which the hostiles always responded: "Do away with all treaties, give us back our lands . . . if not, then we will fight." Stevens reiterated his peace terms: "Throw aside . . . [your] guns and submit to the justice and mercy of the government." On the eighteenth, Colonel Steptoe spoke to the Indians as if there were no war. The polarized attitudes of the military and himself aggravated the governor but did not deter Steptoe, who told the Indians: "My mission is pacific. I have come not to fight you, but to live among you. . . . I trust we shall live together as friends."[15] Not even Steptoe's peaceful words could satisfy Quiltenenock, since there had been no promise to him or the other Indians that their lands would be returned to them.

Stevens set out for The Dalles on September 19, escorted by his Nez Percé and volunteer guards. In the party was William Craig, whom the governor thought it best to remove from among the angry Nez Percés to the Walla Walla Valley near the troops. About three miles out they encountered squads of thirty to fifty painted Indians, who broke off from a main body of four or five hundred and rode down a hill toward them.[16] Aware of their presence, the governor's party continued on its westward way.

At a small spring-fed creek in an open basin about five or six hundred yards wide, the Stevens party stopped, formed a wagon corral, moved the animals inside, and chained the vehicles together. Before all the loose animals had been gathered, a warrior charged to within ten feet of a herder, fired at his head, but

14 Josephy, *Nez Perce Indians*, 375.
15 *Life of Isaac Ingalls Stevens*, II, 218–20.
16 Homily of the Walla Wallas and Stockwhitley the Tenino did not join the warriors. Nor did Kamiakin take an active part; he watched "in the wings."

missed, as did his fellows, who were too far away to be effective. Seven or eight men from the wagons ran to a willow-and-rosebush thicket about seventy-five yards away. "An old Indian, Cayouse [sic] war chief, rode by [the thicket] at a gallop, giving the war whoop at every jump," wrote Pambrun. A bullet crashed into the jaw of the chief's horse and felled the animal; another bullet intended for the chief missed the mark. The horse got to its feet but collapsed after running about a hundred yards—far enough away, however, to save its rider.[17] Another Indian behind some sagebrush made a poor target for one of the governor's men who harmlessly emptied a rifle and two revolvers at him. The Indian returned the fire, shooting a ramrod from his attacker's hand. When the white man stooped to pick it up, the Indian shot him in the back. Two members of the party went out to get him; he died that night.

Several Indians who had stolen up to the thicket were warned to pull back because someone in the wagon corral had tipped off the whites to their movements. There followed a lull, broken only by yelling and gunfire as the combatants watched each other enter a deep washout. The two forces closed, but, after running a short distance, the Indians paused. A white man who rushed up carelessly was shot through the bowels.

Fifty friendly Nez Percés assigned to hold the ridge on the south side of the corral were told by the hostile Indians, "We came not to fight the Nez Perces, but the whites; go to your camp, or we wipe it out."[18] The hostile Indians clustered together, 150 strong, to form a trap, placing an equal number of their men in a nearby ravine between the governor's party and themselves. Into it they drew no less than Colonel Shaw and 24 of his volunteers, who rushed them. The Indians began to run, hoping to draw the whites past the ravine so that the hidden warriors could cut off their retreat. But there was a hitch. An old man, ignorant of the plan, met the braves who were running to attract the troops.

[17] Pambrun, "Story of his life," 153–54.
[18] *Life of Isaac Ingalls Stevens*, II, 221.

Thinking they were in full retreat, he yelled: "You band of squaws, what are you running from a few white men for? Turn on them and kill them all." Disconcerted, as well as stimulated, by this call to arms, the Indians obeyed the old one and thereby spared the lives of the nearly trapped soldiers. With their plan undone, the warriors in the ravine joined the others. When the other whites saw this confusion, they charged. They and the Indians were so intermingled that when it approached the scene, the volunteer "rescue squad" took off in another direction. A lone soldier holding back shot an Indian in the neck. Two warriors immediately carried his body away. Other Indians fired at the volunteer but missed.

At dusk the fighting broke off. After dark the Indians saw the glow of the volunteers' supper fires—good targets for "a perfect storm of bullets" which set the command to emptying coffee pots, frying pans, and assorted kettles on the fires to douse them.[19] The Indians peppered the corral with bullets, and when candlelight illuminated a covered wagon into which the governor had gone to write Steptoe for help, several bullets crashed into it, hitting no one. Surmising correctly that Stevens would again apply to Steptoe for relief, the Indians placed guards along the road to the colonel's command post. As expected, one of the governor's party, Nez Percé Dick, rode east for help, fighting his way through the guards.[20]

It was midnight when Steptoe dispatched troops in response to Stevens' call.[21] Before they could reach the embattled party (between one and two o'clock in the morning), the Indians kept an almost constant stream of bullets whining over the heads of the volunteers picketed in dugout outposts. The men constantly shifted in their pits, for Stevens could not keep them outside the wagon corral for any length of time. One group, running to warn

[19] Pambrun, "Story of his life,"156.
[20] Nez Percé Dick was later killed by a blind man thought to have been hired by vengeance-bent Indians.
[21] Edward J. Steptoe to Nannie [his sister], October 27, 1856, Steptoe Papers.

those inside that the onrushing figures in the dark were Indians, fired at the shadowy forms until someone cried: "Don't shoot, it's us."[22] One group of Indians amused themselves with a fife and drum until fire from Steptoe's reinforcements stilled their revelry.

There was much yoking of oxen and saddling of horses as the expedition formed into a line, reversing itself to move east to the fort. One team at the rear left without its wagon, and the driver was sent back to get it. He made a good target for two Indians, who harassed him with their fire. The wagon halted. An Indian fired in its direction, and two white men from the train crept out a little way. When the Indian fired again, one of them fired toward the gun blaze. The Indian stopped the bullet and fell. His blood-covered horse ran toward the train, where one of the whites caught it, remarking that he had made some "whiskey money."[23]

As the wagon train continued eastward through the dark, the Indians kept it under constant but desultory fire, scaring "a few notorious cowards." Without much experience in night firing, the Indians tended to overshoot their targets. The train halted on Mill Creek, waiting there half an hour before moving on toward Steptoe's command post. Troops scoured the brush for Indians, but most of them were on the brow of a nearby hill, from which vantage point they fired volley after volley at the whites. Thus harassed, the train continued on its way, reaching the fort before daybreak. The Indians continued firing on the troops and herders. Some of their bullets ripped through troopers' tents without hitting anyone. While he waited for the Indians to take the offensive, Steptoe ordered a few shells lobbed into the timber in their direction. Fearing the "fire balls," as they called them, the Indians left the timber and regrouped, unwilling as yet to give up the fight.

The troops maintained sporadic fire, the Indians returning

22 Pambrun, "Story of his life," 157.
23 *Ibid.*, 158.

it, until about 10:00 A.M., when Quiltenenock rode out toward the soldiers—just as his father had a few years earlier on the buffalo plains. The Blackfeet had mortally wounded the father; the son was more fortunate. Coming off with a ball in the hip, he was picked up by his comrades. The sight of the fallen chief discouraged the Indians, already frustrated by the inconclusiveness of their fight, and they rode away.[24]

In writing to his sister about the battle, Steptoe asked that she "tell pa that I had a brush . . . with some Indians not much damage done however, none to my people."[25] Nevertheless, his attitude toward the Indians hardened. "In general terms," he wrote Colonel Wright, "I may say that in my judgment we are reduced to the necessity of waging a vigorous war, striking the Cuyuses [sic] at the Grande Ronde, and Kam-i-ah-kan wherever he may be found."[26] Meanwhile, he set about building a permanent military post, Fort Walla Walla, some six miles up Mill Creek (present-day Walla Walla, Washington).

The Indians attended one more council in the Walla Walla Valley before the year was out. This one was called by Colonel Wright, who arrived there from The Dalles on October 5. Only three prominent Cayuses, two Nez Percé chiefs, and Stockwhitley responded to Wright's invitation; the others refused to make the long journey back from their winter camps but expressed willingness to hear the results of the talk.[27] In council Wright presented General Wool's views that the army regulars understood the Indians' point of view, that he knew they wished to be left alone, that he understood the signing away of their lands at the first Walla Walla council was at the root of the war. Wright

24 As with all military engagements, there are varying estimates of the number of casualties. One account (Pambrun, "Story of his life," 161) placed troop losses at thirty dead, an obvious exaggeration.

25 Steptoe to Nannie, October 27, 1856, Steptoe Papers.

26 Life of Isaac Ingalls Stevens, II, 223.

27 Josephy, Nez Perce Indians, 377; Special Indian agent for Washington Territory A. H. Robie said that Wright did not have that good a turnout. A. H. Robie to Stevens, November 28, 1856, Washington Superintendency, Microfilm No. 5, Roll 17.

assured them that since the treaties were not yet in effect the land was still theirs. Extremely welcome was Wright's promise that the troops would keep whites off Indian lands. "The bloody shirt shall now be washed and not a spot left on it," declared Wright, urging that all past differences be forgotten and peace and friendship established forever.[28] The Indians took these words to mean that the land would be theirs forever. But Wright knew that the federal government, not the Indians, would have the last word on the treaties, and as a servant of that government, he knew that he was duty bound to see that it did. Governor Stevens spoke to the Indians no more. The following year he went to Congress as a territorial delegate to defend the treaties he had made.

With calm restored, the Cayuses pursued their normal activities. Many went to the Grande Ronde,[29] but Camaspelo, his people, and the son of Peopeomoxmox journeyed to the Wallowa Valley to stay with Nez Percé Old Joseph.[30] Howlish Wampo, Tintinemetsa, and Yellow Hawk camped for a while near the military Fort Walla Walla, while Stockwhitley and some twenty of his families moved into winter camps on the Umatilla near Five Crows' old camp. Five Crows, Weatenatenamy, and about thirty-five men rode into the Snake country to the Boise Basin to winter near the Mormons. Palouse Chief Tilcoax was with the Nez Percé Kakamas on the Snake River above the mouth of the Salmon. Kamiakin now lived in the country of his father's Palouses, nursing grudges against his white adversaries and those Yakima chiefs who had sought peace. In December he was visited by Quiltenenock and certain Cayuses out killing cattle belonging to the Nez Percés who had accompanied Stevens to The Dalles; the marauders were soothing their hearts with revenge and their stomachs with food.[31] Some Cayuse hostiles rode into Nez Percé

---

28 Josephy, *Nez Perce Indians*, 377.
29 John F. Noble to Stevens, October 11, 1856, *Washington Superintendency*, Microfilm No. 5, Roll 17.
30 Craig to Stevens, December 5, 1856, *ibid.* Roll 21.
31 Craig to Stevens, December 19, 1856, *ibid.*

country to steal horses from the Indians, horses and mules from the Indian Department, three head of horses from Washington Territorial Militia which Craig had left behind, and thirteen horses and fourteen cattle from the agent himself.

The winter-scattered Cayuses[32] planned to return to their own country in the spring, believing that the army regulars would pose less of a threat to them than had the volunteers. Had not Colonel Wright said that they could have their old lands? By April, 1857, Five Crows, Weatenatenamy, and their people were back in the Grande Ronde harvesting roots, free from another massacre. But there remained the perpetual fear of Snake incursions. That same month word came that the Snakes had pounced upon a Cayuse party, taking a large number of horses and wounding many of their owners in an attack as bad, if not worse, than the attacks of the volunteers.[33] The Cayuses could ill afford to sustain such losses, which were reducing their tribe almost to the threshold of extinction. Soon some of them began to beg food from the federal Indian agent at The Dalles.

That spring the Cayuses' friend (as much as they could be said to have one among the whites), General Wool, left for the East, but his successor as commander of the Department of the Pacific, General Newman S. Clarke, continued Wool's policy of allowing no white settlement east of the Cascade Mountains.[34] Well meaning though it was, the policy made the hostile Cayuses no less hostile. Even the sixty friendly Cayuses under the supervision of Craig, now a subagent for Washington Territory, were unhappy with the military establishment in their country, although the insults they endured from the army regulars were mild compared with those from the volunteers. The friendly Indians continued

[32] Craig to Stevens, January 5, 1857, *ibid.*
[33] Craig to Stevens, April 20, 1857, *ibid.*
[34] In October, 1858, General W. S. Harney arrived at Fort Vancouver to assume command of the northern district, or Department of Oregon, which had been split off from the Department of the Pacific on September 13. General Clarke retained command of the southern district, which became the Department of California.

254

to suffer serious losses through depredations committed by the hostile ones for their refusal to join in the war. The reprisals and dislocations made it impossible for them to attempt to farm, and things promised to be no better with the threatened white occupation.

In reporting to the commissioner of Indian affairs on September 1, 1857, concerning that occupation, James W. Nesmith, now Oregon superintendent of Indian affairs, wrote:

> I would recommend that steps be taken to throw open the Walla-Walla valley to settlement. It is an advanced point in the interior, which, if occupied, would protect and increase the facilities for an overland communication with the States. The Walla-Walla is a rich valley, unsurpassed in its qualities as a grazing country, and a desirable locality for a white settlement.[35]

The superintendent thought that a general solution to the Indian problem would be to move the Indians to reservations, providing subsistence until they could care for their own needs through agriculture.

It was not that easy. The Cayuses did not wish to move, under provisions of an unpopular and unratified treaty, to a reservation they did not like. Although it included their homeland, they complained that it was too small for their herds of livestock, which they hoped to restore if the whites would leave them alone. Moreover, there was too little tillable land on the proposed reserve and too much traffic through it on the Immigrant Road.

During the winter of 1857–58 the Cayuses were annoyed by a multitude of whites taking advantage of the apparent cessation of hostilities to invade their country: discharged soldiers, gamblers, reckless adventurers, and whisky peddlers. The intruders appropriated spots on which the Indians' lodges stood, ordering their occupants to move out. With the whites came some traders licensed to deal with the Cayuses and Walla Wallas; many other whites arrived with no licenses at all. Their so-called farms were

[35] *Annual Report of the Commissioner of Indian Affairs, 1857*, 320.

merely blinds to sell whisky.[36] Scarcely qualifying under Wool's order as missionaries were certain ruffians riding into the valley with bottles, not Bibles, in their saddlebags; nor could they be classified as Hudson's Bay Company employees. Miners, whom Wool envisioned as peacefully traversing Indian land on their way to the diggings, were a constant source of aggravation to the Indians. To make access to the mines easier, the army had commissioned Lieutenant John Mullan to survey a trans–Rocky Mountain military thoroughfare (the Mullan Road) from Fort Walla Walla to Fort Benton on the Missouri River. As Mullan and his party moved from The Dalles to Fort Walla Walla in July, Indians on Willow Creek stole five oxen—a message to him that, not far away nor long before, those "daring villains," the Cayuse Indians, had met soldiers like him in battle.[37]

Still in an ugly mood from their encounters with parties like Mullan's and the territorial volunteers, the Cayuses warned the intruders to get out of their country or be killed and have their property destroyed. To show that they meant business, they chased into the fort a Mr. Combs, a beef contractor for the army.[38] If his retreat to the post tended to cut down on its beef supply, so would Palouse Chief Tilcoax's order to his people to shoot army cattle.[39] On the negative side, the fort made it difficult for the Cayuses to carry out their threats against their unwelcome guests.

The Cayuses finally decided that they had had enough and voted to fight "a war of extermination." The interior tribes had become so menacing that Colonel Steptoe and 150 men left Fort Walla Walla on May 6 to conduct a military reconnaissance at the request of miners in the Colville country.[40] The Spokanes and Coeur d'Alenes, as plagued by gold seekers as the Cayuses,

36 Brevet Major William Grier to Nesmith, October 28, 1858, *Oregon Superintendency*, Microfilm No. 2, Roll 16.

37 John W. Hakola (ed.), *Frontier Omnibus*, 214.

38 Dennison to Nesmith, January 12, 1858, *Oregon Superintendency*, Microfilm No. 2, Roll 15.

39 Snowden, History of Washington, IV, 20.

40 For further details of Steptoe's action, see B. F. Manring, *The Conquest of the Coeur D'Alenes, Spokanes and Palouses*.

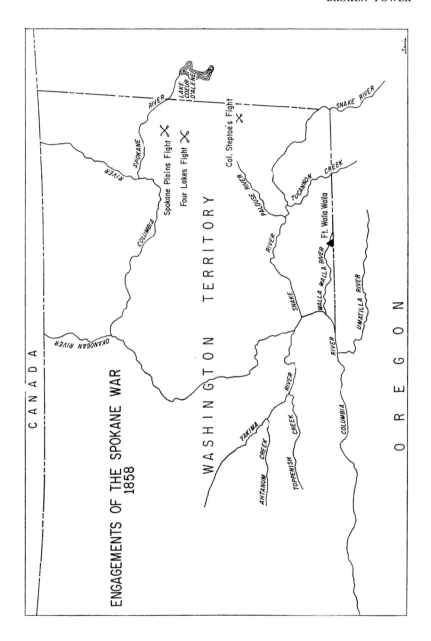

ENGAGEMENTS OF THE SPOKANE WAR
1858

joined elements from other northern tribes—Palouses, Sinkiuses, and a token representation of Cayuses—to jump the poorly prepared expedition in the lower Spokane country, killing eight of its members and chasing it back to Fort Walla Walla. In the command's absence, Cayuses in the valley talked of attacking the unprotected fort but refrained from doing so. Their joy at Steptoe's defeat was offset by increased vigilance at the post. Even at that, the raids continued. In July seventy hostiles attacked W. J. Lindsay, thirteen packers, and Lieutenant Wickliff at the confluence of the Touchet River and Patit Creek. Sweeping downhill, the attackers surrounded the little party, charging it seven times. Despite sharp fighting, the whites escaped.[41]

As was anticipated by the Cayuses and their allies, the whites did not take Steptoe's defeat lying down. Colonel Wright, who had given the Cayuses a measure of reassurance concerning peace, now led a vengeful attack on the tribesmen who had whipped Steptoe. The Cayuses, too battered to aid their northern brothers, could offer only moral support—which was more than they had received from the latter in the recent war. In the upper plateau Wright fought two decisive engagements with Spokanes, Coeur d'Alenes, Palouses, and scattered elements of other bands at Four Lakes on September 1 and at Spokane Plains four days later.[42] Not content with mauling his foe, Wright permitted his men to slaughter nearly a thousand Indian horses, hanged several Indians, and returned to Fort Walla Walla with prisoners. On October 9 he assembled the Cayuses and Walla Wallas at the fort to tell them that if there were any more murders, they would be severely punished. As if to illustrate his lecture, Wright hanged three prisoners for murder and one for inciting the war, which was now over. Lamented Howlish Wampoo: "We had thousands of horses and cattle; the hills and valleys were covered with them; where are they now? Not an animal is to be seen over this wide expanse. . . . we are stripped of everything."

A more powerful force than fear in causing the Cayuses to

41 *Oregonian*, September 24, 1921.

heed Wright's warning was their declining population; they could not wage war now even if they wanted to. Inspector General J. K. F. Mansfield of the United States Army, who was in charge of the hangings, wrote of the Cayuses and Walla Wallas: "Their power is now broken, and they can never again bring about a combination of action."[43] Concerning the judgment meted out to the Cayuses by "The Rider on a Black Horse," Indian agent A. J. Cain, widely known as "the Indians' friend," said in August, 1858:

> They have been much reduced in numbers from war and disease and with the exception of few of the principle men who have some horses and cattle are very much impoverished. . . . Their tribe have lost many of their tribal characteristics and the chiefs have but little influence over their young men, who are much addicted to liquor and wandering over the country creating disturbances with other Indians.[44]

In a flourish of Darwinian exuberance and white racial confidence, White Salmon (Columbia River) Indian agent R. W. Lansdale described the triumph of civilization over savagery:

> Here, indeed, is an epitome, in a few words, of the history of the two races, so called, since the white man first planted his heavy foot upon the North American continent, and came in contact with his red brethren. The weak has been compelled to give way before the strong; the strong man has an impulsive aspiration for dominance and insatiable desire for broad lands and rich domains. He is not satisfied unless he can build a city in every country: a village in every nook and corner, and cover all he claims with farms, and factories, and roads; unless he can plough every river with swift running steamers; thunder through hills and over valleys in the

[42] For further details of the Wright battles, see Robert H. Ruby and John A. Brown, *The Spokane Indians: Children of the Sun*, 114–40.

[43] Colonel Jos. K. F. Mansfield to Major Irving McDowell, October 11, 1858, *Oregon Superintendency*, Microfilm No. 234, Roll 611.

[44] Cain, Annual Report, August 2, 1859, *Washington Superintendency*, Microfilm No. 5, Roll 21.

steam car; fortify every headland with bristling cannon, and cover every sea with canvas.[45]

Cain reported that the Cayuses did not want to leave the Walla Walla Valley but that when forced to it they were willing to go east to join Old Joseph's nontreaty Nez Percés in the Wallowa. He warned that, if the Cayuses were not removed soon, they would go there of their own accord.[46] They knew that their 1855 treaty had assigned them to the Umatilla Reservation, but they also knew that it was as yet unratified, which gave them time to think of options to its stipulations.

When the various treaties were discussed in the United States Senate in 1858, the Indian office sent a special commissioner, C. H. Mott, to inquire into the advisability of establishing reservations as arranged at the Walla Walla council. He was also charged with ascertaining whether changes in the Indian situation in Oregon and Washington territories would necessitate policy adjustments if the treaties were ratified as written.[47] The supposed merits of the agreements with the Cayuses, Umatillas, and Walla Wallas, as with the other tribes, lay in the Indians' removal to isolated areas in order to protect them from "the contaminating influences of bad white men." There they would be introduced to agricultural pursuits, education, training, and other services which the whites enjoyed; in sum, it meant the abandonment of their "roving, thriftless habits" and "barbarous customs" for "civilized life."

Mott scheduled councils with various tribes at various locations. At one held in the fall of 1858, he assured the Cayuses and the Nez Percés that the Great Father would not permit their lands to be taken from them without compensation and provision for

[45] R. W. Lansdale to C. H. Mott, Special Commissioner, October 22, 1858, *Oregon Superintendency*, Microfilm No. 234, Roll 611.

[46] Cain, Annual Report, August 2, 1859, *Washington Superintendency*, Microfilm No. 5, Roll 21.

[47] Mott to Geary, October 4, 1858, *Oregon Superintendency*, Microfilm No. 234, Roll 611.

their comfort on reservations to which they had consented to go.[48] After Looking Glass talked about some of his past hostile actions, Tintinemetsa spoke for the Cayuses. A friendly chief during the recent hostilities, he said that he believed he could speak with some authority. After telling Mott that his (Mott's) talk was good, he said that he had not been one to war against whites and "did not even look at my gun." He spoke at length of the folly of killing, of his love for others. "Let us take each others hands in true friendship," he said, promising amity with his white brothers in a request that the Great Father make good his promises to his children. "All here know," said Tintinemetsa, "I have sustained heavy losses by the war. I have furnished the white soldiers with horses and have not been paid; yet of this I say nothing. My talk is ended."[49]

Certain Indian office personnel did not respond to such expressions with similar gestures of good will, believing, as did many army men, that by going to war the Cayuses had forfeited their lands and that rapid settlement of the country would produce disastrous, uncontrollable, and indiscriminate intermingling of the races, although it was a foregone conclusion that whites would triumph over Indians. Mott, however, appeared sincere in his wish to protect the Cayuses, suggesting that, with some modification of boundaries and location of the public road farther south, the treaties be ratified.[50]

Agent Cain, every bit as concerned about the Cayuses' welfare as Mott, disagreed with the commissioner, recommending instead the abandonment of the proposed Umatilla Reservation as being too near a public highway. Its inhabitants, he said, would be dissatisfied there, even if a military post was built to protect them from rampaging Snakes. Forgoing it would have been no small concession on the part of Cayuses, who might have been expected to give highest priority to protecting themselves from their an-

[48] Mott to J. W. Denver, U.S. Indian Commissioner, February 11, 1859, *ibid.*
[49] *Ibid.*
[50] *Ibid.*

cient enemies. Cain's superior, Edward R. Geary, Washington Territory superintendent of Indian affairs, reported that "enterprising robber" Snakes had reduced the Cayuses to "comparative poverty." Even the more powerful Nez Percés were said to be in "constant apprehension" of their attacks. In August, 1859, Geary noted that Snake marauders had become more daring, ranging as far north as the Bitterroot Valley, from which it was reported they had recently driven large herds of the horses.[51]

Far worse for the Cayuses than their livestock losses was the death of Weatenatenamy, who was killed during the summer in a skirmish with some Snakes.[52] Attempts to quell them could no longer be made by his survivors, who were now forced to depend chiefly upon the whites to do so. Early in 1859, in a move to check Snake raids on the war-weakened Teninos of the Warm Springs Reservation, application was made to the Department of Oregon commander, General W. S. Harney, for rifles, ammunition, and troops to track them down and punish them for murdering peaceful Indians and to recover large numbers of horses and cattle they had stolen from both the Indians and the government. The hunters had their work cut out for them as they searched for the swift-striking Snake horsemen, who were outfitted with short swords, pistols, and carbines.[53]

Despite their incursions, Cain represented the Snakes as no deterrent to Cayuse removal to the Nez Percé country, particularly since the Cayuses spoke the language of the Nez Percés, having intermarried with and been "mostly absorbed" by them.[54] How far and how fast Cayuse–Nez Percé assimilation would proceed depended on how much official attention was given to Cain's proposal. Whatever the decision, it was evident that removal of

[51] Geary to Commissioner, August 19, 1859, *ibid.*
[52] *Annual Report of the Commissioner of Indian Affairs, 1858,* 263.
[53] Geary to Harney, August 15, 1859; Geary to Commissioner, August 19, 1859; Special Order No. 86, August 17, 1859; Geary to H. B. Greenwood, U.S. Indian Commissioner, October 11, 1859, *Oregon Superintendency,* Microfilm No. 234, Roll 611.
[54] Cain to Geary, October 31, 1859; Cain to Geary, November 15, 1859, *Washington Superintendency,* Microfilm No. 5, Roll 21.

the Cayuses would be accomplished at the pleasure of white men, not red.

It could not come too soon. The Cayuses' "urgent propensity to traffic" induced them to trade their horses, often for liquor from peddlers violating federal law before it could be enforced. Trade with lawless frontiersmen resulted not only in conflict but also in dissipation of the Cayuses, diminishing their numbers. Agent Craig, as aware of the problem as Cain was, wrote from Walla Walla in September, 1858:

> Subtly some evil disposed persons have begun to introduce whiskey . . . the pernicious and bad effects of which have become most glaringly apparent within the past few months. From what source they obtain it is impossible to tell . . . many of the Cayuses and Walla Wallas living in this valley have been leading a most dissolute and renegade life lately, under no control whatever.[55]

If the Walla Walla Valley Cayuses were not removed soon, there might be none left to move.

Finally, after four long years of delay, Congress ratified the treaty with the Cayuses, Umatillas, and Walla Wallas on March 8, 1859. The Cayuses would leave the Walla Walla, but until then, they and whites would step on each other's toes. Tension mounted through the remainder of 1859 and the following year. In December, 1860, because of some difficulty, whites confined and threatened to hang two Indians. Actually, they were being held as hostages to force G. H. Abbott, new agent at the Umatilla Reservation, to take all the Cayuses there. The plan worked, for when he received a letter from Major Enoch Steen, commander at Fort Walla Walla, ordering him to gather his Indians, Abbott left to do so the very next day. Arriving in the valley, he found that only complete Cayuse removal would quiet the settlers, and he notified the Cayuse chiefs to be ready to leave in a few days. They complained that there was no way to haul their supplies of corn, wheat, and potatoes, whereupon Abbott secured from

---

[55] Craig, Annual Report, September 20, 1858, *ibid.*

Steen four wagons, teams, and drivers and three more wagons from other sources. He apparently did not have to use wagons offered by the whites to get the Indians out of the valley. Once removal began, the two Indian hostages were released.[56]

In 1845 a government employee wrote of the Pacific Northwest Indians: "They are all savages; and they make no figure on the history of the country, over the destinies of which they have not exerted, and probably never will exert, any influence."[57] As for making "no figure" on history, the white man as well as the red would have to admit that the Cayuses had proved him wrong. Concerning their savagery, the white man would think him right, for the Cayuses emerged from a massacre and two wars with a poor reputation in white eyes. A former captain in the United States Cavalry said: "Of the various tribes the Cayuses were the worst of the whole. They were crafty, cunning, and troublesome, being constantly on some thieving expedition. They were notorious horse thieves, and were despised by all people in their country."[58]

Bumping along the road to the Umatilla, the Cayuses looked upon themselves as victims of white civilization. Having suffered from disease and war, thrown now onto a reservation they did not like with neighbors they did not choose, they could well ask whether they would be able to retain not just the memory of their past glories but their entity as a tribe. Were the wagons rolling them into oblivion?

56 Steen to Abbott, December 23, 1860; Abbott to Geary, January 5, 1861, *Oregon Superintendency*, Microfilm No. 2, Roll 19.
57 Robert Greenhow, *The History of Oregon and California and the Other Territories on the North-West Coast of North America*, 30.
58 J. Lee Humfreville, *Twenty Years Among Our Hostile Indians*, 290.

XVI
Cayuses Corralled

Traveling from their homes in the Walla Walla Valley to the Umatilla Reservation undoubtedly filled the Cayuses with regret. A small group, believing that they would one day repossess the land, avoided the reservation to join Walla Walla Chief Homily near the old Hudson's Bay Company post. Others with similar views went to White Bluffs and Priest Rapids on the Columbia to join "Hump-Backed Dreamer" Smohalla (Big-Talk-on-Four-Mountains), a Wanapum. To white authorities he was the leader of Indian resistance to the government along the Columbia, providing a rendezvous for all "renegades" from Priest Rapids to The Dalles who wanted to avoid the Umatilla, Yakima (Simcoe), and Nez Percé reservations.[1] To his followers he represented the best hope for a return to the old times as expressed in his teachings, which he once summarized for a white preacher: "The Indians were first on earth; . . . all people come from one Indian mother; . . . the water, the grass, the woods and soil are equally free to all."[2]

In the Grande Ronde reservation-shy Cayuses and other Indians espousing the Dreamer religion, having repudiated the

---

[1] For an account of government attempts to track down the Columbia renegades, see Abbott to Geary, February 6, 1861, *Oregon Superintendency*, Microfilm No. 2, Roll 19.

[2] *Pacific Christian Advocate*, May 15, 1873, p. 1. The influence of Chief Smohalla on Indians of the Columbia River and the Yakima and Umatilla reservations caused government officials great concern throughout the rest of the century. See Agent John W. Crawford to Commissioner, December 15, 1891; March 17, 1892; September 28, 1892, *Preliminary Inventory of Records of the Umatilla Agency*, Record Group 75, Federal Records Center, Seattle, Washington (cited hereafter as *Records of the Umatilla Indian Agency*).

1855 treaty, denied the right of government agents to remove them and threatened war on white settlers should they trespass in the valley. Troops of the First Oregon Cavalry under Captain George B. Currey were ordered from Fort Walla Walla in August, 1862, to arrest them. There was a skirmish, and four Indians were reported killed. One of them was known as The Dreamer—not Smohalla, who continued to drum, dream, and attract dissidents to his isolation along the Columbia River.[3]

There was more communication between the so-called renegades and their reservation brothers than government agents thought desirable. Indians accustomed to roaming freely could not have been expected to adjust graciously to reservation life. Consequently, their traditional patterns of seasonal migrations drew many Cayuses from their newly established reservation, if only temporarily, to their old haunts. John Keast Lord, a naturalist with the British Boundary Commission, described their presence in Walla Walla, now a quarter-mile-long town of tawdry barrooms, billiard parlors, a few stores, and horse corrals. "The throng in the streets," he wrote, "consists of half-naked savages, with their squaws and children, gold-miners, settlers, American soldiers, and rowdies of all sorts." Cayuses and members of other tribes dashed "wildly up and down the street—some on bare-backed horses, others having a rude kind of saddle: all ... yelling, whooping, and flourishing their lassos, like maddened fiends." In this "perfect horse-fair," said Lord,

> half-naked savages, one after another (often two or three together), dash up to the rails [of the corral], and fling themselves from off the panting horses [those of the Cayuses had bobbed tails and cropped ears]; run their hands down the length of the horse's back, to show it has no galls or sores; tickle its flanks and creep under its belly, to demonstrate its docility; drag open the lips, to show the teeth; invariably ask four times the sum they intend to take; give

3 Brigadier General Benjamin Alvord to L. H. Rector, August 28, 1862, *Oregon Superintendency*, Microfilm No. 2, Roll 20. See also *Walla Walla Statesman*, August 9, 1862, p. 2; August 23, 1862, p. 2; August 30, 1862, p. 2.

a frantic yell on being offered less; spring again upon the horses' backs, to gallop furiously about, until, tired of further exhibition, and hopeless of exacting a larger sum, they ride quietly to the "Coral," turn in the horses, and receive payment.[4]

The Cayuses viewed the heavy traffic around Walla Walla with mixed feelings. Selling horses to whites, such as the miners, was a good thing, but these invaders were hardly welcome. Disaffected Cayuses went among the Nez Percés, urging them to destroy all miners tramping over Cayuse and Nez Percé lands searching for gold. William H. Gray, talking over old times with the Nez Percés in 1861, said that they asked him whether they and the Cayuses should drive the Americans from the country. He advised them to shun the renegades and let the gold seekers come in peace because if they did not they would encounter all kinds of trouble from the whites.[5] As if to symbolize white persistence, Henry H. Spalding's colleague on the American Board of Commissioners for Foreign Missions, the Reverend Cushing Eells, settled on the very site of the Whitman mission in 1860, a dozen years after being driven from the country in 1847 when Whitman was killed. There he had laid plans for a seminary to be named in honor of his martyred co-laborer.

In their off-reservation rambles, the reservation Cayuses constantly encountered settlers when they visited their old hunting and root grounds. Like their treaty-escaping brothers, they found that, just as miners had killed the game, settlers' hogs had uprooted the camas and kouse, and their fences barred free travel. To avoid conflicts between whites and Indians, agents were warned by their superiors to limit the number of passes issued for off-reservation travel.[6]

Although the traveling reservation Cayuses and their holdout

4 John Keast Lord, *The Naturalist in Vancouver Island and British Columbia*, II, 85–88.
5 Gray, *History of Oregon*, 600.
6 J. W. Perit Huntington, Oregon Superintendent of Indian Affairs Circular to Agents, June 1863, *Oregon Superintendency of Indian Affairs, 1848–1873*, Letter Book H:10, Microfilm No. M-2, Roll 9.

fellow tribesmen faced some of the same problems, the former enjoyed a better reputation with government officials. Umatilla agent G. H. Abbott reported in September, 1861, that the Cayuses were "an industrious and wealthy people, and intellectually . . . superior to the great mass of Oregon Indians." This, of course, in his eyes (and in those of the Cayuses, too, it might be added) would have made them superior to the other Indians on the reservation: the 340 Umatillas, who were "neither so high in the scale of intelligence, wealth and industry as the Cayuses" and the 209 Walla Wallas, who were "debased and poor."

Abbott was impressed by the Cayuses' wealth, amounting to 5,000 head of horses valued at $80,000; divided among 384 Cayuses, that would average more than $200 per capita in horses alone. Also impressive to the agent was their knowledge of agriculture, which enabled them to raise wheat and vegetables.[7] Most Cayuse family heads were reported as cultivating one to five acres, and the agents hoped that the Umatillas and Walla Wallas would follow this example and make the reservation self-subsistent.[8] Even though the Cayuses controlled most of the choice garden sites along the Umatilla River, their cultivated land was only a tiny fraction of the nearly 1,000-square-mile reservation, whose major attraction for the Cayuses lay more in its grazing lands than in the garden sites. Raising horses appealed to them much more than raising grain, which they laboriously threshed with sticks. In 1862 three reservation Indians had log cabins. A few had set out apple trees.[9]

Not all government officials shared Abbott's evaluation of the Cayuses. In his annual report of October, 1860, Superintendent Edward R. Geary wrote that the Cayuses and Umatillas had been

---

[7] Abbott to W. H. Rector, September 10, 1861, *Oregon Superintendency*, Microfilm No. 2, Roll 19. Three days after this letter was sent, the commissioner of Indian affairs issued an order transferring Umatilla Agency to the Washington Superintendency. On May 22, 1862, it was returned to the Oregon Superintendency.

[8] S. M. Black, Superintendent of Farming, to Abbott, September 5, 1861, *ibid.*

[9] T. W. Davenport, "Recollections of an Indian Agent," *Oregon Historical Quarterly*, VIII (March–December, 1907), 13.

General Jonathan Wool clashed repeatedly with Washington Territorial Governor Isaac I. Stevens over Indian policy.

Joel Palmer was appointed Oregon superintendent of
Indian affairs in 1853.

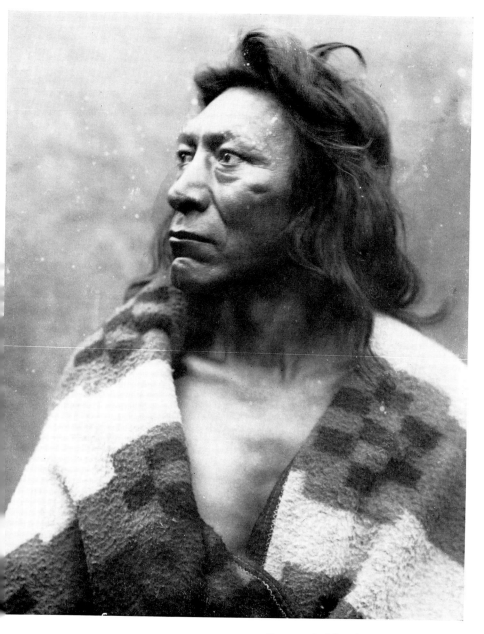

Fish Hawk, son of a Cayuse chief. From a photograph by Lee
Moorhouse.

Chief Sergeant Charley Shaplish of the U.S. Cavalry scouts was
also known as Pai Shamkain and Dr. Whirlwind.

Courtesy Smithsonian Institution

Paul Showaway succeeded Howlish Wampo as chief of a band
of Cayuses when Howlish Wampo died in 1880.

Sergeant Tiloukaikt of the U.S. Cavalry scouts was later known as Captain Sumpkin when he served on the Umatilla Reservation police force.

David Young, a Cayuse chief, in full regalia, including hooded cloak.

These Cayuse twins, Toxelox (*left*) and Alompum, were photographed by Lee Moorhouse in 1898.

greatly reduced in numbers and wealth.[10] Abbott's successor, William W. Barnhart, reported that in late 1861 and early 1862 there were many deficiencies on the reservation. Mills, schools, and hospitals promised to the Indians by Geary on a visit the previous year had not been built. Annuity goods had failed to arrive. Lack of clothing and blankets only aggravated outbreaks of measles and smallpox, which joined a host of Indian diseases.[11] In 1860, Geary had written that the Cayuses and Umatillas were "still comparatively free from the degrading vices to which the Indians have so generally fallen victims." If so, it was not for long. A rising tide of white population was washing over what the government had hoped would be an island of safety. The boundary of the reservation from the head of Wild Horse Creek—a straight line along the crest of the Blue Mountains to an uncertain place known as Lee's Encampment—was continually disputed. The northwestern boundary—a straight line from the mouth of McKay Creek to the mouth of Wild Horse Creek—was in doubt. The latter creek, in fact, had several mouths. Land-hungry settlers chose one to suit themselves on what the Indians believed to be their land.

Not until 1861 was there any effort to fulfill that clause of Article 5 in the 1855 treaty which called for construction of a road around the reservation to give its inhabitants sanctuary from white men.[12] By August 1, 1862, more than four thousand travelers had passed the agency en route to such places as the Powder River mines and the Grande Ronde Valley. They harassed the Indians, often driving off their horses,[13] and of course there was more trouble when the Indians tried to get them back. By late

[10] Geary, Annual Report, October 1, 1860, *Oregon Superintendency of Indian Affairs, 1848–1873,* Letter Book G:10, Microfilm No. M-2, Roll 8 (cited hereafter as *Oregon Superintendency,* G:10, Roll 8).

[11] William W. Barnhart to B. F. Kendall, Washington Territory Superintendent of Indian Affairs, December 3, 1861; December 6, 1861; March 1, 1862; May 23, 1862, *Washington Superintendency,* Microfilm No. 5, Roll 21.

[12] Tucker, "Pilot Rock Emigrant Road."

[13] Barnhart to William H. Rector, August 1, 1862, *Oregon Superintendency,* Microfilm No. 2, Roll 20.

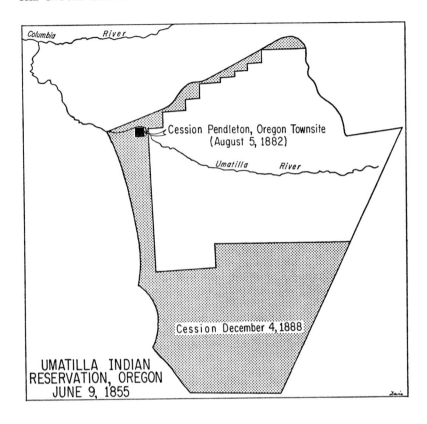

Columbia River

Cession Pendleton, Oregon Townsite
(August 5, 1882)

Umatilla River

Cession December 4, 1888

UMATILLA INDIAN
RESERVATION, OREGON
JUNE 9, 1855

1864 there was a road through the reservation and one on each side of it. Four years later at its western edge, near the mouth of Wild Horse Creek, the town of Pendleton sprang up. Proximity of town and reservation held advantages for both places—and disadvantages, too. Wrote the editor of the *Columbia Press* in 1867: "Never was an Indian reservation left so long to trouble the settlers on the habitable globe, where all the citizens prayed for relief."[14]

Reports by Umatilla agents concerning the liquor traffic became as commonplace as they were dismal. Barnhart, for instance, lamented in June, 1868, that there were no United States troops anywhere within hundreds of miles of the reservation. Furthermore, after hearing Indian testimony, juries at a late term of the district court refused to convict white men for giving liquor to Indians. This tended, Barnhart judged, to embolden infamous men in the traffic. Concluded the agent, "It is getting to be generally understood that there is no law here for the punishment of [drunken] Indians [committing crimes] or if there is any, there are no means of administering it."[15]

Just thirty-two years earlier—or one generation before Barnhart's report—Dr. Lyman Beecher, the well-known divine, had told some Oregon-bound missionaries he met in Cincinnati: "Go on and do the present generation of Indians all the good you can, and get as many to heaven as possible, for you will be the means of sending the next generation all to hell."[16] An increasing number of people, particularly in the East, saw whisky as the ticket sending the American Indian to perdition. A. D. Stillman, who discussed the problem on the Umatilla Reservation at the end of the nineteenth century, attributed it to "natural causes." The Indians know, he said, that

[14] *Columbia Press* (Umatilla, Oregon), December 14, 1867, p. 2.

[15] Barnhart to Huntington, June 10, 1868, *Oregon Superintendency*, Microfilm No. 2, Roll 25.

[16] Myron Eells, "The Decrease of the Indians," *American Antiquarian*, XXV, 3 (May–June, 1903), 145–47.

the exhilerant intoxication produced by strong liquors is the nearest approach they can obtain to the wild exhileration of their ancient business and pastimes, and you may guess something of the strength of their inclination to drink, not for the pleasure of drinking, but for the mental effects produced by strong drink. . . .

The wild desire for the pleasures of the chase, where the mind runs riot and the body runs after the mind, has been ground into them, and for generation after generation has been a part of their very beings. When the spirit moves them, the dangers, their own resolves, the fear of punishment are swept aside and the wild, hilarious drunk follows.[17]

If the Cayuses seemed to be losing population to disease and drink, it also appeared to some officials that they were losing their character as a distinct tribe.[18] One white observer had noted as early as 1842 that the "Ki-oos" and other interior peoples were gradually merging into one tribe speaking the Nez Percé language.[19] Travel, permitted the Cayuses to off-reservation root and fishing grounds and to other reservations, facilitated intertribal amalgamation. Whereas Cayuses had particularly close ties with nontreaty Nez Percés in the Wallowa, the Walla Wallas' ties were with Indians on the Warm Springs Reservation; Umatilla ties were with Indians at Simcoe (Yakima). But working against amalgamation as far as Cayuses were concerned was their fierce pride, cementing their tribal identity. Seventy-five years later an observer noted that not even then had they completely surrendered that identity and were still aristocrats among the Indians.[20]

The government was committed to recognize Umatilla Reservation tribal entities under terms of the 1855 treaty, by which it also recognized and remunerated tribal chiefs. Where at one time the chiefs had been given gratuities by the Hudson's Bay Com-

17 A. D. Stillman, "Eastern Oregon Indians," *Oregon Native Son*, I, 3 (July, 1899), 121–25.

18 Geary to Commissioner, March 1, 1860, *Oregon Superintendency*, G:10, Roll 8.

19 Edwards, *Emigrants' Guide*, 8.

20 Stephen A. Lowell, "Pioneer Lore in Question and Answer Form," in *Reminiscences of Oregon Pioneers*, 136.

pany, they now received gifts and five-hundred-dollar annuities from the Great Father. With pay as well as prestige, the chieftaincy was a prize. The government (as had the fur traders and missionaries) depended on chiefs to act as intermediaries between it and the Indian people, for whom they were expected to set good examples. The government soon found, however, that of all Indians the chiefs had the "worst" record in the matter of work. With their annuities they could well ask, "Why work?" As men in the middle, they also found it difficult to share their loyalties with both government and people.

On February 4, 1861, the Cayuses elected as their chief the white-disposed Howlish Wampo.[21] In attempting to supervise his people, he had some differences with the Indian agent, who was trying to do the same thing. The chief was angry that Barnhart killed a Cayuse in June, 1862, for a murderous assault on an Indian woman.[22] Fearing reprisals, the agent appealed for protection to the commandant of Fort Walla Walla, who promptly dispatched a cavalry detail. Howlish Wampo was still angry in the fall of 1862, when agent T. W. Davenport removed a government doctor, John Teal, without consulting the chiefs or the Indians.[23] In November, for refusing to deliver certain Indian offenders, the chief was placed under custody of the fort commandant, Colonel Justus Steinberger, of the First Washington Territorial Volunteers. The chief's incarceration brought out the paint and feathers among his people. It also excited Oregon Superintendent of Indian Affairs W. H. Rector, who urged Steinberger to treat the chief kindly, since his offense was due more to "ignorance of his duty, than wilful intent to do wrong." But the commandant would have had Howlish Wampo hanged if the

---

[21] Abbott to Geary, February 6, 1861, *Oregon Superintendency*, Microfilm No. 2, Roll 19.

[22] Barnhart to Cornelius, June 13, 1862, *Oregon Superintendency*, Microfilm No. 2, Roll 20. The *Weekly Oregonian* of August 30, 1862, p. 2, stated that the Indian victim was a brother of one of the Indians killed in the Grande Ronde by Currey's command.

[23] Davenport, "Recollections of an Indian Agent," 10–11.

chief had not been cleared on examination. Less fortunate were two Cayuses whom Steinberger hanged at the fort for killing a man (presumably white) on the Umatilla. The pair "met death with their usual coolness and indifference of their race."[24]

On November 18, 1862, the Cayuses met in council to depose Howlish Wampo. Just what tribal politicking brought on his demise is not known. His replacement, Tintinemetsa, did not receive the emoluments of office until the first of the year. Tintinemetsa, who "had not even looked at his gun" in the recent war, proved to be more tractable than his predecessor. It was with regret that Barnhart, in early March, 1868, reported his death from "pulmonary consumption."[25] In the spring of 1868, Howlish Wampo was Cayuse chief again, his salary beginning the first of April.[26]

In the fall of 1871, with fellow chiefs Winampsnoot of the Umatillas and Pierre of the Walla Wallas, Howlish Wampo accompanied agent Narcisse A. Cornoyer to Salem, Oregon, to the annual state fair to see what the white men were doing in their communities. Cornoyer hoped his charges would practice some of what they saw with their people back home.[27] At the fair the chiefs discussed with the new Oregon superintendent of Indian affairs, A. B. Meacham, the problem of Indian "civilization and education." On the basis of an official visit to the reservation on February 18, 1870, Meacham thought the Indians far from these twin goals. He noted that the Dreamers, comprising two-thirds of the reservation's people, refused to send their children to its day schools. Those who did attend, he said, were mostly the children of Roman Catholics, who made up most of the remaining one-third of the population. It was observed that

24 *Washington Statesman* (Walla Walla, Washington Territory), February 21, 1863, p. 2.
25 Barnhart to Huntington, March 7, 1868, *Oregon Superintendency*, Microfilm No. 2, Roll 24.
26 Barnhart to Huntington, April 2, 1868, *ibid.*, Roll 25.
27 Cornoyer to Meacham, November 6, 1871, *Oregon Superintendency*, Microfilm No. 2, Roll 27.

even those Indians whom Whitman had trained were beginning to embrace the Catholic faith. A traveler among the Cayuses in 1871, aware that Whitman had taught them to raise melons and garden vegetables, remarked on their "Protestant farms, and Catholic forms."[28] Meacham thought that the children had progressed very little in school, having learned to speak only a few words of English and these mechanically.[29] A teacher since November 1, 1865, the Reverend Gustav A. Vermeersch zealously sought to enroll children in school, but they avoided it like wild cayuses shying from a corral. After a year's time he had gathered twenty-eight students in a dilapidated log cabin doubling as a chapel.[30]

Since the time of the Whitman massacre the Catholic fathers had been the only Christian missionaries among the Indians at Umatilla Agency. Before establishing a school there, they first sought in the early 1860's to have the people send their children to Catholic institutions in Vancouver, but the Indians' suspicion of sending their children away made the priests realize the importance of bringing education to the reservation. Under the peace policy established by President Ulysses S. Grant in 1870, which assigned reservations to various religious denominations, whose agents were to supervise and aid the Indians in Christianity, civilization, and arts of peace, the Catholics had been permitted to conduct schools on the Umatilla. Inconsistencies in the policy, aggravated by sectarian jealousies, had brought it much criticism. The Methodists, for instance, had been permitted to set up schools on the traditionally Catholic-oriented Yakima Reservation. Protestants complained that Catholics on the Umatilla were claiming "the very ground where Whitman was murdered."

[28] Frances Fuller Victor, "The Oregon Indians," *Overland Monthly*, VII, 5 (October, 1871), 432–33.

[29] Meacham to Colonel Samuel Ross, Washington Territory Superintendent of Indian Affairs, March 22, 1870, *Oregon Superintendency of Indian Affairs, 1848–1873*, Letter Book I:10, Microfilm No. M-2, Roll 10 (cited hereafter as *Oregon Superintendency*, I:10, Roll 10).

[30] Barnhart to Huntington, March 10, 1868, *Oregon Superintendency*, Microfilm No. 2, Roll 24.

Responding in a letter to E. S. Parker, commissioner of Indian affairs, Archbishop Blanchet defended Catholic activities on the Umatilla. He reviewed for the commissioner the founding of Mission St. Anne and resumption of its work after the Cayuse War at the Mission of St. Rose of Lima at Walla Walla, mentioning the baptism of some two hundred Cayuses by Father Chirouse in May, 1852. He explained that the six- or seven-year absence of Catholic teachers on the Umatilla after the Indian wars was due to opposition by the agents until 1865, when Barnhart consented to receive a Catholic priest.[31]

Vermeersch noted in 1871 that a new school had been built and that its children were "more civil, better dressed and more modest in their behavior than they were before." Moreover, he said, there had been an increase in church attendance and membership, providing hope that "the minds of those . . . yet buried in the darkness of paganism" were finally submitting to the "civilizing influences of Christianity."[32] In praising the work of Lieutenant W. H. Boyle, the Catholic Umatilla agent, Vicar General Brouillet noted that the Cayuses were "in a fair way of improvement," working farms, living comfortably, keeping themselves well dressed and clean, both physically and morally.[33] Whatever their progress, Oregon Superintendent of Indian Affairs J. W. Perit Huntington had learned four years earlier what traders and missionaries could have told him: the Cayuses and other Indians were more impressed with the material than the abstract elements in Christianity.[34]

The task of agents and missionaries who worked among Indians on the reservations was to introduce white civilization without bringing in white men. Scarcely had the Cayuses and their fellow tribesmen been settled at Umatilla when a number

31 Catholic Sentinel, March 25, 1871, p. 2.
32 Vermeersch to Cornoyer, September 6, 1871; Lt. W. H. Boyle, Umatilla agent, to Meacham, June 2, 1871, Oregon Superintendency, Microfilm No. 2, Roll 27.
33 Catholic Sentinel, February 25, 1871, p. 2.
34 Huntington, Annual Report, August 20, 1867, Oregon Superintendency, I:10, Roll 10.

of proposals were made to abandon it and locate them elsewhere. With increased travel near and through the reservation and settlement on the edges, it was inevitable that attempts to get rid of the Indians increased each year. In his annual report for 1866, Huntington wrote:

> There are constant attempts to encroach on it . . . constant attempts under various pretexts to locate upon it and occasional attempts to exasperate the Indians into the commission of some overt act which will justify or at least palliate retaliation and thus give excuse for plunging the country into another Indian war, the end of which they well know, would be the expulsion of the Indians from the coveted tract.[35]

During the 1860's the tract was coveted for its grazing land. Public meetings were held in La Grande (in the Ronde), Pendleton, and Walla Walla to devise means of opening it to settlement. Petitions were sent to Congress and the Oregon legislature to that effect. Newspaper editors and office seekers advanced various plans to remove "these useless and unproductive people," to other reservations or to "other places." There was even talk of removing them to the coast.[36] Some of the Indians spoke of going to Canada.

Pressures for removal would have been useless without congressional sanction, which was not long in coming. On July 1, 1870, by joint resolution, Congress approved negotiations with the Indians of the Umatilla for their lands and their removal elsewhere. On June 23, 1871, Superintendent Meacham reported to Commissioner Parker that some of the Cayuses and Umatillas were willing to negotiate with the government, as were all the Walla Wallas, who had few roots there anyway.[37]

From August 7 to 13, 1871, the Umatilla tribes met with commissioners appointed to conduct the negotiations: Meacham, Cornoyer, and J. White, along with Special Commissioner Felix

---

[35] Huntington, Annual Report, October 26, 1866, *ibid.*
[36] *Spirit of the West* (Walla Walla, Washington Territory), October 15, 1875, p. 3.
[37] Meacham to Parker, June 23, 1871, *Oregon Superintendency*, I:10, Roll 10.

Brunot. Meacham was apprehensive that Cornoyer, who was married to a Cayuse woman and had been appointed under Catholic auspices, might express church opinions, which were generally opposed to removal. Six days of meetings gave the chiefs ample time to exercise their skill in palaver.

In all of them Howlish Wampo spoke first and eloquently, as usual, a recognition of his leadership—and that of his people among the tribes—and of his affluence, for he reportedly owned one to two thousand horses (but no more than his fellow Cayuse Tintinemetsa, who was said to have had three thousand), a large herd of cattle, a good farm, and four or five thousand dollars. The privilege of speaking first was recognition, too, of Howlish Wampo's reputation for holding his own with white men, particularly where horseflesh was concerned, on or off the turf. He wagered not only on horse races but also on the presidential election of 1872, offering to put a thousand dollars on the reelection of President Grant.[38] Perhaps he could have bet more on Grant's reelection had the president or his predecessors sent mules laden with money to the reservation, as Howlish Wampo claimed Governor Stevens had promised.

On the last day of the council, Howlish Wampo summarized his opposition to the commissioners' proposals, stressing that the Indians were basically herdsmen and not farmers, as government officials wanted them to become, and that they had no intention of giving up the piece of land they "looked upon as a mother." In conclusion he politely told the commissioners and the white men they represented to tend to their own affairs.[39]

Pressure by the whites to appropriate the reservation did not slacken with the end of the council. During the 1870's they discovered beneath the bunchgrass a soil capable of producing fine crops of wheat—and not in the valley garden spots alone. Before

[38] In *Wigwam and War-Path*, 183–202, Meacham describes Howlish Wampo's skill as a horseman. See also *Walla Walla Union*, August 3, 1872, p. 3; Davenport, "Recollections of an Indian Agent," 12–13.

[39] Secretary of Interior, *Annual Report, 1871, House Exec. Doc.* No. 5, 42 Cong., 2 sess., Serial 1505, pp. 511–32.

the decade was out, the reservation and its environs were recognized as one of the greatest wheat-producing areas on earth. Little wonder that the editor of Pendleton's *East Oregonian* editorialized in 1877: "We favor their removal as it is a burning shame to keep this fine body of land for a few worthless Indians."[40]

The principal chiefs of the three tribes began to harbor second thoughts about remaining on their tract of land. In councils in 1875 they expressed willingness to cede their reserve to the government in exchange for removal to the Wallowa Valley. Invitations to the Cayuses to make this move were extended by Young Joseph (Hinmahtooyahlatkekht), son of Old Joseph of the Nez Percés, and his followers in their ancestral home (they had renounced an 1863 treaty drastically reducing the Nez Percé Reservation as established by the 1855 treaty). Young Joseph was not unmindful that with the removal of Umatilla Reservation Indians to the Wallowa that valley stood a better chance of becoming a reservation, since the government was now pressing him and his people to abandon it and settle on the Nez Percé Reservation. Ties between the Cayuses and the nontreaty Nez Percés remained close, and Nez Percé appeals to the Cayuses to join them were strong. In early 1875, General O. O. Howard, commander of what was now called the Department of the Columbia, met Young Joseph, who had come with some of his people to visit his Cayuse friends. The Cayuses in council that fall complained that because of the white problem they would be compelled to fight to protect themselves if a remedy was not forthcoming. Attending one of the sessions was Father Mesplié, now army chaplain at Fort Boise, to whom the chiefs gave signed depositions to forward to authorities in Washington, D.C.[41]

In late spring, 1877, Howlish Wampo passed through Boise City en route to meet some members of his tribe who had been serving as scouts under General George Crook in the Sioux coun-

---

[40] *East Oregonian* (Pendleton), December 22, 1877, p. 2.
[41] Mesplié to Hon. J. H. Muchret, December 6, 1875, *Records of the Umatilla Indian Agency*; *East Oregonian*, July 7, 1877, p. 2.

try. Cayuses served more or less willingly with the military against their traditional foes. In 1864, for example, Umhowlish, leading ten Cayuse scouts, had joined territorial troops from Fort Walla Walla to chase Snakes into Nevada. In 1873, they had served with Donald McKay, of the fur-trading McKay clan, in a campaign in southern Oregon against the Modocs, from whom they had taken scalps.[42] Now they had sought to even the score with the Sioux for running off their horses.[43]

On his way east, Howlish Wampo told Mesplié that in two years' time hostile feelings had not lessened on the Umatilla and that, although he was peacefully inclined, there was a possibility that his braves might join the Nez Percés in war to keep their homeland. When Howlish Wampo returned through Boise City, he told the priest that he thought war would break out before he got home because the Nez Percés had powwowed with the Bannacks and other tribes of the region. Then, speaking of General Howard, who had conferred with the Nez Percés in late April and early May about the necessity of their removal, Howlish Wampo said:

> The one-armed white chief has a smooth tongue and speaks softly and nicely to the Indians, but his good words have no power to reach their hearts. The Indians laughed at the General and his fine speeches saying that they would never persuade them to give up the Wallowa valley which they were resolved to keep at every hazard.[44]

After the Nez Percé councils, Howard accompanied Awahitin (Owtoyaktin, or Young Chief) to meet scattered Columbia River tribes. Although a Cayuse, Awahitin was the paid chief of the Walla Wallas, whose actual chief, Homily, had been temporarily deposed by the Interior Department for having two wives. How-

42 Joseph Gaston, *The Centennial History of Oregon, 1811–1911*, I, 82.
43 Tintinemetsa, who attended "The Last Great Indian Council" in Montana in 1909 (not the Tintinemetsa mentioned in the text), spoke of the ancient Cayuse-Sioux rivalry. See Joseph Kossuth Dixon, *The Vanishing Race: The Last Great Indian Council*, 61.
44 *East Oregonian*, July 7, 1877, p. 2.

ard exhorted the renegades, such as Smohalla and other Indians roaming the Columbia, "to run to the shelter of the reservations as soon as possible." Anticipating trouble from the Nez Percés, he wished none from the Indians along the Columbia River, knowing that should war erupt the Nez Percés might seek their help.

Lying between these Columbia River peoples and the Nez Percés, the Cayuses and their reservation allies held the key to peace in a large area of the interior. Smarting from their losses in war a quarter of a century earlier and from confinement in the wake of that war, would they now cast their lot with the increasingly hostile members of Young Joseph's band? The one-armed general hoped not.

XVII
Outpost of a Dying Race

Needless to say, the outbreak of the Nez Percé War in mid-June, 1877, caused great excitement among settlers surrounding the Umatilla Reservation. They saw Indians under every bush. To put them at ease, agent Cornoyer and interpreter John McBean rode into Walla Walla on June 27 with a delegation of unarmed Indians. To avoid alarming the townspeople, their coming had been announced by telegraph. Cornoyer told the assembled whites that he had called a council of all reservation Indians over sixteen years of age and that he had brought some of them along to show their friendly disposition. The chiefs made amicable speeches. Said Howlish Wampo: "I have only one heart and tongue." Then Jesse, a Nez Percé who was visiting the reservation when war broke out (and was urged by Cornoyer to remain there until it was over), addressed the group: "Look at me. I am half Cayuse and half Nez Percé. When the blood was spilled over here [at the Whitman mission], my people took Mr. Spaulding and saved him. From that day I have never taken arms against the whites. If you arrest an Indian try him. If he is hostile punish him." The speech brought cheers from the crowd. So did the introduction of braves who had fought under Crook. The scalps they had taken were Indian, not white.[1]

A small group of Cayuses went to join Young Joseph. Many belonged to the Dreamer faith, which had made inroads into the two tribes. The center of Dreamer activities on the reservation—to which Joseph and his people often repaired—was Thorn Hollow

1 *Walla Walla Statesman*, June 30, 1877, p. 2; *East Oregonian*, June 30, 1877, p. 2; *Walla Walla Union*, June 30, 1877, p. 3.

(Leelachpa, or Many Pine Trees) along the middle Umatilla.[2] It was likely at this spot that Joseph's people enticed some of the Cayuses to join their cause. During the war scattered bands of peaceful Nez Percés, fearing Joseph's wrath for their isolation, went to live among the Cayuses, Coeur d'Alenes, and Spokanes.[3] After fleeing eastward across the Rockies, pursued by General Howard, Joseph and his band were captured just short of their destination—Canada. They were taken from the point of their surrender to Indian Territory (present-day Oklahoma). One group of warring Nez Percés under Chief White Bird escaped and for a time remained free to return secretly to the Umatilla Reservation, where they were harbored by its residents. From this band in late July six warriors, one woman, and a child were captured by Captain Evan Miles, of the Twenty-first Infantry.

General Howard related that a Bannack-Snake chief named Buffalo Horn, whom he had employed in pursuit of Joseph, had become dissatisfied with the conduct of the war. For this and "other causes," his people began their own war in 1878. The "other causes," which Howard might have explained, were the ineptness and inefficiency of the Indian Bureau in dealing with these peoples. In the spring some 150 braves under Buffalo Horn moved toward the Malheur Reservation in east-central Oregon to meet dissident Paiutes. With the death of Buffalo Horn and the passage of leadership from Paiute Chief Oits (Oytes) to Egan (Eagan), the combined bands raided north toward the Columbia River, enlisting other Indians along the way.[4]

Howard said that on one occasion, when Egan's Cayuse parents

<hr>

[2] It has been impossible to obtain from white sources the number of Cayuses who went with Joseph. Present-day Indians tell of Cayuses joining the Nez Percé chief. William Minthorn interview, Thornhollow, Oregon, July 16, 1968, and Amie Webb interview, Thornhollow, Oregon, July 17, 1968. See also Spier, *Prophet Dance of the Northwest*, 21, 46, for information about the Dreamer religion among these people. Another group on the Umatilla was the Feather Cult. See Cora DuBois, *The Feather Cult of the Middle Columbia*, 16.

[3] Oliver Otis Howard, *Nez Perce Joseph*, 19.

[4] Oliver Otis Howard, *Famous Indian Chiefs I Have Known*, 270–71. Howard explains the sources of Paiute dissatisfaction.

and a few others from their tribe were gathering roots in a meadow, they were attacked by Indians from the Snake country. After a fierce battle all the Cayuses except the children were killed. Among those captured and scattered among the Snake-Paiutes was Egan. He was subsequently trained by the Paiutes in their best traditions and developed into a strong, athletic man. By warring against other Indians and American soldiers, he gained a Paiute chieftaincy.

What kind of welcome would the Snake-Paiutes receive from the Cayuses? The latter had a long record of conflict with various freebooting bands of the former, and the trouble did not end with the coming of American military forces and the beginning of the reservation era. Because of its own concern with Snake depredations, the army had been pursuing them since the late 1840's. Cayuses serving with Captain Currey's expedition in late spring, 1863, were reported to have killed six Snake Indians on the Owyhee.[5] In the spring of 1865 the army permitted Cayuse and Umatilla scouts to pursue the Snakes and retrieve stolen horses, but the Cayuses were afraid that during their absence the Snakes would return and "gobble up" their horses and cattle. In 1871 the government sought to retrieve Snake captives, some of whom the Cayuses held at Umatilla Agency.[6]

Better armed and provisioned than their Snake enemies, the Cayuses and their reservation allies held their own in attacks against the marauders, but it was difficult to cope with incursions. Cayuse women digging roots in the hills had to keep a sharp lookout for *twelka* ("enemies"). Often disguised in coyote skins, the *twelka* spied out Cayuse camps to steal their stock, women, and children.[7]

In late spring, 1878, Cornoyer received permission for some of his Indians to serve under General Howard as scouts against

[5] For an account of some of the Snake depredations, see Edward R. Geary, *Depredations and Massacre by the Snake River Indians.* See also Barnhart to Huntington, May 28, 1865, *Oregon Superintendency*, Microfilm No. 2, Roll 21.

[6] McKay to Meacham, December 20, 1871, McKay Papers.

[7] Amie Webb interview.

the Snake-Paiutes. It was reported in June, however, that elderly men on the reservation—and even the young ones—were luke-warm to the proposal, preferring a stay-at-home policy. Cornoyer did not explain the Indians' negative attitude, but there was considerable disaffection with the government. The influence of resident priest Louis L. Conrardy (Conrardi), especially among Catholic Cayuses, tended to keep them more tractable, but they were not unmindful of their blood ties with Egan. Now the latter was returning to the land of his birth. Egan and his band moved toward the Columbia River in July, seeking allies and commit-ting depredations east of the agency at Cayuse Station. They were checked about the middle of the month by army regulars. Accord-ing to Cornoyer, on July 14 he received a proposal from one of eleven reservation Indians who, with about fifty from the Colum-bia River, had joined the hostiles. They said that, if he and others who had joined the Snake-Paiutes were granted pardons and that if a party of soldiers and Cayuses were sent to a certain place in the mountains to help them, they would decoy Egan into captivity. The whites accepted the terms. That night forty-three Cayuses went to the designated spot.

The following morning the party returned, Cornoyer reported, with Egan's scalp and those of four others, having killed twelve men and taken five prisoners and about three hundred head of horses. Umatilla Chief Umapine took credit for killing Egan. Since he was not with the Cayuse posse because he was a Umatilla and yet was in on the kill, it is very likely that he and his followers were the Indians who had defected to the hostile Indians. If this was true, then he had apparently helped barter Egan's life for a pardon and restitution to the reservation. Later accounts exon-erated Umapine and his men, making their defection to Egan appear to be a careful ruse, because, although he knew that the Umatillas had promised to come to the Paiute chief's aid, he also knew that they never would.[8]

8 There are numerous and conflicting accounts of this phase of the Snake-Paiute war. For an official account, see Secretary of War, *Annual Report, 1878, House Exec.*

Although the Bannack-Paiutes returned to their homeland, a small band continued to commit depredations. Because they lived on wild sheep in the Salmon River country in Idaho Territory, they were dubbed Sheepeaters, but they were actually "a small band of renegade Bannacks, Shoshones, and Weisers." On July 9 twenty young men on the reservation were recruited for six-month hitches as scouts to hunt down the Sheepeaters. Under Lieutenant E. S. Farrow of the First Regiment, U.S. Infantry, and Lieutenant W. C. Brown, First Cavalry, they rendered invaluable service to the government. Singled out for his work by Brown was Cayuse Chief Sergeant Charley Shaplish (Pai Shamkain, or Dr. Whirlwind, as he was known to the whites). Also cited by Brown was Cayuse Chief Sergeant Yatiniawitz, a lean, wiry, former fighter against the whites, a son-in-law of Howlish Wampo. Another important Cayuse serving as a scout was Sergeant Tiloukaikt, who later went by the name Captain Sumpkin because at one time he was an officer of the Indian reservation police force (organized in 1881).[9]

Perhaps one reason the scouts enlisted more eagerly in the Sheepeater campaign than they had at the beginning of the Snake-

---

Doc. No. 1, 45 Cong., 3 sess., Serial 1843, pp. 224–26. See also Mark V. Weatherford, *Bannack-Piute War: The Campaign and Battles*; George Francis Brimlow, *The Bannock Indian War of 1878*; *Oregonian*, July 20, 1878; J. F. Santee, "Egan of the Piutes," *Washington Historical Quarterly*, XXVI, 1 (January, 1935), 16–25; James Fulton, "The Dalles and Eastern Oregon Events," 16–17; Clarence Hines, "Indian Agent's Letter Book, I: The Piute-Bannock Raid of July, 1878," *Oregon Historical Quarterly*, XXXIX (March–December, 1938), 8–15; William Parsons, *An Illustrated History of Umatilla County*, 217–18. One Cayuse, Ollicut, not Joseph's brother, joined the Snake-Paiutes in the war. When he came home, he was considered such an outcast among whites and Indians alike that he went to Montana, where he enrolled on the Flathead Reservation. David Steve Hall interview, Mission, Oregon, July 18, 1969.
    9 W. C. Brown, "The Sheepeater Campaign," *Tenth Biennial Report of the Board of Trustees of the State Historical Society of Idaho for the Years 1925–1926*, 27–43; Microcopy of Records in the National Archives, *Register of Enlistments of Soldiers Belonging to the First Regiment of United States Infantry, Registers of Enlistments in the United States Army, 1789–1914, Indian Scouts, 1878–1914*, Vols. 152–54, Microfilm No. 233, Roll 71. In 1879 several Umatilla Reservation men were recruited as scouts for three- and five-year hitches but were soon mustered out.

Paiute War was that they believed the government's position was now stronger. On the day of their recruitment there was a council at which their chiefs reported on a recent trip to see the Great Father. Like Chief Moses of the Columbia Sinkiuses, recipient of a reservation, Howlish Wampo was impressed with the power of the government. Cornoyer, with Pambrun interpreting, explained the agreement worked out in Washington giving each Indian the alternative of taking lands on the reservation in severalty (each tribal member of either sex above eighteen years of age was entitled to 160 acres and each below that age 40 acres) or removing to another reservation should he so wish. Father Mesplié reported that, although they were not altogether satisfied with the government proposal, the "older and more civilized" of the tribes would perhaps accept it. Others not so disposed, he added, would go to other reservations or wander off with the wild Indians.[10] Both of the latter alternatives posed problems. None of the Indians liked the idea of living on a reservation with Chief Moses, and wandering was becoming more difficult each year. Settlers in the Wallowa Valley were loudly complaining that Umatilla Reservation Indians were invading their lands.

The whites were relentless in trying to slice chunks from the reservation. Pendleton citizens petitioned for the sale of a portion of it adjoining their town. In council on January 31, 1881, the Indians agreed to sell, but, since they could not agree on a price, they chose to leave the decision to the Great Father. On March 3, 1885, Congress passed the Slater bill, which reduced the reservation and put the Indians under allotment. Special agent Charles H. Dickson sought to obtain the Indians' consent to the measure but failed. In 1885, a commission composed of Judge W. C. La Dow and former Senator James Harvey Slater, attempted to secure their approval but also failed. In the fall of 1886, Colonel William Parsons and Inspector George Pearsons succeeded in gaining the Indians' consent to the Allotment Act of March 3, 1885. The reservation was reduced about one-fourth, with the

[10] *Catholic Sentinel*, July 10, 1879, p. 4.

surplus opened to public sale, and the remainder—about 100,000 acres of excellent agricultural land—was allotted: 160 acres to family heads and 40 or 80 acres to children according to age. An equal amount was set aside for the Indians as grazing and timber land.[11]

The Cayuses, who for a century had sought the white man's material magic, now had more of it than ever before. Some of it they accepted—subsidies, clothing, buildings, tools—and, of course, there was always liquor. Ironically, they could not accept everything the white man had to offer. The one thing which had been their pride, the hallmark of their fame, the cayuse, was becoming anachronistic in an environment now lending itself to farming. Even had their ponies pulled plows and other implements (which the Cayuses had never wanted in the first place), their owners would have preferred the thrill of equestrian life to the boredom of agriculture. Not the least important result of the upstaging of the cayuse by the American workhorse were several years of mange among the former and a corresponding drop in their value. During the early 1860's an average cayuse brought anywhere from thirty to sixty dollars and could be used for riding or packing to the mines. Three years later the price had dropped to as low as fifteen dollars. In 1875, according to the editor of the *Walla Walla Union*, a cayuse brought only five dollars, because "our people don't 'hanker' after Cayuse stock like they used to."[12]

Not only were cayuses becoming anachronistic, but, it appeared to observers, so were their owners. Some thought that the Cayuses were reaping the whirlwind of divine judgment for the

11 For a description of the reservation cessions, see Charles C. Royce, "Indian Land Cessions in the United States," *Eighteenth Annual Report of the Bureau of American Ethnology to the Secretary of the Smithsonian Institution, 1896–97*, 804, 908–909, 928. See also Parsons, *An Illustrated History of Umatilla County*, 244. *Records of the Umatilla Indian Agency* is a rich source of information on the allotting of lands on the reservation.

12 *Walla Walla Statesman*, March 23, 1866, p. 3, and *Walla Walla Union*, April 17, 1875, p. 3. For a description of early farming, see C. A. Barrett, "Early Farming in Umatilla County," *Oregon Historical Quarterly*, XVI (March–December, 1915), 343–49.

Whitman massacre. Kate McBeth, of the Nez Percé Presbyterian mission, wrote in 1908 that "there is no boasting here of their blood. They have heard too often, 'That is the tribe that killed Whitman.' They rejected the message, killed the messenger, and have lost their identity as a tribe."[13] In 1881, General Howard, who was closer to the massacre than Miss McBeth, had said of it: "Blood tells. Why ever forget it?" In 1907 he described as a Cayuse the Umatilla Umapine, referring to the self-declared killer of Egan as "a cruel and wicked man"—an indication of how vividly the Cayuse role in the Whitman massacre was still recalled in the white community sixty years later.[14] Others somewhat less detached than General Howard and Miss McBeth might have agreed with Stephen A. Lowell, who commented about the Cayuses in 1898: "If Providence has so ordered the race will survive, but from a human standpoint the decree seems otherwise."[15]

Fears for the survival of the Indians of the Umatilla were expressed by Archbishop Blanchet in a letter to the commissioner of education in early 1879. He attributed what appeared to him to be their approaching demise to several factors: their failure to remain on reservations, hence their mingling with whites and the attending results; inbreeding resulting from their forced confinement, which perpetuated diseases; premature death from exposure, parental neglect, abortions, and the "noisy and useless *Tamanwas*" over the sick, accompanied by the continued practice of killing medicine men and women; inadequate marriage laws, which opened the door to polygamy and prostitution; diminishing authority of chiefs, whose powers were more nominal than were their annuities; lack of medical care; ardent spirits; and, finally, a "pagan, atheistical and godless education."[16]

In 1885, Father Conrardy proposed a plan to solve the plight of the Umatilla tribesmen. Criticizing the waste of government

[13] Kate C. McBeth, *The Nez Perces Since Lewis and Clark*, 74.
[14] Howard, *Nez Perce Joseph*, 75; Howard, *Famous Indian Chiefs*, 277.
[15] Stephen A. Lowell, "The Indians of the Whitman Massacre," *Whitman College Quarterly*, II, 2 (June, 1898), 20–28.
[16] *Catholic Sentinel*, January 30, 1879, p. 3.

money in "barrels without bottoms" agencies and the "indifference" of the agents, he suggested a "little community of farmers"
as a nucleus around which the Indians could be gathered. The
nucleus, composed of the best families, would receive government help to get started. Sufficient land for the project would be
taken in severalty, and houses and barns would be provided. Careful supervision and direction would be required for some time
to assure that the Indians would become industrious and familiar
with the routine of farm life and thereby become independent.
Agents would be retained, but the government would appoint a
committee of three upstanding citizens to keep the agents honest.
Agent Davenport wrote: "The practice of combining against the
Government for mutual profit is so common that all agents are
regarded in the same unenviable light." In essence, Conrardy's
plan was the Jesuit system, through which the Society of Jesus had
sought to create in Oregon another Paraguay (where it had been
successfully employed).[17]

Oregon proved to be no Paraguay. Influenced by the twin
American philosophies of pragmatism and social Darwinism (off-
setting the protection of the Church), the Umatilla Reservation
in the nineteenth century, like most other American institutions,
was left to evolve in trial and error. Early twentieth-century pro-
gressivism brought to it more governmental concern and attempts
to correct past mistakes. Lowell pictured the Cayuses in 1898 as
clinging to the past but making some concessions to the future.
The women, he wrote, still wore the brilliant kerchief, the *top-
mosh*, and families lived chiefly in circular reed lodges, sleeping
on skins, their feet to open fires. There was considerable "vice and
laziness," although in marital matters the Cayuses followed white
customs; they had learned that at death their lands descended
according to Oregon law and that records of legal marriage and

17 Davenport, "Recollections of an Indian Agent," 18–19. Conrardy's plan ap-
peared in the *Catholic Sentinel*, October 1, 1885, p. 1. For an explanation of the
Jesuit system as proposed in the interior Pacific Northwest, see Robert Ignatius
Burns, *The Jesuits and the Indian Wars of the Northwest*, 36–42.

formal divorce were often essential in settling estates. Lowell observed that tribal chieftaincies had been formally abolished by the government (in 1891).[18]

Chief Howlish Wampo died in March, 1880. His Roman Catholic funeral was attended mostly by whites, although he reportedly willed one horse to each Indian on the reservation.[19] Soon thereafter his brother became chief. The last formally recognized Cayuse chief, Yatiniawitz, crippled earlier in a fall from a horse, died in the mid-1890's. The decline of their office was, of course, a bitter pill for the chiefs to swallow, especially since the man who held it at the time it was abolished was Yatinia-witz, a Cayuse of strong character. When he died, the half-Cayuse, half-Nez Percé Awahitin assumed the chieftaincy, but his claim was not recognized, a situation which caused further friction between the Cayuses and the government.

In one of a widely read series of articles about the Umatilla Reservation at the turn of the century, Charles N. Crewdson stated that when Awahitin died his kinsman and likely heir was the burly Paul Showaway. However, Tow-watoy (Hatswallatakapt), wanting the position, went to see Chief Joseph, who had no official connection with the Cayuse chieftaincy but nonetheless exercised considerable influence among the Cayuse people. Joseph, said Crewdson, sent word to the Cayuses that Tow-watoy should be their leader. About that time a reporter for a West Coast newspaper wrote an article, accompanied by Tow-watoy's picture, telling how he had been made chief. The Cayuses did not immediately confirm Joseph's choice, but, chancing to be shown the page on which Tow-watoy's picture appeared, voted for him at the next powwow. They did so, they said, because "it was in the paper." The magic of the printed page still worked for them in the twentieth century.[20] Some saw in Joseph's interference a move

18 Lowell, "The Indians of the Whitman Massacre," 25–27.
19 *East Oregonian*, March 27, 1880, p. 3.
20 Charles N. Crewdson, "Traits of the Indian Man," *Spokesman-Review* (Spokane, Washington), January 24, 1904, p. 16.

to establish a toehold on the Umatilla, a preliminary step in regaining his old Wallowa home.[21] Former agent Major Lee Moorhouse wrote in 1908 that with Tow-watoy's death no one had cared take up "the empty honor" of the chieftaincy.[22] An Indian wisely remarked: "There will be but one chief, and that is the Government of Washington." So-called chieftains remained on the reservation, making important decisions until the Business Council of the Umatilla Confederated Tribes, through a process of evolution, took over their powers.

The strengthened hand of the Great Father on the reservation gave it a government school in 1890. In 1881, Catholic agent R. H. Fay and Father Conrardy had unsuccessfully resisted the attempts of Captain M. C. Wilkinson to take reservation children to the government Indian school in Forest Grove, Oregon.[23] Another casualty of growing secularization and the breakdown of the Grant peace policy was the temporary loss of the Catholic Indian school in late 1886. Acting on orders from his Washington superiors, Catholic agent Bartholomew Coffey had "the cross removed from the school." His subsequent dismissal (to Catholics "like a judgment of Providence") and the opening of another Catholic school in 1890 could not stem secularism, which the Roman Catholic church bitterly opposed.

Particularly annoying to Catholics was the establishment of a Presbyterian church on the reservation in 1882. Since Spalding's return to the Nez Percés in 1871 under Presbyterian auspices—the "fruition of seed planted by the martyred Whitman"—his teaching had spread to the closely allied Cayuses (in May, 1874, old Chief Umhowlish was baptized Marcus Whitman by the missionary). The church's pastor was the Reverend James Hayes, a Nez Percé Indian. In 1899 the Reverend J. M. Cornelison came

21 A good picture of reservation life at this time can be found in Moorhouse, "Umatilla Indian Reservation," 235–50.

22 Parsons, An Illustrated History of Umatilla County, 225; Moorhouse, "Umatilla Indian Reservation," 235–50.

23 McKay to Wilkinson, October 5, 1881, McKay Papers.

as the first white missionary among the Cayuses since Whitman, to serve the Presbyterian Tutuilla Church.[24]

In an official census about the turn of the century, the Cayuses numbered between four and five hundred. Walla Walla numbers were about the same, for many of their people had come in from the Columbia River. The Umatilla population had dropped because of intermarriage. Increasing governmental concern for the health of the Indians had slowed their death rate. Although many Indians told government officials that they were Cayuses, it is very possible that they were not purely so. Before 1900 the Cayuses (unlike the Walla Wallas, who intermarried with Hudson's Bay Company employees) kept their blood relatively unmixed with that of the whites; they were unable to do so in the case of other Indians. Where disease had failed to diminish Cayuse numbers, intermarriage had. Where at one time intermarriage was primarily with the Nez Percés, life on the reservation had increased such ties with the Walla Wallas and the Umatillas. An indication of this was the growing use of the Umatilla dialect among the Cayuses in the late 1880's, although Nez Percé continued to be the dominant tongue. White observers on the reservation at the turn of the century reported that only a half-dozen oldsters spoke the original Cayuse language.[25] In his report to the commissioner of Indian affairs in 1891, agent Moorhouse said that he could not distinguish between Cayuse and Walla Walla names.

The Cayuses' pride remained strong and carried over into the twentieth century, as did the age-old distinction between them and Columbia River tribes. Lessie L. Cornelison, relating the poignant story of Allen Patawa, son of a Cayuse woman, who visited relatives on the Columbia River about 1895 observed:

[24] The founding and early years of the Presbyterian church on the reservation are described in J. M. Cornelison, "The Seed of the Martyrs."

[25] J. W. Powell, "Indian Linguistic Families of America North of Mexico," *Seventh Annual Report of the Bureau of Ethnology to the Secretary of the Smithsonian Institution, 1885–86*, 128; Stewart Culin, "A Summer Trip Among the Western Indians," *Free Museum of Science and Art, Department of Archaeology, University of Pennsylvania, Bulletin*, III, 3 (May, 1901), 125–43.

The difference in type between these people and the reservation tribes, who had been reared in the greener land of the upper Umatilla was marked. The hard life, restricted diet, the fierce sand storms, and burning desert heat had combined to make comparatively young people old, leathery and lined. The really old looked very aged indeed, with thin gray hair and bleary eyes.[26]

Today on the Umatilla the term Cayuse Tribe is seldom heard; it has been incorporated into Umatilla Confederated Tribes. But seldom has the name of a people so numerically small contributed so much to a regional or national lexicon. Consider these uses to which the name Cayuse has been put: a range horse; a rodeo in the Northwest, the Cayuse Performance; a cold east wind blowing down the Columbia River; a crater on Broken Top Mountain in the Deschutes; a Cascade Mountains pass; a sternwheeler (the *Kiyus*) on the Columbia and Snake rivers in the 1860's; a Frenchman or French-Canadian, married to an Indian woman, known as Cayuse French; a town in eastern Oregon; a type of helicopter used in the Vietnam War; a set of twins made known through the camera wizardry of former agent Lee Moorhouse. In his collection was a photograph of the "Cayuse Twins," Toxelox and Alompum. Complementing the human interest of the photograph in many newspapers, magazines, and travel bulletins was a story. Perhaps more fiction than truth (at this stage of Cayuse history), it described the survival of the only Cayuse twins known to have escaped death at the hands of their people. The Cayuses, said the story, killed twins at birth to appease the Great Spirit.[27]

The Cayuses' hopes of maintaining their heritage steadily faded with the advance of white culture. It was difficult to perpetuate the old ways, for the synthetic fabric of reservation life had enshrouded them. However, the Cayuses' annual participation in the colorful Pendleton Roundup, begun in 1910, brought vicarious renewal of past glories. The whites were happy that

---

[26] Lessie L. Cornelison, "Allen Patawa."

[27] The origin of the twins taboo is explained in Charles N. Crewdson, "Christmas for the Hyas Skookum Papoose," *Seattle Post Intelligencer*, December 20, 1903.

Shaplish, on tour with a medicine show in the late 1890's, was not practicing the arts of his profession, which had brought death to the Whitmans. Yet in December, 1901, two reservation Indians who poisoned a medicine woman were rescued from hanging by a white jury; their attorney had argued that his clients were influenced by mores different from those of whites.[28]

There was sadness, too, that the cayuse had been sidetracked by the mechanical horses of Cyrus H. McCormick, and the Oregon Railway and Navigation Company (a railroad was laid out across the reservation in 1880 and constructed four years later; the Union Pacific subsequently used the line). Reapers cut ripened wheat, and locomotives thundered along the Umatilla, gathering steam at Thorn Hollow for their bold thrust into the Blue Mountains. Free passes given to the Cayuses by the railroad, providing easy travel to the Blue Mountains and to their old fishing grounds at The Dalles, could scarcely repay them for losses on the iron trail: horses, cattle, and occasionally even themselves.[29] Howlish Wampo in his grave was spared the sight of cayuses being rounded up during the Great Depression to be sold as dog food to Portlanders, a fate he might have considered scarcely worse for them than that which befell others: pulling streetcars in Chicago.[30] Death also spared the chief the sight of fishing grounds blotted out by Columbia River dams in the mid-twentieth century and the resulting conflicts over fishing rights on the river. He would have been overjoyed in the 1960's to see members

28 "Indian Doctors Have a Hard Lot," Bagley Scrapbook, No. 5.
29 Information about the application of the Oregon Railway and Navigation Company to build a railroad across the reservation and permission to do so, granted in an executive order dated January 22, 1881, may be found in U.S. Commissioner of Indian Affairs Hal Price to Umatilla Agent R. H. Fay, May 24, 1881, and Acting Commissioner Thomas N. McNichol to Fay, March 8, 1881, *Records of the Umatilla Indian Agency*. In these same records is correspondence between railroad and agency officials relative to Indian stock losses. The former argued that the Indians placed too high values on the stock they lost. Newspapers of the day contained many accounts of Indians killed by trains.
30 Claude Maxwell interview, Ephrata, Washington, November 5, 1969. Maxwell told of going back east with a load of cayuses, to be used in pulling transit cars. They were later replaced by mules.

of the Umatilla Confederated Tribes receive $2,450,000 for lands taken by the government.

What the Cayuses could not do to halt the march of time, history and memory can. One cannot forget a people whose influence extended beyond their existence as a tribe in a historical pageant, staged in the Columbia Empire, which told their story in eras: Aboriginal, Fur Trade, Missionary, Two Wars, Reservation. That the Cayuses' lodge was pitched at an important crossroad of history was due not alone to the accident of time and place but also to their character as a people. In what has been described as his finest Indian portrait, *The Fish Hawk*, Moorhouse's camera captured not only the face of the son of a Cayuse chief but also that of the People of the Flint Rocks: "blanket wrapped, breast bared to meet the storm beating their race to the earth—wind blown hair proudly thrown back—eyes hurling defiance to the world." The last words in "Lonely Outpost of a Dying Race," Ella Higginson's text for the Moorhouse photograph, are a fitting epitaph for the Cayuse Indians:

> *those last dark ones ... drifting silently*
> *and uncomplainingly into the great shadow.*

Appendix A: White's Laws of the Nez Percés

Friction between whites and Indians in the Oregon country, most of it brought on by the Indians' proclivity to do as they pleased, regardless of how the whites might feel about it, made it necessary to establish laws to govern human conduct in everyday life and to punish miscreants. To Dr. Elijah White, an agent of the federal government, fell the task of drawing them up and persuading the Indians to accept them. Called the Laws of the Nez Percés, they were ratified by the Indians in December, 1842:

Art. 1. Whoever wilfully takes life shall be hung.

Art. 2. Whoever burns a dwelling house shall be hung.

Art. 3. Whoever burns an outbuilding shall be imprisoned six months, receive fifty lashes, and pay all damages.

Art. 4. Whoever carelessly burns a house, or any property, shall pay damages.

Art. 5. If any one enter a dwelling, without permission of the occupant, the chiefs shall punish him as they think proper.

Art. 6. If any one steal he shall pay back two fold; and if it be the value of a beaver skin or less, he shall receive twenty-five lashes; and if the value is over a beaver skin he shall pay back two-fold, and receive fifty lashes.

Art. 7. If any one take a horse, and ride it, without permission, or take any article, and use it, without liberty, he shall pay for the use of it, and receive from twenty to fifty lashes, as the chief shall direct.

Art. 8. If any one enter a field, and injure the crops, or throw down the fence, so that cattle or horses go in and do damage, he shall pay all damages, and receive twenty-five lashes for every offence.

Art. 9. Those only may keep dogs who travel or live among the game; if a dog kill a lamb, calf, or any domestic animal, the owner shall pay the damage, and kill the dog.

Art. 10. If an Indian raise a gun or other weapon against a white man, it shall be reported to the chiefs, and they shall punish him. If a white person do the same to an Indian, it shall be reported to Dr. White, and he shall redress it.

Art. 11. If an Indian break these laws, he shall be punished by his chiefs; if a white man break them, he shall be reported to the agent, and be punished at his instance.[1]

[1] White, *Ten Years in Oregon*, 189–90; Victor, *Early Indian Wars of Oregon*, 48.

Appendix B: The Cayuse Indians' Letter to Governor Abernethy

After the massacre at Waiilatpu, the whites wanted to take revenge in an all-out war against the Indians. The latter wanted to talk peace. At a council on December 20, 1847, Cayuse chiefs Tauitau, Five Crows, Camaspelo, and Tiloukaikt proposed six steps toward settling white-Indian differences in a letter to Oregon Provisional Governor George Abernethy:

> The principal chiefs of the Cayuses in council assembled state: That a young Indian, who understands English, and who slept in Dr. Whitman's room, heard the Doctor, his wife, and Mr. Spalding express their desire of possessing the lands and animals of the Indians; that he stated also that Mr. Spalding said to the Doctor, "hurry giving medicines to the Indians, that they may soon die"; that the same Indian told the Cayuses, "if you do not kill the Doctor soon, you will all be dead before next spring"; that they buried six Cayuses on Sunday, November 28th, and three the next day; that the schoolmaster, Mr. Rodgers, stated to them before he died that the Doctor, his wife, and Mr. Spalding poisoned the Indians; that for several years past they had to deplore the death of their children; and that, according to these reports, they were led to believe that the whites had undertaken to kill them all, and that these were the motives which led them to kill the Americans.
>
> The same chiefs ask at present—
>
> 1st. That the Americans may not go to war with the Cayuses.
>
> 2d. That they may forget the lately committed murders, as the Cayuses will forget the murder of the son of the great chief Walla-Walla, committed in California.
>
> 3d. That two or three great men may come up to conclude peace.
>
> 4th. That as soon as these great men have arrived and concluded peace, they may take with them all the wom[e]n and children.
>
> 5th. They give assurance that they will not harm the Americans before the arrival of these two or three great men.

6th. They ask that Americans may not travel any more through their country, as their young men might do them harm.

TILOKAIKT
CAMASPELO
TAWATOWE
ACHEKAIA

Place of Tawatowe, Umatilla
December 20, 1847.[1]

1 *House Exec. Doc.*, No. 38, 35 Cong., 1 sess., Serial 955, p. 45.

Appendix C: Reward Offered the Nez Percés for Capture of the Cayuse Murderers

The whites' search for the Indians who participated in the Waiilatpu affair proved to be a difficult undertaking. The hostile Indians always managed to stay a step ahead of their pursuers. At Lapwai in May, 1848, Colonel Henry A. G. Lee and his 121 men tried a new tactic: they offered the Nez Percés several hundred dollars' worth of enticing merchandise for apprehending the murderers or any two of their principal men:

CLEARWATER CAMP, 23d May, 1848

We, the undersigned, promise to pay to the Nez Percés or other Indians, or their agent, the articles, sums, and amounts annexed to our names, respectively, for the capture and delivery to the authorities of Oregon territory, any two of the following named Indians, viz., Teloukikt, Tamsucy, Tamahas, Joe Lewis, or Edward Teloukikt; or half the amount for any one of them. We also promise to pay one-fourth of the amount as specified above for the capture and delivery of any one of the following, viz., Llou-Llou, Pips, Frank Escaloom, Quiamashouskin, Estools, Showshow, Pahosh, Cupup-Cupup, or any other engaged in the massacre. The same to be paid whenever the service is rendered, and the fact that it has been rendered established: Burrel Davis, two blankets; Edwin F. Stone, two blankets, four shirts; P. F. Thompson, fifty dollars in goods; Harrison C. Johnson, two blankets; A. R. Fox, one blanket; James Etchel, one blanket; D. B. Matheny, one blanket, one shirt; Jeptha Garrison, two shirts; Wm. A. Culberson, two blankets; Jesse Cadwaleder, two blankets; Josiah Nelson, one blanket, one shirt; Martin F. Brown, two blankets; Isaac Walgamot, one blanket; John Eldridge, one blanket; A. S. Wilton, one blanket; J. W. Downer, one blanket, two shirts; Jacob Grazer, one blanket; Thos. J. Jackson, two blankets, two shirts; Clark Rogers, one blanket; John Scales, one blanket; Hiram Carnahan, two shirts; John Copenhaver, one blanket, two shirts; Isaiah C. Matheny, one blanket, one shirt; Benjamin Taylor, one shirt; M. B. Riggs, one blanket, two shirts; E. C. Dice, five shirts; S. E. Elkins, one blanket; J. W. Burch, two blankets, five shirts; M. A. Ford, four shirts; J. Butler, four shirts; John Orchard, four blankets; C. W. Cooke, twelve shirts; J. J. Tomerson, one blanket, one shirt; John Doran, two blankets; William Rogers, one blanket, one shirt; D. D. Duskins, two blankets, two shirts; F. T. McLentick, five shirts; Wm. McKee, one blanket; John McCord, one blanket; J. L. Snook, two blankets; J. Scudder, one blanket, one shirt; R. Mendenhall, one blanket, one shirt; John Carlin, one blanket; Wm. Olds, one blanket, one shirt; Phillip Peters, one blanket, one shirt, Laurence Hall, fifty dollars in goods; A. M. Poe, five dollars in goods; Jas. R. Bean, five dollars in goods; Jackson Reynolds, five dollars in goods; Jason Peters, five dollars in goods; Franklin Martin, one blanket; Robt. Loughlin, one blanket; Geo Frazier, four shirts; James M. Owen, one blanket, one shirt; John Menoia, two shirts; Josiah Lowrey, two shirts; J. J. Louk, two shirts; G. W. Pibern, two shirts; R. Christman, two shirts; Stephen King, one blanket, two shirts; John McLosky, one blanket, one shirt; Aaron Cone, two shirts; Robert Harman, two shirts; Wm. Hailey, one blanket, two shirts; Jas. O. Henderson, one blanket; Fred. Ketchum, two shirts; Joel Welch, four shirts; J. G. Fuller, two shirts; J. C. Robinson, two blankets; F. R. Hill, one blanket; Fred. Paul, wheat, five bushels; Peter A. Wice, one shirt; Charles Bolds, one blanket; Jas. E. Alsop, one blanket, one shirt; Daniel P. Barnes, one blanket, one shirt; Henry Coleman, one blanket; Wm. W. Porter, one blanket, one shirt; A. M. Peak, one blanket; W. Holman, one blanket, one shirt; I. N. Gilbert, two dollars; Fales Howard, one shirt; O. S. Thomas, one shirt; John Monroe, two shirts. Total, one hundred and twenty-five dollars in goods and wheat; blankets, sixty-seven; shirts, one hundred and four.[1]

1 Victor, *Early Indian Wars of Oregon*, 212–13.

Appendix D: Indictment of
Marcus Whitman's Murderers

At Oregon City on May 21, 1850, Tiloukaikt, Kiamasumpkin, Tomahas, Isaiachalakis, and Klokamas were indicted for the murder of Dr. and Mrs. Marcus Whitman and other whites at Waiilatpu on November 29, 1847. They were tried, found guilty, and sentenced to death. On June 3 they were hanged by United States Marshal Joe Meek:

United States of America

District Court of the United States of America, for the District of Oregon, County of Clackamas, SS:

At a District Court of the United States of America, for the District of Oregon, begun and holden at Oregon City in said county within and for said District, on the thirteenth day of May in the year of our Lord one thousand eight hundred and fifty

The Jurors of the United States, within and for said District, on their oath present: That on the twenty ninth day of November in the year of our Lord one thousand eight hundred and forty seven, at Wai-il-at-pu, in said county, the said place being then and there in the Indian country, certain Indians named Telakite, Tomahas otherwise called the Murderer, Clokomas, Issiaasheluckas and Kiamasumkin, with certain other Indians; whose names are to the Jurors unknown, with force and arms in and upon one Marcus Whitman, the said Whitman not then and there being an Indian, did make an assault, and that the said Telakite, Tomahas otherwise called the Murderer, Clokomas, Isiaasheluckas, and Kiamasumkin with other Indians whose names are unknown, certain guns, muskets and pistols, each of the same then and there being loaded and charged with gunpowder and bullets, which guns, muskets and pistols they the said Indians in their hands then and there had and held, to, against and upon the said Marcus Whitman, then and there feloniously wilfully and of their malice aforethought did shoot and discharge, and that the said Indians with the leaden bullets aforesaid, out of the muskets, guns and pistols aforesaid, then and there, by force of the gunpowder shot and sent forth as aforesaid, the said Marcus Whitman, in and upon the body of him, the said Marcus Whitman, then and there feloniously, wilfully and of their malice aforethought, did strike, penetrate and wound, giving to the said Marcus Whitman then and there with the leaden bullets aforesaid, do as aforesaid, shot, discharged, and sent forth out of the muskets, guns, and pistols as aforesaid, by the said Indians, in and upon the body of the said Marcus Whitman, several mortal wounds, of which said mortal wounds, he the said Marcus Whitman, then and there died. And so the Jurors aforesaid, upon their oath aforesaid, do say that the said Telakite, Tomahas otherwise called the Murderer, Clokomas, Isiaasheluckas, and Kiamasumkin, with certain other Indians, whose names to the Jurors, aforesaid are unknown, him the said Marcus Whitman, in manner and form aforesaid, then and there feloniously, wilfully and of their malice aforethought did kill and murder, and did then and there commit the crime of wilful murder upon the body of the said Marcus Whitman, against the peace and dignity of the said United States and contrary to the form of the Statutes in such case made and provided–And the Jurors aforesaid, upon their oath aforesaid, do further present, that certain Indians named Telakite, Tomahas, otherwise called the Murderer, Clokomas, Isiaasheluckas, and Kiamasumkin, with certain other Indians whose names are to the Jurors unknown, on the twenty ninth day of November in the year of our Lord one thousand eight hundred and forty seven, at Wai-il-at-pu, in the county and district aforesaid, the said place being then and there in the Indian country, with force and arms, in and upon one Marcus Whitman, the said Whitman not being then and there an Indian, feloniously, wilfully and of their malice aforethought did make and assault, and that the said Indians, with certain tomahawks, axes and knives, which they then and there in their hands had and held, him the said Marcus Whitman, in and upon the head and neck of him the said Marcus Whitman, in and and there feloniously, wilfully and of their malice aforethought, did strike, cut, stab and thrust, giving to the said Marcus Whitman, with the weapons aforesaid, then and there in and upon his head and neck, several mortal wounds, of which said mortal wounds, he the said Marcus Whitman then and there died. And so to the Jurors aforesaid upon their oath aforesaid do say that the said Telakite, Tomahas, otherwise called the Murderer, Clokomas, Isiaasheluckas and Kiamasumkin, with certain other Indians whose names are to the Jurors unknown, him the said Marcus Whitman, in manner and form aforesaid then and there feloniously, wilfully and of their malice aforethought did kill and murder, and did then and there commit the crimes of wilful murder, upon the body of the said Marcus Whitman, against the peace and dignity of the said United States, and contrary to the form of the Statute in such case made and provided.

And the Jurors aforesaid, upon their oath aforesaid do further present, that the said Telakite, Tomahas otherwise called the Murderer, Clokomas, Isiaasheluckas and Kiamasumkin with certain other Indians whose names are to the said Jurors unknown, at Wai-il-at-pu aforesaid in the county aforesaid, the said county being then and there in the Indian country, on the twenty ninth day of November in the year of our Lord one thousand eight hundred and forty seven, in and upon the said Marcus Whitman he not then and there being an Indian feloniously, wilfully and of their malice aforethought, did make an assault; and him the said Marcus Whitman in some way and manner, and by some means, instruments and weapons, to the Jurors aforesaid unknown did then and there feloniously, wilfully, and of their malice aforethought deprive of life, so that he the said Marcus Whitman then and there died. And so the Jurors aforesaid, upon their oath aforesaid, do say that the said Indians, him the said Marcus Whitman, in the manner and by the means aforesaid to the said Jurors unknown, then and there feloniously, wilfully and of their malice aforethought did kill and murder, and did then and there commit the crime of wilful murder in and upon the body of said Marcus Whitman, against the peace and dignity of the United States aforesaid, and contrary to the form of the Statute in such case made and provided—A true bill, F. W. Pettygrove Foreman, Amory Holbrook U.S. Attorney for the District of Oregon.[1]

[1] "Whitman Massacre Records."

Appendix E: Treaty With the Walla Wallas, Cayuses, and Others, 1855

In June, 1855, the Cayuses, Walla Wallas, Umatillas, Nez Percés, and other tribes of Oregon and Washington territories signed a treaty in which they agreed to cede their lands to the whites and move onto reservations. The ink on the document had scarcely dried before they began to seek ways to avoid the commitment:

> Articles of agreement and convention made and concluded at the treaty-ground, Camp Stevens, in the Walla-Walla Valley, this ninth day of June, in the year one thousand eight hundred and fifty-five, by and between Isaac I. Stevens, governor and superintendent of Indian affairs for the Territory of Washington, and Joel Palmer, superintendent of Indian affairs for Oregon Territory, on the part of the United States, and the undersigned chiefs, head-men, and delegates of the Walla-Wallas, Cayuses, and Umatilla tribes, and bands of Indians, occupying lands partly in Washington and partly in Oregon Territories, and who, for the purposes of this treaty, are to be regarded as one nation acting for and in behalf of the respective bands and tribes, they being duly authorized thereto; it being understood that Superintendent I. I. Stevens assumes to treat with that portion of the above-named bands and tribes residing within the Territory of Washington, and Superintendent Palmer with those residing within Oregon.

> ARTICLE 1. The above-named confederated bands of Indians cede to the United States all their right, title, and claim to all and every part of the country claimed by them included in the following boundaries, to wit: Commencing at the mouth of the Tocannon River, in Washington Territory, running thence up said river to its source; thence easterly along the summit of the Blue Mountains, and on the southern boundaries of the purchase made of the Nez Percés Indians, and easterly along that boundary to the western limits of the country claimed by the Shoshonees or Snake Indians;

thence southerly along that boundary (being the waters of Powder River) to the source of Powder River, thence to the head-waters of Willow Creek, thence down Willow Creek to the Columbia River, thence up the channel of the Columbia River to the lower end of a large island below the mouth of Umatilla River, thence northerly to a point on the Yakama River, called Tomah-luke, thence to Le Lac, thence to the White Banks on the Columbia below Priest's Rapids, thence down the Columbia River to the junction of the Columbia and Snake Rivers, thence up the Snake River to the place of beginning: *Provided, however,* That so much of the country described above as is contained in the following boundaries shall be set apart as a residence for said Indians, which tract for the purposes contemplated shall be held and regarded as an Indian reservation; to wit: Commencing in the middle of the channel of Umatilla River opposite the mouth of Wild Horse Creek, thence up the middle of the channel of said creek to its source, thence southerly to a point in the Blue Mountains, known as Lee's Encampment, thence in a line to the head-waters of Howtome Creek, thence west to the divide between Howtome and Birch Creeks, thence northerly along said divide to a point due west of the southwest corner of William C. McKay's land-claim, thence east along his line to his southeast corner, thence in a line to the place of beginning; all of which tract shall be set apart and, so far as necessary, surveyed and marked out for their exclusive use; nor shall any white person be permitted to reside upon the same without permission of the agent and superintendent. The said tribes and bands agree to remove to and settle upon the same within one year after the ratification of this treaty, without any additional expense to the Government other than is provided by this treaty, and until the expiration of the time specified, the said bands shall be permitted to occupy and reside upon the tracts now possessed by them, guaranteeing to all citizen[s] of the United States, the right to enter upon and occupy as settlers any lands not actually enclosed by said Indians: *Provided, also,* That the exclusive right of taking fish in the streams running through and bordering said reservation is hereby secured to said Indians, and at all other usual and accustomed stations in common with citizens of the United States, and of erecting suitable buildings for curing the same; the privilege of hunting, gathering roots and berries and pasturing their stock on unclaimed lands in common with citizens, is also secured to them. *And provided, also,* That if any band or bands of Indians, residing in and claiming any portion or portions of the country described in this article, shall not accede to the terms of this treaty, then the bands becoming parties hereunto agree to reserve such part of the several and other payments herein named, as a consideration for the entire country described as aforesaid, as shall be in the proportion that their aggregate number may have to the whole number of Indians residing in and claiming the entire country aforesaid, as consideration and payment in full for the tracts in said country claimed by them. *And provided, also,* That when substantial improvements have been made by any member of the bands being parties to this treaty, who are compelled to abandon them in consequence of said treaty, [they] shall be valued under the direction of the President of the United States, and payment made therefor.

ARTICLE 2. In consideration of and payment for the country hereby ceded, the United States agree to pay the bands and tribes of Indians claiming territory and residing in said country, and who remove to and reside upon said reservation, the several sums of money following, to wit: eight thousand dollars per annum for the term of five years, commencing on the first day of September, 1856; six thousand dollars per annum for the term of five years next succeeding the first five; four thousand dollars per annum for the term of five years next succeeding the second five, and two thousand dollars per annum for the term of five years next succeeding the third five; all of which several sums of money shall be expended for the use and benefit of the confederated bands herein named, under the direction of the President of the United States, who may from time to time at his discretion, determine what proportion thereof shall be expended for such objects as in his judgment will promote their well-being, and advance them in civilization, for their moral improvement and education, for buildings, opening and fencing farms, breaking land, purchasing teams, wagons, agricultural implements and seeds, for clothing, provision and tools, for medical purposes, providing mechanics and farmers, and for arms and ammunition.

ARTICLE 3. In addition to the articles advanced the Indians at the time of signing this treaty, the United States agree to expend the sum of fifty thousand dollars during the first and second years after its ratification, for the erection of buildings on the reservation, fencing and opening farms, for the purchase of teams, farming implements, clothing, and provisions, for medicines and tools, for the payment of employés, and for subsisting the Indians the first year after their removal.

ARTICLE 4. In addition to the consideration above specified, the United States agree to erect, at suitable points on the reservation, one saw-mill, and one flouring-mill, a building suitable for a hospital, two school-houses, one blacksmith shop, one building for wagon and plough maker and one carpenter and joiner shop, one dwelling for each, two millers, one farmer, one superintendent of farming operations, two school-teachers, one blacksmith, one wagon and plough maker, one carpenter and joiner, to each of which the necessary out-buildings. To purchase and keep in repair for the term of twenty years all necessary mill fixtures and mechanical tools, medicines and hospital stores, books and stationery for schools, and furniture for employés.

The United States further engage to secure and pay for the services and subsistence, for the term of twenty years, [of] one superintendent of farming operations, one farmer, one blacksmith, one wagon and plough maker, one carpenter and joiner, one physician, and two school teachers.

ARTICLE 5. The United States further engage to build for the head chiefs of the Walla-Walla, Cayuse, and Umatilla bands each one dwelling-house, and to plough and fence ten acres of land for each, and to pay to each five hundred dollars per annum in cash for the term of twenty years. The first payment to the Walla-Walla chief to commence upon the signing of this treaty. To give to the Walla-Walla chief three yoke of oxen, three yokes and four chains, one wagon, two ploughs, twelve hoes, twelve axes, two shovels, and one saddle and bridle, one set of wagon-harness, and one set of plough-harness, within three months after the signing of this treaty.

To build for the son of Pio-Pio-mox-mox one dwelling-house, and plough and fence five acres of land, and to give him a salary for twenty years, one hundred dollars in cash per annum, commencing September first, eighteen hundred and fifty-six.

The improvement named in this section to be completed as soon after the ratification of this treaty as possible.

It is further stipulated that Pio-pio-mox-mox is secured for the term of five years, the right to build and occupy a house at or near the mouth of the Yakama River, to be used as a trading-post in the sale of his bands of wild cattle ranging in that district: *And provided, also,* That in consequence of the immigrant wagon-road from Grand Round to Umatilla, passing through the reservation herein specified, thus leading to turmoils and disputes between Indians and immigrants, and as it is known that a more desirable and practicable route may be had to the south of the present road, that a sum not exceeding ten thousand dollars shall be expended in locating and opening a wagon-road from Powder River or Grand Round, so as to reach the plain at the western base of the Blue Mountain, south of the southern limits of said reservation.

ARTICLE 6. The President may, from time to time at his discretion cause the whole or such portions as he may think proper, of the tract that may now or hereafter be set apart as a permanent home for those Indians, to be surveyed into lots and assigned to such Indians of the confederated bands as may wish to enjoy the privilege, and locate thereon permanently, to a single person over twenty-one years of age, forty acres, to a family of two persons, sixty acres, to a family of three and not exceeding five, eighty acres; to a family of six persons and not exceeding ten, one hundred and twenty acres; and to each family over ten in number, twenty acres to each additional three members; and the President may provide for such rules and regulations as will secure to the family in case of the death of the head thereof, the possession and enjoyment of such permanent home and improvement thereon; and he may at any time, at his discretion, after such person or family has made location on the land assigned as a permanent home, issue a patent to such person or family for such assigned land, conditioned that the tract shall not be aliened or leased for a longer term than two years, and shall be exempt from levy, sale, or forfeiture, which condition shall continue in force until a State constitution, embracing such land within its limits, shall have been formed and the legislature of the State shall remove the restriction: *Provided, however,* That no State legislature shall remove the restriction herein provided for without the consent of Congress: *And provided, also,* That if any person or family, shall at any time, neglect or refuse to occupy or till a portion of the land assigned and on which they have located, or shall roam from place to place, indicating a desire to abandon his home, the President may if the patent shall have been issued, cancel the assignment, and may also withhold from such person or family their portion of the annuities of other money due them, until they shall have returned to such permanent home, and resume the pursuits of industry, and in default of their return the tract may be declared abandoned, and thereafter assigned to some other person or family of Indians residing on said reservation: *And provided, also,* That the head chiefs of the three principal bands, to wit, Pio-Pio-mox-mox, Weyatenatemany, and Wenap-snoot, shall be secured in a tract of at least one hundred and sixty acres of land.

ARTICLE 7. The annuities of the Indians shall not be taken to pay the debts of individuals.

ARTICLE 8. The confederated bands acknowledge their dependence on the Government of the United States and promise to be friendly with all the citizens thereof, and pledge themselves to commit no depredation on the property of such citizens, and should any one or more of the Indians violate this pledge, and the fact be satisfactorily proven before the agent, the property taken shall be returned, or in default thereof, or if injured or destroyed, compensation may be made by the Government out of their annuities; nor will they make war on any other tribe of Indians except in self-defense, but submit all matter of difference between them and other Indians, to the Government of the United States or its agents for decision, and abide thereby; and if any of the said Indians commit any depredations on other Indians, the same rule shall prevail as that prescribed in the article in case of depredations against citizens. Said Indians further engage to submit to and observe all laws, rules, and regulations which may be prescribed by the United States for the government of said Indians.

ARTICLE 9. In order to prevent the evils of intemperance among said Indians, it is hereby provided that if any one of them shall drink liquor, or procure it for others to drink, [such one] may have his or her proportion of the annuities withheld from him or her for such time as the President may determine.

ARTICLE 10. The said confederated bands agree that, whenever in the opinion of the President of the United States the public interest may require it, *that* all roads highways and railroads shall have the right of way through the reservation herein designated or which may at any time hereafter be set apart as a reservation for said Indians.

ARTICLE 11. This treaty shall be obligatory on the contracting parties as soon as the same shall be ratified by the President and Senate of the United States. . . .[1]

[1] C. J. Kappler (comp.), *Indian Affairs. Laws and Treaties. U.S. Doc. No.* 319, 58 Cong., 2 sess., II, 694-97.

Bibliography

UNPUBLISHED MATERIALS

Bagley, Clarence B. Bagley Scrapbooks 5, 6, 12, 58. Suzzallo Library, University of Washington, Seattle.

———. "Miscellaneous Selections of Historical Writings, 1843–1932." Manuscript, Oregon Historical Society, Portland.

Black, Samuel. "Extracts from report by Chief Trader Samuel Black to the Governor and Committee of the Hudson's Bay Company, dated 'Willa Walla,' 25 March 1829." Hudson's Bay Company Archives, B. 146/e/2, fos. 3–5, 6d.–7, and 10. London, England. Published by permission of the Governor and Committee of the Hudson's Bay Company. By order of the Governor and Committee of the Hudson's Bay Company, R. A. Reynolds, Secretary.

Burpee, Isaac. "The Story of John Work." Manuscript 319, Oregon Historical Society, Portland.

Cornelison, J. M. "The Seed of the Martyrs." Typescript copy in possession of Purdy Cornelison, Walla Walla, Washington.

Cornelison, Lessie L. "Allen Patawa." Typescript copy, Umatilla County Library, Pendleton, Oregon.

Davis, William Lyle. "Mission St. Anne of the Cayuse Indians, 1847–1848." Thesis 50804, Bancroft Library, University of California, Berkeley.

"Documents Pertaining to the Whitman Massacre and Trial of the Cayuse." Manuscript 318, Oregon Historical Society, Portland.

Doty, James. "Journal of operations of Governor Isaac Ingalls Stevens, Superintendent of Indian Affairs and Commissioner, treating with the Indian Tribes East of the Cascade Mountains, in Washington Territory, and the Blackfeet and neighboring Tribes, near Great Falls of the Missourie, in the year 1855: including therein details of the celebrated Indian Council at Walla Walla, and of the Blackfoot Council at Fort Benton, and the commencement of the Indian Wars 1855–8. Prepared from the original [sic] journal of James Doty, the Governor's Secretary by Willial[m] S. Lewis,

Corresponding Secretary, Eastern Washington State Historical Society, December 22, 1919." Typescript copy, Washington State Library, Olympia. Original in National Archives, Records of the Bureau of Indian Affairs, Records Group 75, Microcopy T-494, Roll 5.

Douglas, Sir James. Private Papers (First Series), Manuscripts P-C12, P-C13, Bancroft Library, University of California, Berkeley.

Dye, Eva Emery. Eva Emery Dye Papers. Manuscript 1089, Oregon Historical Society, Portland.

Ebberts, G. W. "A Trapper's Life in the Rocky Mountains of Oregon from 1829 to 1839." Manuscript P-A28, Bancroft Library, University of California, Berkeley.

Evans, Elwood. Elwood Evans Papers. Manuscript 173, Beinecke Library, Yale University, New Haven.

Fort Dalles Papers. Huntington Library, San Marino, California.

"Fort Nisqually Journal of Occurrences, 1833–39." Microcopy H867nj, Vol. I, Suzzallo Library, University of Washington, Seattle.

Fulton, James. "The Dalles and Eastern Oregon Events." Manuscript P-A33, Bancroft Library, University of California, Berkeley.

Gatschet, Albert S. "The Molale tribe raided by the Cayuses." Manuscript No. 2029, National Anthropological Archives Collection, Smithsonian Institution, Washington, D.C.

Haller, Granville Owen. Haller Papers. Manuscript AIA3-6, Suzzallo Library, University of Washington, Seattle.

Joset, Joseph. "LXVII A. Account of the Con. Ind[ian] war '58." Manuscript, Crosby Library, Gonzaga University, Spokane, Washington.

Knuth, Priscilla. Letter to authors.

Lee, H. A. G. "An account of the tactics of Col. Gilliam's party on Mar. 11–12 [1848] in the Cayuse War." Manuscript WA 23, Walker Collection. Huntington Library, San Marino, California.

Lee, Jason. Jason Lee Papers. Manuscript 934, Oregon Historical Society, Portland.

McKay, William Cameron. McKay Papers. Umatilla County Library, Pendleton, Oregon.

McKinlay, Archibald. "Narrative of a Chief Factor of the Hudson's Bay Company by Archibald McKinlay." Manuscript P-C25, Bancroft Library, University of California, Berkeley.

McWhorter, Lucullus Virgil. McWhorter Papers. Manuscripts 331, 409, Holland Library, Washington State University, Pullman.
Mary Louise, Sister, O. P. [Nellie Sullivan]. "Eugene Casimir Chirouse, O.M.I., and the Indians of Washington." Thesis 2559, Suzzallo Library, University of Washington, Seattle.
Pambrun, Andrew D. "The story of his life as he tells it." Typescript copy, Washington State Library, Olympia.
Reese, J. W. "The Exciting Story of Fort Henrietta." Typescript copy, Umatilla County Library, Pendleton, Oregon.
Spalding, Henry H. Spalding Papers. Correspondence and American Board File. Manuscript 143/3, Holland Library, Washington State University, Pullman.
Steptoe, Edward J. Steptoe Papers. Manuscript AIA2-1, Suzzallo Library, University of Washington, Seattle.
Tucker, G. J. "Pilot Rock Emigrant Road, 1861 and 1862." Typescript copy, Umatilla County Library, Pendleton, Oregon.
Walker, Elkanah. Walker Papers. Manuscript 57/276, Holland Library, Washington State University, Pullman.
Walter, W. W. "Reminiscences of a Forty-Niner." Manuscript 1741, Holland Library, Washington State University, Pullman.
White, Elijah. "Government and the Emigration to Oregon." Manuscript P-A76, Bancroft Library, Univerity of California, Berkeley.
Whitman, Marcus, to Mrs. Alice Loomis, May 20, 1844. Letter P-A, 231:8, Bancroft Library, University of California, Berkeley.
"Whitman Massacre Records of the trial of the Whitman murderers." Envelope 37, Holland Library, Washington State University, Pullman.

PERSONAL INTERVIEWS

Bergevin, Clem. Walla Walla, Washington, July 19, 1968.
Hall, David Steve. Mission, Oregon, July 18, 1968.
Maxwell, Claude. Ephrata, Washington, November 5, 1969.
Minthorn, William. Thornhollow, Oregon, July 16, 1968.
Webb, Amie. Thornhollow, Oregon, July 17, 1968.
Williams, Lucien. Gibbon, Oregon, July 17, 1968.

GOVERNMENT DOCUMENTS AND PUBLICATIONS

Annual Reports of the Commissioner of Indian Affairs, 1856, 1857, 1858.

Annual Reports of the Secretary of Interior, 1854–55, 1855–56, 1856–57, 1857–58, 1870–71, 1871.

Annual Reports of the Secretary of War, 1855–56, 1856–57, 1878, 1889–90.

Hodge, Frederick Webb (ed.). *Handbook of American Indians North of Mexico. Bureau of American Ethnology Bulletin 30.* 2 vols. Washington, 1910.

Kappler, C. J. (comp.) *Indian Affairs. Laws and Treaties. U.S. Doc. No. 319, 58 Cong., 2 sess., 2 vols.* Washington, 1904.

Laws of a General and Local Nature passed by the Legislative Committee and Legislative Assembly, 1843–49. Salem, Ore., 1853.

Memorial of the Legislature of Oregon praying an appropriation for the payment of expenses incurred by the Provisional Government of Oregon in the Cayuse War. Senate Misc. Doc. No. 29, 31 Cong., 2 sess. Washington, 1851.

Message of the Governor of Washington Territory. Also: The Correspondence with the Secretary of War, Major Gen. Wool, the Officers of the Regular Army, and of the Volunteer Service of Washington Territory. Olympia, Wash., 1857.

Microcopy of Records in the National Archives. *Oregon Superintendency of Indian Affairs, 1848–1873.* Letter Books A:10, Microfilm No. M-2, Roll 3; B:10, Microfilm No. M-2, Roll 3; C:10, Microfilm No. M-2, Roll 4; D:10, Microfilm No. M-2, Roll 5; E:10, Microfilm No. M-2, Roll 6; F:10, Microfilm No. M-2, Roll 7; G:10, Microfilm No. M-2, Roll 8; H:10, Microfilm No. M-2, Roll 9; I:10, Microfilm No. M-2, Roll 10.

———. *Oregon Superintendency of Indian Affairs, 1848–1873,* Microfilm No. 2, Rolls 11–13, 15–16, 19–21, 24, 25, 27.

———. *Oregon Superintendency of Indian Affairs, 1842–1880, 1858–1859,* Microfilm No. 234, Roll 611.

———. *Register of Enlistments of Soldiers Belonging to the First Regiment of United States Infantry, Registers of Enlistments in the United States Army, 1789–1914, Indian Scouts, 1878–1914,* Vols. 152–54, Microfilm No. 233, Roll 71.

———. *The 10th Military Department, 1846–1851,* Microfilm No. 210, Roll 3.

———. *Washington Superintendency of Indian Affairs, 1853–1874,* Microfilm No. 5, Rolls 1, 17, 20, 21, 23.

Mooney, James. *The Aboriginal Population of America North of Mexico.* Publication 2955, *Smithsonian Miscellaneous Collections,* LXXX, 7 (1928).

Powell, J. W. "Indian Linguistic Families of America North of Mexico," *Seventh Annual Report of the Bureau of Ethnology to the Secretary of the Smithsonian Institution 1855–86.* Washington, 1891.

Preliminary Inventory of Records of the Umatilla Indian Agency, Record Group 75, Federal Records Center, Seattle, Washington.

Reports of Explorations and Surveys, to Ascertain the Most Practicable and Economical Route For a Railroad From the Mississippi River to the Pacific Ocean, 1853–5. 12 vols. Washington, 1855–60.

Royce, Charles C. "Indian Land Cessions in the United States," *Eighteenth Annual Report of the Bureau of American Ethnology to the Secretary of the Smithsonian Institution, 1896–97.* Washington, 1899.

Slacum, William A. *Memorial of William A. Slacum praying compensation for his services in obtaining information in relation to the settlements on the Oregon River. Senate Exec. Doc.* No. 24, 25 Cong., 2 sess. Washington, 1837.

Special Report of the Secretary of War, 1855–56.

Stevens, Isaac I. *Speech of Hon. Isaac I. Stevens, Delegate From Washington Territory, on the Washington and Oregon War Claims Delivered in the House of Representatives of the United States, May 31, 1858.* Washington, 1858.

Swanton, John R. *The Indian Tribes of North America.* Bureau of American Ethnology *Bulletin 145.* Washington, 1952.

Teit, James A. "The Salishan Tribes of the Western Plateaus," *Forty-fifth Annual Report of the Bureau of American Ethnology, 1927–1928.* Washington, 1930.

Wool, Major General John E. "General description of the military department of the Pacific." *Topographical Memoir of the Department of the Pacific, House Exec. Doc.* No. 114, 35 Cong., 2 sess. Serial 1014. Washington, 1859.

NEWSPAPERS

Catholic Sentinel. Portland, Oregon Territory, 1851; Portland, Oregon, 1871, 1872, 1875, 1879, 1885.

Columbia Press. Umatilla, Oregon, 1867.
East Oregonian. Pendleton, Oregon, 1877, 1880.
New York Tribune. 1845, 1850, 1872.
Oregonian. Portland, Oregon, 1878, 1921.
Oregon Spectator. Oregon City, Oregon Territory, 1848, 1850, 1853.
Pacific Christian Advocate. Portland, Oregon, 1873.
Prattsburg News. Prattsburg, New York, 1898.
Seattle Post Intelligencer. 1903.
Spirit of the West. Walla Walla, Washington Territory, 1875.
Spokesman-Review. Spokane, Washington, 1904.
St. Louis Republican. 1844.
Walla Walla Statesman. Walla Walla, Washington Territory, 1862, 1863, 1866, 1877.
Walla Walla Union. Walla Walla, Washington Territory, 1872, 1875, 1877.
Washington Statesman. Walla Walla, Washington Territory, 1863, 1877.
Weekly Oregonian. Portland, Oregon Territory, 1853; Portland, Oregon, 1862.

BOOKS AND PAMPHLETS

Armstrong, A. N. *Oregon; Comprising a Brief History and Full Description of the Territories of Oregon and Washington.* Chicago, 1857.
Bancroft, Hubert Howe. *The Works of Hubert Howe Bancroft.* 39 vols. San Francisco, 1882–1890. Vol. I, *The Native Races, Vol. I, Wild Tribes.* San Francisco, 1883. Vol. III, *The Native Races, Vol. III, Myths and Languages.* San Francisco, 1882. Vol. XXIX, *History of Oregon, Vol. I, 1834–1848.* San Francisco, 1886. Vol. XXX, *History of Oregon, Vol. II, 1848–1883.* San Francisco, 1888.
Barker, Burt Brown (ed.). *Letters of Dr. John McLoughlin Written at Fort Vancouver, 1829–1832.* Portland, 1948.
Before the Indian Claims Commission: Confederated Tribes of the Umatilla Indian Reservation, Petitioner, v. United States of America, Defendant. Petitioner's Proposed Findings of Fact and Brief (Claims One and Four). Claims Commission Brief. Docket 264.

Berreman, Joel V. *Tribal Distribution in Oregon.* Memoirs of the American Anthropological Association, No. 47. Menasha, Wis., 1937.

Blanchet, F. N. *Historical Sketches of the Catholic Church in Oregon During the Past Forty Years, 1838–1878.* Portland, 1878.

—— et al. *Notices and Voyages of the Famed Quebec Mission to the Pacific Northwest; Being the Correspondence, Notices, etc., of the Fathers Blanchet and Demers together with those of Fathers Bolduc and Langlois.* Portland, 1956.

Bradbury, John. *Travels in the Interior of America, in the Years 1809, 1810, and 1811.* Liverpool, 1817.

Brimlow, George Francis. *The Bannock Indian War of 1878.* Caldwell, Idaho, 1938.

Brown, William Compton. *The Indian Side of the Story.* Spokane, 1961.

Bryant, Edwin. *What I saw in California: Being the Journal of a Tour, By the Emigrant Route and South Pass of the Rocky Mountains, Across the Continent of North America, the Great Desert Basin, and Through California, in the Years 1846, 1847.* New York, 1849.

Burns, Robert Ignatius. *The Jesuits and the Indian Wars of the Northwest.* New Haven, Conn., 1966.

Clark, Keith, and Lowell Tiller. *Terrible Trail: The Meek Cutoff, 1845.* Caldwell, Idaho, 1967.

Clarke, S. A. *Pioneer Days of Oregon History.* 2 vols. Portland, 1905.

Coke, Henry J. *A Ride Over the Rocky Mountains to Oregon and California.* London, 1852.

Coues, Elliott (ed.). *New Light on the Early History of the Greater Northwest: The Manuscript Journals of Alexander Henry, Fur Trader of the Northwest Company, and of David Thompson, Official Geographer and Explorer of the Same Company, 1799–1814.* 3 vols. New York, 1897.

Cox, Ross. *Adventures on the Columbia River.* 2 vols. London, 1831.

Crawford, Medorem. *Journal of Medorem Crawford.* Fairfield, Wash., 1967.

Cummins, Sarah J. *Autobiography and Reminiscences of Sarah J. Cummins, Touchet, Wash.* La Grande, Ore., 1914.

Curtis, Edward S. *The North American Indian; Being a Series of Volumes Picturing and Describing the Indians of the United States and Alaska*. 20 vols. Norwood, Mass., 1911.

Davies, K. G. (ed.). *Peter Skene Ogden's Snake Country Journal, 1826–27*. London, 1961.

Delaney, Matilda J. Sager. *A Survivor's Recollections of the Whitman Massacre*. Spokane, 1920.

DeVoto, Bernard (ed.). *The Journals of Lewis and Clark*. Boston, 1953.

Dixon, Joseph Kossuth. *The Vanishing Race: The Last Great Indian Council; A Record in Picture and Story of the Last Great Indian Council, Participated in by Eminent Indian Chiefs From Nearly Every Indian Reservation in the United States, Together With the Story of Their Lives as Told by Themselves—Their Speeches and Folklore Tales—Their Solemn Farewell and the Indians' Story of the Custer Fight*. Philadelphia, 1925.

Drury, Clifford Merrill. *First White Women Over the Rockies: Diaries, Letters, and Biographical Sketches of the Six Women of the Oregon Mission Who Made the Overland Journey in 1836 and 1838*. 2 vols. Glendale, Calif., 1963.

———. *Marcus Whitman, M.D., Pioneer and Martyr*. Caldwell, Idaho, 1937.

DuBois, Cora. *The Feather Cult of the Middle Columbia*. General Series in Anthropology, No. 7. Menasha, Wis., 1938.

Dunbar, Seymour, and Paul C. Phillips (eds.). *The Journals and Letters of Major John Owen, Pioneer of the Northwest, 1850–1871*. 2 vols. New York, 1927.

Duniway, Abigail J. *Captain Gray's Company; or, Crossing the Plains and Living in Oregon*. Portland, 1859.

Edwards, P. L. *A Sketch of the Oregon Territory; or, Emigrants' Guide*. Liberty, Mo., 1842.

Eells, Myron. *History of the Indian Missions on the Pacific Coast: Oregon, Washington and Idaho*. Philadelphia, 1882.

Elliott, T. C. *The Earliest Travelers on the Oregon Trail*. Portland, 1912.

Evans, Elwood. *History of the Pacific Northwest: Oregon and Washington*. 2 vols. Portland, 1889.

Farnham, Thomas J. *Travels in the Great Western Prairies, the Ana-*

huac and Rocky Mountains, and in the Oregon Territory. New York, 1843.

Frémont, J. C. *Oregon and California: The Exploring Expedition to the Rocky Mountains, Oregon and California.* Buffalo N.Y., 1850.

Garrison, A. E. *Life and Labour of Rev. A. E. Garrison: Forty Years in Oregon.* N.p., 1943.

Gass, Patrick. *Journal of the Voyages and Travels of a Corps of Discovery, Under the command of Capt. Lewis and Capt. Clarke of the army of the United States, From the Mouth of the River Missouri Through the Interior Parts of North America to the Pacific Ocean, During the Years 1804, 1805, and 1806.* Philadelphia, 1811.

Gaston, Joseph. *The Centennial History of Oregon, 1811–1911.* 4 vols. Chicago, 1912.

Gates, Charles Marvin (ed.). *Messages of the Governors of the Territory of Washington to the Legislative Assembly, 1854–1889.* University of Washington Publications in Social Sciences, Vol. XII. Seattle, 1940.

Geary, Edward R. *Depredations and Massacre by the Snake River Indians.* Fairfield, Wash., 1966.

Gilbert, Frank T. *Historic Sketches of Walla Walla, Whitman, Columbia and Garfield Counties, Washington Territory.* Portland, 1882.

Gray, William H. *A History of Oregon, 1792–1849, Drawn From Personal Observation and Authentic Information.* Portland, 1870.

———. *The Moral and Religious Aspect of the Indian Question: A Letter Addressed to General John Eaton, Department of the Interior, Bureau of Education, Washington D.C.* Astoria, Ore., 1879.

Greenhow, Robert. *The History of Oregon and California, and the Other Territories on the North-West Coast of North America.* 2nd ed. Boston, 1845.

Hakola, John W. (ed.). *Frontier Omnibus.* Missoula, Mont., 1962.

Hastings, Lansford W. *Narratives of the Trans-Mississippi Frontier: The Emigrants' Guide to Oregon and California.* Cincinnati, 1845.

Hines, Gustavus. *Wild Life in Oregon.* New York, 1887.

Hines, H. K. *An Illustrated History of the State of Washington.* Chicago, 1893.

Hosmer, James K. (ed.). *History of the Expedition of Captain Lewis and Clark 1804–5–6.* 2 vols. Chicago, 1902.

321

Howard, Helen Addison. *Saga of Chief Joseph.* Caldwell, Idaho, 1965.

Howard, Oliver Otis. *Famous Indian Chiefs I Have Known.* New York, 1908.

———. *Nez Perce Joseph: An Account of His Ancestors, His Lands, His Confederates, His Enemies, His Murderers, His War, His Pursuit and Capture.* Boston, 1881.

Hulbert, Archer Butler, and Dorothy Printup Hulbert (eds.). *Overland to the Pacific.* Vol. VI, *Marcus Whitman, Crusader, Part One, 1802 to 1839.* Denver, 1936. Vol. VII, *Marcus Whitman, Crusader, Part Two, 1839 to 1843.* Denver, 1939.

Humfreville, J. Lee. *Twenty Years Among Our Hostile Indians.* New York, 1899.

Hunt, G. W. *A History of the Hunt Family From the Norman Conquest, 1066, A.D., to the Year 1890.* Boston, 1890.

Illustrated History of Lane County, Oregon. Portland, 1884.

Irving, Washington. *The Adventures of Captain Bonneville, U.S.A., in the Rocky Mountains and the Far West.* Norman, Okla., 1961.

———. *Astoria; or, Anecdotes of an Enterprise Beyond the Rocky Mountains.* Norman, Okla., 1964.

Jackson, Helen Hunt. *A Century of Dishonor: A Sketch of the United States Government's Dealings with Some of the Indian Tribes.* Boston, 1890.

Jacobs, Melville. *Northern Sahaptin Grammar.* University of Washington Publications in Anthropology, Vol. IV. Seattle, 1931.

Jacobs, Orange. *Memoirs of Orange Jacobs Written By Himself.* Seattle, 1908.

Jesset, Thomas E. *Chief Spokan Garry, 1811–1892, Christian, Statesman, Friend of the White Man.* Minneapolis, 1960.

Johansen, Dorothy O. (ed.). *Robert Newell's Memoranda: Travles in the Territory of Missourie; Travle to the Kayuse War; together with A Report on the Indians South of the Columbia River.* Portland, 1959.

Johnson, Overton, and William H. Winter. *Route Across the Rocky Mountains, With a Description of Oregon and California.* Lafayette, Ind., 1846.

Josephy, Alvin M., Jr. *The Nez Perce Indians and the Opening of the Northwest.* New Haven, Conn., 1965.

The Journal of John Work, January to October, 1835. Archives of British Columbia *Memoir No. X.* Victoria, B.C., 1945.

Kane, Paul. *Wanderings of an Artist Among the Indians of North America From Canada to Vancouver's Island and Oregon Through the Hudson's Bay Company's Territory and Back Again by Paul Kane.* Toronto, 1925.

Kip, Lawrence. *The Indian Council at Walla Walla, May and June, 1855. Sources of History of Oregon, Volume I, Part 2. Contributions of the Department of Economics and History of the University of Oregon.* Eugene, Ore., 1897.

Lang, H. O. (ed.). *History of the Willamette Valley; Being a Description of the Valley and its Resources, with an account of its Discovery and Settlement by White Men, and its Subsequent History: Together with Personal Reminiscences of its Early Pioneers.* Portland, 1885.

Large, R. G. (ed.). *The Journals of William Fraser Tolmie, Physician and Fur Trader.* Vancouver, B.C., 1963.

Laut, Agnes C. *The Overland Trail: The Epic Path of the Pioneers to Oregon.* New York, 1929.

Lee, D., and J. H. Frost. *Ten Years in Oregon.* New York, 1844.

Leonard, Zenas. *Narrative of the Adventures of Zenas Leonard.* March of America Fascimile Series, University of Michigan Microfilms, Ann Arbor, 1966.

Lewis, William S., and Paul C. Phillips. *The Journal of John Work, A chief-trader of the Hudson's Bay Co., during his expedition from Vancouver to the Flatheads and Blackfeet of the Pacific Northwest, 1831–32.* Cleveland, 1923.

Lockley, Fred. *Oregon's Yesterdays.* New York, 1928.

Lord, John Keast. *The Naturalist in Vancouver Island and British Columbia.* 2 vols. London, 1866.

Lyons, Sister Letitia Mary. *Francis Norbert Blanchet and the Founding of the Oregon Missions, 1838–1848.* Catholic University of America Studies in American Church History, Vol. XXXI. Washington, 1940.

McBeth, Kate C. *The Nez Perces Since Lewis and Clark.* New York, 1908.

McWhorter, Lucullus Virgil. *Tragedy of the Wahk-shum: The*

Death of Andrew J. Bolon, Indian Agent to the Yakima Nation, in mid-September, 1855. Fairfield, Wash., 1968.

Madsen, Brigham D. *The Bannock of Idaho.* Caldwell, Idaho, 1958.

Maloney, Alice Bay (ed.). *Fur Brigade to the Bonaventura: John Work's California Expedition, 1832–1833, for the Hudson's Bay Company.* San Francisco, 1945.

Manring, B. F. *The Conquest of the Coeur D'Alenes, Spokanes and Palouses: The Expeditions of Colonels E. J. Steptoe and George Wright Against the "Northern Indians" in 1858.* Spokane, 1912.

Meacham, A. B. *Wigwam and War-Path; or, the Royal Chief in Chains.* Boston, 1875.

Merk, Frederick (ed.). *Fur Trade and Empire: George Simpson's Journal.* Cambridge, Mass., 1931.

Nicolay, Charles Grenfell, *The Oregon Territory: A Geographical and Physical Account of that Country and its Inhabitants; with Outlines of its History and Discovery.* London, 1846.

Ogden, Peter Skene [?]. *Traits of American Indian Life & Character, By a Fur Trader.* San Francisco, 1933.

Palmer, Joel. *Journal of Travels Over the Rocky Mountains, to the Mouth of the Columbia River; Made During the Years 1845 and 1846.* Cincinnati, 1847.

Parker, Samuel. *Journal of an Exploring Tour Beyond the Rocky Mountains, Under the Direction of the A.B.C.F.M.* Ithaca, N.Y., 1844.

Parsons, William. *An Illustrated History of Umatilla County.* Spokane, 1902.

Payette, B. C. (ed.). *Captain John Mullan: His Life Building the Mullan Road As It Is Today and Interesting Tales of Occurrences Along the Road.* Montreal, 1968.

Read, Georgia Willis, and Ruth Gaines (eds.). *Gold Rush: The Journals, Drawings, and Other Papers of J. Goldsborough Bruff, Captain, Washington City and California Mining Association, April 2, 1849–July 20, 1851.* 2 vols. New York, 1944.

Relander, Click. *Strangers on the Land.* Yakima, Wash., 1962.

Reminiscenses of Oregon Pioneers. Pendleton, Ore., 1937.

Revere, Joseph Warren. *Naval Duty in California.* Oakland, Calif., 1947.

Rich, E. E. (ed.). *Eden Colvile's Letters, 1849–52.* Publications of the Hudson's Bay Record Society. London, 1956.

———. *Peter Skene Ogden's Snake Country Journals, 1824–25 and 1825–26.* London, 1950.

———. *Simpson's 1928 Journey to the Columbia.* London, 1947.

Roe, Frank Gilbert. *The Indian and the Horse.* Norman, Okla., 1955.

Rollins, Philip A. (ed.). *The Discovery of the Oregon Trail.* New York, 1935.

Ross, Alexander. *Adventures of the First Settlers on the Oregon or Columbia River.* London, 1849.

———. *The Fur Hunters of the Far West.* Norman, Okla., 1956.

Rousseau, Jacques, M.S.R.C. (ed.). *Caravane vers l'Oregon.* N.p., 1965.

Ruby, Robert H., and John A. Brown. *The Spokane Indians: Children of the Sun.* Norman, Okla., 1970.

Schoolcraft, Henry Rowe. *Information Respecting the Condition and Prospects of the Indian Tribes of the United States.* Philadelphia, 1855.

Settle, Raymond W. (ed.). *The March of the Mounted Riflemen, First United States Military Expedition to travel the full length of the Oregon Trail, From Fort Leavenworth to Fort Vancouver, May to October, 1849, as recorded in the journals of Major Osborne Cross and George Gibbs and the official report of Colonel Loring.* Glendale, Calif., 1940.

Simpson, Sir George. *Narrative of a Journey Round the World, During the Years 1841 and 1842.* 2 vols. London, 1847.

Sketches of Mission Life Among the Indians of Oregon. New York, 1899.

Snowden, Clinton A. *History of Washington: The Rise and Progress of an American State.* 4 vols. New York, 1909.

Spaulding, Kenneth A. (ed.). *On the Oregon Trail: Robert Stuart's Journey of Discovery, 1812–1813.* Norman, Okla., 1953.

Spier, Leslie. *The Prophet Dance of the Northwest and Its Derivatives: The Source of the Ghost Dance.* General Series in Anthropology, No. 1. Menasha, Wis., 1935.

Splawn, A. J. *Ka-mi-akin: Last Hero of the Yakimas.* Portland, 1944.

Steeves, Sarah Hunt. *Book of Remembrance of Marion County, Oregon, Pioneers, 1840–1860.* Portland, 1927.

Stevens, Hazard. *The Life of Isaac Ingalls Stevens.* 2 vols. Boston and New York, 1901.

Swan, James G. *The Northwest Coast; or, Three Years' Residence in Washington Territory.* New York, 1857.

Teit, James H. *The Middle Columbia Salish.* University of Washington Publications in Anthropology, Vol. II, No. 4. Seattle, 1928.

Told by the Pioneers: Reminiscences of Pioneer Life in Washington. 3 vols. Olympia, Wash., 1938.

Townsend, John K. *Narrative of Journey Across the Rocky Mountains, to the Columbia River.* Vol. II in Reuben Gold Thwaites (ed.), *Early Western Travels.* Cleveland, 1905.

Transactions of the Third Annual Re-Union of the Oregon Pioneer Association. Salem, Ore., 1876.

Transactions of the Twelfth Annual Re-Union of the Oregon Pioneer Association for 1884. Salem, Ore., 1885.

Transactions of the Nineteenth Annual Reunion of the Oregon Pioneer Association for 1891. Portland, 1893.

Transactions of the Twenty-First Annual Reunion of the Oregon Pioneer Association for 1893. Portland, 1894.

Transactions of the Twenty-Seventh Annual Reunion of the Oregon Pioneer Association for 1899. Portland, 1900.

Tyrrell, J. B. (ed.). *David Thompson's Narrative of His Explorations in Western America, 1784–1812.* Publications of the Champlain Society. Toronto, 1916.

Umatilla Indian Reservation Then and Now. Pendleton, Ore., n.d.

Victor, Frances Fuller. *The Early Indian Wars of Oregon; Compiled from the Oregon Archives and Other Original Sources with Muster Rolls.* Salem, Ore., 1894.

———. *The River of the West.* Hartford, Conn., 1870.

Weatherford, Mark V. *Bannack-Piute War: The Campaign and Battles.* Corvallis, Ore., 1957.

White, Elijah. *Ten Years in Oregon: Travels and Adventures of Doctor E. White and Lady West of the Rocky Mountains.* Ithaca, N.Y., 1848.

Wilbur, Marguerite Eyer (ed.). *Duflot de Mofras' Travels on the Pacific Coast.* Santa Ana, Calif., 1937.

Wilkes, Charles. *Narrative of the United States Exploring Expedition*

During the Years 1838, 1839, 1840, 1841, 1842. 5 vols. Philadelphia, 1849.

Wood, Charles Erskine Scott. *A Book of Tales; Being Some Myths of the North American Indians Retold by Charles Erskine Scott Wood, One Time Lieutenant U.S. Army.* New York, 1929.

ARTICLES

Bagley, Clarence B. "The Cayuse, or First Indian War in the Northwest," *Washington Historical Quarterly,* I, 1 (October, 1906).

Barrett, C. A. "Early Farming in Umatilla County," *Oregon Historical Quarterly,* XVI (March–December, 1915).

Brandon, William. "Two Thousand Miles from the Counting House: Wilson Price Hunt and the Founding of Astoria," *The American West,* V, 4 (July, 1968).

Brown, W. C. "The Sheepeater Campaign," *Tenth Biennial Report of the Board of Trustees of the State Historical Society of Idaho for the Years 1925–1926.*

Burgunder, Ben. "Recollections of the Inland Empire," *Washington Historical Quarterly,* XVII, 3 (July, 1926).

"Chief Factors P. S. Ogden and James Douglas to Sir George Simpson. Fort Vancouver, March 16, 1848," in "Notes and Documents: Whitman Material in the Hudson's Bay Company Archives," *Pacific Northwest Quarterly,* XXXIII, 1 (January, 1942).

Clark, Robert Carlton. "Military History of Oregon, 1848–59," *Oregon Historical Quarterly,* XXXVI (March–December, 1935).

Coan, C. F. "The Adoption of the Reservation Policy in the Pacific Northwest, 1835–1855," *Oregon Historical Quarterly,* XXIII (March–December, 1922).

———. "The First Stage of the Federal Indian Policy in the Pacific Northwest, 1849–1852," *Oregon Historical Quarterly, XXII* (March–December, 1921).

Conn, Richard T. "The Iroquois in the West," *The Pacific Northwesterner,* IV, 4 (Fall, 1960).

Cullin, Stewart. "A Summer Trip Among the Western Indians," *Free Museum of Science and Art, Department of Archaeology, University of Pennsylvania, Bulletin,* III, 3 (May, 1901).

Davenport, T. W. "Recollections of an Indian Agent," *Oregon Historical Quarterly,* VIII (March–December, 1907).

Driver, Harold E., and William C. Massey. "Comparative Studies of North American Indians," *Transactions of the American Philosophical Society Held at Philadelphia for Promoting Useful Knowledge*, N.S., XLVII (1957).

Drury, Clifford Merrill. "Marcus Whitman—A Reappraisal," *The Record*, XXXI (1970).

Eells, Myron. "The Decrease of the Indians," *American Antiquarian*, XXV, 3 (May–June, 1903).

———. "Indian War History Errors," *Oregon Native Son*, II, 3 (July–August, 1900).

Elliott, T. C. "The Coming of the White Women, 1836," *Oregon Historical Quarterly*, XXXVII (March–December, 1936).

———. " 'Doctor' Robert Newell: Pioneer," *Oregon Historical Quarterly*, IX (March–December, 1908).

Ellison, Joseph. "The Covered Wagon Centennial," *Washington Historical Quarterly*, XXI, 3 (July, 1930).

Gairdner, Meredith, M.D. "Notes on the Geography of the Columbia River," *Journal of the Royal Geographical Society*, XI (1841).

Garth, Thomas R. "Archeological Excavations at Fort Walla Walla," *Pacific Northwest Quarterly*, XLIII, 1 (January, 1952).

———. "Early Nineteenth Century Tribal Relations in the Columbia Plateau," *Southwestern Journal of Anthropology*, XX, 1 (Spring, 1964).

———. "Waiilatpu after the Massacre," *Pacific Northwest Quarterly*, XXXVIII, 4 (October, 1947).

Gathke, Robert Moulton (ed.). "Documentary: The Letters of the Rev. William M. Roberts, Third Superintendent of the Oregon Mission," *Oregon Historical Quarterly*, XXI (March–December, 1920).

Heizer, Robert Fleming. "Walla Walla Indian Expeditions to the Sacramento Valley," *California Historical Quarterly*, XXI, 1 (March, 1942).

Hewitt, Rosetta W. "Joseph L. Meek," *Washington Historical Quarterly*, XX, 3 (July, 1929).

Hilaire, Theodore J. "Pedagogy in the Wilderness," *Oregon Historical Quarterly*, LXIII (March–December, 1962).

Hines, Clarence. "Indian Agent's Letter Book, I: The Piute-Bannock

Raid of July, 1878," *Oregon Historical Quarterly*, XXIX (March–December, 1938).

Holman, Frederick V. "A Brief History of the Oregon Provisional Government and What Caused Its Formation," *Oregon Historical Quarterly*, XIII (March–December, 1912).

Holmes, Kenneth L. "Mount St. Helens' Recent Eruptions," *Oregon Historical Quarterly*, LVI (March–December, 1955).

Hussey, John Adam, and George Walcott Ames, Jr. "California Preparations to Meet the Walla Walla Invasion, 1846," *California Historical Quarterly*, XXI, 1 (March, 1942).

Jacobs, Melville, "Historical Perspectives in Indian Languages of Oregon and Washington," *Pacific Northwest Quarterly*, XXVIII, 1 (January, 1937).

Johansen, Dorothy O. "McLoughlin and the Indians," *The Beaver*, Outfit 277, No. 1 (June, 1946).

Knuth, Priscilla, and Charles M. Gates. "Oregon Territory in 1849–1850," *Pacific Northwest Quarterly*, XL, 1 (January, 1949).

Lewis, William S. (ed.). "Oscar Canfield's Pioneer Reminiscences," *Washington Historical Quarterly*, VIII, 4 (October, 1917).

Light, E. A. "Incidents of the Early Days," *Tacoma Weekly Ledger*, June 24, 1892.

Lowell, Stephen A. "The Indians of the Whitman Massacre," *Whitman College Quarterly*, II, 2 (June, 1898).

Lyman, H. S. "Reminiscences of F. X. Matthieu," *Oregon Historical Quarterly*, I (March–December, 1900).

Moorhouse, Lee. "The Umatilla Indian Reservation," *The Coast Alaska and Greater Northwest*, XV, 4 (April, 1908).

Painter, H. M. "The Coming of the Horse," *Pacific Northwest Quarterly*, XXXVII, 2 (April, 1946).

Ray, Verne F. "Native Villages and Groupings of the Columbia Basin," *Pacific Northwest Quarterly*, XXVII, 2 (April, 1936).

———— et al. "Tribal Distribution in Eastern Oregon and Adjacent Regions," *American Anthropologist*, N.S., XL, 2–4 (1938).

Santee, J. F. "Egan of the Piutes," *Washington Historical Quarterly*, XXVI, 1 (January, 1935).

————. "Pio-Pio-Mox-Mox," *Oregon Historical Quarterly*, XXXIV (March–December, 1933).

Saylor, F. H. "Legendary Lore of the Indians," *Oregon Native Son,* II (May, 1900–April, 1901).

Stevens, Hazard. "The Pioneers and Patriotism," *Washington Historical Quarterly,* VIII, 3 (July, 1917).

Steward, Julian H. "Linguistic Distribution and Political Groups of the Great Basin Shoshoneans," *American Anthropologist,* N.S., XXXIX, 4 (October–December, 1937).

Stillman, A. D. "Eastern Oregon Indians," *Oregon Native Son,* I, 3 (July, 1899).

"A Story of Oregon," *Colliers Weekly,* June 29, 1912.

Teiser, Sidney. "First Associate Justice of Oregon Territory: O. C. Pratt," *Oregon Historical Quarterly,* XLIX (March–December, 1948).

Victor, Frances Fuller. "The First Oregon Cavalry," *Oregon Historical Quarterly,* III (March–December, 1902).

——. "The Oregon Indians," *Overland Monthly,* VII, 2 (October, 1871).

Wissler, Clark. "The Influence of the Horse in the Development of Plains Culture," *American Anthropologist,* N.S., XVI, 1 (January, 1914).

Wood, Charles Erskine Scott. "Famous Indians: Portraits of Some Indian Chiefs," *Century Magazine,* O.S., XLVI, 3 (July, 1893).

Wood, T. A. "The Cayuse War," *Oregon Native Son,* II (May, 1900–April, 1901).

Index

Lewis River: *see* Snake River
Lindsay, W. J.: 258
Liquor: 19, 49, 79, 206, 263, 271, 272
Llou-Llou (Indian): 149
Looking Glass (Nez Percé): 158, 160, 203, 204, 225, 230, 236, 261
Lord, John Keast: 266
Lowell, Stephen A.: 289–91
Lutuamian linguistic group: 4

McBean, John: 222, 282
McBean, William: 106, 115, 116, 126, 132, 156–61
McBeth, Kate: 289
McClellan, Capt. George: 187
McDonald, Angus: 234
McFarland, John: 176
McGillivray, Simon: 58
McKay, Alexander: 126
McKay, Charles: 208
McKay, Donald: 280
McKay, Thomas: 87, 107, 126ff., 139, 203
McKay, Dr. William Cameron: 203, 212, 216
McKay Creek: 27, 211, 212, 269
McKenzie, Donald: 32, 41, 44
McKinlay, Archibald: 60, 61 & n., 82
McKinlay, Mrs. Archibald: 82n.
McLouglin, Dr. John: 50, 52ff., 82, 88ff., 105n., 166, 170
Magone, Maj. Joseph: 147, 148
Malheur Lake: 54
Malheur River: 7, 101
Mansfield, J. K. F.: 259
Marsh, Walter: 111
Martin, Capt. William: 150
Mason, Gov. Charles H.: 227
Massachusetts (ship): 161
Maxon, Capt. H. J. G.: 130, 141, 144
May Dacre (ship): 56, 57
Meacham, A. B.: 274, 277
Medicine men: 16, 74, 75, 100, 289
Meek, Helen: 112
Meek, Joe: 101, 133, 153, 163, 167–70
Menetrey, Rev. Joseph, S.J.: 197
Mesplié, Rev. Toussaint: 174, 181, 226, 279, 280, 287
Methodist missions: 142; Willamette, 68–70, 89, Wascopum (on The Dalles),

84, 85; on the Yakima Reservation, 275
Mexican War: 153
Miles, Capt. Evan: 283
Military troops: Oregon Territory volunteers, 116, 120, 121, 122 & n., 126, 129, 136, 139, 145, 154, 155; 215 & n., 227, 238; Washington Territory volunteers, 240, 246, 254, 273; Oregon cavalry, 266
Mill Creek: 7, 192, 214, 221, 224, 246, 251
Missouri River: 21
Moath (Cayuse): 160
Modoc Indians: 124, 280
Mollalah Indians: 4–6, 7n., 124
Mono-Paviotso Indians: 4n., 5
Montana: 286n.
Montour, George: 246
Mool Mool (on Columbia River): 180
Moorhouse, Maj. Lee: 292, 293, 296
Mormons: 163n., 181, 182n., 253
Moses, Chief (Columbia): 287
Mott, C. H.: 260, 261
Mount Hood: 4, 21, 31
Mount St. Helens: 21, 85
Mount Shasta: 54, 55, 58
Mullan, Lieut. John: 256
Mullan Road: 256
Munson, Capt. L. B.: 215n.

Naches River: 236
Narrows, The (of Columbia River): 9
Nesmith, Col. James W.: 215 & n., 255
Nevada: 280
Newell, Robert: 125, 136, 155
Nez Percé Indians: 8ff., 23, 41ff., 48ff., 57ff., 71, 86, 88, 101, 116ff., 131–38, 141ff., 150ff., 162, 180ff., 201ff., 218, 222, 224, 233ff., 240ff., 260, 267, 281, 293
Nez Percé Trail: 136
Nisqually Indians: 180
Noble, John: 178, 192, 211, 212
North West Fur Company: 25, 29, 32, 34, 63

Ococtuin (Cayuse): 7
Ogden, Peter Skene: 4n., 54, 82n., 119, 120 & n., 121, 186

Waiilatpu (Place of the Rye Grass and mission): 67ff., 86–89, 106ff., 124, 132–34, 138, 143, 156, 176, 192, 211, 214, 220, 267, 282; school at, 77, 78; agriculture at, 78, 79, 89
Waiilatpuan linguistic group: 3
Waiilatpu Indians: *see* Cayuse Indians
Waileptuleek (Cayuse): 68, 69
Waitsburg, Wash.: 138
Walker, Elkanah: 75, 102, 147, 173, 174
Walla Walla, Washington Territory: 266, 267, 277, 282
Walla Walla Indians: 8, 14, 22, 33, 48, 61, 78ff., 98, 125, 134, 138, 141, 156, 180, 182ff., 191ff., 210, 211, 237, 268, 293
Walla Walla River: 8, 30, 35, 51, 53, 71, 80, 132, 175, 224
Walla Walla Valley: 7n., 12, 62, 71, 75, 93, 98, 132, 142, 151, 185, 192, 194, 208ff., 218ff., 232ff., 248, 255, 260, 265
Wallowa Valley: 142, 253, 260, 279, 280, 287, 292
Walpapi Indians: 5n.
Wampole, Elias: 177, 178, 183
Waptashtakmahl (Feathercap, Cayuse): 68, 80, 87, 89
Warm Springs River: 4
War of 1812: 29
Warrarica Indians: 45, 46
Wars and skirmishes, Indian: 43; on The Dalles, 121, 122; on Deschutes River, 122, 123; at Sand Hollow, 128–31; on Tucannon River, 138, 139; at Touchet Crossing, 140, 141; on Toppenish River, 207; at Union Gap, 213, 214; at Fort Henrietta, 218; in Walla Walla Valley, 219; on Touchet River, 219, 220; at LaRoque cabin, 220; in Grande Ronde Valley, 239–40; in Walla Walla Valley, 248–52; with Col. Steptoe, 258; at Four Lakes, 258; on Spokane Plains, 258; Nez Percé, 282, 283 & n.; Paiute, 284–87; Sheepeater, 286
Wascopum Indians: 121
Wascopum Mission: 84, 85
Washington, D.C.: 133, 153, 176, 198
Watashchenownan (Afraid of the Earth, Walla Walla): 60

Waters, Maj. James: 134, 145–47, 151
Watshtamena (Cayuse): 212
Wattastuartite (Cayuse): 208
Weatenatenamy (Young Chief, Cayuse): 184, 187, 196ff., 205ff., 218, 219, 235, 253, 254, 262
Weiser Indians: 286
Welaptulket (Tenino): 121, 126, 131, 144
Wells Springs (on Immigrant Road): 127, 128
White, Dr. Elijah: 57n., 69, 85, 88, 92, 93; Indian laws of, 86, 87, 80–94, 297, 298
White, J.: 277
White Bird (Nez Percé): 283
White Bluffs (on Columbia River): 265
Whitman, Dr. Marcus: 68, 70ff., 135ff., 151, 157, 160ff., 212, 275; eastern journey of, 82, 83, 94, 102; massacre of, 109–14, 119–21, 134–39, 146–49, 154–57, 159, 164–68, 170, 171, 202–205, 289, 301, 302
Whitman, Narcissa (Mrs. Marcus Whitman): 72, 74ff., 84, 88, 92, 93, 111, 157, 164–66
Whitman, Perrin: 124, 173
Wiecat (Cayuse): 208
Wild Horse Creek: 215n., 269, 270
Wilkes, Lieut. Charles: 84
Wilkinson, Lieut. M. C.: 292
Willamette Falls: 32
Willamette River: 32, 69
Willamette Valley: 4, 6, 14, 21, 66, 86, 98, 101, 105, 111ff., 136, 145, 151, 153, 165, 172, 178, 182
Willatmotkin (Cayuse): 64
Williams, Thomas: 183
Willow Creek: 8, 126, 256
Wilson, Capt. Alfred B.: 215n., 220
Winampsnoot (Umatilla): 206, 208, 274
Wool, Gen. Jonathan: 214, 215, 220, 226–28, 230, 236, 240, 241, 252, 254, 256
Work, John: 50, 51
Wright, Col. George: 228, 233ff., 247, 252ff.
Wyeth, Nathaniel J.: 56, 57 & n., 64, 65

Yahuskin Indians: 5n.

339

of which *The Cayuse Indians: Imperial Tribesmen of Old Oregon* is Volume 120, was inaugurated in 1932 by the University of Oklahoma Press, and has as its purpose the reconstruction of American Indian civilization by presenting aboriginal, historical, and contemporary Indian life. The following list is complete as of the date of publication of this volume.

1. *Forgotten Frontiers:* A Study of the Spanish Indian Policy of Don Juan Bautista de Anza, Governor of New Mexico, *1777–1787.* Translated and edited by Alfred Barnaby Thomas.
2. Grant Foreman. *Indian Removal:* The Emigration of the Five Civilized Tribes of Indians.
3. John Joseph Mathews. *Wah'Kon-Tah:* The Osage and the White Man's Road.
4. Grant Foreman. *Advancing the Frontier, 1830–1860.*
5. John H. Seger. *Early Days Among the Cheyenne and Arapahoe Indians.* Edited by Stanley Vestal. Out of print.
6. Angie Debo. *The Rise and Fall of the Choctaw Republic.*
7. Stanley Vestal. *New Sources of Indian History, 1850–1891:* A Miscellany. Out of print.
8. Grant Foreman. *The Five Civilized Tribes.*
9. *After Coronado:* Spanish Exploration Northeast of New Mexico, *1696–1727.* Translated and edited by Alfred Barnaby Thomas.
10. Frank G. Speck. *Naskapi:* The Savage Hunters of the Labrador Peninsula. Out of print.
11. Elaine Goodale Eastman. *Pratt:* The Red Man's Moses. Out of print.
12. Althea Bass. *Cherokee Messenger:* A Life of Samuel Austin Worcester.
13. Thomas Wildcat Alford. *Civilization.* As told to Florence Drake. Out of print.
14. Grant Foreman. *Indians and Pioneers:* The Story of the American Southwest Before 1830.
15. George E. Hyde. *Red Cloud's Folk:* A History of the Oglala Sioux Indians.
16. Grant Foreman. *Sequoyah.*
17. Morris L. Wardell. *A Political History of the Cherokee Nation, 1838–1907.* Out of print.
18. John Walton Caughey. *McGillivray of the Creeks.* Out of print.
19. Edward Everett Dale and Gaston Litton. *Cherokee Cavaliers:* Forty Years of Cherokee History as Told in the Correspondence of the Ridge-Watie-Boudinot Family.
20. Ralph Henry Gabriel. *Elias Boudinot, Cherokee, and His America.* Out of print.
21. Karl N. Llewellyn and E. Adamson Hoebel. *The Cheyenne Way:* Conflict and Case Law in Primitive Jurisprudence.
22. Angie Debo. *The Road to Disappearance.*
23. Oliver La Farge and others. *The Changing Indian.* Out of print.
24. Carolyn Thomas Foreman. *Indians Abroad.* Out of print.
25. John Adair. *The Navajo and Pueblo Silversmiths.*

26. Alice Marriott. *The Ten Grandmothers*.
27. Alice Marriott. *María*: The Potter of San Ildefonso.
28. Edward Everett Dale. *The Indians of the Southwest:* A Century of Development Under the United States.
29. *Popol Vuh:* The Sacred Book of the Ancient Quiché Maya. English version by Delia Goetz and Sylvanus G. Morley from the translation of Adrián Recinos.
30. Walter Collins O'Kane. *Sun in the Sky*.
31. Stanley A. Stubbs. *Bird's-Eye View of the Pueblos*. Out of print.
32. Katharine C. Turner. *Red Men Calling on the Great White Father*.
33. Muriel H. Wright. *A Guide to the Indian Tribes of Oklahoma*.
34. Ernest Wallace and E. Adamson Hoebel. *The Comanches:* Lords of the South Plains.
35. Walter Collins O'Kane. *The Hopis:* Portrait of a Desert People.
36. *The Sacred Pipe:* Black Elk's Account of the Seven Rites of the Oglala Sioux. Edited by Joseph Epes Brown.
37. *The Annals of the Cakchiquels*, translated from the Cakchiquel Maya by Adrián Recinos and Delia Goetz, with *Title of the Lords of Totonicapán*, translated from the Quiché text into Spanish by Dionisio José Chonay, English version by Delia Goetz.
38. R. S. Cotterill. *The Southern Indians:* The Story of the Civilized Tribes Before Removal.
39. J. Eric S. Thompson. *The Rise and Fall of Maya Civilization*. (Revised Edition).
40. Robert Emmitt. *The Last War Trail:* The Utes and the Settlement of Colorado. Out of print.
41. Frank Gilbert Roe. *The Indian and the Horse*.
42. Francis Haines. *The Nez Percés:* Tribesmen of the Columbia Plateau.
43. Ruth M. Underhill. *The Navajos*.
44. George Bird Grinnell. *The Fighting Cheyennes*.
45. George E. Hyde. *A Sioux Chronicle*. Out of print.
46. Stanley Vestal. *Sitting Bull, Champion of the Sioux:* A Biography.
47. Edwin C. McReynolds. *The Seminoles*.
48. William T. Hagan. *The Sac and Fox Indians*.
49. John C. Ewers. *The Blackfeet:* Raiders on the Northwestern Plains.
50. Alfonso Caso. *The Aztecs:* People of the Sun. Translated by Lowell Dunham.
51. C. L. Sonnichsen. *The Mescalero Apaches*.
52. Keith A. Murray. *The Modocs and Their War*.
53. *The Incas of Pedro de Cieza de León*. Edited by Victor Wolfgang von Hagen and translated by Harriet de Onis.
54. George E. Hyde. *Indians of the High Plains:* From the Prehistoric Period to the Coming of Europeans.
55. *George Catlin:* Episodes from "Life Among the Indians" and "Last Rambles." Edited by Marvin C. Ross. Out of print.
56. J. Eric S. Thompson. *Maya Hieroglyphic Writing:* An Introduction.
57. George E. Hyde. *Spotted Tail's Folk:* A History of the Brulé Sioux.

58. James Larpenteur Long. *The Assiniboines:* From the Accounts of the Old Ones Told to First Boy (James Larpenteur Long). Edited and with an introduction by Michael Stephen Kennedy. Out of print.
59. Edwin Thompson Denig. *Five Indian Tribes of the Upper Missouri:* Sioux, Arickaras, Assiniboines, Crees, Crows. Edited and with an introduction by John C. Ewers.
60. John Joseph Mathews. *The Osages:* Children of the Middle Waters.
61. Mary Elizabeth Young. *Redskins, Ruffleshirts, and Rednecks:* Indian Allotments in Alabama and Mississippi, 1830–1860.
62. J. Eric S. Thompson. *A Catalog of Maya Hieroglyphs.*
63. Mildred P. Mayhall. *The Kiowas.*
64. George E. Hyde. *Indians of the Woodlands:* From Prehistoric Times to 1725.
65. Grace Steele Woodward. *The Cherokees.*
66. Donald J. Berthrong. *The Southern Cheyennes.*
67. Miguel León-Portilla. *Aztec Thought and Culture:* A Study of the Ancient Nahuatl Mind. Translated by Jack Emory Davis.
68. T. D. Allen. *Navahos Have Five Fingers.*
69. Burr Cartwright Brundage. *Empire of the Inca.*
70. A. M. Gibson. *The Kickapoos:* Lords of the Middle Border.
71. Hamilton A. Tyler. *Pueblo Gods and Myths.*
72. Royal B. Hassrick. *The Sioux:* Life and Customs of a Warrior Society.
73. Franc Johnson Newcomb. *Hosteen Klah:* Navaho Medicine Man and Sand Painter.
74. Virginia Cole Trenholm and Maurine Carley. *The Shoshonis:* Sentinels of the Rockies.
75. Cohoe. *A Cheyenne Sketchbook.* Commentary by E. Adamson Hoebel and Karen Daniels Petersen. Out of print.
76. Jack D. Forbes. *Warriors of the Colorado:* The Yumas of the Quechan Nation and Their Neighbors.
77. *Ritual of the Bacabs.* Translated and edited by Ralph L. Roys.
78. Lillian Estelle Fisher. *The Last Inca Revolt, 1780–1783.*
79. Lilly de Jongh Osborne. *Indian Crafts of Guatemala and El Salvador.*
80. Robert H. Ruby and John A. Brown. *Half-Sun on the Columbia:* A Biography of Chief Moses.
81. *The Shadow of Sequoyah:* Social Documents of the Cherokees. Translated and edited by Jack Frederick and Anna Gritts Kilpatrick.
82. Ella E. Clark. *Indian Legends from the Northern Rockies.*
83. *The Indian:* America's Unfinished Business. Compiled by William A. Brophy and Sophie D. Aberle, M.D.
84. M. Inez Hilger, with Margaret A. Mondloch. *Huenun Ñamku:* An Araucanian Indian of the Andes Remembers the Past.
85. Ronald Spores. *The Mixtec Kings and Their People.*
86. David H. Corkran. *The Creek Frontier, 1540–1783.*
87. *The Book of Chilam Balam of Chumayel.* Translated and edited by Ralph L. Roys.

88. Burr Cartwright Brundage. *Lords of Cuzco:* A History and Description of the Inca People in Their Final Days.

89. John C. Ewers. *Indian Life on the Upper Missouri.*

90. Max L. Moorhead. *The Apache Frontier:* Jacobo Ugarte and Spanish-Indian Relations in Northern New Spain, 1769–1791.

91. France Scholes and Ralph L. Roys. *The Maya Chontal Indians of Acalan-Tixchel.*

92. Miguel León-Portilla. *Pre-Columbian Literatures of Mexico.* Translated from the Spanish by Grace Lobanov and the Author.

93. Grace Steele Woodward. *Pocahontas.*

94. Gottfried Hotz. *Eighteenth-Century Skin Paintings.* Translated by Johannes Malthaner.

95. Virgil J. Vogel. *American Indian Medicine.*

96. Bill Vaudrin. *Tanaina Tales from Alaska.* With an introduction by Joan Broom Townsend.

97. Georgiana C. Nammack. *Fraud, Politics, and Dispossession of the Indians:* The Iroquois Land Frontier in the Colonial Period.

98. *The Chronicles of Michoacán.* Translated and edited by Eugene R. Craine and Reginald C. Reindorp.

99. J. Eric S. Thompson. *Maya History and Religion.*

100. Peter J. Powell. *Sweet Medicine:* The Continuing Role of the Sacred Arrows, the Sun Dance, and the Sacred Buffalo Hat in Northern Cheyenne History.

101. Karen Daniels Petersen. *Plains Indian Art from Fort Marion.*

102. Fray Diego Durán. *Book of the Gods and Rites and The Ancient Calendar.* Translated and edited by Fernando Horcasitas and Doris Heyden. Foreword by Miguel León-Portilla.

103. Bert Anson. *The Miami Indians:* Sovereigns of the Wabash-Maumee.

104. Robert H. Ruby and John A. Brown. *The Spokane Indians:* Children of the Sun. Foreword by Robert L. Bennett.

105. Virginia Cole Trenholm. *The Arapahoes, Our People.*

106. Angie Debo. *A History of the Indians of the United States.*

107. Herman Grey. *Tales from the Mohaves.*

108. Stephen Dow Beckham. *Requiem for a People:* The Rogue Indians and the Frontiersmen.

109. Arrell M. Gibson. *The Chickasaws.*

110. *Indian Oratory:* Famous Speeches by Noted Indian Chieftains, compiled by W. C. Vanderwerth.

111. *The Sioux of the Rosebud:* A History in Pictures. Photographs by John A. Anderson, text by Henry W. Hamilton and Jean Tyree Hamilton.

112. Howard L. Harrod. *Mission Among the Blackfeet.*

113. Mary Whatley Clarke. *Chief Bowles and the Texas Cherokees.*

114. William E. Unrau. *The Kansa Indians:* A History of the Wind People.

115. Jack D. Forbes. *Apache, Navaho, and Spaniard.*

116. W. David Baird. *Peter Pitchlynn: Chief of the Choctaws.*

117. *Life and Death in Milpa Alta:* A Nahuatl Chronicle of Díaz and Zapata.

Translated and edited by Fernando Horcasitas, with a foreword by Miguel León-Portilla.

118. Ralph L. Roys. *The Indian Background of Colonial Yucatán*. With an introduction by J. Eric S. Thompson.

119. *Cry of the Thunderbird:* The American Indian's Own Story. Edited by Charles Hamilton.

120. Robert H. Ruby and John A. Brown. *The Cayuse Indians:* Imperial Tribesmen of Old Oregon.